TO PLAY AT WILL

by

K. Edmonds Gateley

Published and printed by Herald Press, York House, 17 Rother Street, Stratford-upon-Avon.

1988

ACKNOWLEDGEMENTS

I owe many debts of thanks but I fear that this list cannot help but be inadequate payment of them.

Firstly, I thank Professor Arthur Colby Sprague, great American scholar and the world's leading authority on Shakespeare in performance. It was his high valuation of the work of the Southsea Shakespeare Actors and his continually insisting that I must write this book that drove me on. The great warmth of Arthur's friendship (and I was long ago invited to use his Christian name) has been one of my major delights and inspirations.

What I owed during my twenty-five years as Director of the company to Donald and Rosalind Wolfit must be abundantly clear in the pages of this book. The dedication shows the value I set on the contributions that were made during the same two-and-a-half decades by my great friends, John Fulcher and Prue Higham.

More recently, very practical help has been given me by my other greatest friend, Chris Bloxsom, who tackled vast amounts of duplicating for me and, as he loves words as I do, helpfully spotted oddities of syntax and examples of my erratic spelling. My special friends, Edgar and Betty King, heard every word of the book read aloud to them and made many valuable suggestions for improvements; he having observed the SSA from the inside and she from the outside. The references in the text of this book to Chris and his dear wife, Jenny, and to Edgar and Betty, are too sparse to give any idea of how important my love for them and theirs for me are in my daily life. Nor does it adequately do justice to the years of devoted service that they gave the SSA from the mid-fifties onwards. Alas, that applies to all too many members, some of whom cannot even be named at all.

The negatives no longer existing, many of the photographs have had to be reproduced from the originals and this work has been done by my old friend of many years, Ken Marchant, and I owe him great thanks too. All the photographs except, I believe, three, were taken by Kenneth Pratt who endeared himself to the company so quickly in 1948 that he automatically became part of it. The three exceptions are the ones on pages 213, 221 and 265: these are from the Portsmouth newspapers.

Permission to quote and reproduce photographs from the *Portsmouth Evening News, The News* and the *Hampshire Telegraph* was kindly granted by the Editor, R C C Poulton, on behalf of Portsmouth and Sunderland Newspapers Ltd. and I am most grateful. My thanks, too, for the permission of *The Observer* to reprint Ivor Brown's comments on our plight in 1948. *The Other Theatre* by Norman Marshall, from which there are a few quotations, was published in 1947 by John Lehmann Ltd. I would also like to thank the publishers of the Norwich newspapers, the *Eastern Evening News* and the *Eastern Daily Press,* for their kind permission to quote from their theatre reviews.

ISBN 0 9513782 0 1

This book would not be here for you to read at all had it not been for the generosity and kindness of my friend of more than four decades, Ken Boyden of the Herald Press at Stratford-upon-Avon. His decision to publish it was a natural manifestation of the unfailing warmth of his friendship. His firm did all the company's printing for over thirty years and our dealings always felt like acts of kindness and never like business matters.

For anyone in so eminent a position in the professional theatre as Donald Sinden, old personal friend though he is, to put his seal on this work by writing a Preface for it, is, I am sure, more than it deserves. His support and advice have been an enormous encouragement and I am deeply grateful to him—as I am for his suggesting that I should find a more catchy title than the one I already had. Even that was not its original one and my thanks to John Kane for improving on the first of the three.

Where do I stop? My sister, Gwen, and Melita Martin (then Moon) worked long and tirelessly at what seemed to the rest of us to be boring jobs and no list would be complete without my heartfelt thanks to them. I can only crave the forgiveness of the legion of others who deserve mention but who have been omitted through lack of space.

K. Edmonds Gateley

CHARACTERS FROM EVERY ONE OF SHAKESPEARE'S PLAYS

as they appeared in Southsea Shakespeare Actors productions
(from the October 1966 theatre programme)
Left to right, line by line, from top to bottom

THE TWO GENTLEMEN OF VERONA	Launce (and his dog)	*Eric Greenwood*
TWELFTH NIGHT	Malvolio	*Clifford Allen*
KING RICHARD III	King Richard III	*KEG*
KING HENRY VIII	King Henry VIII	*Leonard Russell*
THE COMEDY OF ERRORS	Luciana	*Mavis Whyte*
KING HENRY IV, PART I	King Henry IV	*Leonard Russell*
MACBETH	Macbeth	*KEG*
KING HENRY VI, PART III	Queen Margaret	*Stella Miller*
ANTONY AND CLEOPATRA	Cleopatra	*Nancy Glenister*
CORIOLANUS	Titus Lartius	*Charles Biggerstaff*
TITUS ANDRONICUS	Aaron	*John Fulcher*
KING JOHN	King John	*Ronald Mills*
THE WINTER'S TALE	Hermione	*Nora Turner*
LOVE'S LABOUR'S LOST	Sir Nathaniel	*John Pearce*
THE MERRY WIVES OF WINDSOR	Ford	*Kenneth Barnard*
THE TEMPEST	Ariel	*Sunya Webster*
KING RICHARD II	King Richard II	*KEG*
KING HENRY V	Pistol	*William EM Smith*
PERICLES, PRINCE OF TYRE	The Bawd	*Prue Higham*
KING LEAR	King Lear	*KEG*
MUCH ADO ABOUT NOTHING	Beatrice	*Anne Nicolle*
MEASURE OF MEASURE	Angelo	*KEG*
TROILUS AND CRESSIDA	Troilus	*John Fulcher*
TIMON OF ATHENS	Flavius	*David Lippiett*
KING HENRY IV, PART II	Sir John Falstaff	*Ben Keen*
ROMEO AND JULIET	Juliet	*Mavis Whyte*
HAMLET	Hamlet	*KEG*
KING HENRY VI, PART I	King Henry VI	*Ian Burton*
OTHELLO	Othello	*Leonard Russell*
ALL'S WELL THAT ENDS WELL	Parolles	*John Fulcher*
AS YOU LIKE IT	Audrey	*Prue Higham*
JULIUS CAESAR	Portia	*Anne Nicolle*
A MIDSUMMER NIGHT'S DREAM	Peter Quince	*Clifford Allen*
CYMBELINE	Guiderius	*Chris Bloxsom*
KING HENRY VI, PART II	Jack Cade	*Edgar King*
THE TAMING OF THE SHREW	Christopher Sly	*Eric Greenwood*
THE MERCHANT OF VENICE	Bassanio	*David Lippiett*

PREFACE
by
Donald Sinden

Why was I being subjected to this? Was it my fault? The stainless steel chair into which I apprehensively lowered myself was thinly padded and had a rexine cover. A girl in white overalls moved purposefully about the room consulting files and straightening instruments on a tray beside me. An unseen hand pressed a button and a tumbler on my other side filled slowly with a pink liquid. The girl was joined by a man also in white and together they held an ominously whispered conversation. The man then seated himself on a stool behind me and pressed another button causing my chair to assume a reclining position—up went my legs, back went my head and neatly fitted into a pre-formed indentation in the chair-back. A powerful light stabbed into my face. Over the top of my head appeared the face of the man, now looking like Cyclops, peering through what seemed to be a pair of opera glasses attached to spectacle frames. He forced several cotton-wool chipolatas between my teeth and my cheeks while the previously charming girl hooked a rubber-tipped suction tube in the shape of a question mark over my lower teeth and under my tongue. She then forced a small vacuum cleaner into the region of my uvula. Cyclops appeared again over my head and, with one hand, insinuated a steel mirror into what remained of my mouth. The other hand moved slowly but firmly towards the same gaping cavity, holding a drill revolving at such speed that it needed to be cooled by a fine spray of water which the girl gleefully sucked up . . . At the precise moment when all nerves were exposed, the man spoke to me for the first time: "Will you make an after-dinner speech for me?"!

It came as no surprise to me to discover that the author of this book, K. Edmonds Gateley, was a dentist by profession. From what other profession could come a man who could coerce a group of sober-minded citizens of Portsmouth and Southsea to perform—free, gratis and for nothing—three plays by William Shakespeare every year for forty years? You can picture the scene, similar to my own experience: the decayed molar; the white coated figures; the screaming drill; then "Will you play Othello next month?". Or the pretty girl about to have her four front teeth cosmetically capped, her own teeth having already been ground to Dracula fangs . . . "I could leave you like this unless you agree to play Juliet".

K. EDMONDS GATELEY. The very name reminds me of the old actors of my youth—many of them old Bensonians—D. A. Clark-Smith; Meadows White; E. Martin Browne; C. Rivers Gadsby. The fact that his friends are encouraged to call him Peter Gateley, cannot disguise the sonorous K. EDMONDS GATELEY. The man had to be a Thespian.

I first met K. Edmonds—Peter—in 1969 and was enormously impressed by his vast knowledge of Shakespeare's plays and details of previous productions. Gradually I learned his story: how he had attended every season of plays at Stratford-upon-Avon since 1934: how, finding himself stationed in Norfolk during the war, he met and became a disciple of Nugent Monck: how he determined to form his own amateur company of actors committed to perform the works of Shakespeare—a formidable task when you remember that most amateur companies have to provide a fairly light diet for their patrons: how, in Aleppo once, his admiration for the late great Donald Wolfit blossomed into friendship. (When Peter played King Lear, Wolfit gave him his own costume, wig and beard. Years later, when I played Lear, Peter loaned me that same beard.) To be entertained by Peter at his house in Southsea is a memorable experience; the other guests are usually members of his company, the food is excellent and the talk is always of Shakespeare—more informed than one is likely to find in the houses of most professional actors.

Peter is unique—he holds a triple record: he is the only man (professional or amateur) to have acted in every one of Shakespeare's plays, to have directed every one of the plays and to have designed the scenery for every one of the plays. He has done the state some service, and they know it, but let K. Edmonds Gateley, MBE, Dentist, Scholar, Actor, Director, Designer, Man of the Theatre, tell you his own story—nothing extenuate—while I assure the reader that I was not his patient with my mouth full of ironwork when he asked me to write this preface to his astonishing book. I do it voluntarily and with great pleasure.

Donald Sinden

For
John Fulcher
and
in memory of
Prue Higham

CONTENTS

(With Preface by DONALD SINDEN)

A very trick for them *to play at will*
The Winter's Tale, II,1

PROLOGUE
Enter Right

CHAPTER 1
Curtains going up

I must begin at the end. It came in November, 1972, when I retired from the Directorship of the unique Shakespearean company that I had created 25 years before. During that quarter century, it had become the only completely amateur one in the world ever to have staged, under an amateur director, every one of the plays of Shakespeare. At the same time, I found myself to be the first person, amateur or professional, who had at any time, anywhere, acted in, as well as directed and designed sets for, the entire Shakespeare canon. That introductory burst of trumpet blowing now being over, I will attempt to explain how it all came about.

These earnest statistics make it look as if the whole thing must have been conceived as a deliberate marathon but it was not by any means. It might better be thought of as my progeny—I have been careful not to call it a prodigy!—because it was, in fact, born of four parents. They were, however, events rather than people.

The earliest of them was, not surprisingly, my first visit to a theatre which I like to think was the most important event of my childhood. The words, 'That's Cinderella!', whispered by my mother during that afternoon in the early 1920s, acted like a starting gun and set me off in the pursuit of what was to become a lifelong passion. She, my sister and myself were half-way down one side of the long U-shaped circle in the theatre on the South Parade Pier, Southsea, and I, being very small, had my chin pressed on to the padded crimson velvet edging.

In those days, the Pier Theatre was ornately baroque with a superb, high proscenium flanked by draped statues of strong male figures holding tridents in their off-stage hands. With their others, they reached out towards each other and held the ends of a swag of gilded plaster leaves that linked them in festoons across the top of the arch. The dark crimson velvet curtains, with their heavy interlaced and tasselled fringes, were topped by a pelmet of the same material. They swung up or, more particularly, down with a majestic and rather frightening swoosh. The great curtain at the Royal Opera House, Covent

Garden, which now in later life gives me so much pleasure to watch, never fails to remind me of that seaside pier.

I can still see in my mind's eye, even after more than sixty years, that brightly lit stage. Sitting in the dark auditorium and looking through the gilded frame was a magical enough experience in itself, but to see the very green woodland flooded with brilliant sunshine on the other side of it, made the wonder even more dazzling. The modern child becomes used to the sight of such visions in miniature on television from the moment it is born and so, poor dear, can never have quite such a revelation on first going to a theatre.

My little heart beat faster as the Principal Girl walked forward in a circle of light that moved as she did so that she was always in its beam. This was the first star entrance I ever saw and I have been enjoying them ever since! The words, 'That's Cinderella!' crystalised for the rest of my life that intoxicating moment. In more recent years, I took two of my little godsons, Antony and Richard Fulcher—a surname that will recur many times in this book—to their first pantomime. It happened to be the same fairy tale, though this time at Southsea's King's Theatre, and it was no accident that, at the appropriate moment, I whispered to Antony, who was sitting on my lap, 'That's Cinderella!'

As soon as I got home after my own very first matinee, my sister and I made a toy theatre from a cardboard box. The curtain and the scenery had to be reproduced with the greatest accuracy possible as these were what mattered to me most. I also tried my hand at brief impersonations of some of the performances that I had seen that afternoon. I blush to mention that I do not seem to have minded about the sex of some of the originals: the fairy's wand was, perhaps, my favourite theatrical 'prop'! However, it should be remembered that I was only about 5 years old at the time! (Rest, rest, perturbéd psychoanalysts!)

From before this time, I had been greatly fascinated by posters. It was from avidly copying every one that I saw on to sheets from endless supplies of writing pads, that I developed any small skill I may later have had as a designer. In those days, one saw more hoardings because our cities were not so closely built up and there were plenty of vacant sites and allotments to screen. Complicated colour printing was economical and so theatres and cinemas advertised very extensively with huge pictorial posters. The twenties were the great years of touring and, as there were then hundreds of provincial theatres, a popular West End success might have three or four companies playing it on the road whilst the original was still running. Many of their posters were copies of the London ones and those for Drury Lane musicals such as *The Desert Song* and *Rose Marie* had realistic pictures of scenes from these shows. Particular favourites of mine were the ones for the D'Oyly Carte Opera Company which were black with scarlet wording. They also had a few of the Charles Ricketts costume designs on some of their others and I especially remember those for *The Mikado*. For many years, I thought that D'Oyly Carte meant, 'All one sees that's Japanese'! Occasionally the Carl Rosa Opera sported large decorative displays as well. I recollect one with many classically-draped ladies reclining in a rocky landscape. I think now that it probably represented the then current view of the erotic delights of the Venusberg in *Tannhauser* but I expect that I assumed it was a scene in an open-air bathroom!

My toy theatre, and its many successors made out of ever bigger and better discarded cardboard boxes, were my continual obsession until eventually I was

South Parade Pier Theatre, Southsea, as it was before the stage was rebuilt in 1933-4

shamed out of them in my early teens. For several years, my theatre-going was confined to more pantomimes and also to the concert parties that came to the Pier in the early part of each summer. However, I had also started going to cinemas and their posters were often more gorgeous than the theatrical ones. The show that I had on at my toy theatre would usually be something that was being either played or shown locally during the same week. I knew the title and I could copy the poster. It could be either stage or screen and I made up my own story from those two basic pieces of information. It had no bearing on the original, of course, although, occasionally, I did get a hint of what a current play or film was about from hearing my family talk. I wonder now what sort of childish domestic plot I attached to my stage versions of films such as *The Sorrows of Satan* or *Flaming Youth*. What, too, had been the crime of the heroine in my account of the much-toured drama, *The Trial of Mary Dugan*? Such titles must have been strange bedfellows for my scenes of Dame Durden's Kitchen and Prince Charming's Palace!

As a side-line, I made cinemas by drawing their interiors on sheets from my ever-present writing pads. Through a slit on either side of the screen I used to slide a strip on which I had sketched about half a dozen pictures. The all-important matters were the posters and the act of putting on a show. Throwing together some sort of plot was almost a tiresome afterthought.

I was not totally innocent about the ways of adult life. My parents were keen golfers and my education was helped by being taken by them every weekend to the club at Waterlooville, just outside Portsmouth. The members were not blinkered sport fanatics but were all part of the social circle within which we moved. My little ears worked like radar saucers and nobody seemed to notice. I did not know about sex and, in any case, in those days it was not openly discussed. It was implied but I was too young to be able to read the signals. However, I did reasonably understand about people falling in love and how some marriages fell apart. Unlike my contemporaries at school I did not find these matters funny and so when I was taken to fairly sophisticated plays and films before I was much older, I had a pretty good idea of what they were all about.

I quickly picked up the knack of enjoying theatrically effective moments. For example, on one occasion I made a joke of the sort that I had heard in many a pier show although I could not understand at the time why my parents blushed and everyone else roared with laughter. It was one of my earliest tastes of the joy of getting a good laugh from an audience. It took place in the golf club house where my seniors were watching a spinster, who had seen a good many mid-winters, gazing fervently into the middle distance. One of them said that she was looking so agitated, there must surely be a man approaching! As her name happened to be Miss Nightingale, I took this as my cue to shoot in my 'gag'. 'Yes', I said in my piping treble, 'she's like all the hens; she gets excited when there's a cock about!' As Wilde's Canon Chasuble might have said, 'My metaphor was drawn from birds'!

My father spent his whole career with Cadbury's, the chocolate firm, but one of his brothers and several of his cousins were lawyers. My paternal great-grandfather was even more on the side of the law: he was Superintendent of Police at Aston in early Victorian times. On my mother's side there was a Recorder and one of my cousins, E. N. Clulee, was an actor in his youth. The Edmonds branch, my paternal grandmother's, were rather learned and were mostly involved with languages and the church. More of them anon.

Our family consisted of five: my mother and father; my sister and brother—and me. In many ways, we fell into those three separate groups. I was almost like an only child and something of a loner. Both my parents were mid-Victorians and my father was ten years my mother's senior. Her first child, my sister, Gwen, was born when she was only 21 and my brother, Geoffrey, followed within the next two years. I did not arrive, however, until my mother was nearly 38 and so there an enormous age gap. The result was that in my childhood I had a grown-up sister and a middle-aged mother. My father was in many ways more like a grandfather and I was constantly being told that he must not be disturbed because either he was working or else he had just finished. He had a sharp and sudden, though fairly rare, temper and was somewhat repressingly unexcitable. He once declared that he was not very interested in foreign travel as, wherever one went, it was 'all just earth, sea and sky'. He was shrewd, reasonably thrifty at a time when this was an essential virtue if one wished to have a comfortable old age, and had a business man's mind without any artistic frills. A hard-working breadwinner with good principles, he also had a calm sense of justice. His many irritating ways included chopping up all his food noisily on his plate and then chewing every mouthful indefinitely. My mother always said that this was because Mr. Gladstone had pronounced that this was the recipe for long life. Such family rows as there were, usually happened because one or other of us could not conceal our irritation any longer.

My mother was the driving force. She always wanted to have her own way and usually got it. If in nothing else, I am certainly her son in this. I do not put that forward as being a particularly likeable quality but I do know that if I had not possessed it, my Shakespearean company of later years would never have survived; probably, never even have started. My mother, although possessive and dominating, clearly adored me and our relationship was an enjoyable and happy one. I had to keep strictly toeing her line but we had many splendid times together. Mother's boy? Yes, I suppose I was.

My sister, always hypersensitive to slights or disapproval, much of it imagined rather than real, was quite beautiful in the, and her, twenties. She tended towards the darkly statuesque but she would have preferred, I think, to have been a fluffy blonde. She was not intellectual and she has always been easily wounded by life's realities as she yearns for a romantic world where all is love and happy ever after.

My brother looked something like the film star, Ronald Colman. He enjoyed wine, women and—no, not song. He was, like his father, in no way artistic. 'Travel' and 'golf' could vie to replace the word, 'song'. We never quarrelled, as far as I can remember, but I often found him intolerant of the things that interested me. We were always strangers. I did not see him until I was about six or seven as he had been abroad in places like Marseilles and Alexandria in the Eastern Telegraph Company, later to be known as Cable and Wireless. Whenever I misbehaved or fell short of the standards expected of me, this brother whom I had never seen was always described as a paragon who at my age would never have dreamed of doing such things. I have always known how the youth who became King John must have felt having a brother known as the Lion-hearted! When he died in 1973 he did not leave me a penny in his will. I am not complaining because he was not mentioned in mine either.

We lived in a fairly substantial late nineteenth-century house in Southsea but when I was eight my parents started to have a smaller one built. My mother found a delightful site which had been an allotment and which faced ornamental gardens and the sea front across a junction of roads. She pushed my father into buying it and then, having selected an architect, she stood over him until he had produced the plans of what virtually she had designed. The result was a very attractive house which was called, appropriately, 'Crossways'. It was typical of its period, the late twenties, and it had a spacious garage and a large garden. The former, which for so many years had scenery stored in it, has had a long amateur theatrical history. The garden has been splashed with so much scene paint over the years that it could be compared with that of the Queen of Hearts—except that in hers the roses were being painted deliberately!

We moved into the house when I was nine and within three years the garage had been converted into a theatre where I put on my first show with live actors. With the help of my sister, Gwen, I had made a pair of crimson curtains out of crepe paper which my father and I had put up on one of the tie beams of the garage roof. The setting consisted of a background of bedspreads hanging from a clothes-line tightly stretched across from wall to wall. As the actors were all my contemporaries, it did not need to be very high. The audience was seated on chairs from the house.

The show was called, *The Revelling Beans Vaudeville Company*. It, and its title, were based on the concert parties that I had seen week after week at the South Parade Pier. The term 'concert party' is now probably archaic and so I had better explain. It was a standard form of seaside entertainment which was at its peak during the first third of this century. The setting was a curtain surround and each company toured its own. The one essential item within this was a grand piano, often with a Spanish shawl tastefully draped across it so that a large embroidered and fringed triangle hung down over the side. An optional extra was a standard lamp to give a drawing-room atmosphere. The cast invariably consisted of seven; the lead being the man who owned the show and he was usually the comedian. His wife was often the soubrette or even the soprano. There had to be, of course, a pianist and the rest also had various specialist talents. Many of these troupes wore pierrot costumes until the one interval and then changed into evening dress. Some of the more superior ones were in white tie and tails with the girls in long ball gowns throughout. They had names like *The Manx Mascots, The Town Topics, The Modern Follies* and *The Ne'er-do-wells,* but by my time they were no longer calling themselves 'concert parties': they were 'vaudeville companies'!

My show in the garage started with a dance by a ten-year-old girl and some conjuring tricks by a little boy of about the same age. I appeared later in two playlets and also pretended at one point that a member of the cast was missing. That meant that it would be necessary to rehearse an understudy for one of the sketches in front of the audience. In it a little girl had to say, 'I have been unfaithful to you' but I protested that she could not get her performance right without an actor to whom she could speak the line. I therefore called on to the stage an equally small boy for her to try it out on. Enter the infant actor. 'I have been unfaithful to you', said the little tot once more but looking at me. 'You fool', said the boy, 'why did you tell him?'

I had picked this up from a concert party, of course. As none of the players was over the age of 12, the audience of parents was noticeably shocked! To my surprise I had managed to create something of a sensation the very first time I had tried my hand at putting on a stage show! I spent the rest of my life hoping to do it again! The title I gave for the sketch that we were supposedly rehearsing was *Passionate Hearts*. My own invention! I was obviously learning fast from my visits to theatres and cinemas!

Looking back at the programme now after all these years, I am struck by two things which seem to show that I had a professional egotism even then. Not only does it say boldly at the top, 'Presented by Kenneth Edmonds Gateley' (no sign of democracy!) but at the bottom it reads, 'Stage Manager, *for K. E. Gateley,* C. P. W. Hayward'. I made it clear that he was employed by the Management and emphasised for a second time just who the Management was!

By this time, my theatre-going had expanded as I had now also been taken to the Portsmouth Theatre Royal, a playhouse destined to have a complicated future in which I should eventually become entangled. The Pier, for all its gilt and red plush, was a long rectangular Edwardian music hall with a single circle. The late-Victorian Theatre Royal had three galleries and eight boxes and it was like going into a tall, round tower; overpowering in its way and very thrilling. The picture that I carry in my mind of it then is of its being wholly encrusted with dark gold ornamentation which glowed in a dim amber light. Although the Pier pantomimes were professional, the ones at the Royal were obviously grander and, before long, I was being taken to plays there as well. One of the first was *Treasure Island* with the old trouper, Charles Doran, as Long John Silver, and I also saw two great and gracious stars, Fred Terry and Julia Neilson, in *Sweet Nell of Old Drury*. Grand, spectacular, richly romantic theatre that clearly owed more to the Victorians than to the new spirits who were forging ahead elsewhere with fresh ideas. I would encounter them in due course but what I had seen laid the foundations for much of my future attitude towards the theatre.

The Royal was, in my earliest days, the 'No. 1' house but there was also the King's Theatre, Southsea, which was Edwardian and larger. It was a twice-nightly music hall; a term which, by that time, had come to mean a theatre that had variety shows and revues on roughly alternate weeks. Occasionally there would be a silent film even though 'talkies' were starting in the regular cinemas. My first visit to the King's was to see one called, *Simba,* which was about lions in Africa. I was taken by friends and we were stuffily packed in somewhere near the back of the Upper Circle. I was a terrible snob and thought that it was, contradictory as it may sound, as awful come-down to go up so high! I was used either to the Stalls or the Dress Circle. At the Pier, one could not go higher than the one circle anyway unless one sat with the seagulls on the roof! My first impression of the King's was that its colouring was too palid and that it lacked the exciting dark golden embrace of the Theatre Royal. As bigger and more expensive shows toured during the late twenties, it gradually became once-nightly and took over the role of being the 'No. 1' from the Royal which declined into becoming a twice-nightly weekly repertory theatre.

Portsmouth, and its residential area, Southsea, had a total of five theatres at that time. Of the remaining three, two were, as the King's had been, variety houses. By far the better of these was the Hippodrome which was very pleasant and had a graceful auditorium of pale brown and white marble but, sadly, it was reduced to rubble by enemy bombs during World War II. The other was the Coliseum which was regarded as the sailors' music hall and to which people like us, moving as we did only within our own very narrow social boundaries, never went. Ironically, many decades later, I did actually appear there in two rather chaste Sunday evening entertainments!

The fifth and last in the list was the South Parade Pier and, as this was only a few hundred yards from Crossways, as I grew older I went to it frequently. I never lost the love for it that had been kindled by those first pantomimes and when, tragically, it was totally destroyed by fire whilst Ken Russell was shooting a sequence for his film *Tommy* in the theatre in 1974, I was very deeply saddened.

After the end of the run of the Christmas pantomime, it was mostly 'dark' until Easter except for occasional performances by amateurs. There were also Travelogues, usually about the far-flung Empire and illustrated with lantern slides, in the Minor Hall. This was a large room with a dance floor that also did service as the foyer of the theatre which, round about Easter, the local amateur operatic society, the Portsmouth Players, reopened for the summer season. That continued until the middle of July with the succession of weekly concert parties. From then until mid-September, it became again, as it had been during its pantomime, a fully-fledged theatre rivalling the Royal and the King's. It was during these two months of high summer that, throughout my schooldays, I was able to digest very concentrated doses of what the commercial theatre had on offer. I lapped up everything from the French windows and bedroom doors of *Rookery Nook* to the sinister oak panelling in Edgar Wallace's thriller, *The Man Who Changed His Name;* and from the Chinese villainy in *The Silent House* to the cockney merriment of *Alf's Button*.

I had seen my first great actor by the time I was only ten, even before seeing Fred Terry and Julia Neilson. He was another of the actor-managers who constantly toured. It was Sir John Martin Harvey and I saw him in the charming Pier Theatre at Eastbourne which an arsonist heartlessly tried to destroy some years ago. The play was his famous Lyceum drama, *The Only Way,* based on Dickens's *A Tale of Two Cities*: an actual Victorian production still on the road! It was also in that same theatre that I remember being made to cry for the first time! Then the play was *The Yellow Streak* and the star was Jeanne de Casalis who in later years became famous for her delightful comedy act of Mrs Feather.

However, it was during the play seasons on our own home pier that I saw most of my earliest professional theatre. Every summer it was two months of sheer delight! I was even excited by the fact that, instead of the solitary piano of the concert parties, there was a real live orchestra in the pit to provide the interval music. For musical comedies—the term 'musical' by itself is post-war, of course—it was considerably augmented, especially with brass and percussion. My first such shows, seen on the Pier, were ones that are now forgotten such as *My Son John, Queen High* and *The Blue Train*. My very first play was *Just Married,* a farcical romp set on a pleasure cruise, and the following week I was taken to see *The Unfair Sex*. I have always been so grateful to my mother for letting me go straight in at the deep end: she obviously saw nothing wrong with those titles as fare for a small child! Others started with *Where the Rainbow Ends* and *Pinkie and the Fairies*. Kids' stuff!

I was taken to most of these shows on the Pier by my sister who taught me not to fidget. The consequence is that I have spent the rest of my life becoming neurotic whenever I am in a theatre because someone near me will always do just that. I sometimes wish she had not been such a successful teacher! As I entered my teens, she became involved in the alternative pleasure of being engaged and then married—rather short-lived delights as will become evident in

Theatre Royal, Portsmouth

due course. I then started going to cinemas and theatres with school friends and also with my mother who loved both forms of entertainment.

We went to all sorts of plays and films but we became particularly enthusiastic supporters of the Denville Players, the repertory company at the Theatre Royal. Having abandoned, many years before, all idea of becoming a tram driver when I left school, I now wanted to be a repertory actor—preferably at the Theatre Royal for life!

Friday was usually the night for going to the King's Theatre and that meant evening dress. Such formality, especially in the provinces, must seem rather pretentious these many years later but it had a certain style and charm. I am old-fashioned enough to think that today we have gone too far the other way. The theatre is always the more exciting by being something of an occasion—and one need not go any the less often simply because one bothers to wear a tie!

My theatrical education was strongly supplemented on these Friday nights by seeing many famous stars including such people as Ivor Novello, Marie Tempest, Owen Nares, Fay Compton, Zena Dare, Seymour Hicks, Sybil Thorndike, Jack Buchanan, Binnie Hale, Edna Best and Matheson Lang as well as the later Aldwych farces which were always 'tried out' at the King's. When I was fifteen, however, one particular production played there which changed my whole theatrical outlook. Up till this point I had known only purely commercial theatre but here, for the first time, I encountered something which was primarily intellectual and artistic. I was stunned and delighted. It was my theatrical Damascus Road; this particular blinding flash showed me the way for the rest of my life.

It was Max Reinhardt's production of *The Miracle,* a spectacular semi-religious mime with music by Humperdinck, which Cochran had staged at the Lyceum Theatre where the auditorium had been transformed into a representation of the interior of a cathedral. The London run had ended and it was now on tour.

As we went into the theatre, we found that the curtain was already up—a familiar device today but then startlingly stark. The set that greeted us was an incredibly realistic one of a great church. It was solid and three-dimensional with a complete absence of the flapping garishness that I had been brought up on. The lighting, too, was absolutely natural as there were no footlights.

The orchestra was hidden and broad steps connected the floor of the stalls with the stage. An organ had been installed and there was a smell of incense. One of the much publicised features of the production was the performance by Lady Diana Cooper who, as the statue of the Madonna that comes to life, had to stand completely motionless for three-quarters of an hour. Oliver Messel had designed what appeared to me to be ravishingly beautiful costumes and Oscar Strnad the equally magnificent scenery. Religious processions filed through the stalls and up into the cathedral, the organ played, a hidden choir sang and this great and marvellous spectacle absolutely bowled me over. Perhaps the most important effect it had on me was to make me see at one stroke just how vulgar so much of what I had previously enjoyed in the theatre had been. Showiness had been replaced by beauty.

'Not a word of Costard yet', says the rustic in *Love's Labour's Lost* when he is listening to the reading of a long letter that has still not reached the main subject. Not a word of Shakespeare yet, my reader might well echo. In the words of Prospero—to quote again—''Tis time I should inform thee further'.

CHAPTER 2
Shakespeare on my shoulder

The second 'parent' of my eventual Shakespearean feat was the discovery of the Great Man Himself.

I do not remember hearing his name mentioned at home when I was a small child but I suppose it must have been occasionally. I first had my attention drawn to it when I was only about four or five years old. I went to a children's Christmas party and when we arrived we each had a piece of paper bearing a famous name pinned on to our shoulders. We then had to ask the other children questions about it—short of the outright 'Who the blazes is it?'—to discover what the name was. I cannot remember what I asked or what answers I got but I do know that I could not guess mine. What is more, I recollect not having much idea who the so-called famous name might be when finally I did find out.

It was, of course, Shakespeare. There would have been little point in telling this story if it had not been but it may well sound too convenient a yarn to be true. Actually, it is: absolutely so. At that early age, I had Shakespeare on my shoulder and he has been there ever since. I do not think of him as being in any way a burden to carry but more like a splendid cloak of myriad colours that it has been an endless enchantment to wear. However, there was no blinding flash that afternoon: this miracle took rather longer to work!

The next contact was *Lamb's Tales from Shakespeare*. Just how they appeared on the scene I do not remember: probably at school, I should think. Once having been introduced to them, I dived in on my own accord because I knew that these were the stories of plays and therefore they could be adapted to my toy theatre. There must have been some lapse of time as I certainly could not read more than 'cat' and 'rat' when the slip of paper was pinned on to my shoulder. I soon decided that they had no feel of the theatre about them and gave them up. At this point, my sister, Gwen, comes back into the story. She was engaged to be married no less than three times: first of all to a Welsh solicitor; then to the charming but impecunious scion of a family with famous naval connections and, finally, to a bank clerk. The Welsh solicitor was often generous and amongst the presents that he gave her was Volume One of *The Works of Shakespeare.* I never knew why he never gave her Volumes Two and Three! I think that they would probably have been wasted on her as she gave me Volume One, obviously without a pang, as soon as I said that I wanted to read it because it contained plays and not just those untheatrical tales. Perhaps the engagement was over by then and the presents had lost their savour.

This time a kind of miracle did happen. I was totally captivated by what I read although I did not understand it. It was rather like listening to an opera in a foreign language that one does not speak, after having heard the plot in English. I started with *The Winter's Tale.* I have learned since that by the time he wrote this play, Shakespeare had evolved an incredibly complicated syntax and that I could hardly have chosen a more difficult one to be my first. I had read the story in Lamb and so I found myself saying such things as, 'This must be about the place where such and such happens'. The important thing was that I found it all absolutely intoxicating and felt as if I were under some magical compulsion to keep going. With Hermione, I could truly say, 'Sir, you speak a language that I understand not', but I loved it and could not put the book down.

This state of blissful but frustrating ignorance did not last long: Shakespeare started coming at me from many different directions. For example, every month there was a broadcast on the radio of one of the plays on a Sunday afternoon and I never missed any of them if I could possibly help it. I even managed to get a dispensation from the obligatory family trek to the golf course. The better the weather the more difficult this was to obtain: family discipline was strict in those days. Sometimes I listened to these broadcasts alone at home, whilst my parents endlessly chased those little white balls, but on other occasions I went across the road to the home of my oldest friend, Paul Hayward. His mother was a prim little woman of whom I was very fond. She read good books and as a family they listened to a lot of classical music. At home, my sister's tastes were essentially popular. In the twenties, she had been a 'flapper' with short skirts, cloche hats and low waists and the pieces that she played on the piano were only the latest dance tunes. My mother was more intellectual and her tastes developed still further as she got older. She, too, was a pianist but her repertoire was restricted to gentle works like Schumann's *Traumerei,* Chopin and the drawing-room ballads that she used to sing to her own accompaniment. She was a trained singer although she had never appeared in public. When she performed at home, even as a very small child I was always deeply moved and I invariably cried. She was adventurous enough to tackle Elisabeth's Prayer from *Tannhauser* and she liked good, as opposed to classical, books.

My father was entirely uninterested in the arts and my brother, abroad most of the time anyway, was a quite positive non-starter. I had instinctively been attracted by the something special about the visits of the opera companies, even as far back as my pantomimes-and-posters days, and now these contacts with the Hayward family opened up the world of classical music to me. There was hardly any to be heard live in Portsmouth and Southsea but we had the blessing of the radio. Most of what I learned at school bored me and I have always maintained that I was primarily educated by the BBC. I certainly learned about Shakespeare by leaps and bounds from that very great British institution. As might be expected, at this time I also started collecting records.

One of the amateur companies to perform at the Pier during those mainly 'dark' winter months was the Portsmouth Teachers' Dramatic Society. Through them I was able to see my first Shakespeare plays on the stage. There was a lull at that time in the professional touring of them, certainly as far as our local theatres were concerned. The Benson Company had come to the end of the road and Harold V. Neilson's had not yet reached us.

My first play was *Twelfth Night* and it was set in a surround of purplish curtains with odd cut-outs of box trees and so forth. After that, I saw them do several others and, although I enjoyed them up to a point—the mere process of going to a theatre was still a great thrill—they did strike me as smelling of the schoolroom. There surely had to be a better way of staging them. I knew that the stuffy old bore who played Brutus and Prospero like a rather repressive headmaster was not giving me what I had imagined when I had read those parts. Even at that age, I realised that much of the production was bad and so I had no conscience pricking me when I joined the other schoolboys in laughing aloud at one of the goddesses, a dreary unattractive woman, who, when she raised her arm to welcome Juno, revealed that she had not shaved where a lady who is going to do that in front of several thousand people should! I still do not regret the laugh: the director should have spotted it and told her to pull her blue stockings up. Occasionally there was actual painted scenery but it was very uninspiring. If the other plays that I was seeing had scenery that I liked, why could not Shakespeare have some, too? I realise now, of course, that it was largely a matter of economics. They could hire only what they could afford and that clearly did not amount to much. Above all, there was, as I should also understand in the years to come, a good deal of artistic poverty.

Eventually, I saw a professional company, led by one Gerald Cooper, give a schools performance in the Wesley Central Hall in Portsmouth; a Methodist church with an open concert platform. It was very spartan and the only attempt at a setting was a small screen at the back on which was a vague mediaeval hunting scene. The play was *The Tempest* and I enjoyed it far more than any Shakespeare play I had yet seen. I realised that the scenery had not really mattered very much after all and that it had been the quality of the acting and the imaginative direction that had raised it so far above the teachers' stodgy efforts.

I had by now long since out-grown my initiation with Volume One. Someone had given me a battered and cumbersome set of the *Library Shakespeare* which had been published in nine books round about the 1870s. It was rather grand and was spaciously set out with nearly 800 splendid engravings by Sir John Gilbert and George Cruickshank. Their rich and dramatic plates were full of very attractive architectural details, elaborate brocade draperies and superb voluminous costumes. There was a fine Renaissance feel about them even if the heavily-moustached, earnest-looking young men and the rather imperious women, gave them a veneer of the 19th century. My original set disappeared long ago but a very kind retired teacher has given me another in recent years. Strange to say, Olivia looks demure and fragile in these pictures whereas at the time when they were done, and even when I was young, the words, 'marble breasted' were usually regarded as the key to the character. Like Gertrude in those days, she was often imagined as being played by an actress of the mould of Mrs Crummles!

When I first acquired the Whole Works, I was slightly daunted by that solid mass of Henries in the middle! There is little to choose between V, IV and VI or between two lots of Parts 1 and 2 and a single Part 3 when you do not know one from the other. When I staged these plays in later years, I always tried to remember that there would be many prospective patrons who would be in the same state of ignorance. They had to be attracted and it is all too easy to be repelled by those forbidding titles. None the less, I had ploughed very happily on and by the time I was eighteen I had read every one of Shakespeare's plays at least once.

School! Yes, between all these bouts of theatre- and cinema-going and reading of Shakespeare, I did have to go to school. After a *kindergarten,* I went as a day boy to St. Helen's College in Southsea; the sort of private establishment that liked to think that it was a minor public school. In fact, it was not but, I suppose, in a small way it was run as an imitation of one. It had been considered at one time to be the best of its kind anywhere in the area but whilst I was there it began to decline and in the end became rather seedy. The lease of the playing fields on the sea front ran out a few years after I left and the whole school moved to a Georgian house at Thames Ditton. I had hated it and so I had no interest in keeping in touch.

I was a reasonably fit child but, not being strong in the muscular sense, I was very bad at games and 'gym'. I dreaded them and this made me unpopular with the toughs who, being even more insensitive than average children to the feelings of their fellows, found me a good subject for bullying. I was, and still am, a bad mathematician and so automatically that whole range of subjects became a torture. I liked geography and would have enjoyed history if it had dealt with more than just politics, wars and dates. The way people lived and dressed, how they designed and built their houses, what they wrote and in which ways they enriched their own times as well as ours with their paintings and their plays—all these matters were untouched. I liked Shakespeare, of course, and I was unique in that I seemed to be the only boy in the school who did. During most of my time, our English master was an amiable man named Collins who was obviously fond of his subject but taught it rather tamely. In fact, we did surprisingly little Shakespeare and only one of the plays was ever considered for production during all my years there. A charming master named Rendell was going to put on *Twelfth Night,* with me as Sebastian, but, tragically, he died before it could be staged.

My first appearance on the boards had been when I was 6. It took place at St. Peter's Hall—of which a very great deal later—when I was a troll king in a mime for tiny tots in one of the *kindergarten's* end-of-term concerts. The first time that I opened my mouth on the stage was when I was at St. Helen's College; though, even then, it has to be admitted that I did not open it very far or produce any particularly significant sounds! I cannot sing. That plain, categorical statement is just not capable of being denied, but when I was about ten I believed otherwise. One of the mediaeval plays of *Noah's Flood* was being cast and foolishly I volunteered for one of the parts that involved singing a song.

I auditioned with 'Two little bluebirds' from *Sunny,* which I thought that I knew after hearing my sister play it on the piano; it was the latest 'hit'. I remember being terrible but, strange to say, I got the part which was one of Noah's Wife's Gossips.

How they let me get through the rehearsals, I do not know, but I suppose they kept me in the part simply because it was 'bound to be right on the'—no, not night; the afternoon. The performance took place in the assembly hall in front of the whole school and when I got to my solo moment, which was about all I had to do, I just gazed ahead in silence. It was not that I had forgotten (or 'dried', to use the theatrical term); I simply could not face it!

I was also in two plays, each put on by the school dramatic society for one performance only, in my beloved Pier Theatre. The great thrill of appearing on that stage was one of the highlights of my school life. I was still very junior and so they were non-speaking parts: the seniors were the only ones who spoke. I was a schoolgirl in *The Strange Adventures of Miss Brown,* a farce set in a girls' school which had originally been staged at the Vaudeville Theatre, London, in 1895. I quail now when I think back to all those small boys dressed up as girls! *The Brass Bottle,* another farce from the same theatre but this time dating from 1909, saw me as an Arabian slave!

I played various other parts in plays at school, ranging from an elderly lady in *The Bathroom Door* (a favourite one-acter at that time) to a headmaster in *The Man with a Cane.* After Mr Rendell had died, the dramatic society had more or less lapsed. This was my chance. By now, I was becoming fairly senior and the days of fighting and bullying had died out. With my interest in the arts being well-known, I was regarded as something of an intellectual and this was fine because, to a certain extent, it isolated me. The very characteristics that had made me unpopular as a junior were now seen in a different light and actually earned me some respect. This was quite apart from my school work which was pretty indifferent because it bored me. Our headmaster, T. Barrick Askew, MA, was the prototype of what all of his ilk are supposed to look like. He was big and impressive with a quelling gaze, a slow rumbling way of clearing his throat and a quiet step. It was therefore with trepidation that I approached him to see if he would allow me to be the first boy ever to run the school dramatic society and put on a show. To my surprise he agreed. Under the watchful eye of a master called Denis Bates, I put on a concert party after handing the musical side of it over to a schoolfriend of the name of Maguire. As far as I can remember, it was all remarkably successful.

I was now old enough to appreciate, or otherwise, schoolmasters as human beings and not just as creatures of infinite age living aside from the world of men. Denis Bates was quite different from any other that I had come across: he looked a lot like today's talented American actor, David Soul—tall, good-looking and Scandinavian blonde—and he had humour and a breadth of spirit that brought sunshine and air into the dusty atmosphere of the school. I used to 'cut' the twice-weekly 'gym' on the pretext that I had a health dispensation and somehow I got away with it. During these periods, I went instead to the study shared by Denis Bates and another master to listen to records of the classics. At first I chattered through them, as we did at home, but, to my surprise, they told me to be quiet and give the music a chance. So simple a thing, unlikely though it may seem, opened up yet another new world. I learned to listen! After some time they gave me a most exciting experience by taking me to my first operas; the double bill of *Cavalleria Rusticana* and *Pagliacci* performed by the Carl Rosa company at the King's. I already knew a reasonable amount of opera from what used to be referred to on gramophone records as 'vocal gems' and from listening to radio relays from Covent Garden and the Wagner nights at the Proms, and so this was the fulfilment of a long-standing dream. Another memorable occasion was when Denis Bates and I went together to the King's to see the play, *Richard of Bordeaux*. Much as we enjoyed it, I well remember him soundly prophesying as we came out, 'You'll find Shakespeare's *Richard II* is much better'.

I was now in my last year at St. Helen's College and I could see that his bright and imaginative personality was chafing against its dusty confinement and petty discipline. He left at the end of the same term as I did and went to Africa as a geologist. We corresponded for a while and it is one of my life's regrets that eventually we lost touch. When I last saw him, he could not wait to escape from the school to reach 'a world elsewhere'. Nor could I.

CHAPTER 3
The building site

The third progenitor of my future Shakespeare world record made its first appearance as a muddy building site on a wet day.

When I was about 13, I was travelling with my parents from Bournville, where we had been staying with friends, down to Portsmouth. On the way, we made a brief stop in Stratford-upon-Avon because my parents thought that I would like to see Shakespeare's birthplace as I was already such a devoted admirer of his plays. It was one of those days of continual rain that seem to be unnaturally dark but, none the less, it lit a flame in my life that has burned steadily ever since.

I have always been very sensitive to the almost electric atmosphere in a consecrated building and I find the feeling of the presence of God in an old church quite literally breath-taking. Other places and less cosmic presences have stirred me deeply too and so my heart beat hard and my throat dried when I stood, little lad though I still was, in the house in which Shakespeare must have been born. We know for certain that his parents were living there at the time and, in those centuries before maternity wards existed, middle-class people always had their children at home. Those respectable burghers, the Shakespeares, would have been no exception.

Although no man's writings throb more with the warm pulse of humanity than Shakespeare's, it has always seemed to me that he is too often thought of quite impersonally. It is as if the plays had been produced by a speaking marble monument like the Commendatore in *Don Giovanni.* 'When he breathed, he was a man' says Don Adriano. In recent times, I have taken part each year in the Birthday Celebrations at Stratford and whenever I have done so I have always felt that I am honouring a friend whom I have known and loved ever since that grey day when I first met him in the house where he lived as a child and which eventually he owned.

When we came out of the Birthplace, my mother bought me a little china bust of Shakespeare which I still treasure. Today it gazes at a lifetime's collection of books, playbills and other theatrical bits and pieces—most of them connected with him. Beware, Sir Oracle, of mocking such tourist souvenirs! Many of them are purchased for, or by, the devoted and any one of them could be the key to the door of Shakespeare's world.

The purchase having been made, we then walked down the town to the river. There on the bank was the building site that I have mentioned and a very large one it was, too. The walls were up to about the height of the first storey and it was still of an indeterminate shape which could have been anything from a power station to a factory. Entirely in red brick, it was surrounded by a vast chaos of scaffolding, lorries, workmen, cranes and, most universally of all, mud. I was told that this must be the new Shakespeare Memorial Theatre but I had not even heard of the old one, much less that there was to be another. How wonderfully exciting! A theatre! Any sort of theatre will do but this was to be a *theatre for Shakespeare!* I was beside myself with sheer delight!

We walked along Waterside towards this great, sprawling embryo and then went into the barn-like building that still stands just opposite. It now houses the constructors of scenery but then it was the reading room of some sort of club connected with the Shakespeare Festivals. Elderly people sitting about inside looked up at us as if we were invaders of the Atheneum! The room was virtually a small hall with the far end completely partitioned off by cretonne curtains of floral design. I assumed incorrectly that these were part of a stage and that this must be where they were putting on the plays whilst waiting for the new theatre across the road to be completed. The whole concept of Stratford as a place where they were constantly being performed captured my imagination and from that moment I wanted to find out as much as I could about this marvellous place.

Before I had learned how to escape from the embarrassing 'gym' sessions at school, I found myself one afternoon 'standing easy' in the ranks next to a boy called Kustner. We were awaiting our turns to take flying leaps over the vaulting horse. I would fail, as always, and either stop short or else do a sort of belly-flop on to the top of it! Whilst we were chatting, he happened to mention that he had an aunt who lived in Stratford and that he had quite often been taken to see the plays there. Here, at last, was a first-hand informant but to my great frustration he did not possess my eye for detail. I realised much later that he must have been taken to the cinema which was used as a temporary theatre after the original Memorial had been burned down in 1926.

Shakespeare's birthday, 23 April, was chosen as the date for the opening of the new one in 1932. As the day drew nearer, so it built up more and more as a news item. I do not remember any building since that created quite such a sensation or so much controversy, except the new cathedral at Coventry. Theatres were in a serious decline largely because the 'talkies' had arrived only a few years before and the Golden Age of the Cinema was well under way. Film with sound was acclaimed as the new medium that had tolled the death knell of the theatre. Cinemas were being built and were sure of good business whilst theatres were going down like flies. Some closed and were destroyed but the majority of them, including the Southsea King's and the Portsmouth Royal, became cinemas. The latter appeared to have gone permanently but the former soon started to have stage shows again. Not surprisingly, I made a bit of a scene in the dress circle foyer at the Theatre Royal on its last night as a live theatre in protest at its going over to films!

Hardly any theatres, therefore, had been built during the past decade and those that already existed were either Victorian or were in the washed-out, half-hearted semi-classical styles of the earlier years of this century. The decision had been made—and wisely, of course—that the new Shakespeare Memorial Theatre must be of its own time and incorporate all the latest in stage machinery, lighting, decor and comfort. Today we live far enough away from the 19th century to be able to enjoy its best architecture and to delight in the flamboyance of its heavy, ornate decoration. The era of my boyhood was too close to it and it was condemned wholesale. Everything must be of the cleanest lines with adornment totally omitted unless there was some special cause for it. Even then it must be light and airy without any suspicion of fussiness. The Stratford theatre was designed and built according to these principles.

The new playhouse that had arisen on the banks of the Avon was of startling modernity. It was a blaze of new brick and had, in an age that was not used to such things, the stark hard edges and rectangular blocks of a toy fort enormously enlarged. Those who know it today as the Royal Shakespeare Theatre, the less funereal name it acquired in 1961, see brickwork that has weathered to a gentler colour and contours much softened by the graceful enlargements of the restaurant terraces over the river. Even as this is written, the theatre is now well over half a century old and we are used to such a design. Although many changes have been made over the years, especially to the auditorium, it remains basically the same and now we can enjoy it as a splendid piece of Art Deco of the thirties. It still has, none the less, a very modern look in spite of its age. In 1932, now well over half a century ago, its design was so revolutionary that it was often described as 'futuristic'—which, in a sense, it was.

This did not suit the Great British Public! The popular abusive epithet was, 'Jam factory!' When asked what they would have preferred, most people seemed to think that it should have been like the old theatres that they already knew or even something on the lines of Ye Olde Tudor. However, they all agreed that even if it had been the latter it should still have all the latest 'mod. cons.' for both audience and actors. Quite how these irreconcilables could be fitted together, no one seemed to know. On the other hand, I was greatly excited by everything that I heard about it and desperately hoped that one day I should actually be able to go and see it.

The day of the opening arrived at last and I sat with both ears glued to the fretwork-fronted speaker of the family radio. Everyone, it seemed, was there except King George V who had gone to the Cup Final! The fashions were described and I remember being particularly impressed by the account of a lady's hat that was composed entirely of live violets. The Prince of Wales, no more of a Shakespearean than his father but only second down the list of the royalty available, arrived by aircraft which landed in the fields on the other side of the river. He made his speech and, after receiving a gold key from the architect, Miss Elizabeth Scott, he opened the new theatre. Little did he know—and less would he have cared even if he had known—that he had inaugurated a temple that I should continue to worship almost as much as the god whose works were performed within. It was built at the perfect stage in my formative years and I have had a love affair with it ever since.

In November of the same year, we again found ourselves travelling south through Stratford-upon-Avon. This time it was a frosty but brilliantly sunny day. What I had last seen as a muddy building site now stood dazzling and stark as an iceberg that had somehow managed to exchange its expected whiteness for brick red. The surrounding apparent muddle had given place to smooth lawns and unruffled autumnal trees. To my delight, I discovered that for a small sum one could have a guided tour of this latest marvel. Whatever criticisms had been levelled against it, there was no doubt that it was a great sensation and crowds of people wanted to see the wonders of the interior. These had been tantalisingly described in the Radio Times and in most newspapers and so, as I went in, my throat was parched and I was trembling through sheer ecstacy.

Theatre foyers had been, up to this moment, dirty cream and gilt; cramped places vulgarised with posters for next week's *No No Nanette* or *Mother Goose.* Now I stepped into a new world. It was dignified, cool and quite extraordinarily fresh and clean, without a poster or photograph anywhere. It was austere and immensely impressive. This high foyer, with its almost ashen brick walls, pale green marble pilasters and steel box office took my breath away. In recent years, it has been overpoweringly cluttered with posters and giant photographs to make it friendly and comfortable but, for me, this is a mistake. Whenever I went into the Stratford theatre in those early days, I tingled with excitement because it was so different and filled me with the most pleasurable awe. The powerful and dignified performance that the building itself gave was greatly thrilling. I am still excited by it even now but I do believe that today's desire to remove anything that might be felt to be more impressive and magnificent than pop-culture-everypeople would find comfortable, is to rob theatres of the wonder that is their very essence.

I went on to see the beautiful green marble staircase winding round the mosaic-floored fountain and then into the auditorium. It had the simplicity of the inside of a giant egg and was all in subdued colours. The circle and the gallery went straight across, as in most cinemas, and the walls were one smooth sweep almost from floor to floor right across the ceiling which was broken by three bands of concealed light. On either side of the proscenium were tall panelled doors which became known affectionately as the 'wardrobes' and indeed they did look something like giant versions of such articles of furniture. The dark grey apron stage was backed by a most attractive safety curtain. On a white ground, Vladimir Polunin had painted in pastel shades a full-length portrait of Shakespeare surrounded by sepia sketches of scenes from the plays.

Since that time the auditorium has been altered almost totally out of recognition. The smooth walls have disappeared behind side extensions of the circle and the gallery which embrace the stage and which have made it altogether more intimate. These alterations have been quite exciting in their way but I do sometimes find myself yearning for the charm of the original decor when I look at today's black studio functionalism. Most of the alterations have, in fact, been made to try to eradicate various faults in its design as a working theatre that in the earlier years had either not been discovered or were not admitted. For these, of course, we must be thankful.

Two years later, having passed my 'School Cert', I thankfully left school. To celebrate, my parents gave me a visit to Stratford and a performance at my beloved theatre. I sent for the programme and we chose *Romeo and Juliet.* We booked seats in the Dress Circle because I wanted a good view of the theatre as well as a chance to see the play. After being used to a small orchestra churning out popular tunes whilst we looked at the footlight glow on the curtain, the cool good taste of what was now set before us had a serene beauty that seemed to me to be almost spiritual. There was no music other than that specifically related to the play, no footlights and a refreshing absence of brashness. Only *The Miracle* before this had given me even the slightest hint that anything on so high an artistic level existed in the theatre. Even the Carl Rosa Opera, with its travel-worn multi-purpose scenery, was a nearer relation to the provincial touring companies than to this.

Instead of a curtain, there was, for this production, a simple arrangement of doors, balconies and an inner stage, all matching the dark grey of the apron and the plain square proscenium. As parts or all of these areas were opened, brightly coloured sets, like the backgrounds of Rennaisance paintings, were revealed. The standard of the Stratford company in those days was often criticised for not being on the high international level that it later reached, but we had accidentally chosen particularly well. This production had been acclaimed by the critics but, in any case, it was just all so wonderful to me that it exceeded everything that I had imagined. This occasion still remains in my memory as one of the great nights of my life.

Next year, a week's family holiday was spent in Stratford. My mother enjoyed both the town and the theatre and continued to do so for more than twenty years but my father got rather bored. We saw Catherine Lacey in an Elizabethan-style production of *The Taming of the Shrew* and in a fine and spectacular *Antony and Cleopatra.* Then followed a visually beautiful staging of *The Tempest* and Komisarjevsky's fantastic treatment of *The Merry Wives of Windsor.* In it, a marvellous Shakespearean comedian, Roy Byford, was a Falstaff who was made to look like the Emperor Franz Josef and the frisky gambol was set in a small square of pastel-coloured dolls' houses. Herne's oak was little more than a shrub and Windsor Park consisted of the houses' roofs supported on slender white poles after the walls had been removed. I was horrified and said so! From now on, although my adoration of the Stratford theatre remained little short of idolatrous, I could be critical and apply judgements.

I wanted to go back to Stratford during the following year but my parents said 'no' and so that was the end of that. We went instead to Cornwall but my father was so querulous that my mother and I decided that in future she and I would go away together and he could go off on his own. In 1937, we did just that. This time we went to Stratford for a fortnight.

Although I have seen, no doubt, many greater productions than the average offering that year, it remains my *favourite* even after over five decades. It was a golden year! My mother's and my relationship was at its best and we explored all the lovely surrounding country from Warwick to Chipping Campden and from Broadway to Kenilworth. What was more, I went to the Shakespeare Memorial Theatre no less than ten times.

There were two people involved in the 1937 Festival (as the Shakespeare Season there was called right up till 1950) that were to have a great deal of influence on me. One was Komisarjevsky and the other, by far the more important in the story I have to tell, was Donald Wolfit.

Komisarjevsky's production of *King Lear* that year was his greatest Stratford success. The wilful and irreverent Russian director staged several plays there during the thirties and each one of them produced strong reactions from the public. The purists were appalled at the liberties he had taken but those who cared more for lively theatre than textual accuracy adored them. They were never dull, however far they may sometimes have strayed from the author's intentions, and, what is more, they were money-spinners at the box office! *King Lear,* which seemed to impress everyone, was played on a permanent set of complicated blocks of golden steps in a series of quite staggering lighting effects. Even when I strip away the rosy haze of youthful inexperience and the bright film that time tends to cast on to productions long past, I know that this was indeed one of the finest pieces of theatre that I have ever seen. Komisarjevsky and his methods had more influence on my future directing and designing than anyone else whose work I have known solely through being a member of the audience.

Donald Wolfit was the leading actor of the Festival and played a wide range of parts that included Hamlet, Kent, Iachimo, Autolycus, Ford and the *Henry V* Chorus. His Hamlet, whilst he was still in his thirties, was dynamic and brilliant and he immediately became a great hero to me. One day, when I was out with someone from where we were staying, we met him and I was introduced. It was a great thrill for me, of course, but I expect he forgot the meeting as soon as I was out of sight. Neither of us could possibly have guessed that in due course we should enjoy a friendship that was to last for 30 years.

Seeing the plays at Stratford every year now became part of my way of life. 1938 brought, amongst other memorable performances, Phyllis Neilson-Terry as Queen Katherine and Lady Macbeth. The former music hall comedian, Jay Laurier—for many years afterwards a great Stratford favourite—was Launce in a lovely production of *The Two Gentlemen of Verona* that was all mauves, dove greys and primrose yellows. Komisarjevsky did a brilliant *Comedy of Errors* and then followed it in 1939 with a Commedia del'Arte *Taming of the Shrew.* On 2 September, 1939, *The Comedy of Errors* was played in the Memorial Theatre and the next day, Neville Chamberlain announced, after weeks of unbearable tension, that we were at war with Germany. The title of the last play always seemed to me to be ironical. It echoes Canio's line after the tragic butchery at the end of *Pagliacci,* 'La commedia è finita!'

In the autumn of 1940, I had my first holiday alone in Stratford. It was a long weekend at the time when the terrible bombing of our cities was just beginning. On the Saturday, I saw a matinee of *King John* and found, as we all did at that time, that the lines about how England never did nor never shall lie at the proud foot of a conqueror, were tremendously emotive. In the evening there was a most enjoyable *As You Like It* in which everyone shuffled about on a stage covered with fallen leaves. Perhaps that filled me even more with a love of England than the history had done at the matinee. When I came out of the theatre, I went and stood on the bridge over the Avon. I was quite alone and all buildings were, of course, blacked out but there was, however, intensely brilliant moonlight. The dark river moved beneath me, a few ghost-grey swans drifted about and the great mass of the theatre rose silvery-solid, looking terribly exposed, on the far bank. The scene was incredibly beautiful. Would I ever see any of it again? I was only just into my twenties and so much had opened up for me during the previous few years: the arts, music, Shakespeare, theatre, Stratford—wonderful new worlds had expanded my own personal universe like flowers opening in speeded-up films. Was it all to be smashed and destroyed by the war? Where should we all be this time next year? Above all, I was thinking at that moment, would that theatre, which I loved so much, be bombed into a heap of rubble? Only the man in the moon saw the tears that streamed down my cheeks.

CHAPTER 4
Laying my foundations

The mother of one of my schoolfriends once said to mine, in tones both smug and spiteful, 'What a pity Peter is so fond of the theatre!' (I must explain at this point that I am Peter. My parents wanted to call me that but at the last minute my father had the not-very-good-idea that I might not like a biblical name and so they christened me Kenneth instead. Even so, I have never been called anything but Peter ever since.)

'What a pity Peter is so fond of the theatre' was, in many ways, the key-note of my search for a career. I wanted to go into the theatre but my mother was determined that I should do something less precarious.

One of my possible alternatives came about partly because my father was a principle shareholder in a local chain of cinemas. An old family friend named Charles Fowley had, with two pals of his from the trenches of World War I, built a small cinema called the Palace and the company had grown from there. It was a delightful building with a Moorish facade topped by domes and minarets and I had a free pass. It has now been converted into a disco after declining into an 'X Films' house but in my youth, which was during the Hollywood Golden Age, it showed the usual run of family fare.

As a schoolboy I had a very simple theory about Crime and Punishment. I do not think that I ever deliberately did anything that I believed was morally wrong but I did not include in that category the misdeeds that were simply a matter of not obeying headmaster-made rules. If the severity of the punishment was greater than the pleasure of the misdemeanour, then I would not risk it. I could not keep away from the Palace! This meant 'cutting' football and cricket on Wednesday afternoons and skimping my homework on at least one evening a week. This was the only major misdeed for which I would gamble on being caned!

Having been persuaded that an actor's life was not for me, I next decided that I wanted to own a cinema—preferably the Palace! We actually got as far as discussing it seriously with Charles Fowley but he advised against it. He prophesied, correctly as eventually one saw, that cinemas would all fall into the hands of the great multi-million corporations and that the management of them would become simply caretaking and housekeeping.

Other things were considered: estate agent, quantity surveyor, photographer—all these appeared as possibilities and quickly disappeared. In those days before Social Security it was vital to have a job that was safe and had prospects of enough money for eventual retirement. The real answer, it was decided, was a profession. Whatever happened, one would then be *qualified.* Eventually, dentistry was suggested. Well, perhaps. 'Perhaps' was enough to signify 'yes' and I was committed. I felt no particular desire to do it but we knew several dentists who seemed to be reasonably prosperous and not too bowed down by their work.

It was at about this time that I started to become interested in my relations and ancestors. Both my parents had come from King's Norton in Warwickshire, then apparently a charming village but now swallowed up to become a suburb of Birmingham. My father had no interest in the family history and consequently could not tell me anything about it. I turned to his brother and sister in Birmingham, my Uncle Ernest and Aunt Nan. They were full of it and only too happy to tell me all they could. It transpired that in the line of my paternal grandmother (née Mary Ann Edmonds) there was a long stream of forbears all interested in Shakespeare, the theatre and various forms of public speaking and tub-thumping. A letter from my paternal grandmother to this uncle, thanking him for the book of Ellen Terry's memoirs, says,

> 'I find it very interesting . . . as most of the actors and actresses are of my young days, so that I have seen most of them play their parts. Pa used to take me once a week to the theatre and often go without me, he was so fond of the play. My grandfather Bland was an amazing man for the play and Grandma Bland was the same, always quoting Shakespeare . . .'

'Pa' was my own grandfather, of course, and the Blands (actually the name was Ward-Bland) were therefore my great-great-grandparents. A great-uncle, Edward Edmonds, was a lecturer in French, German and Spanish for 40 years and was also a devoted Shakespearean. His splendidly erudite letters contain delightful passages such as the following:

> 'It is a pity we do not get more Shakespeare on the stage at this tragic time' (writing in 1917 at the age of 66) 'It would be more refreshing this wartime than some of the evanescent vanities that occupy the boards nowadays'.

The ancestor of whom I am most proud was my great-great-uncle, George Edmonds (1788-1868), who started as a schoolmaster but soon transferred to the law. He became Birmingham's first Clerk of the Peace and was a fiery political agitator. His first wife was apparently aptly named Patience. After she had died, he married Mary Fairfax of Barford, not far from Stratford-upon-Avon and Charlecote, in 1867 when he was 79. His bride was 74 but the marriage lasted for only three weeks as they could not stand each other. Remarkably advanced and liberated for mid-Victorian times!

His work was in no small part responsible for the passing of the Reform Bill of 1832 but his most lasting claim to fame was his creation and publication in 1855 of a complete and very extensive language contained in a large volume of some

400 pages. This mind-boggling, monumental work anticipated by many years the later attempts such as Esperanto. George's father, who was another Edward Edmonds, and his grandfather, Amos Edmonds (who died in 1797) were Baptist ministers at a time when hell-fire histrionics from the pulpit were the order of the day. They were my great-great and great-great-great grandfathers!

It might very reasonably be said that these ancestors of mine completely explain my own interests and character. The seeds of my devotion to Shakespeare, to the English language, to the theatre and to appearing in public—if only to voice my own opinions!—are all here. Add to these the only two references I have found in the far past to the name of Gateley, which is a rare one, and one seems to have all the necessary ingredients to create me. The first of them, kindly discovered for me by Miss Sybil Rosenfeld of the Society for Theatre Research, was to a Roger Gately (the second 'e' is missing but that is obviously unimportant) in 1702. Miss Rosenfeld says, 'He is mentioned among the stage players, mountebanks, ropedancers, etc., who were operating without a licence from the Master of the Revels and whom all constables, etc., were desired to oppose unless they paid two shillings a day'. The other was to an actor called Gately who was in the travelling company of William Smith, known as Canterbury Smith, on the Kentish circuit in the mid-eighteenth century. In 1752 he appeared at the Canterbury theatre in *Romeo and Juliet.* Ironically, he played 'Peter'!

Heredity; certainly. Influence; none whatever. I had exhibited all my great interests without having known any of this family history or having been influenced by those relatives who were similarly inclined. My father, through whom all these characteristics have come to me was, as I have already stated, totally uninterested in these subjects and I never discussed them with my aunt and uncle until later years. It obviously all missed one generation, namely my father, and came out in me again without any prompting.

However, dentistry it was to be and there seemed no prospect of escape. My student days began at the Portsmouth college that has now developed into the Polytechnic. Before I could go to Guy's Hospital in London, to which I already had an entrance, I had to pass examinations in Botany, Zoology, Chemistry and Physics. I quite liked the first two, even if I was sickened by having to cut up rabbits whilst they were still warm and by the vile smell of dogfish soaked in formalin, but the others were for me just drudgery. As I failed chemistry the first time, I had to go and stay in London twice for exams. This enabled me to visit my first theatres there. The fare was popular but it was very exciting to be going at last to the ones that had sounded so magical on the provincial posters. All touring companies were either 'Direct from the Such-and-Such Theatre' or 'Prior to West End production at . . .' I saw Maurice Chevalier in *Stop Press* at the Adelphi, *1066 and All That* at the Strand and Eugenie Leontovitch with Cedric Hardwicke at the Lyric in *Tovarich.*

My chemistry lecturer had once said to me, 'You will probably prescribe your patients Nitric Acid!' I had been more interested in appearing in a blazer and white flannels in the college dramatic society's production of *The Fourth Wall* by A. A. Milne and in running a little Shakespeare play-reading circle during the lunch breaks, than in my scientific formulae.

Once these exams had been passed, I had to spend two years as a premiumed pupil in the laboratory of the practice of which I ultimately became the senior partner. During this period I formed a small group called *The Shakespeareans,* the average age of whom was about 19. We were five boys and two girls but I automatically organised every aspect of the shows: I chose the name of the group, selected the scenes that we were to perform, booked the first venue, directed the rehearsals and designed the programme. We opened with an arena-style performance in a local café which was appropriately enough called the Academy. We lads wore dinner jackets and the girls were in long evening dresses.

The performance began with a shortened version of Mendelssohn's overture to *A Midsummer Night's Dream* on the piano and was followed by my old schoolfriend, Paul Hayward, now at Cambridge but temporarily at home during the 'long vac', speaking the first Chorus from *King Henry V*. I then staggered on, battle-wounded and near death but in reality clean and fresh in my dinner jacket, and collapsed on to the carpet as York in *King Henry VI, Part III*. Even at that age, my Shakespearean taste ranged wide! This must have been something of a surprise as the lesser-known plays were then hardly ever performed anywhere. That particular one had not been staged at Stratford since 1906; a situation difficult to imagine today when every play in the canon can be sure of a fairly frequent airing. The whole entertainment was all very respectable and, no doubt, rather prim but I think that it did have some style and it was a great change from the usual amateur offering which then was usually an inadequate copy of a West End success.

A year later we were invited to provide the second half of a performance in a church hall. The first part was given by members of the local branch of the British Empire Shakespeare Society and was on the same lines as our own. However, I used a few simple properties and we felt that our approach was livelier and more colourful than their rather starchy evangelistic presentation. It was said that they complained that we had cheated! I played Hamlet, Autolycus and the *Henry V* Chorus—all parts which I had seen Wolfit do and so I tried to copy him. I cannot have been very good because as an actor I was very raw and untrained but my eyes were full of stardust.

I had already begun to formulate plans for the future: I wanted to create an amateur company and put on Shakespeare plays at the Pier after I had qualified. They would have imaginative sets and productions and would, I felt with all the confidence of a teenager, be many times better than the staid teachers' productions of my schooldays. None the less, there was a nagging at the back of my mind that what I really wanted to be was a professional actor. 'What a pity Peter is so fond of the theatre!'

Even so, the part of me that was settling for being an amateur had an unexpected fillip when I saw in the Radio Times a photograph of what was to be the fourth parent of the Shakespearean work that did in fact lie ahead. It was the interior of the Maddermarket Theatre in Norwich and it was there because the founder and director, Nugent Monck, was to give a talk about staging Shakespeare with amateurs. It looked enchanting and immediately I started to dream of creating just such another theatre and company. The former never happened but the company that I brought into being was, I suppose, as near as I could have hoped to the ideal that Monck's work inspired. The Maddermarket was a heavily half-timbered reproduction of an Elizabethan theatre and the Norwich Players had staged there the entire Shakespeare canon. Nugent Monck, who was a professional director, had settled in Norwich and was running this marvellous little playhouse with a paid staff but with amateur players. The open platform had a canopy over the back half of it supported by two sturdy timber pillars and was backed by a balcony forming upper and lower inner stages. There were side doors with lattice windows over them and the auditorium had a gallery round three sides.

In the autumn of this same year, 1937, Donald Wolfit had formed his company which was to tour Shakespeare, and later other classics, until the 1950s. He brought it to the King's and I went every night, seeing him play Macbeth, Shylock, Malvolio, Petruchio and a repeat of his Stratford Hamlet. His productions were well costumed and the sets bright and fresh, even though obviously economically done. They were in marked contrast to those of the other two touring Shakespearean companies that I had already seen. One was led by the veteran, Sir Philip Ben Greet, who had been a director at the Old Vic in its earliest days and whom I saw as Duncan and Shylock, and the other was Harold V. Neilson's. In a way, they corresponded to professional versions of those amateur teachers in comparison with the Stratfordian fresh air that Wolfit brought. Although I usually want to run anything to which I belong, I have always been shy socially. I have a very thin skin and dread snubs. Although I had been introduced to Donald Wolfit and enormously admired him, strange as it may seem, I did not contact him during his week in Southsea. Immediately afterwards, however, I wrote to say how much I had enjoyed his work. Perhaps there was something infectious about my enthusiasm but right from the start it appeared that he did not regard me as simply just another writer of 'fan' letters. A moderate correspondence soon began but, although I saw him act several more times, I was still too shy to attempt to meet him again.

At the beginning of 1938 I went to London to become a dental student at Guy's Hospital. I knew that I must study hard and so I promised myself that I would not go to more than three West End theatres each year; one a term. How strong and diligent of me! However, intention is one thing and performance quite another. It happened that I was free on my second afternoon and so I spent it standing at the back of the gallery at the Queen's Theatre (my snobbery about being up high having long since evaporated!) watching John Gielgud, Peggy Ashcroft, Michael Redgrave and an incredibly glittering cast in *The School for Scandal.* To cut a long story short, during that first year at Guy's I went to a total of 44 theatres! Allowing for vacations, this was just about one a week instead of one a term. All those in the West End, together with Sadler's Wells, the Old Vic, the Regent's Park Open Air Theatre and even the gallery at Covent Garden, were there for the taking.

Just as it took me no time at all to discover these temptations, so my realisation that I was not interested in dentistry happened equally speedily. However, I was now deeply involved and I felt that I must make the best of it. For one thing, my father was paying a great deal of money for my training and I could not throw this aside without conscience as if it were some public grant issued by an impersonal body and supplied by anonymous taxpayers. Even if it had been, I am sure that I would still have felt a responsibility not to let down the suppliers. None the less, the pull of the theatre grew ever stronger and ideas of dropping dentistry before I got too much further were taking deeper root.

The fuse was lit by a week's theatre-going in Stratford followed immediately by a performance of Bernard Shaw's *Saint Joan,* with Elisabeth Bergner and Donald Wolfit in it, at the Malvern Festival Theatre. My mother and I were on our way from Stratford to Symonds Yat for the second week of our summer holiday. Once there, we had seven days of golden sunshine which glittered through the leaves in the woods that tumble down the sides of that lovely gorge to the sparkling waters below. Nearly every afternoon, my mother retired to sleep whilst I lazed in the hotel garden looking down on these idyllic scenes. In contrast to them, my heart beat too fast and my mind was black with doubts and foreboding. The combination of Stratford and Malvern had been too much for me and the break must be made before my return to Guy's the following week.

After we got home, I had only two days left in which to do it. On the second of them, my mother asked me if I minded going back to London. Perhaps I had been dropping hints to pave the way but it felt to me as if she had some suspicion that all was not well. This was my cue and so I told her that I hated dentistry and wanted to go on the stage or try to get into the BBC. Had I guessed what a passion and tornado I should let loose, I would never have risked it. My mother was a woman of very strong will and she had decided that I would become a brilliant social success as a prosperous dental surgeon. Although, apart from golf, she had no time for such a life herself, she saw me as a professional man at the centre of fashionable bridge parties, golf and tennis clubs and all the best dances. Even if I could have lived up to these expectations, this sort of existence belonged to a pre-war world and its set of values that would be swept away in just over another year's time. I hated the stiff, snobbish circle in which such pasteboard dummies moved and felt an outsider when I had to mix, however briefly, with them. She displayed an astounding range of the appropriate emotions. She was furiously angry; she was heart-brokenly disappointed; she condemned me as being incurably weak-willed and she used every wile to ensure that she got her own way. I quailed under the onslaught and could hardly wait to escape back to London. She had won and I was mentally very bruised.

Only a week later, the Czechoslovakia crisis began and just two and a half weeks after that came the Munich Agreement and Neville Chamberlain with his promise from Hitler that there would be 'Peace in our time'. It is very easy for historians, especially those who were not alive at the time, to declare that throughout the thirties we all knew that war was inevitable. Likewise, a great many of my contemporaries, talking now with hindsight, like to show how perceptive they were by stating the same thing. This was just not true, especially amongst young people like myself. Of course, it was immensely worrying as the clouds of threatening war became thicker and blacker but people of my age had the eternal optimism of youth that such insane mass slaughter and destruction could never happen again. World War I had been part of the incredible folly of our elders and things were different now; the old barriers were down and all this bad news must simply be dangerous sabre-rattling. Had I really believed that there would be a war, I should not have considered going into the theatre. At least as a dental student I would be allowed to carry on until I had qualified and then go into the Army, doing my job as a dental surgeon, with an immediate commission. As a budding actor, my career would disappear over night and I should find myself as a war-time soldier without any sort of qualification or future. I really did believe in the scrap of paper that Chamberlain waved when he got off his aircraft.

I made some very good friends amongst my fellow students at Guy's, many of them being fond, though not so passionately as I was, of plays and music. One in particular, who was to become a lifelong friend, was Norman Punt. He was doing dentistry but later transferred to the Medical School and, after the war, became a very distinguished throat specialist. He introduced himself to me because he heard my voice cry out above all the others in the laboratory at Guy's, 'Oh! do hurry up or else I shall be late for my matinee'. He knew at once that here was a kindred spirit whom he wanted to meet.

On July 1, 1939, he and his parents took me to the last night of the Lyceum as a theatre. It was to be demolished to make way for a roundabout but, as it happened, the war intervened and the project was never even started. This special occasion was marked by the presentation of *Hamlet* with a company led by John Gielgud, Fay Compton, Jack Hawkins and several other fine artists. It was a highly emotional evening as it was the finale of such a famous theatre. All of Irving's Lyceum had gone except the magnificent pillared portico and the back wall but, none the less, his and Ellen Terry's spirits seemed to be abroad in the newer building that night. Hitler was threatening the Free City of Danzig and the papers were full of the possibility of his attacking the Polish Corridor. The atmosphere in the theatre was electric when the Captain told Hamlet that Fortinbras was marching 'against some part of Poland . . . a little patch of ground that hath in it no profit but the name'. Hamlet assumed that 'the Polack never will defend it' but was assured that 'it is already garrisoned'.

'I see
The imminent death of twenty thousand men,
That for a fantasy and trick of fame
Go to their graves like beds; fight for a plot
Whereon the numbers cannot try the cause,
Which is not tomb enough and continent
To high the slain'.

Shakespeare, the prophet! I have no doubt that all of us in the Lyceum Theatre that night felt that he was talking about us there and then. Alas, 'twenty thousand' would prove to be a tragic underestimate for the years to come. When John Gielgud spoke those ominous lines, my heart sank for, at that moment, the brutal truth hit me that we really were on the very brink of war. It began 64 days later.

CHAPTER 5
The benefits of War

Besides being dramatic, war has several other things in common with a good play. The plot keeps you guessing throughout, it maintains an uncomfortable tension and it continually springs surprises.

The first of these in World War II was the fact that for a whole year, in Britain at any rate, nothing much seemed to happen. We expected the devastating bombing of London, which did in fact come in 1940, to happen sooner. Immediately after war had been declared, Guy's Hospital Dental School 'evacuated' to a disused clinic in Tunbridge Wells where, for a time, a new rusticated form of student life was very pleasant. During it, I fell in love with an attractive girl named Bridget; a honey pot around whom several other of my fellow students also buzzed. She was pretty and vivacious and, for me, one of her great virtues was that she was a 'resting' actress. However, as soon as word of this reached home, it was heavily stamped upon. I must not become involved as nothing—repeat nothing—must get in the way of my career.

The winter of 1939-40 was particularly severe and during it I had a bad attack of 'flu which developed into mastoiditis. Modern antibiotics have virtually abolished this condition but then it was very serious, especially in adults. I was operated upon at Pembury Hospital, to which the Medical School had 'evacuated', and then eventually invalided back to Crossways in Southsea with my head so elaborately bandaged that I was occasionally mistaken for a war hero!

By the time I was fit to resume my studies, my year had been transferred back to the hospital in London just in time for the 'Blitzkrieg', Hitler's torrential rain of bombs. It was so terrible a time that when one recalls it now it is almost impossible to believe that it really happened. The world is automatically divided into those who have lived through a war and those who have not. I do not say this in a patronising way or mean to suggest that we who passed through the fire are in any way the better for it. I have to admit that, although I hated it at the time, now that I can look back in the knowledge that I survived, I know that I would not have missed it. To spend six years, confined by necessary strict regulations that seem unbelieveable in peace time and not knowing from day to day, or even from hour to hour, whether or not all that one treasures, including one's own life, will be destroyed by fire and explosion, is an unnatural experience that has to be lived through to be understood. And yet there was a cameraderie and a degree of trust and honesty about that has almost vanished without trace today.

When the raids began, most London theatres closed. The famous Windmill, however, with its nude revues, became even more famous by being the only one that never did so. There was a time during the heaviest raids when there was only one straight theatre open in the whole of central London. It was the Vaudeville and Robert Atkins put on one of the rarest of all Shakespeare's plays, the optimistically-titled, *All's Well that Ends Well*! To my delight, he produced it in what was almost a copy of the Maddermarket stage except that it was done with painted scenery within the proscenium arch. He followed this a few weeks later with *King Henry IV, Part I,* in the same setting. The fact that he managed to do so big a play with only 14 men encouraged me for the future: if one tried one could obviously stage any of the plays with a small cast and a simple permanent set.

It looked very strange to see the long column of London theatres in each national newspaper reduced to a single entry when the first of these plays was put on.

THEATRE

VAUDEVILLE. Daily at 2.30. Mats. only. ALL'S WELL THAT ENDS WELL.

Within ten days, however, the heading of the column was back in the plural and there were now two entries; both Shakespeare. He was therefore the only dramatist whose plays could be seen in London at that time; a situation which had not existed since the Restoration.

THEATRES

STRAND. 1 to 2 pm. Adm. 1/-. LUNCHTIME SHAKESPEARE. Snack bar open 12.30.
VAUDEVILLE. Daily at 2.30. Mats. only. ALL'S WELL THAT ENDS WELL.

There is no prize for guessing whether or not I was there in the audience at the Strand, especially when it is mentioned that this venture was being put on by Donald Wolfit. The reason why these two lone theatres were open for matinees only was because the bombing in the evenings reduced the West End to a dangerous battleground with the likelihood of buildings crashing in ruins at any time. It was bad enough in daylight and at first I made a point of sitting only in the back stalls so that I should be underneath the dress circle if any other part of the theatre had a direct hit during the performance. At the Strand, though, I threw caution to the wind and sat near the front of the stalls. Just how risky this was may be guessed from the fact that the day after Wolfit opened, the back of the theatre was blown out by a bomb and part of the stage was damaged. The company continued—a mere war was not enough to stop the man who was later to become the greatest Lear of our time!—with no heat or water in the building and no dressing rooms fit to use.

The performances were very simply staged without any use of the front curtain. All the audience sat in the stalls whilst coffee and sandwiches were served in the bar at the back. There were scenes, individual speeches and a few songs and many of the important parts were played by Rosalind Iden, the future Mrs Wolfit. I enjoyed it all immensely and went several times each week.

During our three years correspondence, Donald Wolfit had said that he would like to meet me again and so I went round to the stage door after one of the earliest of these lunchtime shows. I was directed to the stage where I found him taking off his make-up. Within the first few moments, I encountered the two Wolfits that inhabited the same body. Although he often gave the impression of being tall, he was, in fact, only of medium height and I saw at once that he was already heavier, both in stature and in personality, than the young Hamlet who had dazzled me at Stratford three years before.

The first of the two Wolfits that I saw that day was the captain of his ship rather imperiously giving orders in a slightly operatic manner. The dark, electric atmosphere of a theatre stage was a perfect setting in which to meet again this actor of such great vitality. As I approached, the other Wolfit turned towards me. This was a very gentle man, rather like a large, black-browed teddy bear overflowing with warmth and kindliness. Many who knew him only as an actor manager with, or for, whom they worked, found him difficult because they saw solely that first dominating figure. Those of us who were privileged to know him as a friend, held the second one deep in our hearts.

The affinity between us that I had detected in our correspondence soon developed into an undoubted rapport. Having once been round backstage to see him, I went again and again. Looking back, I think now that I must surely have been something of a nuisance but he did keep encouraging me. In fact, very soon he invited me to spend the night at Frensham where he and his second wife were then living. He thought that I was still lodging in London where at that time it was impossible to get a good night's sleep. The bombing raids happened night after night and most people spent their so-called sleeping hours in the air-raid shelters. My parents had left Crossways as Portsmouth was one of Hitler's prime targets and had gone to stay temporarily at Billingshurst where my sister was living with her husband. I had joined them and was commuting between there and Guy's—except when the previous night's bombs had blown up the railway tracks! As I, therefore, already had a bed in a relatively peaceful place, I did not accept the invitation although afterwards I regretted not having done so as I am sure it would have been a most memorable experience.

When the Battle of Britain had been won and the air raids became more sporadic, Donald Wolfit and his company, between playing to troops on various battlefronts and in service camps, had normal London seasons at the Strand and elsewhere. Now he was staging his full-length productions again. One of the most memorable was *King Richard III* not long before Laurence Olivier's famous portrayal. I always preferred Wolfit's as I found it stronger and bloodier and I believed in the character more than I did in Olivier's highly-stylised figure.

Another play that I was grateful to Donald Wolfit for was Ford's rare, *'Tis Pity She's a Whore.* During those war years I saw him in many different plays and places, varying from *Much Ado About Nothing* at an East End barn of a community centre called the People's Palace to his towering and magnificent performance as Lear at the Winter Garden Theatre.

My other life (I am not a Gemini for nothing!) was proceeding satisfactorily. As I was working so hard with my studies and as no other job which I should have preferred would have been open to me at that time, I did not stop to bother about whether I liked it or not. I ploughed through a welter of text books and lectures; anatomy with the first dead bodies I had ever seen; surrealistic patterns through the cinema-like eye of the microscope and ghoulish arrays of artificial teeth. I discovered that the human mouth is a dangerous and inaccessible black hole that is never still and I learned how to perform surgery within its maddening confines and endure the feel of someone else's blood on my hands. The reward of my labours was the passing of my Finals in June, 1941: I was now a Licenciate in Dental Surgery of the Royal College of Surgeons of England. I was free and a professional man with qualifications that would always enable me to earn a living. Free? Well, no, not exactly. I had either to go into one of the services or register as a conscientious objector. Although war in all its forms was totally abhorent to me, I had no intention of doing the latter. Everyone and everything that I most valued was in daily danger of extinction and the future could, if we lost the war, bring the slavery and annihilation that was to be the fate in Germany of six million Jews. I did not hesitate although, of course, I dreaded what my lot might eventually be. This is not jingoism or the sort of flag-waving that is now so generally derided but a simple, unheroic, honest conviction.

Two months elapsed between the attachment of *LDS, RCS Eng.* to the end of my name and *Lieutenant, AD Corps* to the beginning. I spent part of this time as a real dentist who was scared out of his wits because he was supposed to know it all but who no longer had the Guy's experts to oversee his inexperience. I did a locum at Newmarket and at least enjoyed the freedom from family and hospital restraint. I was in East Anglia with a free weekend in the middle of my stay and so I decided to go over to Norwich for the sole purpose of having a look at the Maddermarket Theatre. If I did no more than look at the outside, I would be satisfied.

When I got there, I stood in the courtyard and gazed at the imitation half-timbering of the facade and was very thrilled. There was no play on at the time but the door stood half open. I peeped inside and a charming middle-aged man stepped out of the darkness and asked me if I would like to see over it. He did not have to ask me twice and soon I was standing on the stage. It exceeded expectation! It was so beautiful and I was tremendously excited to find myself inside what was to all intents and purposes a playhouse of Shakespeare's time. The photograph in the Radio Times and Nugent Monck's BBC talk three years before had left a deep impression but this day's excursion from Newmarket made an even greater one. Both before and after that trip, I was constantly making sketches of the sort of little Elizabethan theatre I hoped that I should be able to build for myself after the war. It could be in Southsea but I had a grander idea! I would live in an Elizabethan house in the Cotswolds, perhaps near Chipping Campden or Broadway, and I would build it in the garden. Professional Shakespeare summer seasons would be given there and they would be a fringe attraction for the visitors to the Stratford area. Alas, those dreams never materialised but someone else created exactly the theatre that I had in mind many years later. It is the enchanting Watermill Theatre at Bagnor, near Newbury. I go there from time to time and feast my eyes upon it with a mixture of nostalgic delight—and sheer jealousy!

During my last few weeks as a civilian, my 'Officer's Service Dress Uniform' was made by a tailor in Horsham, the nearest town to Billingshurst where we were still temporarily living. My first Army posting was to Bulford on Salisbury Plain and I had to travel there wearing it. The experience was rather like the dream that most actors, amateur and professional, get of being on a stage in front of an audience without any idea of the words or even what the play is. I knew that there was a complicated set of rules of behaviour but was almost totally ignorant of the details. I felt quite sure that if I broke any of them I should be in the Tower by the end of my first day!

I travelled by train and eventually arrived at the small station of Amesbury in Wiltshire. I had managed to get through the bustling crowds at Waterloo and Salisbury without problems because, if I saw anyone who looked as if they could be hanging matters if they were not saluted, I managed to be conveniently distracted. I walked on to this tiny country platform and it was packed with troops! Panic seized me because I had no idea how to sort out those who should be saluted from the ones who should not. I had visions of awful humiliation as ignored generals burst blood vessels as they did in H. M. Bateman's cartoons or the possibility of laughter as I grovelled to Acting Unpaid Lance-Corporals. I felt that I needed time to inspect each epaulette or sleeve. I made an instant decision: I sat on the nearest bench and appeared to be very short-sighted as I bent right over and peered into the first piece of reading matter that I could extract from my pocket. I stayed paralysed in this position until they had all got on to their train when eventually it arrived. With no one in sight, I then straightened myself and left the station to find the stop for the country bus that was to take me to the camp.

The sun poured down and for a time there was not a soul about. At last, however, I espied along the road a distant, solitary airman. Please Heaven, do let the bus get here first! My prayer was not answered and so, as the harmless little man got closer, I blushed a deeper and deeper red. Finally, it being impossible to convince him any longer that I did not know that he was there, he saluted me very efficiently. I had to respond but I have a feeling that as I was so inexperienced my returned salute was probably more of a wave. I quote these stories to sum up the sort of Mack Sennett soldier that the Allied Forces had to put up with for five years. Even after I had been in the Army for about four of them and my saluting had become one of my better performances, at the end of giving a heel-clicking display at a court of enquiry, I turned smartly to leave, tripped over a small obstacle and fell flat on my face. As at school in my later years, I got away with a lot by being accepted as something of an eccentric.

After a short time at Bulford, I was posted to Perham Down where I was attached to a very superior unit, the 11th Hussars, known as the 'Cherry Pickers', who lived in a marvellous mess that could have passed for a four-star hotel. Once settled in, bits of my theatrical side began to show through as when, for example, I gave a lecture on the Elizabethan Theatre to one of the small educational groups that sprang up in every camp. I had already had minor experience in this field as I had talked to the Portsmouth branch of the British Empire Shakespeare Society about the history of the two Stratford theatres when I was still only 21. I also joined a playreading group and landed myself with the part of the Thane himself in what superstitious (and which of them is not?) members of the theatrical profession call 'The Scottish Play'. I thought that I had picked up a very professional technique and I used it because I seemed to have heard old actors speak in that way. It sounded good to me but several fellow officers, who had been on the stage before being called up, gently tried to show me the error of my ways. I was sure that they were wrong. One officer whom I knew there was John Le Mesurier who would delight us in the years to come with many distinguished performances including Sergeant Wilson in *Dad's Army* on television. I cannot remember whether or not he was one of my mentors but I do recollect that he was a man of great good sense in contrast to the youthful silliness of some of the rest of us. When I was much older, with acting training and experience behind me, I realised how awful my reading must have been. I spoke something like this: 'Is this a dagger which' *(breathy pause before crashing on and deliberately ignoring the punctuation, especially the full stops)* 'I see before me the handle toward my' *(same sort of break before the next meaningless hurtle)* 'hand come let me clutch' *(same old trick ad infinitum)* 'thee I have . . .' I was just copying tricks and not really attempting to act from within myself at all. My punishment followed, however! During nearly 30 years afterwards I would be plagued by having to cope with many amateur actors who would be just as bad but who would also think that they were marvellous and be equally impervious to the truth.

Eventually I moved on to other camps on the Plain. There was no shortage of plays or music as Garrison Theatres abounded and most of the big stars toured. At Bulford I saw John Gielgud and a dazzling cast in J. M. Barrie's *Dear Brutus,* a whimsical play totally unsuited to the troops. The bar had to be closed during the week because so many of the soldiers gave up the play after the first half hour and preferred to spend the rest of the evening noisily drinking. A week of Sadler's Wells Opera in *The Barber of Seville* emptied the house but overblown gypsies playing accordians for community singing invariably drew gales of applause and kept every seat filled. Symphony concerts in the camps and in Salisbury were, on the contrary, very well attended. It seemed to be serious drama and opera that appealed least to the majority. In Salisbury, lovely city to which I went whenever I could to escape from too much Army, there was chamber music in the Old Deanery during which one could gaze at that serene cathedral spire and believe that all was well with the world. Eric Fenby, who had been amanuensis to Delius for many years, was much involved in these concerts.

After I had been in the Army for a year, it became known that the American troops would be arriving soon and that they would occupy nearly all the camps in Southern England. We all wondered where we would be sent. The north of England, perhaps, or some God-forsaken hole that one could not even find on the map? At last the posting came through. When I saw where I was to go, I just could not believe my eyes. Of all the thousands, perhaps tens of thousands, of places in Britain and the rest of the free world where there were British troops, it was Norwich! The notice said, 'Britannia Barracks', but it might just as well have read, "Maddermarket Theatre' because within three days of my arrival there I had been auditioned by Nugent Monck and he had given me a part in his next production. I had become an Associate Member of the Norwich Players in that dream theatre that I had seen all those years before in a Radio Times photograph!

The play was the first production in this country of *Summer at Nohant* by Jaroslav Iwaszkiewicz and dealt with the love affair between Chopin and the novelist, Madame George Sand, in 1840. I was a lovesick young man for ever chasing one of that lady's daughters. Like many other nations that had been over-run by the Nazis, Poland had based its Free Army in this country and those Poles who had managed to escape in time from their native land were made welcome here. The Polish Ministry of Information took a great interest in the play and so my initiation into the Maddermarket happened with a particularly interesting production.

From my first rehearsal I became aware that I had entered yet another new world. Here in Norwich I realised at once that I was in a professionally-run theatre and that there were traditions and a code of behaviour to be slighted at one's peril. There was a hierarchy amongst the Players and its elders made it clear that they were aware of their importance in the theatre's scheme of things. The director, the scene designer and painter, the wardrobe department and all the rest of the staff were professional and even though the actors were not, they behaved as if they were too. There was a seriousness of purpose and a dedication, though not in a solemn or pompous way, that was new to me and which turned the fun of 'amateur dramatics' into the satisfaction and deep enjoyment of real theatre.

Nugent Monck was 64 at this time. He was a short, partly bald man who made much of the fact that he was half Irish. He had originally planned to be a musician but whilst at the Royal Academy of Music had transferred to drama. In his early years as an actor he had worked with the pioneer in the revival of Elizabethan staging, William Poel, and had also played at the Abbey Theatre, Dublin, in the great days of W. B. Yeats and Lady Gregory. He settled in Norwich before the First World War and created the Norwich Players in 1911. The Maddermarket Theatre was converted in 1921 from a disused Roman Catholic chapel which dated from 1794.

Monck had pale, wistful eyes which he used with often devastating effect. They frequently twinkled with mockery and they excelled those of anyone I have ever known at showing humorous, but total, disbelief. His wide, rather loose mouth had lips that curled with the enjoyment of irony but could also set in a hard line if exhibiting steely determination. When he was really angry they somewhat failed him and he tended to splutter. His relaxed way of moving gave him a slightly sagging appearance and his walk was flat-footed. He had most expressive hands and when he wanted to be at his most beguiling he clasped them gently in front of him. He liked to be thought to be something of a mystic and he beamed with calculated modesty whenever he was treated as being famous. A bemused whimsicality often covered a good deal of cunning and even some ruthlessness. He was usually referred to as 'The Little Man' and was always addressed by those of us who knew him well as 'Moncklet'. He had a wit reminiscent of that of Bernard Shaw who was, in fact, one of his friends. I remember when one of the actresses, who had made a hobby of chasing every man in sight, eventually produced an engagement ring which she showed to Moncklet, he drifted away muttering, "The reward of industry"! On another occasion, there was a rather listless young actor who could not respond to direction and play the part of a lover with any sign of passion. Moncklet walked helplessly off the stage and said in a whisper calculated to be heard by everyone, "Oh! dear! I do wish that someone would rape Patrick". He once announced to an audience whilst I was there that he intended to have a green spotlight trained on to future late-comers to show them to their seats. He smilingly pointed out in dove-like tones that lady members of the audience would look their very worst illuminated in that particular colour.

Life as an officer in the Army Dental Corps ('Royal' was not attached until later), even in wartime, proved to be a weekdays only, 9 to 5 job. What is more, I was immediately placed on the Lodging List, which meant that I slept out of barracks more or less wherever I chose. This ensured that I was free every evening and weekend and so could devote all my spare time to the Maddermarket and much else of the cultural life of that civilised city.

Within a few days, I found myself agreeing to sleep in the theatre one night each week. Someone did so in nearly every building of any importance in order to be on the spot should there be an air raid. It was known as Fire-watching and was primarily in case of incendiary bombs in the hopes that one could put the flames out before they got too much of a hold.

I soon discovered that Maddermarket people were something of an elite in Norwich. Whereas I had known many individuals with whom I could discuss the arts, this was the first time that I had found myself in quite a large cultured community. The talk amongst all these people was automatically and unselfconsciously about books, plays, music, painting and acting. Quite often we went in groups to symphony concerts at the Theatre Royal or to showings of foreign films presented by the local Film Society at one of the cinemas. Nugent Monck was usually with us. Graciously he would make a quiet but royal entrance and we would be very conscious that we were the special palace entourage. We felt that we were stars even if twinkling in only a very tiny provincial sky. We hoped that everybody would be looking at us—and they usually were!

By now I had been promoted to the rank of Captain and as it was war-time I had to go everywhere in uniform. I was in my middle twenties and, if I may be permitted to say it now that I am so much older, I was not bad looking. I am sure that I was very conceited but this new life seemed to me to be quite marvellous. Of course I fell in love with the actress opposite whom I acted in the first play; a rather longer attack than the quite passionate one on Salisbury Plain with a revue artiste whose show moved on all too soon. This latest was a little married blonde who gently, but very firmly, rejected me. There was another leading lady in the company and she taught me more in the long grass on a summer afternoon than any girl had ever done before. We all developed later in those days: perhaps I was tardier than most. It was not until I went into the Army that I really learned about how not to drink. Again, this was a somewhat late development and was largely because my strict upbringing had overshielded me against such things. During my concentrated three years in Norwich I was taught more about Life and Living than in any comparable period before or since. I also became very aware, sometimes to my alarm, that there are two sexes to which a young man can be attractive. This took me very much by surprise. Here was something that was both strange and alien that put me on my guard. These matters were almost totally buried in the dark until long after that time and most of us were absolutely ignorant about them.

Each Norwich Players' production ran for ten performances and the opening weekend of *Summer at Nohant* was very exciting. The Polish Ministry of Information arranged for Stanislas Balinski, a friend of the author, to speak before both performances on the Saturday and, on the Sunday afternoon, there was a Chopin recital by Jerzy Sulikowski preceded by a talk from the writer, Dr Z. Grabowski. The translator of the play, a lovely and serene lady of the name of Celina Wieniewska, was also present. After having given only my first three performances at the Maddermarket, on that Sunday afternoon I already felt that I was part of the elite. The Ministry also sent a pianist, Maria Geist, to play parts of Chopin's B Minor Sonata off-stage during the play when the composer was supposed to be in the next room working on its composition. Monck's house was in many ways like a club as so many of us were constantly in and out. Maria, a delightful but very vigorous person, stayed with him during the period of the play and on one occasion she and I had a wrestling match in Moncklet's dining room which she won easily. I will tantalisingly leave my reader to guess how all that came about!

I had no cause to be particularly pleased with myself whilst we were rehearsing. The old hands made it quite clear that I was a novice with a great deal to learn. My old tricks were stripped off me ruthlessly and Moncklet, whose gods, apart from Shakespeare, were the prophets of the new theatre such as Ibsen, soon toppled many of my old heroes. As Shaw had done before him, he declared that Irving could not act and he had no time for the old romantic theatre that had seemed so royal to me as a youngster. I shuddered at this blasphemy but it made me think and helped to teach me to analyse plays and acting more clearly. I read Stanislavsky and learned something of his revolutionary creation of a real acting style to sweep away the old clichés. I also studied the designs and methods of Gordon Craig and Appia to try to understand their ideas about stage scenery and lighting. Theatres everywhere still had photographically realistic trees painted on to cut-outs of flapping canvas lit by the old footlights and overhead battens. Stratford, the Old Vic and the Maddermarket were amongst the very few that I knew where the new methods were practiced: there were no such old-fashioned devices at any of them. Monck was one of the pioneers of the use of carefully directed spotlighting to bring out the three-dimensionalism of modern sets.

The Maddermarket stage proved to be very versatile. Not only could it be used as itself, which was an Elizabethan open platform, but, not unlike the Chichester Festival Theatre of more recent years, it could take modern scenery. For the Chopin play we had to have a French drawing-room of the early 19th century. Flats covered all the Elizabethan trappings and French windows looked out into a garden which was in fact the lower inner stage skilfully disguised.

One of the banes of amateur acting is the partisan adoration of so many of the supporters. There was no danger, for me at any rate, of this happening in Norwich. I had two particular friends whose stringent comments were critical almost to the point of cynicism. The elder of the two was Peter Taylor Smith who was the man who had stepped out of the darkness to show me over the theatre when I had made my day-trip from Newmarket. He had been Wardrobe Master at the Old Vic at one time but had now retired to a small house off one corner of the Maddermarket courtyard. He had great charm, kindliness and a wit that was gentle until he got on to the subject of Moncklet when it became waspishly hilarious. The other was Jack Mitchley, one of the actors in the company and a man of about my own age. He was a very live wire who ran his own amateur group as well and was much involved in the Norfolk Education Committee's youth drama projects. On my fire-watching nights, usually after a rehearsal and when everyone else had gone home, he, his wife, Peter and I used to have picnic suppers in the Green Room of the theatre. These were immensely enjoyable sessions of criticism and gossip.

My second play was G. K. Chesterton's *Magic,* the climax of which was a seance. I have no time for spiritualism of the sort that has the voices of infants speaking through shabby old women in trances and talking about roses on the mantlepiece, but I have always deeply believed that 'there are more things in heaven and earth than are dreamt of'. Never was I more aware of this than in Norwich.

The first occasion was one of my earliest fire-watching nights. I had made up my camp bed in the Green Room and the theatre was silent and otherwise dark. It was very late but I decided that I would do a little part-learning before I went to sleep. Remembering that my script was on the far side of the stage, I set off in the darkness to fetch it. Unfortunately I could not find the light switches but I knew exactly where to go and that there were no obstructions in my path. Half way across the stage I suddenly froze with terror as I came up against something very large and frightening. I felt nothing and could see nothing but to this day I am certain of that terrifying presence. I turned back as soon as my trembling legs would let me and I could not sleep for a long time after as every nocturnal creak of the old building kept reinforcing my fear. It was not until after this that I was told that a great many people regarded the theatre as haunted and that several previously complete sceptics had had very frightening experiences when alone in there. I was told, I do not know whether rightly or wrongly, that it had ceased to be a Roman Catholic chapel after it had been desecrated by a priest being murdered in it in the 19th century. The side chapel where the deed was said to have been committed was where the 'stage right' wings now were and that was where I had left my script.

Nugent Monck's house was 16th century and was very beautiful with a wealth of great beams, odd nooks and corners and twisty staircases. The door to the brick-vaulted cellar was in his hall and had come from the old Norwich prison. It looked sinister and was no doubt a Door of Sighs. One winter night, several of us were talking to the Little Man round the fire in his upstairs sitting room. After a time, he began to ease himself out of his high-backed armchair as if he were 20 years older than he really was and said that he must go down to the cellar to get some more coal and logs. Gallantly, I offered to get them instead. Downstairs was in darkness but I was so familiar with my way across the hall that there was no problem. Again, a similar presence, this time not just frightening but somehow evil, blocked my way. In terror I rushed for the switches and found that there was no visible obstruction but that both the front and back doors, carefully locked before we went upstairs earlier, were wide open to the night air. The sceptic may well find perfectly prosaic explanations for all this but Moncklet had no doubts concerning these matters and, when I spent a night there on one occasion, he said to me as he showed me to my room, "If anything brushes against your face during the night do not worry; it will only be the man who hanged himself from the beam over your head many years ago. He is quite harmless!"

The third play was Shakespeare, his particular speciality. Norman Marshall in his book, *The Other Theatre,* wrote, 'Monck at his best deserves to be ranked amongst the first half dozen producers in England. His interpretation of a play is subtle, fastidious and exact. Trained as a musician, his productions have infinite variety of tone and tempo'. The play was *Hamlet* and I was cast as Horatio. George Hagan, whom I had seen at Stratford in 1937-8 as Lysander, Paris, Trinculo and Sebastian, was in Norwich serving with the RAF. He came along to the theatre and gave me a good deal of very valuable professional instruction. This was the first full-scale Shakespeare play in which I had acted and it launched a struggle within me that was to be life-long. Instead of the play being as clear as it was when I read it or saw a good production, the whole thing was blurred by the trappings of the theatre. Was one's make-up right? Where is my cloak for the next scene? I must not trip over those electric leads in the wings and do remember to stand on the third step or else I shall not be in the correct lighting. From then on, and especially when I came to direct my own productions, I should find the purity of the text on the printed page pulling me in one direction and my love of the business of the theatre tugging in the other.

A Shavian double-bill came next: *The Shewing-up of Blanco Posnet,* in which I played an old Westerner called Waggoner Joe, and the comedy, *Village Wooing.* George Hagan could not get away from the RAF to play every night and so he and I shared the part of the man in it, each playing five performances. The audience's laughs were an intoxicating experience and suddenly one night I realised for the first time that I had complete control over all those people. They hung on to whatever I did or said and, if I paused, they paused with me. Before this, all my acting had been as if they were sitting behind glass. Now I was in contact with them and discovering the very essence that makes a live performance so special. When it works, there is a complete, almost electrical, charge generated between player and audience. That night, a window had opened for me.

The local press came to my performance; not George's. To my delight, the critic of the Eastern Evening News said, 'We made some criticism of the man in a previous play and it is doubly pleasing to have from him this time an excellent performance . . . a tour de force for which it is a pity more members of the company cannot be praised'. Norwich Players were anonymous on the programme and so notices could refer only to the characters.

I then went on to play Bob Acres in *The Rivals* by Sheridan, a blood-thirsty priest in a 13th century Chinese play, *The Western Chamber* (known to the cast because of its initials as 'Far Po'!) and Cloten in *Cymbeline.*

The Army then posted me to my own one-man dental centre at the camp at Ludham, 12 miles away. I was still on the Lodging List and so I continued to live in Norwich. I had to provide my own transport and after a nerve-wracking spell of hitch-hiking at a time when private cars were off the road, occasional Army transport if there was any going and buses that were too few, I bought my first motorcycle. It was a 350cc Royal Enfield and I was taught to ride by a despatch rider from a nearby anti-aircraft battery who was a patient of mine. I managed to get just enough petrol coupons out of the Transport Officer of the unit to which I was then attached. I was very fortunate to have a sympathetic commanding officer who once admitted to me that his early dream had been to be a professional violinist. He had a soft spot for my activities and once gave me a week's leave to be on the staff of a residential drama course, directed by Jack Mitchley for the Norfolk Education Committee, at a time in 1944 when it had all been stopped because of the invasion of Europe. I was very friendly with Jack and his wife and I was living, very innocently, with his sister, Judith. She was a kind, warm-hearted woman, somewhat older than me, who had the sort of looks that made her right for the part of Lady Bracknell which she played in her brother's amateur production of *The Importance of Being Earnest* which toured service camps on Sunday nights. I belonged to his company, the Conesford Players, as well and played Canon Chasuble, a small part in *Hay Fever* and acted as Stage Manager for *Private Lives.*

Eventually, I was posted still further away. This time it was to Great Yarmouth but, with a little cheating on my part—I was not supposed to be living quite so far away as Norwich—and some turning of a blind eye by my commanding officer, I kept going at the Maddermarket. I appeared there in three more plays by Bernard Shaw: *The Apple Cart, Misalliance* and *Major*

Barbara. The cast of the second of them included Hugh Manning and that of the third, Alec McCowen; both of them to score considerable fame after the war. In *Misalliance* I was supposed to be tough and beefy and in *Major Barbara* I tried to do Stephen in the parsonical tones of the Aldwych comedian, Robertson Hare. They were both dismal failures. Alec McCowen and I got on very well together and even corresponded for a short time after he left Norwich. As so often with these war-time friendships, we soon lost touch and went our separate ways. I played in three more Shakespeares: *The Merchant of Venice* (Bassanio), *The Taming of the Shrew* (Tranio) and *The Merry Wives of Windsor* (Dr Caius). I loved the 18th century elegance and superb costumes for Charles Surface in *The School for Scandal* and the King Charles spaniel-like wigs for Congreve's *The Way of the World*. A particular honour and thrill was giving the first English performance of Chekhov's one-man play, *The Tobacco Evil* ('excellent piece of make-up and sensitive technique' said the local press). We also did Ben Jonson's *The Silent Woman* ('the most polished performance'), Ibsen's *Rosmersholm*, Machiavelli's *Mandragola* ('virile acting . . . as though he were galloping a four-in-hand'), Wilde's *Lady Windermere's Fan* and the premiere of Edward Thompson's *Essex and Elizabeth*. As well as these, there were two American plays, *The Silver Cord* and the first English production of Saroyan's *The Time of Your Life* in which I played a sleazy plain-clothes 'cop'. In some ways, the most important of all were two Chekhov productions, *The Seagull*, of which more later, and *Uncle Vanya*.

Nugent Monck always said that it took him three years to train an actor to professional standards. I had been there precisely that length of time and had played in 25 of his productions when, at last, the posting came that was to take me right out of the reach of Norwich. I had to go to Maidstone in Kent. By now, VE Day, when the war in Europe ceased and we danced in the streets at Norwich with complete strangers, had already passed. The final hostilities, those in the Far East, ended during my time in Kent. My old friend, Norman Punt, by then an ear, nose and throat surgeon, was at Maidstone Hospital and I spent most of the day of celebration with him. He was operating all the afternoon and, in theory, I assisted him, thinly disguised, to justify my being there, as a superfluous extra anaesthetist.

My final posting was to Lincoln where I was introduced by a fellow officer to Michael and Rae Goodwin who were in the repertory company at the Theatre Royal there. We became very friendly and I used to sit in the front row of the stalls every Wednesday night. Afterwards, I would go back with them to their lodgings to have supper and to tear to pieces the other members of the cast in the play that I had just seen.

When, at last, in July, 1946, I was demobilised, I had to go all the way up to York to get my free civilian clothes and be officially released. It was a very hot day and the train was so crowded that I had to travel down to London afterwards in the corridor on the sunny side. I sat on my suitcase which contained an oven-ready chicken that Michael and Rae had given me to bring home; a rare treat at that time when food was still short. My parents had long since returned to Crossways and so home was Southsea again.

On the day after I got back, we cooked the chicken as a celebration of my being a civilian once more. When we cut into it, we found that the hot, sat-upon suitcase had acted, not surprisingly when one thought about it, an an incubator. The joints were full of maggots!

When I threw it away, it reminded me of the legendary curate's egg of the old Punch joke. It was good in parts! It seemed to me to be symbolic of the war. When I put the lid on the dustbin, I felt that I had disposed of both of them at the same time.

ACT ONE
St. Peter's

CHAPTER 6
The springtime of Peace

A few weeks after my release from the Army, I was visited by an exuberant man with seemingly unseeing eyes behind horn-rimmed spectacles that were as thick as pebbles. His light, sibilant voice had the rolling silkiness that appears to be the prerogative of the Welsh. His name was Ronald Mills.

He said that he was putting on an amateur production of *The Merchant of Venice* and would I like to be in it. He was going to direct it himself and the other members of the cast would be drawn from the local branches of the Workers' Education Association and the British Empire Shakespeare Society. It all sounded dauntingly untheatrical and amateurish. However, as I had not had time to do anything about forming my own company and had not become involved in any other activity, I agreed. I had a choice of parts and decided to do Bassanio again.

In the meantime, I had to settle back into life at home and to start work as a civilian. The former was not as easy as I had hoped it would be as my mother was just 67 and my father almost 77. I soon found that their old desire to treat me as if I were still a boy was almost as strong as ever. As far as dental practice was concerned, I had previously negotiated with the one in which I had long ago been a pupil, to go to them as an assistant with a view to partnership after two years. I had six weeks of the nearest to real freedom that I had ever had in my life and then returned to the squirrel's cage when I resumed working as a dental surgeon.

One was very much a professional servant as an assistant in those days and little better as a junior partner. Ten days after I started, I was so unhappy with the prospect that I wrote to Donald Wolfit. As far back as 1943, when I was at the Maddermarket, he had said to me, 'I am glad to know that you are getting such good training in the theatre. I always felt that you should be more active in the work and, who knows, I may have a corner for you when this is all over'. I reminded him of this suggestion and said that I was committed for the next two years but would he take me on as an actor after that? He replied, 'Who knows whether I shall even be in management in two years' time and by then you may be looking after the mouths of the most beautiful ladies in the world and would rather do anything than give up dentistry. After all, it must have its attractive side as well as its unattractive one!'

That was my last attempt to become a professional actor.

The Merchant of Venice plumbed what were for me previously uncharted depths of amateur theatricals. At the Maddermarket we had rehearsed each play every night, except Sundays, for three weeks. It was concentrated hard work that kept the whole thing 'on the boil' and resulted in performances that were fresh and lively. Now we amiably bumbled along on about one night a week all through the winter. We rehearsed in people's houses with the furniture pushed back or in dismal schoolrooms that had been gloomily out-of-date before the war.

The play was eventually put on in the hall of the Portsmouth teachers' training college. The stage had a permanent setting of beige velvet curtains, which must not be removed or tampered with, inadequate wings and lighting consisting of the inevitable footlights below and battens overhead. Apart from one or two small cut-outs to indicate different locations that was the full extent of the staging of the play.

Ronald Mills had done what the Victorians often did to reduce the number of intervals between their various big set changes: he had strung all the scenes of each sort together. For example, all four casket scenes (Morocco has two) were played as one. Shakespeare knew what he was doing when he interlaced Venice and Belmont so that we keep moving from one to the other and back again. To destroy that balance is to wreck the play. Many of the cast were just about as bad as amateurs can be but there was some interesting talent amongst the leads. The Portia was Nora Turner, a pale girl with hair of the lightest auburn, who had been on the stage professionally and, although her acting was sometimes inclined to be a little too intimate, she had the grace, smoothness and style that training and experience can bring. The Shylock, a man some 20 years older than myself, was also excellent and an attractive Irish girl, Brenda Cosgrave, was a vivacious Jessica. They had all been got together just for this one play and afterwards were to be disbanded. Whilst we were rehearsing, it occurred to me that the best of them could well form the nucleus of the company that I was now in a hurry to start. I asked Ronald Mills if he would mind my asking them if they would join me and he seemed delighted that they would still be kept together. I went ahead and most of them accepted.

The war years, with their massive restrictions and shortages, had been like a dark winter of six years' duration. It was as if we had been snowed up in our isolated cabins in the mountains. Now, it seemed to be springtime with everything ready to burst into leaf. We wanted to rush out into the sunshine full of high spirits and hopes for the summer ahead. Although much of the rationing of food and goods would remain with us for several years yet, there was a general contentment and goodwill that it is impossible to imagine these several decades later. One has only to see films of the crowds dancing at the South Bank Exhibition of the Festival of Britain, that joyous explosion of colour and national delight in 1951, to capture some of the feeling. Today such things are at war with vandals before they open and degenerate into violence as soon as they get going. In those immediately post-war years, things were very different. There was a great burst of energy: people had felt cramped and had spent so much time planning the wonderful things that they would do when peace came, that they embraced every activity that presented itself. Neither television nor the long-playing gramophone record had yet arrived and they were keen to go out to find their pastimes. What is more, older people were not afraid to venture forth at night to plays and concerts as the reign of the mugger had not yet made them fear the streets.

Amateur companies of all sorts were springing up out of this fertile soil. The Portsmouth and Southsea scene was dominated by two groups. The pre-war stagers of popular musicals, the Portsmouth Players, had started again and were already going strong. Amateur operatic societies, however, seem to belong very much to a world of their own; they are extremely popular but seem to be even more narcissistic than those that put on straight plays. The others were the Portsmouth Little Theatre Society. Formed in 1945, they were hell-bent from the outset on being accepted as Civic Establishment and in those early years many people did regard them as such. For example, they were allowed to use Corporation property for scenery work, storage and for rehearsals. This was almost entirely in the City Library and it was not surprising as their Stage and Business Manager was the City Librarian. He was a sombre little man named Harry Sargeant and he had been at school with Wolfit.

There was already a company called the Little Theatre Entertainers. They had started as an amateur concert party in 1943 but were now presenting plays instead. Naturally they protested to the new society about their taking over the name by which they themselves were already known. The arrogant reply was that the Little Theatre *Society* intended to be the premier company in the city and that they, the already established group, had better change their name. The smaller and older company very rightly resisted this bulldozing and did no more than add the word 'Southsea' to the beginning of their title. In 1950 the newer group altered theirs to the Arts Theatre, Portsmouth. It was a pity they had not thought of that or some other alternative in the first place but the incident does serve to pinpoint their big-headedness at that time.

The Arts Theatre, as I shall call them henceforth to avoid confusion, presented the usual amateur fare of plays that had been commercial successes in the West End like *Robert's Wife, The Flashing Stream* and *The Sacred Flame.* Their rare excursions into costume drama only went as far as the inevitable *The Importance of Being Earnest* and *The School for Scandal:* a policy which was no more adventurous or consciously artistic than most other amateur societies. There was an active social side which was well supported by the wives of city councillors and officals as well as those of the business and professional men. At performances and parties, these bustling ladies, with their pearls and twin-sets, accompanied by their locally important but rather dull husbands, mingled in a way more attuned to the cocktail party than the cultural event. Most people seemed to assume that I would join them but I saw several of their productions and I knew that I wanted to do something quite different and that I must run it all myself. I was not afraid of any competition that they had to offer.

Just as I was about to start my own company, something else appeared on the scene that, if it had developed as planned, could have been a serious threat to me. It was announced that there would be a Southsea Theatre Club. It was to have its own premises and sounded as if it might tackle just the same sort of repertoire as I had in mind. It was being organised by a young man whose surname, unfortunately, did not sound unlike part of mine. He began by announcing that he was approaching practically every great star in the theatrical profession to become a patron. He succeeded in getting Ellen Pollock and the comedian, Ronald Shiner. I decided that the time had come to answer with a broadside! I wrote to Donald Wolfit and invited him to become my patron. He replied:

> 'My dear Peter Gateley,
> I shall be delighted to accept your very kind suggestion and if I can help in any way in addition to lending my name, I shall be only too happy.
> *Good fortune to you* and let me know how you get on. Is my friend Sargeant still Librarian at the Portsmouth Library? He is a dear friend of mine and I am sure he will help you if you want it.
>
> Every good wish, in haste,
> Donald Wolfit.
>
> P.S. Rosalind Iden will be glad to add her name to mine if you would like it—equals Pollock and Shiner, doesn't it?

I was delighted that this threat of possible opposition had been instrumental in bringing us these two marvellous patrons. As far as the venture itself was concerned, however, it turned out that I need not have worried about it as it faded away before it ever even happened.

During the war, Alec Clunes had run the little Arts Theatre Club in London as a miniature blueprint for a National Theatre. Its Maddermarket-type repertoire was the sort that I was planning and the name of his company suggested an idea to me. I wanted to avoid the over-worn word, 'Players', and even 'Portsmouth' seemed to have become too popular a label.

Alec Clunes's company was called the theatre's 'Group of Actors'—we would be *The Southsea Actors.*

Whilst I was still in the Army, I wrote to Alex Kinnear who was then Entertainments Manager for Portsmouth Corporation. He controlled the South Parade Pier and I told him that I wanted to stage plays there as soon as the Army would release me. He replied disappointingly that he had formed a new policy. Dancing was very popular then and so from each autumn until the following spring all the seating of the ground floor of the theatre was being removed to convert it into a dance hall. The remaining summer season would be devoted to live performances but the only amateur company that they would have would be the Portsmouth Players with their musicals in the first and last weeks. The Portsmouth Arts Theatre, when they started, played in the inadequate hall where we did *The Merchant of Venice.* There was one more possible place but that was not available. The Theatre Royal was still a cinema and the King's, which was flourishing in the immediately post-war theatre boom, was not even considered. It would have been impossibly expensive and at that time the idea of an amateur straight play there was entirely out of the question.

After World War I, there had been a plan to drive a main road, full of shops, right across the heart of the city. It would cut through various backwaters and bring them new prosperity. In one of these stood St. Peter's Church. Its authorities decided that this was too good an opportunity to miss and so they built a very grand church institute with a view to its becoming a paying proposition when the thriving new road materialised. Its main feature was a large hall with a stage worthy of a small theatre. It even had a fly-tower so that scenery, providing it was not too large, could be taken up out of sight without rolling or folding. As is the way so often with municipal projects, the road scheme was dropped. St. Peter's Church was thus left with something of a white elephant which was doomed to remain for ever off the beaten track. This was the St. Peter's Hall where I had made my stage debut at the age of six as a troll king in the *kindergarten* mime. Between the wars it had been a popular venue for the smaller amateur societies that could not afford the grandeur of the Pier and for schools. For a short time it even housed a professional repertory company. They had called themselves the Free Theatre and their income had been derived from taking a silver collection; a slightly more profitable method then than it would be today! I remember seeing them perform *Almost a Honeymoon* when I was a schoolboy.

The Vicar of St. Peter's, a splendid broad-minded man with a rich sense of humour, the Reverend Jack Smithers, had, like Alex Kinnear at the Pier, decided on a different policy. The new ideas that flourished in such profusion at the end of the war were not always good ones as far as I was concerned! He was not going to let the hall out for hire; it was to be used solely for parish activities as the amateurs before the war had been more nuisance than they were worth. St. Peter's Hall was the other possible home for the Southsea Actors that I mentioned earlier and this was why it was not available. However, I went to see the vicar and, after much hard pleading on my part, he relented and reversed his policy.

I announced my first season. First season, please note; not just first play! St. Peter's Hall was booked for four separate weeks between October, 1947, and the following March. We were to open with *Twelfth Night* and follow this in late November with Goldsmith's *She Stoops to Conquer.* At the end of January, Ibsen's *Ghosts* was planned and the season would end in March with *Othello.* Ten people from Ron Mills's play had agreed to join me but, of course, I needed more. I went talent-spotting to school plays looking for those who were just about to leave. At that time, far fewer went on to higher education than they do now several decades later and so there were good pickings to be had. However, for two of the most vital members I did not have to look further afield than my surgery.

My first dental nurse was a girl in her teens called Prue Higham. Dark haired and with a chubby face, she was the younger of two daughters of a retired Naval officer. Even after the war, Service families like hers kept very strictly to their own social stratum and tended to have rather well-developed superiority complexes. Her parents, with an eye to her eventually making a 'good marriage', disliked her mixing with those civilians whom they considered to be on a lower social level. It did not take me long to discover that Prue had a warm and generous personality that only needed a little stimulus for it to want to break out from its social cage and expand. I, her new and first employer, with my theatrical plans and essentially civilian outlook, provided what she needed. Like me, she was stage-struck! Between patients and in coffee breaks there was very little talk of dentistry. I do not think that my partners greatly approved as it savoured of an officer hobnobbing with the troops! In view of her family's outlook, this was an ironical reversal. However, the partners had already begun to realise, I think, that in me they had taken on a bit of a maverick as far as the profession was concerned.

The other person was the practice secretary: Melita Moon, also the daughter of a retired Naval officer. She was a few years older than me and had no desire whatever to appear before an audience. Her enthusiasm, which was very great, was channeled into the role of Hon. Secretary and Treasurer. Her father, a Paymaster Captain, automatically became the Auditor. Prue, Melita and I thus formed a triumvirate which was able to discuss the new company practically every day.

Like Pooh-Bah I intended to be Lord High Everything. I therefore produced a Constitution which was a tough, iron-clad affair designed to ward off any would-be intruders into my proposed dictatorship. Ronald Mills had asked if he could have some official post and so I called him my Assistant Director. The most important paragraph was the following:

> 'The company shall be under the sole direction of K. Edmonds Gateley, the Director, who shall be entirely responsible for the company's finances. He shall be assisted in the artistic policy only by Ronald Mills, the Assistant Director. Neither they, nor anyone else connected with the company, shall receive any remuneration. The profits shall be devoted entirely to the bettering of productions or to recognised charities. The accounts shall be in the hands of the Hon. Treasurer and shall be audited annually by the Hon. Auditor. They shall be open to inspection by anyone who wishes to see them. *There shall be no committees.*'

The final sentence was because at that time I believed so very firmily in the two well-known clichés about them: that a camel is a horse designed by such a body and that the best sort of committee is one that has only two members providing half of them stay away. All too often, the only things they produce successfully are lowest common denominators.

All public performances were still subject to Entertainment Tax which was levied on each ticket sold, but cultural non-profit-making organisations could obtain complete exemption. This would be no problem: all I had to do was to write to the Customs and Excise people in London to explain what I was doing and the authorisation would follow automatically. What, in fact, did follow was a letter saying, 'The Commissioners . . . cannot regard . . . the Southsea Actors . . . as entitled to exemption from entertainments duty on the grounds on which you claim. Duty must therefore be paid . . . It is pointed out that exemption may not be granted to individuals and the entertainments are personally financed and controlled by you.'

I wrote at once to my Member of Parliament, Sir Jocelyn Lucas, and poured out my heart and spleen. He replied from the House of Commons the very next day saying that he would do all that he could. In due course he wrote again and this time enclosed a letter from Glenvil Hall, the Financial Secretary at the Treasury, no less. He said that they were *legally* unable to grant exemption unless I would set up a committee who would take an active share in the running of the company. This was the exact opposite of what I wanted to do: it was a very real blow. However, I climbed down to the extent of saying that I would have one after all although I was secretly determined that they should have virtually no say. This was not enough for H.M. C. and E., however! They said that they had in mind a committee 'consisting of disinterested persons not connected with the Company who would have effective control of its affairs'. They continued, 'The fact that the suggested members of the committee consist of players'—and surely this would have been reasonable enough—'suggest that the effective control of the Company is to remain in the hands of one person'. What could be more idiotic than a controlling body that was 'disinterested' and, of all nonsensical phrases, 'not connected with the Company'? More correspondence took place but eventually I had to go and see them.

A lot of details are now forgotten but I do remember sitting on an isolated, upright chair in the middle of the room whilst the officials—two, I seem to recollect—literally prowled round me asking questions. There was no bright light in my face but I did find it quite an alarming experience. I must have convinced them of my honesty, or perhaps simply of my naivity, because they eventually gave in and granted exemption. The one concession that I had to make was that three of the members of the committee would be what they had described as 'disinterested'.

An elderly spinster, a middle-aged housewife and an old friend from my earliest childhood were our first such members. The word 'disinterested' always seemed to us to be inapt and rather silly: in fact, it became a long-standing running joke amongst the committee members. We all believed that it was the cultural quality of the work that was produced by any theatre group that entitled it to exemption. In this case it looked very much as if all the fuss had been solely about bureaucracy. I do not remember the fact that we proposed to produce only plays by Shakespeare and other distinguished writers ever being mentioned at all. It had been necessary to sacrifice on the altar of red tape before the curtain could rise on our first production!

CHAPTER 7
First and Twelfth Nights

Eyes before ears—we all look first and listen second. If there is something to see and to hear at the same time, it will be the looking we shall do rather than the listening. This was to be the key to my plan to make the Southsea Actors superior to the other local companies as I realised that the standard of acting was not likely to be noticeably better. It was with scenery and lighting that I felt sure that I could score.

Before that, however, came the printing. I liked the work that a London firm had done for the Alec Clunes venture and so I got them to do our first job, the notepaper. It was well done but expensive and somehow they seemed rather remote people to deal with. I did not care for the printing of the local firms at that time and besides, if they produced something attractive for me, the other companies could more easily copy us. I then realised that no firm could suit me better than the one that supplied the Shakespeare Memorial Theatre, the Stratford-upon-Avon Herald Press. I had been taking their newspaper every week for nearly ten years and so I was immediately amongst friends. A happy relationship began and, like the best of wines, it has matured to even greater excellence with the passing of the years.

Good printing on a paper of a high quality was, therefore, the first manifestation of my policy that the public saw. I was following Nugent Monck as well as my own feelings on this matter: the Maddermarket programmes and publicity were always discreet and in good taste.

The modern principles of stage setting and lighting are now fairly generally understood but in the middle 1940s few more than a handful of theatres had any idea of them. Basically things had never changed since the very first indoor playhouses. Until the advent of electricity, all lighting, of course, had to be by naked flames; at first candles and then gas. As it is difficult to get such a source of light to throw its beams downwards, the natural place for the illumination of the stage was along its front edge below the feet of the actors. These footlights, or 'floats', as they were often called because the candles floated in water for safety, cast over the whole stage a completely even light which had a flattening effect. The arrival of electricity had simply meant that each light source had been replaced by a bulb and so illumination was still coming, apparently, from underground. Because this flood of light was so uniform, all shadows, depths and reliefs had to be painted on flat surfaces in the photographic convention of nearly all painting from the Rennaisance to the development of the camera. Even the Pier Theatre in the twenties, and St. Peter's Hall when we first went there, had inner prosceniums—adjustable to mask the edges of sets that are smaller than the actual solid frame of the stage opening—that were of draped curtains and golden, tasselled ropes all painted as pictures on flat canvas.

As far back as the late 19th century, Adolphe Appia, stimulated by what he regarded as the thoroughly unsatisfactory realistic painted scenery at Bayreuth, formulated two basic essentials. The first was that lighting must emphasise the three dimensions of the actor instead of flattening him and the second was that scenery must be solid to give movement its full value. The former can only be done by using individual light sources, such as 'spots', directed at the actors and at three-dimensional sets from angles that will bring out their solidity. A strong point made by another theatrical revolutionary, Ellen Terry's son, Gordon Craig, was that illusion is false and bogus. Things on the stage must look genuine and true. If a tree is needed, for example, when it is painted with photographic naturalism, it still remains a flat device of wood, paint and canvas standing on a wooden floor. The one thing that it is not, in spite of every trick that the painter can use, is a tree. It is therefore much truer to accept the materials and physical limitations of the stage and make instead a decorative or stylised tree that one can recognise as simply an artistic representation. Similarly, a plain or attractively designed background to such items will be much more of a genuine article than a photograph-like picture masquerading as the real thing. If realism was to be attempted, as it could be, for example, with a room, then it must be truthfully solid.

Another movement that had swept all before it was the equally drastic change in the method of producing Shakespeare. His plays had been written for continuous presentation on an open stage without scenery but from the Restoration onwards they had been acted in a series of elaborate realistic sets. This had necessitated cutting the texts very heavily for two reasons. In the first place, scenes had to go that could not be fitted into the scheme of scenery and, in the second, there were so many breaks with the curtain down, whilst these huge scenic extravaganzas were changed, that even more of the play had to be cut to keep the performance to a manageable length. Round about 1895, William Poel, whose eccentricity sometimes unfortunately prevented the more general acceptance of his ideals by the public, started presenting Shakespeare's plays as they were written, in imitations of Elizabethan theatres. Nugent Monck was his stage manager for a time and acted in many of his productions. The Maddermarket was very much the outcome of all that he had absorbed from, and most admired in, Poel's work and, likewise, my methods of staging Shakespeare, having been inherited directly from Monck, were themselves simply only one remove further from him.

Harley Granville-Barker, with his series of Shakespearean revivals at the Savoy Theatre in 1912-14, made more impact. He used a theatre of his own time as he found it but presented the plays uncut, unbroken save for one interval, and employing the modern methods of staging. He used a permanent set that was sufficiently abstract for it not to clash with any location in which the scene was supposed to be taking place but which, by the addition of some minor item such as a stylised tree or a gold curtain with a throne, could indicate a precise place. This new treatment meant that Shakespeare's plays could be acted, as they were originally, in a continuous sweep using a text that was more complete than it had been since the author's lifetime.

Before we could put on our first play, much necessary equipment had to be bought but I faced limitations of funds and space. It was no use having fresh sets for each production as, even if I could have afforded them, where would they go after they had been used? There was some space available in the garage at Crossways, where my *Revelling Beans* had performed when I was 12, but the family car had the first claim to the lion's share of it. There was also a fairly large garden shed at the back of the house which my mother very nobly gave up for me to use as an additional store. I felt that I had room for, and so would have made, seven 'flats'; four plain, two with practical doors in them and the third a tall arch. They were just over three metres high and nearly two wide. The plan was for them to be used like the children's toy, 'Lot's Bricks', in an infinite number of combinations with each other and to be repainted to look different each time they appeared in another production. Ronald Mills was a master at the Portsmouth Building School and he persuaded the carpentry teacher to make the frames for us with the help of some of the boys. Canvas was in short supply so soon after the war and so I bought a lot of old naval mattress covers from a surplus store and cut them up. I also decided to buy from a professional firm, two backcloths with rollers at the bottom so that they could be taken up out of sight whilst hanging in position. The fly-tower at St. Peter's Hall was not quite high enough for them to go up (or, to use the correct term, be taken out) completely from view without rolling. Final and very useful items were a pair of full-stage black curtains (known as 'tabs'), a professional track for them to run on and sets of black wings and overhead borders.

As far as lighting was concerned, the hall could only offer footlights and battens which I was determined not to touch at any price. Even at the King's at that time I should have found little more and so I bought several spotlights and floods with stands for them to go on to so that they could throw their beams down from a good height. I also designed, and had professionally made, a portable switchboard. Nowadays, such equipment is normal and this amount that I started out with would appear to be extremely modest but then the other local amateurs thought it was extraordinary and eccentric.

In Norfolk, during my spare time from the Maddermarket and Army dentistry, I did a lot of youth drama instruction with Jack Mitchley. During week-end courses, the 1944 seven-day one and even single evenings, we preached the new methods of setting and lighting with almost fanatical fervour. Consequently, when I approached the designing of the sets for the inaugural production of *Twelfth Night,* I was filled with the best of intentions and the highest Gateley-Mitchley, to say nothing of Stanislavsky-Appia, ideals. Alas! my courage failed me and my lofty principles tottered!

It is often said that a little black dress is an indispensable feature of every well-dressed woman's wardrobe. If it is really good it can look superb but, if it is not, nothing can appear to be cheaper or more insignificant. Would the public think that my sparse modern sets were poor and cheese-paring simply because the stage was so much barer than they were used to? I wanted the first that they saw of us to be rich, expensive-looking and quite different from their expectation. Would the simplicity that had been artistically rather good for Norfolk youth clubs and schools achieve the dazzling effect that I was after here? I funked it and decided that the answer was 'no'.

The set that I designed had a blue, vine-covered Tudor building on one side and high hedges with an opening in them on the other. Both the new backcloths were used; one for Orsino's palace and the other for Olivia's garden. The former had white Ionic pilasters and graceful pink drapes on a blue background but the other was considerably more fantastic. A pale weeping willow stood out against a towering curve of dark arches and from a gnarled tree stump arose a single branch of flaming foliage swirling like a Catherine Wheel. The significance of that oddity would emerge towards the end of the play. The hall possessed a battered old backcloth, so I turned it round and used its dirty reverse as a plain wall for the drinking scene. I borrowed some real barrels from a brewery and, by lighting the stage from a single deep amber flood in the rejected footlight trough, gave, I hoped, the impression that the drinkers were in the cellar sitting round a fire. As everything must startle and amaze, I used far too many colours in my spots and floods so that the lighting was not only bewilderingly unusual but had a bizarre quality that went much too far.

There is one sure test of a good stage setting: it should look empty when there are no actors in it. My two main scenes, with their elaborately painted backcloths, did the opposite. They filled the eye with busy detail and over-use of colour—especially with my somewhat harlequin lighting!—and were complete in themselves. When actors were added to the picture it all looked desperately overcrowded. The public may not all have liked it but at least it achieved one of its objectives; it struck everyone as being extraordinary! It was also quite obvious that the company had been launched with a big splash. I am sure it is no use starting anything of this nature like Cinderella: the trouble with that story is that you do not reach riches and the palace until the end! Jack Mitchley and his sister, Judith, travelled down from Norwich to see the production and obviously hated it.

My father, my sister—who had been coming home from Sussex more and more frequently as her marriage grew threadbare—and I painted the sets in the garden at Crossways. It was a beautiful summer and so we were able to lay the backcloths out on the lawn. I squared them with chalk and sketched in the details proportionally from my original designs. My father, then only two years short of 80, and Gwen filled in blocks of colour or traced lines under my instruction and I completed the more complicated areas.

Rehearsal space was a problem as funds were short in view of the expenditure on equipment and printing. We had four venues. One was the large sitting room at Crossways. Looking back, I wonder now at my gall as the use of this meant that the family had to be banished to the tiny dining room where they sat on upright chairs throughout the time of the rehearsal. Quite reasonably, they soon began to protest and it became obvious that we must find somewhere else. We also rehearsed in the Mills's flat but, although they were rather more Bohemian and so perhaps more tolerant of the invasion, they too got tired of the heavy-footed horde. Our other two rehearsal rooms were the Victorian drawing room of Miss Lily Flowers, the elderly spinster on the Committee—but here one was too frightened of knocking over occasional tables loaded with family photographs in silver frames—and the main room of the Portsmouth South

Conservative Association headquarters. This last was the most suitable but, on the other hand, was the one that cost money to hire. My Antonio, Howard Wood, who had been Gratiano in Ron Mills's *Merchant,* was a vigorous Socialist who caused a great deal of amusement by his dislike of rehearsing under the disdainful glares of the portraits of eminent Tory leaders of the past.

Prue Higham was to be my Maria, Ronald Mills Sir Andrew, Charles Biggerstaff (Ron's Shylock) Sir Toby, Nora Turner was Viola and Brenda Cosgrave Olivia. I cast myself as Malvolio with the actor manager's prerogative of picking what he wanted. As everyone began to collect at Crossways for the first rehearsal on Monday, 8 September, 1947, a stranger arrived at the door. He had come to see if he could join the company and his name was John Pearce. He and his mother ran the Little Theatre Entertainers who had crossed swords with the big guns—and hand weapons had stood little chance against gunpowder! He turned out to be one of the most delightful natural clowns that I have ever had the pleasure of working with. Slim and with a dancer's movements, he had sandy hair over a small merry face on a long neck. In later years, I would fail to direct him successfully in serious roles—Nature had given him a great gift which could not be concealed—but in parts like Flute he was incomparable and audiences loved him.

The lad originally cast as Fabian had to drop out and so Ronald Mills got the head boy of his school to take over the part for me. He was in his last few terms and so, no doubt, homework made demands on his spare time as it did upon that of the players of parts like Curio and Valentine. They spent their rehearsals at Crossways, when not actually performing, sitting under the grand piano immersed in their studies for the next day's school. The new Fabian was a teenager with Mediterranean good looks and a rich but rather thick voice. His name was John Fulcher and his unobtrusive entrance into the company did not give the slightest hint of the important part he would be destined to play in the story that lies ahead.

With this first production, I knew that I must do more than just put the play on the stage successfully. I had to establish myself right from the start as an unassailable dictator and get myself accepted as being far more artistically advanced and better trained than anyone else on the local theatrical scene. I also knew that no matter how efficient I was, I could only succeed if the company liked me enough personally. They were not starving employees desperate for jobs! I must find time to be kind and polite even if at the end of my tether through overwork and tiredness. Alas, through the years to come, this admirable ambition was all too often not achieved! I wanted to go on playing at toy theatres and I expected the live people who were now my actors to be as obedient and docile as the cardboard cut-outs had been. Above all, I was determined to run everything my own way and scotch any attempts that might be made to democratise the company and so rob me of power or control. This may sound terribly cold-blooded and ruthless. However, I believe that my burning enthusiasm counteracted those unattractive qualities to a certain extent and, in any case, two things must be remembered. The first is that the enterprise did succeed and, secondly, that I am not advising what should be done in an ideal society but simply reporting what in fact did happen.

Komisarjevsky had not only designed the sets and costumes for all his own productions but he had always arrived at his first rehearsal with every detail of movement and interpretation worked out and recorded in his own annotated copy of the play. I determined to do the same and, although in time I would know the value of being flexible and of discussing details with the actors, at first I felt that I must insist upon there being no variations from what I had laid down. I was afraid that any giving-in to contrary ideas that might be put to me would weaken my position. I needed to be much more firmly established and accepted before I could afford to do that. Strange to say, when in due course I felt safe to come out from behind my defences, those who had been in the company longest upbraided me for not being as tough as they liked me to be.

The costumes had to be hired from a London firm. I had learned a lot at the Maddermarket about historical clothes and dressing a play, especially from Peter Taylor Smith who was a considerable expert on the subject. I appointed a Wardrobe Mistress with several helpers so that the costumes would be ironed after they had been taken out of the baskets and so that there would be someone constantly watching to make sure that they were being worn correctly.

The rehearsals went reasonably well and I insisted upon two things. One was that they should start punctually and the other that parts must be learnt as early as possible. The older members of my cast lacked the Maddermarket discipline and the malleability of the youth group teenagers and so I found them tougher to mould than I had expected. This particular Rome was not going to be built in a play. The thought that seems to have come to me throughout my life as a director stood me in good stead then as it has since. Unbidden it has always said, 'Now I know that I shall not make that mistake again, next time will be absolutely right'. It never has been but the recurrence of the urge has constantly kept me optimistically pressing on.

The day arrived for us to move into the hall. It was the Monday and I had planned that we should have two dress rehearsals as we had done at the Maddermarket. The first performance was to be on the Wednesday. A local electrician, who was devoted to St. Peter's Hall and was its official stage manager, had assured me that he and his men would get all our lighting equipment installed and scenery up during the day so that it would be more or less ready when I arrived in the late afternoon. A removal firm had collected these items from Crossways first thing in the morning. Prue and I left the practice at about 4 and went straight to the hall. Nothing had been done. Everything had arrived safely and the men were all there but the only thing that anybody seemed to be doing with any efficiency was standing about. However, even though it meant starting from scratch, I assumed that it would not take too long to get it all set up. I soon realised how very wrong I was, especially as it became clear that there would be a great deal more work to do than I had envisaged beforehand. Almost at once it was 'knocking-off' time for the electrician and his men and so my own inexperienced stage manager, the son of our head dental technician and himself one, and I had to carry on as best we could with the few helpers that we were able to press-gang from the cast.

For hours there was chaos and pandemonium. Everywhere there were dangling ropes and entanglements of electric leads and, whilst the huge fragile bulbs were being screwed into the spotlights, voluminous unrolled backcloths billowed perilously as they were being hung from the overhead grid. Unwieldy flats toppled and all was a maelstrom of disordered activity. My stage manager, John Hewison, and I, frustrated and desperate, crossly barked orders; the wardrobe mistress interrupted with problems as she unpacked and saw for the first time what the London costumiers had sent; actors and actresses arrived and, wandering through the muddle, were each quite sure that their own questions about what they wore or how they made up were all that mattered. Even the least theatrical of them seemed to assume with ease the actor's self-importance which leads him to say, "Why isn't everything ready for *me*? How much longer have *I* got to wait?"

As the evening wore on, some sort of order seemed to be emerging and then the photographers arrived; one from the press and the other from a portrait studio. I had to rush down to the dressing room under the stage and throw myself into my costume and make-up for Malvolio. By the time I was ready, the stage was sufficiently clear for a start to be made. The press photos were soon done but the posed portraits and the scenes from the play took far too long. The young man from the studio had little idea of how to cope with the situation and his delays caused the cross, self-pitying actors to become even more supercilious and irritating and me to feel that my grip on the whole affair was slipping perilously. Prue and John Hewison were towers of strength and between us we just about managed to keep control.

At last, not far short of 10 o'clock, the dress rehearsal began and ran through into the small hours. I slept very little that night even though I was exhausted. My head throbbed with tension and worries. Tuesday's second dress rehearsal went comparatively smoothly and many faults that on Monday had passed unchecked, because the one desire had been to get through it somehow, were sorted out. Future get-ins and dress rehearsals would have their problems of various sorts but, having learned a great many lessons during that hideous first day, the company would never again be afflicted with quite such a nightmare.

The first night, Wednesday, 8 October, was solely for schools. Every one of the 400 seats had been sold and the noise of a packed house of excited youngsters through the curtain was thrilling and encouraging. Memories of Monday's tempers and chaos were obliterated by the actors' pre-performance sick feeling known as 'Butterflies in the tummy'.

I had designed the programmes to be as much like the Shakespeare Memorial Theatre ones as possible. They were discreetly in black on rough cream paper and had arrived safely from the Stratford printers. In correcting a mistake in the proof, they had created another one and my name was spelt on the front as 'K. Edm*u*nds Gateley'. Damn! Especially when I wanted everything to be absolutely right!

As at Stratford in those days, we began with the National Anthem. The music was from marked discs on a turntable in the stage manager's corner—and I have a feeling that the girl who was Sound Operator found herself doing a deal of ASM (Assistant Stage Manager) jobs as well! Necessity was the mother of versatility and we had no time for demarcation disputes! The houselights went out and, after a few bars of Vaughan Williams's *Fantasia on Greensleeves,* not then as much of a cliché as it has since become, the curtain went up in complete blackness. Slowly the light from a pale blue flood, suggesting soft moonlight, came on through the high arch to reveal the Duke sitting listening, with the blue pillared backcloth behind him. When he spoke, a pink glow gradually brightened the area where he and his courtiers were grouped.

At the end of the scene, the black tabs closed and Viola's arrival with the Sea Captain was played in front of them. This was dull visually but in the years to come I would manage scenes like this, I think, to rather better effect. When the tabs opened again, the garden backcloth was in view and the lighting suggested

Twelfth Night St. Peter's Hall, 1947

Sir Toby, Fabian and Sir Andrew (Charles Biggerstaff, John Fulcher and Ronald Mills) watch Malvolio (KEG) reading the letter

that it was dawn. Maria entered with a feather duster to show that she was busily at work before anyone else was up and thus the play continued.

I had the final scene in Olivia's garden at night with deep blue on the backcloth, a general effect of moonlight and an amber glow coming from inside the house. After the discomfiture of Malvolio, Feste jumped on to a seat at the back and everyone turned suddenly to face upstage, all with their backs to the audience except Feste. He was immediately in front of the swirling tree and with a sweep of his arms indicated its form as he said, 'Thus the whirligig of time brings in his revenges'. The revengeful Time Tree had dominated all that had happened up to that point. Now that I look back on it, the idea seems to me to be rather obscure and heavy-handed. I doubt if many of the audience understood it anyway!

I tried to play Malvolio as a parchmenty dried stick of a man, rather like a Dickensian lawyer, and before my final exit I took off my steward's chain and ceremoniously—and, I hope, cynically—laid it at Sebastian's feet. The enormous enthusiasm of that first sold-out house was a wonderful send-off for our venture. They may not have been very discriminating but I shall never forget the tremendous roar that I received when I entered in the drinking scene wearing a nightshirt. It had more of music hall beer about it than the dry, pale wine of the artistic theatre, but it was irresistible.

The houses were very good for the rest of the week and we covered our running expenses. The initial outlay became the start of a debt to me that would grow steadily larger throughout the next eleven years. The performances were a very mixed bag. The Orsino, a lad named Victor Goodings, who had been one of my students in Norfolk but was now doing National Service near Portsmouth, was stiff and unromantic but spoke well. The Feste was wholly inadequate though he sang passably. The Sir Toby was a nice enough old buffer but lacked the seediness and the alcoholism of this arch sponger. I found Ronald Mills to be a wild, bubbling, undisciplined actor whose knowledge of the text was often alarmingly inaccurate. I tried very hard to get him to play the part straight as this is not a farce. Both the comedy and the pathos of this great play will emerge only when the characters are people and not exaggerated into clowns and buffoons. He guyed it for all he was worth, especially when spurred on by the undiscriminating in the audience. The Viola and the Olivia were both excellent and gave quite professional performances; the former achieved wistful sadness and the other a glittering emotionalism which explains so much of Olivia's behaviour and changes of mood.

To me this first production had been rough and broad where I had hoped for smoothness and subtlety but it had been generally well received. Whatever my private misgivings, it had to be accounted a success and we were all happy and justifiably pleased with ourselves when the curtain came down on the last performance. As we were beginning to strike the set and pack the costumes and lighting equipment, three members of the Portsmouth Arts Theatre walked through the midst of us as if we were not there. They then proceeded to inspect the stage for their own possible future use without a word to, or a look at, any of us. I was very, very angry at this cavalier behaviour and remembered anew their insufferable attitude to the little company that had dared to use their original name before them.

I wrote, of course, to Donald Wolfit and told him how the first production had gone. 'Keep it up and fight for all the good things you know of', he replied from

His Majesty's Theatre, Aberdeen, where he was on tour. 'Do not go down for lack of funds', he continued. 'Tell the public how much money you want, rattle a box under their noses . . . and I am sure you will win through. Keep your standards high and make your actors rehearse'.

This was all good advice, though I did not need to 'rattle a box' at this stage as I was not particularly worried about funds. As far as standards were concerned, I had been irritated when some people told me how good they had thought that Ronald Mills had been as Sir Andrew. I knew that his performance had been contrary to what I had tried to get him to give and that each night had seen the addition of some impromptu and irrelevant extravagance. Hamlet's advice to 'those that play your clowns' suggests that Shakespeare himself knew about this type of thing that will 'set on some quantity of barren spectators to laugh'.

Yes, Donald, I will make my actors rehearse and, in future, I will see to it that they perform no more than they have rehearsed. *Twelfth Night,* even though it seemed to have given pleasure to most of those who saw it, had been too undisciplined to satisfy me. Donald Wolfit told me to keep my standards high. Yes, I would—but I must get them up there first!

CHAPTER 8
Ghosts and the invisible man

The incessant rains and high winds in the autumn of 1947 soon turned the trees into the bare ruined choirs of Shakespeare's sonnet. The dark lace of the branches was flecked with golden sovereigns of leaves which glittered against tumbling grey skies. This romantic picture of the third season represents how I would normally see it but, in this particular year, to my scene-painter's eye it was one of singularly mellow unfruitfulness. Each aspect of it that was usually a delight to gaze upon became simply one further nuisance.

There were several flats and one backcloth to be repainted as something quite different for *She Stoops to Conquer,* the next play. Gone were the good, sunny drying days that had made the painting of the *Twelfth Night* sets a pleasure. The car had to be banished to the pouring rain whilst all the work was done in the garage. The flats were difficult enough because they had to be done on their sides and there was room for only two at a time. Gwen and my father helped, as before, but we were so cramped for space that we kept backing into each other; though somehow we did just manage to avoid kicking over, or putting our feet into, the buckets of paint. The backcloth was a nightmare! The only thing to do was to secure its top batten as high as possible on one wall and then let it roll down to, and across, the floor. The bottom roller almost reached the opposite wall and so for most of the time we were walking about on the lower half of the cloth. When we reached the stage of painting the final few inches we were pressed so hard against that wall, with barely any space for our feet, that it was all we could do to prevent ourselves from losing our balances and falling face downwards into the wet paint.

The resultant set did not betray its troublesome gestation, however. It was the proscenium of an 18th century theatre with doors on to the front stage on either side and reclining figures, vaguely copied from Inigo Jones, in the central pediment. There was a chandelier and one of the backcloths was used as a flat, painted front curtain (or act drop) that rolled up from the bottom. The hall's own curtain was up when the audience came in and the effect was quite good except for one thing. Over the side doors I had painted the theatre boxes that would have been there in that period but, unfortunately, the flats being each only a little over three metres high, the space available was very limited and they looked like Punch and Judy booths.

Lovely ladies have been amongst the most precious jewels of our theatre since the Restoration but they are not always as much of a delight to a director. Very many of them are more interested in showing their beauty to its best advantage than in concealing it when a character requires that they should. A pretty woman, who was perhaps just past *ingénue* roles, had to step in to take over the part of Mrs. Hardcastle, the play's domineering older woman. Would she make up accordingly? She would not : I fought long and lost. Four tiny lines, hardly visible even to the front rows, were all I could ever get! I soon learned that it is very dangerous to cast a woman who is pretty as an ugly one and almost as great a problem when someone who is unattractive is expected to look like herself!

The original actress for the part had been met accidentally in a shop by Ronald Mills. She would have been disastrously bad but fortunately she embarrassed herself out of the company. She puffed and stumbled her way through the script, which she seemed to be unable to learn, until one night she reached the line, 'Indeed, Madam, you are the pink of circumspection'. By some Freudian slip she substituted for the last word one that refers to a surgical operation that dates back to the Old Testament! She stopped dead and went crimson. There was utter silence. It should be remembered that this was in the late 1940s, long before four-letter words had become obligatory in all new plays. We were in the Conservative headquarters and so perhaps it was suitable that the person who broke the silence by giggling was our strong Labour man. The gale of laughter that followed made the poor woman rush out, never to return. I believe that even the dusty portrait of Lord Salisbury smiled.

School parties again packed out the first night but the public was less interested. The first flourish was over and both play and performance were mildly pleasant but little more. I directed but did not appear in it so that I could keep an eye on things from the front of the house.

The side of me that still rather enjoyed the brash publicity of the commercial theatre prompted me to put, 'No longer banned but its terrible problem is still today's' on the advertisements for the next play, Ibsen's *Ghosts*. My better judgement, influenced by the cool good taste of Stratford and the Maddermarket, made me keep it in small type, however. I had long wanted to play the part of the young man who, going out of his mind as a result of his inherited venereal disease, blindly cries for the sun when it makes its solitary appearance as the final curtain falls. In any case, a great play by Ibsen was completely in keeping with the type of programme that I wanted to present.

During the previous two years, Sir Barry Jackson had been the Director at Stratford and had instituted what was to be a brave new world there of productions better than ever before. Like many another immediately post-war intention, it turned out to be very little different from what we had had in the late thirties. One part of his policy was to have a different director for each play. Incidentally, one of these was Nugent Monck who did *Cymbeline* in 1946 and *Pericles* the year after. As Stratford was so much my model, I decided to have different directors for the third and fourth plays of this first season. I invited Ronald Mills to tackle *Ghosts* and he made a very good job of it. He designed a splendidly gloomy 19th century room and I did the lighting. I was able to produce varying degrees of greyness for the daytime scenes and pools of lamplight contrasted with dark corners for the night. There was also, of course, the effect of the glow from the distant burning of the orphanage and the eventual rising of the sun.

In the afternoon of the dress rehearsal day, I had a telephone call from the Chief Constable of Portsmouth Police. 'I am very sorry to tell you', he said, 'but I am afraid that you cannot put your play on tomorrow. A Common Informer has laid information before me and I am compelled by law to act on it'. I assumed that the reason was the Lord Chamberlain's ban and so hastened to explain that it had been removed over 30 years before. No, it was nothing to do with that. The Common Informer, who could legally remain completely anonymous, had objected that St. Peter's Hall was not licenced as a theatre. This seemed to be ridiculous because no hall that I knew of did comply with professional theatre regulations and thousands of amateur productions had been staged in such buildings since long before the law had been put on to the Statute Book over 100 years earlier.

I told the cast when it gathered for the dress rehearsal and spread the news as far and wide as possible in the small amount of time available. Supporters immediately promised all sorts of help and one elderly lady of renowned battling disposition offered £25, quite a lot of money then, to start a fund to pay our fine if we went ahead and defied the law. Nothing much could be done that night so we went ahead with our dress rehearsal but with the heavy hearts of people who thought that they were performing it for the last time.

The next morning, I sent the following telegram to the Home Secretary at the House of Commons:

> AMATEUR IBSENS GHOSTS DUE TO OPEN TONIGHT IN ST PETERS CHURCH HALL HERE USED 23 YEARS FOR AMATEUR PLAYS ETC STOPPED BY PORTSMOUTH POLICE YESTERDAY BECAUSE HALL DOES NOT COMPLY WITH PROFESSIONAL THEATRE REGULATIONS NO SAFETY CURTAIN MUSICAL SHOWS ALLOWED BUT ALL AMATEUR PLAYS IN CITY FORBIDDEN IF MUST BE DONE HERE SURELY MEANS ALL AMATEUR PLAYS THROUGHOUT COUNTRY IN CHURCH AND TOWN HALLS BANNED UNLESS IN THEATRES MAY WE HAVE PERMISSION TO OPEN TONIGHT PLEASE

By lunchtime, I had the following reply:

> YOUR TELEGRAM AMATEUR STAGE PLAYS STOP MATTER IS ONE FOR THE LOCAL LICENCING AUTHORITY UNDER THE THEATRES ACT 1843 AND SECRETARY OF STATE REGRETS THAT HE CANNOT INTERVENE - UNDER SECRETARY HOME OFFICE

Immediately I telephoned the Chief Constable with the bad news from London. He thought for a while and then decided that he would use special powers that he had and defy the law himself. He permitted the play to go on after all on the grounds that it would be prejudicial to the public good to have people, who would be unaware of the ban, coming out on cold winter nights only to discover that they had to go home again.

A mere 507 people came to see the play over the three nights and this has remained the record lowest attendance. The company was still very new and this was the first time that there had not been any school performances. No sooner had the curtain come down on Ibsen than the Common Informer's balloon—to use a colloquial expression of the time—went up. The Portsmouth Evening

News gave the ban considerable coverage but it also got into several of the national papers and no less than three Members of Parliament asked questions in the House and received answers from Chuter Ede, the Home Secretary. The Daily Mirror devoted part of its leader to the case, Beachcomber in the Daily Express merrily poked fun at the law and Ivor Brown in the Observer wrote, 'There is still a strong minority in this country which sincerely detests the theatre and is determined to harass it. Witness the Common Informer at Portsmouth who has managed to pull out of its grave a bit of mouldering legislation and so prevent the amateur actors performing in their usual premises'.

Nothing could be done: the Common Informer had succeeded. The church halls had no alternative but to apply for theatre licences and so we had to postpone *Othello*.

Words like 'frivolous' and 'busybody' had been used about the Common Informer but I never believed, and still do not, that his intentions were as trivial as those words suggest. Why should anyone do such a thing unless they had a serious motive? The trouble, I think, was that the amateur movement was thriving and growing rapidly: we and the Arts Theatre, who had now moved into St. Peter's Hall as well, alone were providing eight weeks a year of straight theatre. I have always thought that this person was probably someone with a vested interest in professional entertainment. The Pier was not suspected and, in any case, at this time of the year its theatre had been stripped for the winter ballroom dancing. I am sure the sailors' music hall, the Coliseum, did not care either. This left the city's one live straight theatre, the King's, with, as an outsider, one of the cinemas that had had its application for a licence to have live acts between films turned down. Nobody ever admitted to being the Common Informer but, likewise, no one who could reasonably have expected to be under suspicion ever came forward to assure us that they were not responsible.

A quarter of a century after the event, I had an article under the heading of *Viewpoint* in the now-defunct weekly newspaper, the Hampshire Telegraph, every fourth week. I chose as my subject on one occasion, this whole business. I wrote to the Secretariat of Portsmouth Corporation and also to the present Chief Constable to ask if they could now, after all this time, reveal to me who it was—even if only for my private information. The first replied that they knew no more than I did and the second that all such information had been destroyed when the Portsmouth and Hampshire Constabularies had combined a few years before. Now no one knows and, presumably, no one ever will. He remains what he has always been; an invisible man.

Six weeks later, St. Peter's Hall became officially a theatre. It was impossible to install a proper iron safety curtain but the old actual front curtain, which was blue with simulated gold embroidery painted on it, had to be replaced by a new, very thick, lined fireproof plush one. Wooden doors gave place to steel and there were iron escape ladders in all directions. The church authorities were faced with a very large bill! The Watch Committee had recommended to the Portsmouth City Council, the body which granted the licence, that they should restrict it to amateur performances. How odd! Why? Was my suspicion about the motive of the Common Informer correct? Had he been able in some way to influence the members of the Watch Committee to help him to curb the possibility of the hall's developing still more as a theatre in competition to whatever his interest may have been? Justice prevailed and the recommendation was defeated.

I invited a highly intellectual young woman of the name of Valerie Bechervaise to direct *Othello* for me. She was tall, dark, had a certain striking beauty and was well-known locally as an amateur actress and producer of some standing. She had accepted when I asked her in the spring of 1947 but before the end of the autumn she had tragically died of cancer. The new director of the play, also a woman, was an English lecturer at the local teachers' training college. I soon discovered that I had made a mistake as the lady seemed to have no sense of the theatre and spent most of her rehearsal time with her eyes covered as she beat out the rhythm of the verse to ensure that we were metronomically accurate! I had no alternative but to interfere. The result, after only a little friction, was a reasonably satisfactory but rather unimaginative production. I designed a vaguely Moorish set which was carried out in pink and black with touches of emerald; colours which might suggest the decor of a twenties tea-shop. In fact it looked quite well and a central feature of it, which was repeated later in miniature over the bed, was a green mask that was intended to symbolise the 'green-eyed monster' that is at the centre of the tragedy. It came from my same mental stable as the Revenge Tree in *Twelfth Night* and probably meant just as little to the audience as that brain-child had done!

Additions to the stock of scenery had to be strictly limited because of the shortage of storage space at Crossways. I did not want anything that could not be repainted and used as something else. In any case, the money had to come out of my not-particularly-deep pocket and be added to the mounting debt and so I dug my heels in over the matter of the bed canopy which was cheap and nasty. A decorative cross-piece of wood and cardboard was hung by ropes from the roof of the fly-tower and curtains were attached to it. When the stage was empty and still, it looked sufficient but, when it received the slightest touch, it swung about like a mad thing. Everybody hated it, particularly Ronald Mills, who played the Moor, because he had to cope with it and the murder of Desdemona simultaneously. Even though I knew it was a disaster, I stubbornly would not alter it as I was still ruthlessly pursuing my policy of not giving in over any of my decisions. I have even heard of this situation in the professional theatre: the actors become temperamental because the director is asking for something which they think is quite ridiculous and he becomes even more obstinate in a desperate attempt to justify his decision.

Nora played Emilia and it proved to be one of her best parts. I was Iago, a role which I was to tackle again in two further productions. He is one of the most fascinating characters to play with his alternations between his 'honest' public face and his actual evil, but the prose is difficult to learn: the variations on the theme of 'Put money in thy purse', for example, can be very hazardous. Ronald Mills was a flambouyant Othello. There were touches of 'haminess' but generally his performance was well liked. We on the stage with him were delighted that he had learned to curb his weakness for spontaneous embellishments but he was still alarmingly erratic.

The notices in the local paper up to this time had been clearly the work of uninterested reporters who were without much knowledge of the theatre. The Goldsmith play had received the headline, 'Amateurs give comedy' and the level of criticism did not rise above, 'Leading parts were played by . . .' Now, for *Othello,* we got a report with very slightly more substance. 'In a season that has been all too short, the Southsea Actors . . . have made a valuable and important contribution to the cultural life of the city . . . Perhaps their best achievement so far was . . . *Othello* . . . Ronald Mills as the generous and noble-hearted Moor gave a performance that was all the more creditable in its unexpectedness'—a remark that, at last, actually sounded like dramatic criticism.

The new fire regulations caused the seating capacity of the hall to be reduced to 320 but that did not matter for some time yet. The audiences for *Othello* had crept up a little on the Ibsen but still did not reach the figures for the first two plays. Donald Wolfit said, 'Do not forget the old Chinese proverb, "It is very easy to open a shop but it is very hard to keep it open" '. The Wolfits—he and Rosalind Iden had married only a month before—seemed genuinely pleased. 'What a splendid record for your first year', he wrote. 'Rosalind and I are delighted with your success'. He asked for a balance sheet and, having enquired how much I had had to spend on basic equipment, sent me a cheque as a donation to the funds. Talking about the actors, he gave me some very good advice that I did not really need. It was a recommendation that Nugent Monk could equally well have given but was something which I already firmly believed myself. 'Do not let them flag', he said, 'and if you get a clique of self-satisfied amateurs who begin to think that they are more important than the play, take my advice and get rid of them and find some fresh ones'.

CHAPTER 9
Sacred and profane

No sooner had my first season been launched than I was already teeming with ideas for the second. Again there should be two Shakespeares: I decided on *The Merry Wives of Windsor* and *King Richard III.* The other two should be a modern English play—but no, not a West End commercial success—and a continental classic: T S Eliot's *Murder in the Cathedral* and Molière's *Tartuffe; or, The Imposter.* However, by the time we were rehearsing *Ghosts* I was so impatient to do even more that I decided to extend this next season to five plays. I felt sure Nora would be good as Beatrice—and I was dying to play Benedick!—so the extra one was to be *Much Ado About Nothing*. I would direct four of them this time and my one 'guest producer' (the word, 'producer' meant then what 'director' does now) would be Margaret Dewey, who had been our Mrs. Alving. She was to undertake the Shakespeare history.

Looking back from a more sedate time of life, I am amazed to think of the boundless energy that I had then. As I preferred to cope myself with the mountains of correspondence that running the company involved, Melita Moon's secretarial work was largely concerned with ticket sales and accounts. Under the umbrella title of 'Hon. Secretary and Treasurer' she was also our very busy, and efficient, Box Office and Front-of-House Managers. I should have been glad, one might think, to have had time for rest and reassessment after the first hectic season had ended, but not so. A charming little old churchman, straight out of a 19th century novel, Canon Grigg-Smith, approached me to see if I would stage a play in the nave of Portsmouth Cathedral during the summer to celebrate the 21st anniversary of the foundation of the diocese. This was really quite a remarkable tribute to the reputation I appeared to have built up within the space of this one inaugural season. I accepted. The play was to be Dorothy M. Sayers's piece about the building of the Chapter House of Canterbury Cathedral in the 12th century, *The Zeal of Thy House.*

If I had had any doubts about the wisdom of running everything myself, my dealings with the Diocesan Drama Committee, on to which I was co-opted, would very rapidly have dispelled them. It was cumbrous, slow and succeeded in damping down every bright idea. They had hoped that the whole cast would be practicing members of the Church of England and it was assumed that all the parishes would provide hordes of enthusiasts to walk-on as the monks and pilgrims. In fact, they provided 5. In the end, we had a professed atheist in one of the leads and Ronald Mills, a Roman Catholic, in the principal part. On the other hand, I arranged to be well and truly on the side of the angels: I cast myself as the Archangel Gabriel and the Reverend Gerald Ellison, then vicar of St. Mark's Church in Portsmouth, as the Archangel Michael. The latter went on to become the Bishop of London. I am still waiting.

Soon after we had started to rehearse, the Provost, the Very Reverend Eric Porter-Goff, feeling perhaps that he had not been sufficiently consulted, interposed what were to me impossible conditions. The Cathedral could not be blacked out and every trace of the production, including the lighting, must be removed during the daytime between the performances. Canon Grigg-Smith had agreed to the exact opposite when I accepted the task. The day was saved by the arrival on the scene of our old enemy, the Invisible Man. This time the news seemed to spread even further and wider. A headline in the South African paper, the Cape Argus, read, 'Old Forgotten British Law Stops Play in Cathedral'! I have a feeling that this time it might, perhaps, have been appropriate to have thanked our heretofore villain.

An announcement in the Portsmouth Evening News in April will tell its own story.

> 'Among work of leading stage designers displayed at the British Theatre Exhibition at Norwich Castle are designs of sets by two local producers-actors, Mr. K. Edmonds Gateley (director of the Southsea Actors) and Mr. Ronald Mills (assistant director). Mr. Gateley exhibits his designs for the company's *Twelfth Night* and *She Stoops to Conquer* and Mr. Mills his designs for *Ghosts.'*

I had four productions to design and prepare, to cast and to write endless letters about to all sorts of people varying from professional suppliers of stage equipment to tiros who would be fit only to hold spears but who would pester me for leading parts. None the less, when Jack Mitchley invited me to be on the staff of a week's residential drama course in King's Lynn in August, I accepted that, too, without hesitation.

Again I was in charge of the setting and lighting department but I also had a choral verse-speaking class and directed half the students in theatre-in-the-round productions. These consisted of the Cade Rebellion episodes from *King Henry VI, Part II* and the Wrestling Scene from *As You Like It* as I thought that they were particularly suited to this type of presentation.

As soon as I returned to Southsea, we began rehearsing for *The Merry Wives of Windsor.* Captain Moon had audited our accounts and found that we had just managed to keep within our income if we ignored the debt for equipment that was still owing to me. It stood at nearly £200. If one bears in mind that the top price at Stratford that year was 10s. 6d. (52 pence in new money) and that at the time of writing it is £17 one will realise the value of the sum then. Later in the summer, Captain Moon had died suddenly and had been replaced as our auditor by Ronald Mills's father-in-law. The rehearsal room situation had taken a sudden turn for the better. My partners at the dental practice had agreed to let us use an empty surgery and this was a great help. The one thing that made it different from being simply an empty room was that in the middle of the floor there projected a cluster of pipes leading respectively to the gasworks, the power station and the sewers. So long as we continued to rehearse in that room, there must always have been—had any member of the audience been sharp enough to spot it—a small patch in the middle of the stage where no one ever stood.

Since no chattering was allowed during rehearsals, the sitting-out area for the actors had to be the landing and the stairs outside. We had there a wonderful, almost Dickensian, faithful caretaker of the old school. She was a small, elderly woman of the name of Mrs. Furlong and, ironically, she would never wear any teeth. If we rehearsed, and consequently made noise on the landing, beyond what she considered to be the correct hour to finish, she would come out of her damp basement and start banging every door on the ground floor with such vigour that it sounded like a rival company rehearsing a battle with heavy guns! However, the new room was a great improvement as we were now able to mark out the stage and the positions of the scenery on the floor for the first time.

I have always been particularly fond of *The Merry Wives of Windsor* in spite of the condemnation of scholars. It seems to me that every time it is staged it is rediscovered by critics and audiences who are amazed how well it acts. The extraordinary thing is that they never learn and go through this process of being surprised over and over again. The trouble is that the scholars want it to be *King Henry IV, Part III* and complain because it is something quite different.

Falstaff in this comedy is a delightful, rollicking old buffer who is splendid company. If one can accept him as that and stop looking for the magnificent rogue of the *Henry IV* plays, then all is well. It is a pity that names like Mistress Quickly, Justice Shallow, Pistol, Bardolph and the addition that was yet to come in *King Henry V,* Nym, were used for characters that bear only the faintest resemblance to their counterparts in the histories. Had they been called by other names, or if one can dismiss all ideas of those other different people, then one can enjoy the play on its own very considerable merits. Alternatively, see them as cartoon characters in 'holiday humour' and add to them delights such as the weedy Cousin Slender, the enchanting Welsh parson, the fun of the French doctor and those most likable housewives and one has a joyous concoction that I should hate to be without. Above all, in this, Shakespeare's only *bourgeois* play, we see a wonderful picture of small town life. Surely this is Shakespeare's own Stratford in terms of affectionate, light-hearted comedy. If it is not, then he never came nearer to it. His own schoolmaster at Stratford's Edward VI Grammar School was, whilst he was between the ages of 11 and 15, of the name of Thomas Jenkins. Although it has been shown that he came from London, it is a very Welsh name and for me it is too much of a coincidence that Shakespeare's Windsor-Stratford schoolmaster should be Welsh without there being a connection. Many a very Welsh Welshman today can be found to have been born outside the principality!

As a teenage purist—not to say, puritan—I had enjoyed being outraged by what I then considered to be Komisarjevsky's Austrian dolls' house travesty at Stratford in 1935. In maturer years I think that I would have appreciated it more. Its one great virtue was that it was performed in a permanent set which kept all the relevant houses of Windsor before our eyes. I decided that I would base mine on this same principle except that I wanted it to look English mediaeval. Whenever possible, the Windsor houses should also all remain visible at the same time. To help to make 'Merry' the operative word, I designed my sets in the style of Walt Disney film cartoons. With flats I created the interior of Ford's house on the left-hand third of the stage and the Garter Inn on the right third. Through the central gap one could see the backcloth which had a street of old cottages in pastel shades which I had based on a photograph of the Elizabethan manor house, Grimshaw Hall. To get to the street from either house, there was a doorway leading to the central space.

This all worked remarkably well but the effect was weakened by having to play scenes such as the duel in the fields and the visit to the French doctor's house, before my very useful but rather dull, set of black curtains. I had an interval just before the last act so that we could strike the houses and replace the backcloth with our other one. This meant having a further earlier interval otherwise the first part of the play would have been much too long. The last scene by Herne's Oak at midnight had a deep blue sky against which could be seen a black silhouette of Windsor Castle. The tree itself was also black but outlined with pale blue whilst the foreground was scattered with Walt Disney plants and leaves sketched in white.

When the curtain rose, I had my three-part set in full use. Mistress Ford was laying the table in her house and sending Anne out with a jug. Mistress Page was sitting and chatting. Falstaff and the rogues were being served with tankards by the Host in the inn on the opposite side of the stage, whilst, in the central space, Dr. Caius, with his servant Rugby, was meeting Mistress Quickly. Here I hoped was an immediate cross-section of everyday life in Windsor; three areas all occupied by people doing different things. When the first characters to speak came down through the centre because they were supposed to be in the street, the lights faded in Ford's house and the inn and the people inside them became quite still. It is, of course, an unforgivable sin—or to put it more bluntly, thoroughly bad stagecraft—for actors to move or fidget when anyone else is speaking or when what Hamlet called 'necessary business of the play' is going on.

In the Park at midnight, I followed Shakespeare's instruction, as indeed Komisarjevsky had done but many directors do not, and had head-dresses for some of the supposed fairies with circlets of candles on them. These and the hand-held tapers were, of course, tiny electric lamps with concealed batteries: splendid work, as too were some lanterns that we already possessed, by John Hewison in our dental laboratory.

I played Dr. Caius, and so repeated a performance that I had given under Nugent Monck, and the Falstaff was Howard Wood, known hitherto to my readers as the actor with the left-wing views. It might have sounded as if all the rest of us were deep blue Tories. I am sure that, in fact, we represented every shade of political thought but he was the only one who ever appeared to bring the subject up at rehearsals. Nowadays we are so used to left-wing directors and actors who seem to be more interested in distorting plays to propagate their ideals than in the honest interpretation of what their non-politically motivated authors have written for them, that it is strange to look back to a time before they were rife. Maybe Howard was the advance guard! Anyway, he was a rare breed in the amateur theatre at the time. As Falstaff he looked well because the costume, padding and wig from Nathan's, whose wardrobe hire department we had been using since *Ghosts*, were absolutely excellent. Our original firm had arrogantly refused to supply us after the first two plays solely, so they said, because I told them what I hoped they could send me instead of leaving it entirely to them. Nathan's, who supplied us for many years to come, were always marvellously co-operative and seemed to enjoy doing all they could to realise my mental picture and so match the colour schemes and styles of the sets. Howard had a rumbustious manner which suited the *Merry Wives* Falstaff but he had a provincial burr to his voice which, though it was an asset for his excellent Tony Lumpkin, was to his disadvantage as the knight.

After the abortive attempt to stage a religious play in Portsmouth Cathedral, we had romped in bright colours with Sir John Profanity. Now we returned to the sacred again: *Murder in the Cathedral.* As it is constructed on the classical lines of Greek tragedy, I devised a production to match its formality of structure and speech. The set consisted of black and grey panels marked with inverted J's to suggest the reveals of otherwise invisible Norman arches, a plain cross and a simple line drawing of Christ which was based on a 12th century sculpture in Malmesbury Abbey; all in white. The groupings of the seven Women of Canterbury, the spoken chorus, were all deliberate patterns. For example, to listen to the sermon, they formed a single line across the stage with their heads making a continuous curve from that of Becket, high in the pulpit, down almost to the ground. The tallest stood nearest to him, then the next tallest and so on to a kneeler, a croucher and finally one almost lying flat. Ronald Mills, a devout Catholic, seemed to be inspired by the part of Becket and gave by far his best performance.

Becket to Crookback was a reversal of the switch from the earthly to the heavenly for most of the cast but it was hardly so for me as I changed the mediaeval armour of the Fourth Tempter-Knight for the crown and humped shoulder of another murderer, Richard III. Laurence Olivier had created his famous portrayal on the stage of the New Theatre only five years before and visually I copied him as closely as possible. Even in the professional theatre no one dared to attempt to look very much different from him for many years. It seems to me to be a bad thing when such a performance becomes so definitive in the general public's minds that any variation, however textually justified, is thoughtlessly and automatically barred from consideration. Margaret Dewey, who was a speech therapist, directed well considering the vastness of the play and the smallness of the stage. I designed a set of Decorated Gothic arches blocked in with sombre reds and greens. The rehearsals were rather too schoolmistressly conducted to be particularly enjoyable. There are often moments when giggles set in or the concentration is lost for some reason or other and I have always realised that one must give in to them. The company remains in better health ultimately and amateurs will not stay in one where they find that they do not actually *enjoy* the rehearsals.

March, 1949, brought Molière's *Tartuffe; or, The Imposter;* using the full title to make it sound more interesting to those who did not know it. My French is not good enough for me to appreciate this play in the original language and so, like many similarly placed Britons, I have never really been able to understand why it is thought to be so great. English translations are always relatively trivial and the Anstey one that we used was no exception. All we could offer our audiences was a delightful comedy about a religious hypocrite working havoc in a French family but there is obviously a lot more to it than that. Ronald Mills forgot some of his discipline that had made his Becket remarkably good and 'hammed' Tartuffe for all he was worth. I have to admit, however, that a large number of undemanding members of the audiences, who did not care whether the play was by Molière or Ben Travers, were delighted. I contented myself with a tiny 'cameo'—a euphemism for a very small part in which one hopes to be able to make an instant success—of a catarrhal bailiff which was, I feel sure, instantly forgettable. The great success was the scenery! It was designed—and painted in the drive at Crossways in biting weather which included a few flakes of snow—by Aileen Wyllie, the daughter of the great marine artist, W. L. Wyllie, RA. She did an enchanting dove grey courtyard with swirling magnolias against its walls. I cannot overestimate the amount that I learned from watching her at work and although by this time I was quite an experienced scene painter and designer, my techniques were revolutionised by what I gleaned on those icy afternoons. Aileen was also a good actress and played Queen Margaret in *King Richard III*. However, she disappeared to do missionary work in Africa after *Tartuffe* and so we lost her all too quickly.

During this season, I had managed to add to our scenic equipment. The carpentry master and his boys at the Portsmouth Building School had come up trumps again. We now had some rostra and steps which I had designed to match the measurements of the bases of our flats. Storage was no longer a problem as far as they were concerned because they were able to live their off-stage lives in our rehearsal room at the surgery. The rostra which we had used in *Ghosts* and *Othello* had been botched-up contraptions made of anything that we could borrow or disguise. I had also managed to buy a plain backcloth for use as a flat cyclorama—something of a contradiction in terms! It was at least third-hand but it would serve until we could afford something better which, in due course, we were able to do.

At last, with the final production of this second season, I had the courage to do what my conscience had told me that I ought to have done right from the start. I practised what I had preached and designed a set of modern simplicity. For *Much Ado About Nothing* I had two short white pillars, each topped by a cut-out figure blowing a trumpet held by one hand. White fish-net, suspended from the flies, was held by the figures' other hands to form a simple arch. The statues with their swags over the Pier Theatre proscenium and their counterparts holding trumpets out over that at the Theatre Royal, had been the parents in my mind of this device. These things had branded such deep impressions into my brain as a very small child that I never stopped incorporating reflections of them into my designs.

This simple structure had the lightweight quality of an icing decoration on a wedding cake and stood out against glowing colours, differing according to the moods of each scene, on the plain skycloth. Within the white arch were placed occasional necessary props such as a trellis entwined with flowering climbers for the 'pleached bower' and a large cross for the wedding scene. My father helped with many of the simpler carpentry jobs. One of these was the construction of this cross which, when it was standing upright, was a good deal taller than he was. One day I went into the garage to call him in to lunch and was immediately quite overwhelmed by the drama of what I saw. He was doing nothing more extraordinary than finishing his work on it. It was, however, between noon and 3 o'clock, the time of the Crucifixion, and the day was Good Friday!

My sister's marriage had finally disintegrated in the Divorce Court during the winter and so she was now living locally and thus able to give even more help than she had before. Donning old clothes, she painted scenery under my guidance and did such boring, but necessary, jobs as sticking numbered tabs on to all the seats in St. Peter's Hall every time we went there. The worst work that I ever gave her was the making of the flowering climbers for the bower. The stems were electric cable, as I could not think of anything else that would be stiff enough, with flowers and leaves made of felt. Her poor hands were soon terribly sore and blistered as the wire was very tough indeed. She has never let me forget just how much she suffered for my art!

At last a real critic had appeared on the scene. He was Gordon Jeffery and he wrote for a short-lived magazine called *Mercury* which proclaimed that it covered 'The Arts in Wessex'. As his first article began, 'Of the professional theatre in Portsmouth, the less said the better' and went on to describe the Arts Theatre as 'something of a disappointment', I decided that any praise that came from his pen might be well earned. He said that the Arts Theatre 'may even live down their 1947-8 efforts' but added, 'The Southsea Actors are, I think, of greater significance'. He was 'moved and held' by *Murder in the Cathedral* in spite of never liking the play. He described Ron Mills in it as 'an actor of far above average skill'. 'K. Edmonds Gateley', he said 'is the Director and, in some respects, the Dictator of the company. Without this *single'* (the italics are his) 'directing force I doubt that the Southsea Actors would flourish as they do . . . Mr Gateley, I understand, once worked with Nugent Monck and certainly his sets and lighting and his emphasis upon stage-grouping reveal his own preoccupation with the need for setting, lighting and playing to be attuned'. When he wrote about *King Richard III* he said that he paid us the compliment of judging us by professional standards and that he had to admit that there was 'awkwardness' in many of the small-part players. He went on to say, 'It is Richard who makes or mars the play and here the Southsea Actors were on firm ground. K. Edmonds Gateley makes no mistakes from his first entrance . . . For as long as he held the stage—and there's little time in *Richard* when he does not—it is easy to forget the odd lapses; even to overlook the miscast Buckingham . . . So good, so right was Mr Gateley that I forgot too the small stage but was instead on Bosworth Field and, on Bosworth Field, I felt that fugitive pity for the Crookback creeping in. Did Shakespeare intend it that way? I believe that Mr Gateley did—that he managed to convey it was the measure of his remarkable performance'. Needless to say, I liked that.

In May I adjudicated the Portsmouth Schools Drama Festival. After the high standards of such affairs in Norfolk, I was appalled by the mediocrity of play after play. Most of the productions showed practically no imagination and some of the choices were simply very silly. In a festival in which both sexes are taking part, why, for example, choose Dogberry, Verges and the Watch—tough, mostly ageing, male character parts—for a team of little girls? In a speech of thanks to me at the end of the week, probably not very heartily endorsed by the teachers whose efforts I had blasted, I was described as being either a devil in disguise or else an avenging angel. They were not sure which. I must say that I rather liked that too!

CHAPTER 10
The Wolfit season

As oil and water do not mix, it is a terrible job trying to apply distemper to a surface that has previously been covered with oil-bound paint. This was the situation that my sister and I had to struggle with when we worked on the *Othello* set. Ron Mills had let the carpentry master and the boys at his school paint his *Ghosts* scenery but, in spite of pleas from me, they had used the wrong materials. They had, however, employed distemper on the backcloth of the misty fjord but, having bound it with too little size, it powdered off whenever it was touched and was therefore equally difficult to paint over.

When I asked Ron to direct the first play of the third season, *The Taming of the Shrew,* I therefore stipulated that Gwen and I must be the scene painters. Once bitten with oil paint and too little size, twice shy! He set his production in the colourful Spain of operetta and gave us a very complicated picture in merging mauves, pinks and oranges to copy. We growled constantly about its complexity whilst we were painting it on the lawn in the summer sun. We growled even more when we saw it set up on the stage and discovered just how much time had been wasted because only half our work could be seen through three arches that separated it from the audience. Finally I reached the ultimate in growling when I made the further discovery that he had copied it from Doris Zinkeisen's scenery for the production at the New Theatre in 1938—even to details such as how a flag was blowing on one of the buildings.

There were some good performances in the leading parts, notably from Brenda Cosgrave who did Katherina with the great vivacity that was her forte, and Geoffrey Eagar, a very polished and professional new man who played Petruchio. Far too many of the small parts were given to boys from Ron's school and he let his own natural, extrovert exuberance loose on the production. It was wildly farcical, especially in a scene with a pantomime horse, but none the less, in spite of its shortcomings, it had bubbling vitality and the schools, of course, loved it.

In March, 1944, I had had an emotional experience in Norwich that was so extraordinary and beautiful that perhaps it would be truer to call it a spiritual one. I was cast as Konstantin, the sensitive young writer who eventually shoots himself, in *The Seagull* by Chekhov, whom I have always rated as the world's second greatest dramatist. Norman Marshall said in his book, *The Other Theatre,* 'Apart from Shakespeare, Monck is at his best in the production of a Chekhov play. The mood of these plays is perfectly in tune with the gentle melancholy of his own character'. Nothing could be more true. Throughout the whole production we were caught up in Moncklet's mystical sadness and even found ourselves living our daily lives in that elusive atmosphere of heartache, wry humour and resignation that is the very breath of these marvellous plays. Strange to say, nothing in which I have ever acted, not even my beloved Shakespeare, has swept me along and held me in its thrall as did this Maddermarket production of *The Seagull.* I am uncomfortable when I see it played professionally and can never face the emotional trauma of seeing other amateurs perform it; I am utterly possessive about it. I called the atmosphere elusive because sometimes directors decide that these plays should be done without the melancholy. In my experience, all they succeed in doing is to reveal their own insensitivity and give us the bones of the plays stripped of the warm flesh and the peculiarly Russian minds that inhabited them. They are not plays for the emotionally tone-deaf.

One of the Norwich newspapers said, 'Two parts were outstanding—Konstantin Treplev, the youthful, potential genius warped and tortured by his mother's egotism and suffocating theatrical conventions and Nina . . . the last scene' (the one between these two characters) 'was as well played as anything I have ever seen at the Maddermarket'.

I had to do *The Seagull* again. I knew that it could never be quite the same as the Norwich miracle but it was worth a try and so I chose it for the second play of the season. I did not repeat my own experience nor was I able to exert the magical influence over my cast that Moncklet had upon us, but I did not regret the attempt.

Earlier in the year, Donald Wolfit had said, 'If my wardrobe is not in use and we can help to reduce your costs on any play, let me know and we will get together on it. Give me some idea as to what you have to pay for costumes and we will see if we can't cut it down'. He added a nice postscript: 'Let me have your dates and if we are free we will come down to see you at it'.

When he heard that the next play was to be *King John,* he kindly followed up his suggestion about letting us use his costumes. 'The only possible way is for you to come up to London on a Sunday', he said, 'and together with my secretary we could open up the wardrobe, look out what we have and basket it up there and then. Alterations you would have to do down there if necessary. Cleaning would be done here when it was returned. String mail, tabards, cloaks, etc. and long gowns—I am sure we could help and save you money—but we shall have to do it ourselves as I have no staff at all at present until the late spring. Let me know if this is any good'. It had to be a Sunday as he was playing Long John Silver in *Treasure Island* twice daily in the West End. He asked me to send a list of characters and told me that the costumes would come from his *King Richard III* and *Merry Wives* wardrobes. 'Near enough, I think', he said.

Before the date we settled on, he received the CBE in the 1950 New Year Honours. I sent him a congratulatory telegram and got the following reply.

'Dear Peter,
Bless you for your kind telegram. It is a high honour and one that has given great pleasure to Rosalind and myself. My one hope is that we may continue to be worthy of it in our simple fashion.
With every good wish and many thanks,
Donald Wolfit.
P.S. I have most of the clothes laid out for Sunday at 11.30 a.m. They will want airing when you get them—be sure to do that'.

It was a letter with some nice expressions in it of the kind that he used in normal speech. I particularly liked the homely postscript.

Boils are strange things and their comings and goings are often difficult to explain. Whether or not it was due to the accumulated tensions and frenzied overwork in putting on all these plays as well as coping with my job as a dental surgeon, I do not know, but during this season I had a quite dreadful run of them. When the day arrived to go up to meet Donald at his store, I had a large, throbbing, crimson boil right on the tip of my nose! Not only is it one of the most exquisitely painful places to have one—the merest touch causes the eyes to stream—but it makes people laugh because it looks like a clown's make-up! I always found Donald a very easy person to get on with; he was warm and surprisingly gentle. However, one could never be unaware of the great size and rich quality of his personality and so I always liked to be on the top of my form when we met. This ridiculously placed boil could not have been a bigger morale-destroyer!

I went up to London on the appointed day with William E. M. Smith ('Bill', of course): a very versatile actor who had played Chekhov's Trigorin excellently and who was also a great help in the off-stage activities of the company. The Wolfit stores of scenery and costumes were housed in a building called the Athenaeum which had once been some sort of arts centre but had now become rather dank and dreary. Donald worked with great energy, sorting through the various garments, making suggestions about what each character could wear but always with a sense of drama. That voice of dark gold made the display of each long gown or piece of string mail sound as if it were part of a performance. This was natural to him; it was not in any way an act. This kind man could not have been further removed from the egotistical, over-powering, even tyrannical, actor-manager of legend whom many of his profession found difficult. I have forgotten what he charged us for hire but it was nominal compared with what we normally paid.

I realised that *King John* would be a box office risk and so my routine letter to the schools contained a prod instead of the usual slightly obsequious appeal for their support. I was rash enough to say that those of them that had an enlightened outlook sent parties to see us even if the play was not an examination favourite. I hammered it well and truly home that if theirs was one of the backward seats of learning, they had better look to their laurels and support *King John*. Not very tactful, perhaps, but goading the public into thinking that it is missing something is a fairly stock form of advertising. It was quite a shock when the local teachers' union secretary, or some similar spokesman, telephoned and told me that his members had demanded that I should make a public apology. He was a charming man who gently suggested that I ought to apply the soft pedal in future and made it clear that he felt that there had been some unnecessary over-reaction. It made me more cautious but even so there would be various times in the future when I would clash again with teachers.

Only 18 months before, I had seen Michael Benthall's brilliant production of *King John* at Stratford with Robert Helpmann as the King and Anthony Quayle as the Bastard. I have always been convinced that one must see the shape of a play as a whole and this production succeeded in doing that largely because of its cleverly thought-out set. In the first of the three parts into which the play was divided, it consisted of seemingly indestructible stone steps and walls with a scarlet drape slung overhead. In the second part, the drape had a tear in it and the stonework was cracking badly; whilst in the third, the drape was in tatters and the masonry had crumbled into ruins. My set would have been a perfect model for my lectures on the virtues of Gordon Craig and Appia. It consisted of two great Stonehenge-like monoliths; one had the English lion against a red ground on it and the other with the fleur-de-lys on blue. These were moved about into various positions and different relationships with platforms that were made to look like granite. It was completely three-dimensional and I was able to light it with a wide range of dramatic effects. I think that it was my most successful, artistic and ingenious staging up to that point but neither the press, whose notices sounded as if they had been written by the office boy again, Gordon Jeffery with his keen observation, not the Assistant Regional Director of the Arts Council of Great Britain, who came to look us over, so much as mentioned it! The only person who did was a grubby little man who pushed his way into the men's dressing room one night just before a performance to show me his designs of sets that he had done for other companies. They were the worst sort of amateur scenery with dangling rows of sheeting overhead that looked like washing out to dry, crudely painted to represent foliage. 'I could see from what you have got up on the stage that you badly need a designer', he said! C'est la vie!—or would 'C'est la guerre!' be nearer the mark?

I pointed out in my programme note that 'realistic castles and battlefields' were 'not only impracticable here but also inartistic and old-fashioned'. I then went on to explain my use of formalised groupings and unrealistic setting and lighting. Gordon Jeffery in *Mercury* said, 'It is this careful preparation, this acceptance of limitations—and, for that matter, the turning to good account of limitations—which lifts their work above the level of many amateur, and not a few professional productions. Certainly it showed to the full in *King John*'. He went on to praise the generally high level of acting and particularly picked out Ron and myself who played the King and the Bastard respectively. William Lyon Brown, the man from the Arts Council of Great Britain, spoke to me after the performance that he saw and then in writing later with great enthusiasm. There was no money forthcoming and I do not know really why he came. I suppose it was to help them to create an overall picture of theatre, both amateur and professional, in the provinces. Anyway, it was nice to feel that we had merited a visit. One of the great pleasures for me with my strong love of the history of the theatre, was to be able to use the lion's skin and the swords that Donald lent us. The former, in fact a leopard but heraldically justified perhaps, had belonged to Sir John Martin Harvey, the famous old actor manager whom I had first seen as Sydney Carton on Eastbourne Pier when I was a child, and the latter to Sir Johnstone Forbes-Robertson, a great Lyceum Hamlet in 1897.

The costumes worked very well and it had been a considerable help to be able to select them. With our usual hiring, although I let Nathan's know as clearly as possible what I wanted, we did not see what we should actually be wearing until the baskets from London were opened a few hours before the dress rehearsal. The wigs for the play were hired as usual. They were always a very tricky matter as actors, and particularly actresses, are even more sensitive about how their heads will look than their bodies. Two things had to be guarded against. The first was the impact of the initial trying-on. This was usually done under inadequate, and therefore unflattering, dressing room lighting, with the face un-made-up and with shabby old clothes worn because of the inevitable dirty conditions backstage. Invariably the reaction was 'Oh! this is awful! I can't and won't wear it!' This was about as sound a way of judging the final effect of a wig in context with the proper lighting, setting, costume and make-up as pronouncing judgement on a dress when it is submerged in a bowl of soap suds! The other snare to be watched for was the thoughtless, heartless—and perhaps sometimes even deliberately spiteful—on-looker who would burst out laughing and say, 'Oh! you do look a scream in that wig! Isn't it terrible?'

However much a director may listen to the opinions of his cast, the final decisions must be his. Gordon Jeffery had spoken of my '*single* directing force' being the strength of the Southsea Actors and he was, of course, right. I do not say this in any sense of arrogance: it is the importance of the result being the judgement of a sole mind that I am stressing. I doubt if western ballet, the Royal Shakespeare Company and Glyndebourne would exist today if Diaghilev, Charles Flower and John Christie had been the names of committees. I am not seeking to elevate my own name to those Olympian heights: I simply quote them as examples on the highest plane. For this reason, one of the laws that I had to establish in my company was that one must wear what is provided, without argument, unless the Wardrobe Mistress and I, after consultation, said otherwise. The moment one person had been allowed to discard a wig or a costume for no better reason than that they themselves did not like it, the whole fabric—and therefore the strength—of the company would begin to disintegrate. Everyone else who did not like anything would come tumbling into this first person's slipstream and all too rapidly the dislikes would get more and more trivial until everyone was wearing just what pleased them. What a nice and happy situation that would be! In theory, of course, it undoubtedly would be but what a mess the production would look without the director's co-ordinating eye to give it all unity. It would be like six people all painting the same picture without any relationship between them.

This law was strained almost to breaking point by the wig that arrived for Constance. Margaret Dewey, who played the part, was a rather imposing woman and the wig—I suppose it must have been what I asked for, else why should it have been sent?—was straw blonde, parted in the middle and with plaits hanging down on either side. It was all very unfortunate! There was no alternative to her wearing it as it was too late to get another from London in time. Her own hair was a short modern style and the dialogue demanded long 'tresses' that could be bound up or unbound as Constance raves about them. An experienced actress in the company, who should have known better, said, 'My dear, you looked just like Marguerite in a German opera company!' Fortunately, over the years, all the other dislikes were much more minor and, in any case, the senior members soon became knowledgable enough to realise that ingenuity and a bit of thought could usually work the necessary wonders for it to be, according to that weary old cliché, 'alright on the night'.

Donald Wolfit's run at the Fortune Theatre in *Treasure Island* having ended, he went out with it on tour and February brought him, with Rosalind in the only woman's part, to the King's Theatre, Southsea. Would they come to Crossways one evening to meet the Southsea Actors over cocktails before going on to the theatre? Yes, they would be delighted to do so, they said. When he wrote to confirm the times of the party, Donald commented on the visit and letter that we had had from the Arts Council of Great Britain official. He had no time for such people as he had fared very badly whenever he had tried to get subsidies or other help for his own work. He said, 'I have never heard of Brown—just another of the salaried snoopers we pay for! Of course you are doing *splendid* work and your public knows it without an Arts Council representative to tell them so—or you!!' Words in italics in my quotes from his letters are the ones that he had underlined. He was a great underliner and it was perhaps his way of acting on paper, making sure that one got the stresses that he would have used in speech.

The cocktail party went off successfully as most of the company came and the star guests mingled delightfully. Later in the week, my parents and I went to the King's to see *Treasure Island* and then, as pre-arranged, went backstage afterwards to collect the Wolfits and take them home to Crossways for a private session with just the five of us. We all talked far into the night. Donald and Rosalind were such enchanting, easy company and he, even more than she, was full of marvellous theatrical stories. What a treasury one would have, could the conversation have been recorded or even, after all these years, have been remembered in detail. Alas, Time leaves only the flavour. 'Time hath, my lord, a wallet at his back, wherein he puts alms for oblivion' says Ulysses in a speech that I remember Donald speaking superbly in one of those lunchtime shows at the bombed Strand Theatre during the blitz. My mother told me afterwards that, at one point when I had gone out of the room, Donald Wolfit said to her, 'That boy's a genius!' I know that this was a theatrical exaggeration but it was wonderfully kind of him to say it. My parents were very thrilled, of course, and I cannot resist repeating the remark even though I must decline to believe in its truth. Some time later he wrote, 'I meant to write and thank you for that happy evening—I think (we both do) that your parents are quite delightful. You lucky man'.

The pattern of post-war life now having established itself, I began to find, as most of us did, that I was forming an almost completely new circle of friends. Those who had been close in the school and student days were now widely scattered and I had not seen many of them for ten years or more. The war had been a great separator. Foremost amongst my new ones was Prue Higham, my dental nurse. Her devotion to the company was boundless and, in spite of her background, she had an earthy quality which enabled her to revel in the rough and tumble of the theatre. She found it to be more fun than the parties where her parents probably hoped she would find an elegible young man amongst the junior Naval officers who had been invited.

Two characters in *Measure for Measure* seem particularly to worry the critics although, as is usually the way with such matters, rather less audiences. One of them is the Duke. Because he sets himself up as an all-seeing unseen power for good, it is often thought that he should carry out his plans with God-like

Measure for Measure   St. Peter's Hall, 1950

Isabella (Nora Turner) pleads unsuccessfully with Angelo (KEG)

perfection. That he bungles them and then shows what looks to us like cruelty when he lets Isabella think that her brother is dead, when he knows that he is not, appear to be inexplicable faults in the writing of the play and the creation of the character. Michael Pennington, in an otherwise patchy production at Stratford in 1978, captured the man perfectly to my mind. He gave us a Duke who was youngish, the sort of studious idealist who often appears to be slightly eccentric, and who turned out to be as puzzled as anyone when his bright ideas did not always work as planned. I believe that this is the fallible human being that Shakespeare created and not the faultless *deus ex machina* that the critics think he ought to have been.

The trouble with Isabella is that she is too often judged by the standards of today. In the 20th century there cannot be many people who will condone her saying that she would rather have her brother killed than herself go to bed with Angelo, if those are the only possible alternatives. In the first year of James I's reign attitudes were different: the traditions of virginal honour were still very strong. Many a girl of Shakespeare's time would have killed herself rather than submit to an Angelo. Our problem is that it is not her own life that Isabella is prepared to sacrifice but her brother's! However, if she is seen as a girl of 1604 rather than as one of nearly four centuries later, understanding is easier. We all know how hysterics and fanatics can become dominated by their particular fetishes; clearly Isabella is such a person. She is not just any girl; she is on the brink of becoming a nun. She is swept up in a passion—and I think a particularly *young* girl's passion—for religion and absolute purity. Seen in this light, I think that the character holds far fewer problems. I am sure that one must always go back to the conditions and attitudes of Shakespeare's own time before one can begin to understand his intentions and so the plays themselves. However relevant to our day we may wish to make them—and often this can be done only by distorting them—we must start by trying to read them with an Elizabethan's mind and outlook.

Stratford was now in the midst of its most lavish scenic era of all time. There were few productions that were not luxuriously beautiful to look at but most of them had strong enough casts to be able to stand up to all this rich decoration. Godfrey Tearle, the greatest Othello I have seen, and John Gielgud, the perfect Benedick, to quote two examples, did not need to be worried that they might be swamped by their settings. Michael Benthall's Victorian *Hamlet,* set in sumptuous Gothic surroundings straight out of Winterhalter, was one of the most successful productions of these years. I had seen it only 12 months before I started to plan my *Measure for Measure* and it gave me the idea to use the same period. 'Set in the Vienna of 100 Years Ago', the advertisements could read, and we might use Richard Strauss's *Der Rosenkavalier* for the incidental music. The Duke's desire to 'clean up' Vienna could be seen as a Victorian influence!

At that time, the play's natural darkness was enough to suggest the corruption of the city's brothel life. Nowadays, no production is complete without as sordid a parade of filthy, diseased scum as each new director can devise to out-do his predecessor. The one character who can fit that description is the drunken dreg of humanity, Barnadine. The part is short and effective and be it to my shame that I cut it completely. This was presumably because of difficulty with casting: I seem to remember that I had not got quite enough actors available to go round. I even cut, 'I hear his straw rustle'—a wonderful line in its context.

My basic setting was a room entirely of dark brown panelling. It became a city square when sections of it were removed to reveal a brown, blue and white street scene sketched on the backcloth. The prison and Mariana's grange had the cyclorama, dully lit, instead of the view of old Vienna. I made Angelo cold and Byronic and wore a black wig with stiff locks curling on to my forehead. I saw him as a man proud of his severity and who was, when he gave in to his lust, voracious but clumsy. I am sure that it is a mistake for Angelo to seem to know the techniques of experienced lovers. 'Ever till now', he says, 'when men were fond, I smiled, and wondered how'. Here is a man who is responding to something which is quite new to him; he will have little knowledge of how to cope with it. When finally he is made to marry Mariana, I can never believe that they will live happily ever after. I therefore ended my production with Angelo striding off without her as she pathetically called after him. The Lucio was played as being charmingly lascivious without the visible signs of venereal disease which seem to be obligatory nowadays. We were still using our imaginations in 1950!

'I see you are doing *Measure for Measure'*, wrote Donald Wolfit. 'I want to come and see it as we are free, so please reserve the best seats for my wife and myself and we will pay for them in the usual manner at the box office on arrival. We shall come on the 30th (Thursday) but we shall see you before then but that date fits our plans'. Pay for the tickets at the box office, forsooth! This must be a State Occasion and we must advertise that the famous Donald Wolfit and Rosalind Iden will be in the audience!

The hall was decorated with flowers and cushions were provided for their seats. In spite of the excellent, though small, stage, the auditorium was as bleak as any other church hall and the seats were murderously hard. We were very nervous; especially when the news came round to us backstage, 'They're here!' They had been met at the entrance by a small committee. Melita Moon and Ronald Mills beamed whilst John Hyde, our youngest actor, presented Rosalind with a bouquet of irises, tulips and carnations. Photographers were there and their flashes added to the general excitement. All eyes were upon our two stars as they were escorted down the centre gangway to sit in the third row with my parents and Gwen.

Whilst we were taking our curtain calls at the end, Donald was brought round, as pre-arranged, to join me after I had made a speech to introduce him. He strode on to the stage, amidst great applause, with hand outstretched to shake mine, quoting Vincent Crummles at the Portsmouth theatre in *Nicholas Nickleby,* 'Bravo! My noble, my lion-hearted boy!' He then made a speech which the local press reported very fully. Amongst other things, he said:

> 'This venture must be supported to the full. It is a tremendous undertaking. I know, as one of the patrons, of the support it receives, and I know that this support has been growing. I know, too, that this hall is still large enough to accommodate all the people who want to come here. I think that you have here in Mr Gateley and his players a real enthusiasm and a nucleus of classical drama, to which I contend children in this city should be brought. It would be perfectly simple for the Education Authority to book out this hall for six or eight performances and so provide something for the coffers of the Southsea Actors. This would mean that they would not have to press on so quickly with fresh productions. We are proud

to be associated with this tremendous venture. Here in this hall I think you have a quite remarkable achievement and something of which Portsmouth and Southsea should be very, very proud'.

As soon as the curtain was finally down, Donald and the cast were joined on the stage by Rosalind and those other members of the Actors who had been in the audience. The Wolfits held court and were again great company. They told stories, gave advice to the performers whom they had been watching and were enormously enjoyed. As we all mingled behind the curtain, which was left down, it could have been the stage in a professional theatre. The clutter of scenery, looking garish at close quarters, contrasted with the dark, untidy areas in the wings filled with spotlights, ropes and the props that had been used in the play. In the midst of all this jostled the visitors from the audience and the cast still in their Victorian costumes and make-up but, above all, there was the electric presence of our two stars.

Donald's speech had reminded me of the one that he had made at the end of his week's visit to the King's in 1937 during his first tour as an actor manager. He had played to thin houses and had told us with great force what he thought of those who had not come. 'I must record the fact that support here has been very poor indeed', he said. 'That a city which has the proud reputation of carrying the name and tradition of all that is best in the British character to the ends of the earth should be so lacking in the appreciation of a dramatist who has done just as much for the service of his country in the world of letters, and which is the proud heritage of all English-speaking peoples, is to me a very sad thing'. Our audiences were strengthening in numbers but very slowly and I often felt as he had done all those years before.

The letter that he wrote to me soon afterwards was a largely confidential one and so I had to provide a very much shortened and edited version for the cast who were keen to know what had been said. He pressed, as he had done in his speech, for official civic support and then went on to say that he allowed for nerves but 'what comes through is always positive'.

'Your Angelo is an excellent study', he said. 'I don't believe in him any more than any other Angelo I have seen—he runs away from the story so badly does our Shakespeare in this play. Attempted suicide would have done the trick'. He commented on various individuals with remarks like, 'If he *wouldn't* look on the floor' (the Duke); 'A *professional* touch here—*hold on to him like death*' (an elderly speech trainer named John Gardener who played Escalus); 'A good Danny Kaye shot, useful' (John Pearce, my natural clown, as Pompey); and 'Your women are far below your men in standard . . . Mistress Overdone' (Prue) 'was the best and I should say can do better'. Lighting was 'first class, never too much'; the setting was 'Very ingenious and simple, the room was most convincing' and under the heading of 'Costumes' he put, 'Expensive I am sure. You dress very well all through. (I *can* do *Hamlet* for you if you want it)'. I had told him that I had that play up my sleeve for the next season. Unfortunately, he did not like Isabella at all. She was played by the very polished Nora Turner who was a calm, gentle person of about my own age group. 'Isa *must* be young, my friend', he said. '*Miscast;* she spoke sensitively but never felt a thing'. Nora was terribly upset as she regarded this as one of her best performances and spoke of giving up acting altogether but, I am glad to say, I managed to talk her out of it. Donald's letter finished with one of his endearingly, homely remarks:

Donald Wolfit and his wife, Rosalind Iden, arriving at St. Peter's Hall on 30 March, 1950, to see *Measure for Measure.* Ronald Mills and Melita Moon greet them and the youngest member, John Hyde, presents flowers

'Congratulations—and your parents are a joy, my lad'.

Nora directed the fifth and last play of the season, Congreve's *Love for Love.* I did the sets—clear-cut water colours of 18th century rooms; cherry and white for Valentine, two shades of blue for Foresight—and we enjoyed wearing the rich, elegant costumes and the elaborate curled wigs that looked like overgrown spaniels. I did Tattle, a companion piece to my Petulant in *The Way of the World* at the Maddermarket, but I was not too well. The strain of putting on 14 plays in under 3 years was beginning to take its toll. My boils reached their climax with a revolting many-headed carbuncle on the back of my neck. This was to be the last play in our surgery rehearsal room as my partners and I wanted it to go back to its original use, but, as I was ill, I had to miss the final rehearsal there.

Before the curtain went up on the first night, the scene in the men's dressing room presented a picture that could hardly have been less like the one of grace and good manners that would be seen later on the stage. Knowing how short of time I was, a dear old friend of mine, Dr Aston Key, had come to the hall with his little black bag to minister to the directorial invalid. I could have been seen bending over with my bare behind fully exposed as he subjected me to the indignity of a having an injection of penicillin into it!

CHAPTER 11
Unlucky 21st — Part I

The Southsea Actors had never been part of the city's social scene in the coffee and cocktail party sense, although we had a certain following amongst the less fashionable intelligencia. Nugent Monck maintained that it was so long before any of the top people of Norwich took any notice of him that when, at last, he was invited to some function, he replied, 'Sorry, but I am afraid your invitation is 20 years too late!'

Feeling that it was high time we did something about getting ourselves at least into the margin of the local social register, I thought that it might be a good idea to make the opening performance of our fourth season a Civic Night if the Lord Mayor would agree. It would be useful publicity and bring people to see us who might not otherwise come. There was just the chance that some of them, having enjoyed, perhaps to their surprise, what we had to offer, would return for more. The Lord Mayor of Portsmouth, Alderman Sir Denis Daley, and Lady Daley, both popular figures as they had done heroic work during the appalling bombing raids on the city during the war, accepted our invitation, as did Admiral Sir Arthur Power, GCB, GBE, CVO, the Commander-in-Chief, and Lady Power. Two knights and two Ladies are enough to give a good deal of lustre to an amateur play in a provincial hall! When it was known that they were all coming, almost everybody else of any note who was invited also accepted. This brought the other inevitable hangers-on as well and so the exercise was clearly working.

As when the Wolfits came, there was much presenting of bouquets and photographers' flashes going off as distinguished guests arrived. The evening ended with a reception for the notabilities behind the curtain after the rest of the audience had left the hall and passed the waiting Rolls Royces and their chauffeurs on their way to catch their humble buses.

The play was that precious stone set in a magical sea, *The Tempest:* always one of my favourites. In the years to come I would delve deeper into it but at this time I followed the then current practice of making it a scenic extravaganza. I did a full-stage set in the grand old manner; a fantastic island shore overgrown with imaginary plants in brilliant colours and complete with a backcloth showing the sea and strange rock formations. There was also a front scene of a cliff top with an alarming perspective down to the beach below. The storm was done against the ubiquitous black tabs and a swinging lantern. Then, as since, there has only ever been one work for me to use for incidental music: Ravel's *Daphnis and Chloe.* I was Prospero; Brenda Cosgrave a rather too sophisticated Miranda; Bill Smith a padded, red nosed Stephano and Ron Mills a shaggy Caliban. A sensitive girl named Raie Hardy, who moved particularly well, played Ariel.

However smoothly the final runs-through of the whole play have gone, certain details always deteriorate at the dress rehearsal. One desperately hopes that they will have done so for that one night only! The unfamiliarity of performing in costume, perhaps with swords sticking out behind and getting in the way when the actor tries to sit down—especially if he is wearing a long cloak that he is not yet used to—together with the dazzle of the stage lights, will bewilder even the fairly experienced. These snags can be irritating out of all proportion to a director who is on the edge of his nerves and taut with frustrations at seeing his well-laid plans fraying at the edges. A typical example of this sort of thing occurred near the end of this particular play's dress rehearsal. Caliban, Stephano and Trinculo knew perfectly well where to exit when told by Prospero to go into his cave. The sets were so entirely realistic that the actors, even if they had momentarily forgotten their moves, could see the painted rocky opening clearly enough. On this occasion they walked straight into the equally visible sea!

By now I had come to the conclusion that five plays each season were too many and so I decided that we should revert to the original idea of doing four. I was already discovering that, especially now the initial excitement of three years before had somewhat dimmed, they were getting more difficult to cast. Apart from a very few faithfuls, the majority of the company was not prepared to be available for every play.

John Hewison had left our dental laboratory and the area, so we had stage staff changes. Bill Vaughan Sherrin, whose wife, June, was particularly suited to post-Shakespearean artificial comedy and had made a delightful Mrs Frail in the Congreve play, was a scientist at the Admiralty Establishment. He had become our new Stage Manager and was one of those rare backstage helpers in the amateur theatre—someone who did not want to use it as a stepping stone towards being given an acting part! Not so Jack Eastwood Lewis, a local government architect, who became our Electrician and Carpenter. Good amateur stage staff are difficult to acquire and so one's heart sinks when one discovers that a first-class electrician, mover of scenery and hauler on ropes in dark corners is yearning to leap into the bright lights. However, he was a person of great energy and enthusiasm and, as his talents as an actor were very modest, his conflicting interests never seriously clashed.

Our new rehearsal room to which we moved was over Ron and Win Mills's flat. They had a very pleasant one with high, spacious rooms, near the sea front at Southsea. It was part of a crumbling mansion that had not only seen better days but looked as if its last of all could not be too far hence! The floor over it had obviously been used for the servants' bedrooms in the more gracious yesteryears and, being in the eaves, its rooms were low-ceilinged and had walls that bent sharply inwards. They were also let as a flat and we managed, through

Ron, to acquire two of them. The smaller became our sitting-out area which I quickly christened 'The Gossip Room', a term that became a permanent tradition. Before very long, we were able to add a few more of the rooms and then, finally, the whole flat. It was a relief to have, at last, some more space in which to store our ever-increasing stock of properties and various pieces of equipment. Some of these things were also finding resting places in the similar attics over my surgery. The floor space of the rehearsal room was smaller than even the acting area on the St Peter's Hall stage but we managed to increase its size slightly by knocking down a wall and incorporating a passage that ran along its full length. The ceilings were so low that if we rehearsed on a high rostrum, we could do so only by bending double. One had to remember to stand upright when one actually performed those parts of the play on the stage itself!

In those days, men still wore shirts with separate collars. During the week of *The Tempest* I noticed that I seemed to be getting an exceptional amount of make-up on mine each night. The weather was cold and the washing arrangements in the hall were very primitive and so, I supposed, I had been rather inefficient over washing my neck after the performances. I therefore decided on one occasion to go home without my collar but, after getting hot during the play, I found that when I got out into the night air my neck felt exceptionally cold. I was, therefore, not surprised when the next day I had a stiff neck and rather swollen glands. Although I took care, the condition got worse but I assumed it was all due simply to the exposure of my uncollared neck but I was wrong. I felt really ill, went to bed and called the doctor. I had mumps! A very nasty thing to have as an adult and something which could easily have caused an epidemic affecting the entire population of Prospero's island!

Fortunately, the moves and all the other details of our next offering had been worked out during the summer and recorded in my 'Production Copy', a thick exercise book interleaved with the text of the play. This meant that I was able to hand over the first rehearsals to Nora as I was still in quarantine. I was soon about again, however, and able to start on the next lot of scenery in the drive at Crossways as usual. After the first autumn's tribulations with repainting the backcloths, I had come to the conclusion that it would be best to have only two done each season and that they must both be painted in the summer. *The Tempest* had used up both of them already but this second play, which needed another tropical island setting, this time in the distant future, would have the cyclorama whilst the remaining couple of plays would each have box sets made of flats.

I have always greatly enjoyed Bernard Shaw's plays to read, see in the theatre or listen to on the radio but, apart from *Village Wooing* in Norwich, which worked so well for me, I had always been very bad in them on the stage. For this reason, when I chose for the second play of the season his neglected, but for me clever and very funny, *The Simpleton of the Unexpected Isles,* I decided to direct it and design the sets but not to act in it. I could enjoy playing at being a front-of-house manager for only the second time in 16 plays.

I was short of actors but, as is so often the way in amateur companies, I had quite a lot of actresses who felt that they were not getting enough parts. I therefore wrote to Shaw to ask him if I could have the sophisticated and sharp-tongued angel, who arrives on Judgement Day shaking machine-gun bullets out of his wings, played by a woman instead of a man. Shaw was well-known for refusing to allow alterations to be made to his plays. I had a reply from his famous secretary who had been with him for 30 years. It read as follows:

> 'Dear Mr Gateley,
>
> Mr Bernard Shaw can only suggest that you make the best you can of the material—or cast—that you have at hand. He never interferes with provincial revivals of his plays; but as St Joan has often been played by schoolboys there is no reason why the part of the Angel in *The Simpleton* should not be taken by a woman.
>
> Yours faithfully,
>
> Blanche Patch (secretary)'.

I hoped that I saw a double meaning in this. Was there a tonque-in-cheek suggestion that, although an angel should normally be a man, one could perhaps stretch credulity and for once have a woman angel? Anyway, I regarded this as my own personal Shavianism and have treasured the letter ever since. June Vaughan Sherrin, wearing a superb pair of wings that Jack Lewis had made, horn-rimmed spectacles, and with her own very blonde hair, made a great success in the part.

Having spent hundreds of pounds on hiring costumes with neither rag nor ribbon to show for them in our store rooms, we made our first step towards creating our own wardrobe. I designed two black and scarlet bikini-type costumes, with long flowing panels, for the priest and priestess, and our Wardrobe Mistress, Eileen Hall, produced costumes for the Angel and for the four perfect children who had been created by six parents in these fantastic islands.

After we had been rehearsing for only a very short time, I had to send a programme alteration to the printers. It was for the insertion of a heavily black-edged box containing the following:

> 'In common with all lovers of the Theatre and Literature, the Southsea Actors sadly mourn the death of Mr George Bernard Shaw which took place on 2 November, 1950, and dedicate this production, which was in rehearsal at the time of his death, to his memory'.

Perhaps because of this unintended topicality, this production drew larger audiences than any other non-Shakespearean play that we had done. Even so, the figure of 666 was only half the number that had come to *The Tempest.*

Now that people knew that I was prepared to tackle *Hamlet,* they began to realise that I intended to go full steam ahead into anything that the Shakespearean canon had to offer. Lips were pursed and eyebrows raised because my confidence was not wholly shared. The idea of doing the *King Henry VI* trilogy was so outrageous that it was not even mentioned. I, too, secretly wondered if I should ever be able to stage any of that vast, and then virtually unknown, work in any form. Nugent Monck had done it at the Maddermarket, so perhaps . . . The chief warnings that I received were that it would be impossible to find amateurs who could play either Lear or Cleopatra. As for the former—well, I had ideas about that but intended to keep quiet for the time being. My Cleopatra would be Brenda Cosgrave; I had every confidence in her ability to play the part. She was attractive, colourful, vivacious and both her comedy and tragedy were theatrical in the best sense, but she and I had begun to have disagreements. Much of her best acting was, I think, intuitive rather than calculated and consequently she greatly admired the wild and often unpredictable acting style of her fellow Roman Catholic, Ronald Mills. Perhaps my colder Anglo-Saxon temperament was the wrong one for dealing with either of them but I began to be aware of a feeling that there was an almost intangible opposition party in the company. There seemed to be Ron's people and mine, although I am sure that he would have been the last person to foster such a state of affairs and probably was totally unaware of it.

I had expected that when I asked other people to direct plays for me, I should be interested in the differences between their interpretations and what mine would have been. It was, however, quite the contrary; I became more and more irritated and found it ever harder not to interfere or show my disapproval. I had asked Ron to do *Hamlet* and, true to form, I found myself disliking much of the production and most of his setting. The latter was a realistic stone hall with every block and mortar joint clearly defined like the stock sets that Benson toured at the turn of the century. Added to this there was a rostrum near the front of the stage which made everyone standing behind it look as if they were in a ditch. He made his own Claudius drunk in the prayer scene—when surely this is his most sober moment—and, as the local press put it, 'had a slight tendency to overdo the bye-play', but Brenda was excellent as the Queen.

Donald Wolfit could not costume the play for us after all as he had to move his company's stores at that time. 'I wish you had come to Malvern; we had a fine season there', he said. 'What! Two visits to Stratford and not one to your patron? Shame on you'. He thought that he and Rosalind would be able to come and see this production and went as far as to ask me to book two seats for the Saturday night. Unfortunately, they could not manage it when the time came. However, he did lend me his own Hamlet cloak: black, of course, but lined with purple silk. When the production was over, he sent me one of the most splendid of all his letters. Here it is, starting with a line written above the address.

> 'All Hamlets lose their voice before rehearsals or have fever during them.
>
> Garrick Club, WC2
> 28.2.51.
>
> My dear Gateley,
>
> I played in eight *Hamlet* productions and Hamlet as a part over 700 times. There was never a production that satisfied me, nor a supporting cast. Ophelia and the Queen were always good. The King never was and when I played Claudius my Hamlet loathed me as I loathed him. These things are eternal and so is the exhaustion after the play. If you don't give yourself a rest you will kill yourself, and tell your Mother and Father that I say so!
>
> All these frictions mentioned above are part of the mystery of *Hamlet* the play. No one ever remembers the supporting cast or wants to do so.
>
> The part is all-embracing—you reach the core of the audience or you don't—in any case you are worn out trying to find them. From Cairo to Vancouver I know these things for truth and revere the mystery.
>
> I am glad you gave such happiness—that cloak can almost speak "How all occasions" on its own. It is back safely.
>
> In haste, alas—yours with all good wishes,
> Donald Wolfit.'

We ended the season in April with Ben Jonson's *The Alchemist* in which Prue gave a brilliant performance by any standards in what was to remain her second favourite part, Doll Common. Bill Smith was also just about at his best as the shabby old charlatan of the title and I enjoyed being the dashing rogue, Face. My set was a half-timbered room filled with hired antique furniture and we all had a great time. It would be nice to be able to report that the audience did so too, but that is more questionable. 'Surprising that so few of the audience managed to raise more than a chuckle', complained the Portsmouth Evening News. 'The cast did very well indeed', it went on, 'although they must have felt a little lonely'.

In the theatre, there are so many superstitions connected with *Macbeth* that it is often known as 'The Scottish Play' in order to avoid actually having to say the spell-charged word. It must not be quoted backstage and productions of it have frequently been dogged with real disasters. Lilian Baylis, founder of the Old Vic, one of the world's most celebrated Shakespearean theatres, died on the eve of its opening there in 1937 and when Stratford started its seasons with it in 1938 and 1949, there were bad accidents on both first nights. Wolfit said that it was always a lucky play for him. 'I could make your hair stand on end about the first nights I have been in', he said to me; but went on, 'I produced it on Friday 13th my first year in management and still survive'. I chose it for the opening play and something bad happened to each of the four productions of that season.

At this point in the writing of this book, my typewriter, which had served me throughout my entire quarter century of my Shakespeare company and which, in fact, I bought when I was starting at the Maddermarket, broke down beyond repair. Could it be that mysterious play at work again? Am I really as superstitious as all that? No, of course not—and yet! How strange that of all the 37 plays of Shakespeare about which I might have been writing, it just happened to be this one. One could lengthen the odds considerably by adding all the other theatre works that I have mentioned and the many incidents that are not actually to do with plays.

However, to continue with my first production of this suspect drama. I cast Ron Mills as Macbeth but, as his eyesight was extremely bad, I gave him a very unhappy time! My set consisted of black and scarlet monoliths rising out of a complicated collection of steps and rostra all painted in the deepest black. Even in bright lighting they would have been difficult to manoeuvre but in the stygian gloom that I imposed upon them, they were absolutely impossible to see. Even I, with reasonably good sight and having designed the wretched things, moved from one level to another in terror. Ron did not seem to be able to get the feel of the part at all and fell back on a rather 'hammy' bluster. Added to this was the almost total blindness that my black set forced upon him so that every time he moved he must have been terrified that he would break a leg or even his neck. I played Banquo and Brenda the Lady. This was the sort of blazing drama that suited her perfectly and again I saw her as my future Cleopatra. However, we were still not getting along very well: there was a lot of surface banter but it always had an uncomfortable, not very funny, edge to it.

The boys from Ron's school supported the play in large, and rather rowdy, numbers. I got steadily more and more bad tempered as the week wore on. During the curtain call on one of the nights, there was wild cheering from these lads and loud shouts of 'Good old Ron'! Things had gone too far. The people I suspected of being my unseen opposition loved it but this was not the

The Alchemist St. Peter's Hall, 1951

The three rogues: Subtle, the alchemist (William EM Smith), Doll Common (Prue Higham) and Face (KEG) in Ben Jonson's comedy

atmosphere at which I was aiming. When the curtain came down, I signalled to the Stage Manager that it was not to go up again. He did not understand me and so I broke ranks to go and tell him. At that point, the curtains parted in the centre to reveal us to the audience once more and I was caught in the act of marching off the stage looking very angry. This was seen to be my making a public display of my jealousy of Ron's success and produced a nasty atmosphere that lasted for the rest of the week. It also made the division in the company, which I had hoped was entirely imaginary, visible.

As soon as the run was over, Brenda and I had a very fierce row. She claimed that in our sparring I had said something that had been very hurtful and that my stalking off the stage had brought to a head, as far as she was concerned, all the things that she most disliked about me and the way I ran the company. She resigned, of course, and so sadly we lost one of our best actresses and my hopes for a Cleopatra seemed to disappear into thin air. However, as one sun set, another was shortly to appear over another horizon!

The production had looked quite striking. I had used one of the backcloths as a special act drop in place of the hall's usual rose-coloured velvet curtain. From a crown on it shot three jagged shafts of lightning. Each descended to the elongated first finger of a witch's hand rising out of swirling black clouds. The costumes that we had hired had been made that year for the production at Pitlochry in Scotland and they were quite magnificent. It was only when the bill arrived that I realised that they would cost us something like double what we normally paid. The play had done well at the box office but, for the first time, I was getting worried about the finances.

My over-riding passion was then, still is, and I have no doubt for ever will be, Shakespeare. Our productions of plays by other authors still always drew considerably smaller audiences and I had now done many of the things that I had wanted to do. I had put on *The Seagull* again; I had staged Congreve, Shaw, Molière and had also played Oswald in *Ghosts*. At the same time, coupled with the discouraging box office returns for these non-Shakespearean plays, was a growing feeling in my mind that my ambitions in those areas were dwindling. Less and less did I want to copy the Maddermarket with its varied programme, and ever more was the Shakespeare Memorial Theatre my ideal. There was also a rumour that our rivals, the Portsmouth Arts Theatre, were thinking of doing a Shakespeare play. I was desperate to hold the monopoly and would have gone to almost any lengths to prevent them. I even wrote to their Business Manager, Harry Sargeant, Wolfit's school friend and a man with whom I got on very well, and asked him if he could help to discourage them. In fact, they never did do a Shakespeare play after all, but, not having the gift of prophesy, I decided not to take any chances. As a broad hint I pushed our particular line by advertising this season as being *Four Elizabethan Plays.* The one non-Shakespearean was the second and it was Marlowe's *Doctor Faustus.* I wanted to do one of his plays and the title role was just about the last part outside Shakespeare that I had a particular desire to tackle. I had seen Robert Harris give a fine performance of it at Stratford in 1946 and I made the terrible mistake of trying to copy his voice and way of speaking. The result was disastrous as it is when directors try to get actors to give impersonations of themselves. The actor becomes a marionette making sounds and carrying out movements that have been imposed from outside. No performance can ever work unless it comes from within and is in terms of that person's own voice, personality and body.

We had an 'Education Night' to open the run. This was a version of our previous 'Civic Night' except that this time all the guests were heads of schools and colleges. I got some quite good stage effects, such as having the Seven Deadly Sins crawling all over each other like maggots in a fisherman's bait tin, but the production was not popular. The houses were terribly thin and the press notice, the worst that I have ever had, must have discouraged all but the most devoted from coming. The headline read across two columns, 'This Faustus had no soul to sell to Devil'! The article began, 'If Doctor Faustus had been as soul-less as K. Edmonds Gateley made him last night . . . I hardly think Lucifer or Mephistophilis would have bothered themselves about him'. At the time I felt rather sorry that at last the local paper had got a writer about plays who was knowledgeable enough to justify being called 'Our Theatre Critic'! After tearing me to shreds, he did say that he thought I managed to 'assume the right stature' just at the end. The one sop of comfort was the following, 'I have often praised his acting and producing. There can be few amateurs in the country that are his equal and, because I know this, I am sorry to have to say that the play has more power in cold print than it had on the stage at St. Peter's Hall'. I should have learned but I did not: I would make the same mistake again just over a year later.

With 39 characters, the costume bill was again enormous and the trickle of money at the box office sadly small. The 'National Debt', as the money that was owing to me was being called, now stood at about £500. Another financial failure might well mean that the Southsea Actors would have to close down. Donald Wolfit was scoring one of the great triumphs of his career at this time: he was playing the title role in Marlowe's *Tamburlaine* (a dazzling performance in Tyrone Guthrie's brilliant production) and Lord Ogleby in *The Clandestine Marriage* by Coleman and Garrick at the Old Vic.

I went to see him in both plays and poured out my troubles to him in his dressing room after one of the performances. He advised me to put on Victorian comedies and the mediaeval mystery play, *Everyman,* ('You'll get your churches and you'll get your schools') as a means of making money and so fill up our bank account again! I did not take his advice as I believe that if I had we should have been even more speedily ruined!

In my heart of hearts there was one aspect of this serious situation that was, because the time was ripe, absolutely delighting me. With a solemn brow I was able to announce that, with regret, I had decided that in future the company would present only the plays of Shakespeare. Everyone, including the local press, seemed very sorry. I shook my head sadly but secretly I was very relieved. I had reached a stage when I wanted my company to be solely Shakespearean. Perhaps I had always wanted this but had feared at the start that local audiences would not support four Shakespeare plays a year. It was assumed by many people that I had not told the truth about the reasons for my decision. This was correct, of course, but they were wrong about what they believed my true motive had been. They put it down to my anger at having been so man-handled by the press when I played Faustus. As with the walking-off-the-stage incident, I was accused of peevish temperamentalism and a public display of bad temper at being crossed. Once again, my opponents were incorrect although, naturally enough, the critic's strictures had stung quite considerably.

The next play was the 21st and so it had to be a success. I chose *As You Like It* and asked Ronald Mills to direct it. Having had those various troubles with the scenery for his previous three productions, I stipulated that I must design the set. This restriction, coupled perhaps with his sensing that I was offering him the job rather grudgingly, was presumably why he suggested that it would probably be better if, in future, I gave up the idea of inviting other people to direct and did them all myself. He said this at one of our committee meetings and gained the approval of the majority of, if not all, the members. These events took place twice a year because the law still insisted we had them. When, eventually, Entertainment Tax disappeared I kept the committee in being, although it was no longer legally necessary, and called it thereafter the Advisory Committee. The meetings consisted mainly of long speeches from me explaining what the future held for everyone. I was given a fair amount of advice and occasionally I took some of it. However, the members had no actual power though it was understood that if I died or became incapable of carrying on for some reason, they would be the body to take over the running of the company. Having the committee's approval of my directing and designing all the productions henceforth was absolutely marvellous. It was just what I wanted.

The nicknames that schoolchildren invent for their teachers are usually far from complimentary. On the other hand, has there ever been a more marvellous tribute than the universal name in the Portsmouth High School for the one whom I asked to play Rosalind? She was the new sun that was coming up in the Southsea Actors and her school nickname was 'Glamorous Nancy'! Nancy Glenister, to give her her correct name, was tall, dark, attractive and very polished. She dressed beautifully and could wear bold, clear colours. She was indeed glamorous and many of the High School girls idolised her. She had been one of the Women of Canterbury in *Murder in the Cathedral* but that was about all. Brenda's departure opened the gate for Nancy and over the next decade she would play most of the great women's parts for us. She was ideal for Rosalind and was one of a strong cast. I played Touchstone, with a turned-up nose and small raised eyebrows, whilst Prue scored considerable success as Audrey. I wanted both the backcloths but one had already been used for the *Macbeth* act drop. However, I risked winter painting in my drive and garage and fortunately struck some fine weather. Painted backcloths were on their way out and so I cut one of them up to make a 'cut-cloth'—a group of trees with the spaces between them actually removed so that actors could pass through and the rest of the set could be seen behind. I did an airy pavilion against clear sky for the Duke's court and a forest of flat blocks of different bright greens with stylised black trunks and branches.

It was a happy production and all was set for a sunshine success that would wipe away the troubles of the season's first two plays.

I was in my surgery working on a patient during the morning before the first night when Prue, now the practice's secretary, came in with a long face. 'I have some very bad news', she said, 'the King is dead!' The result was that all places of entertainment were closed for that day. The opening night of our 21st production was cancelled! I thought quickly and decided to put an advertisement in the paper immediately saying that we would have a matinee (our first ever) on the Saturday afternoon and that tickets booked would be available for that. Normally a royal death has a very depressing affect on theatre and cinema attendances but from our opening on what would normally have been our second night we did very well indeed. The matinee also played to a good house and so I decreed that henceforth we should have a Saturday matinee for every play. Donald Wolfit had costumed it for us from his own production which had been the work of Max Reinhardt's designer, Ernst Stern. This was a tremendous financial saving and we had the bonus of being able to put on display in the hall a collection of Stern's original designs, which Donald lent us. In spite of the King's death, we were back on our feet again—or, at any rate, facing in the right direction.

The next play was a feat of mountaineering over an untidy huddle of rostra, flanked by wings with Roman emblems and pillars on them. Not, I think, my most inspired set, especially as it was chiefly carried out in mauve! That in itself seems to suggest an air of artistic desperation! The play was *Coriolanus* with myself in the lead. The hired costumes had all the gold and crimson of Rome in its grandest days although, for this play, everything should have looked earlier and more primitive. Hirers cannot always be choosers! This time 'Our Theatre Critic' felt that I was back on form and said that I 'thrust home the intolerant aspect of Coriolanus's character with flashing mockery that cut deeper than his sword'. He continued, 'He also mastered the essential boyishness that explains his renunciation of victory . . . This scene was in my opinion not only the Southsea Actors' finest moment, but as memorable an experience as I can remember in any amateur production'. Praise indeed! We seemed, after a sticky start to the season, to be on the road back. However, this was still the one that we had had the temerity to start with the Scottish Play so something had to go wrong somewhere. At the dress rehearsal, John Gardener, the frail and rather elderly speech trainer whom Wolfit had liked as Escalus, was so ill with 'flu' that he was swaying about on the stage and appeared to be on the point of collapse. He had to be sent home and a young man from the crowd, who was usually better suited to playing the more proper juveniles, read the part of Menenius for the whole run of the play. This was a considerable blight on what might otherwise have been an overall success.

So many silly people had referred to stage blood as tomato ketchup that I decided, as an economy measure, to try it. Never again! It was intolerably sticky, it was the wrong colour under the lights and, perhaps worst of all, it made the stage smell like a transport cafe! Actually, the season very nearly did finish with a real disaster. When I was killed at the end of the play, I had devised a spectacular fall backwards from the top of the heap of rostra. We had rehearsed it carefully so that in fact I was caught by a group of Volscian soldiers. At the dress rehearsal, one of them lost his cloak at the vital moment and thoughtlessly turned away to pick it up. The result was that I fell on my back, upside down on a flight of steps. No serious harm had been done, I am glad to have survived to be able to say, beyond a severe shaking and some purple bruises but I could easily have done myself a permanent back injury or even broken my neck!

Thus ended one of our two unluckiest seasons. This one had included our 21st production and the other one would be our 21st season. Maybe it was the number 21 and *Macbeth* had nothing to do with it! However, another era was about to begin: henceforth I would be doing all the designing and directing myself and my beloved Shakespeare would be our sole author. William and I had effected what in big business would have been referred to as the Shakespeare Take-over.

CHAPTER 12
The Shakespeare take-over

Romance was in the air! Bill Smith, who had played Aufidius to my Coriolanus, got married just before the sixth season began and the leading lady of the first play in it was on the brink of following suit. The programme that I chose for this first wholly Shakespearean season reflected the prevailing mood. The opening play was to be *Romeo and Juliet* and the second, *A Midsummer Night's Dream*. *King Richard II* and *The Winter's Tale* were planned to follow in the early months of 1953.

A new spirit was stirring. Amongst other activities was the publication of a booklet called, *Five Seasons 1947-52,* which contained ten photographs of scenes from our productions and a two-page article about us by Nora Turner and Bill Smith. For the first time I put an advertisement in the paper announcing that auditions would be held for the coming season's plays. A particularly bright spot was the discovery that our reputation had reached the other side of the Atlantic! Dr Louis Marder, an American Shakespearean scholar, had written from New York and asked me to send him all the information I could about our activities.

Shakespeare's own company was what would nowadays be called repertory. So, too, in an amateur way, was ours. Each time he presented the Lord Chamberlain's Men, or as they were later known, the King's Men, with a new play, they must have cast it out of their stock, resident company. We did the same thing, of course. However, I soon learned that there are certain plays that one should not attempt unless one has absolutely the right people available for the key parts. The Falstaff plays are a case in point; *Romeo and Juliet* is another. It is not enough simply to use the two most personable youngsters available; the parts are too demanding. I had, at that time, as near to the perfect couple as I could wish for. My Juliet was Anne Martin, a tall, quite beautiful girl who had been professionally trained at the Webber-Douglas Drama School, and who had first appeared with us as Lady Macduff and then afterwards as Phebe in *As You Like It.* She was exceptionally talented and always conveyed great warmth. The Romeo was John Fulcher who had been the boy who had taken over the part of

Fabian in the company's initial production five years before. Since then he had developed from a slightly plummy youth into an extraordinarily good-looking young man with almost black hair and slightly Latin features. His voice had become deep and rich in tone and he had lost his earlier thickness of sound. He had already given some very good performances, notably as the two Claudios, the one in *Much Ado* and the other in *Measure for Measure.*

The critic in the Portsmouth paper, now using the initials, 'R. T.', but, none the less, the same person as before, seemed to bear out my own feelings about these two players. He wrote, 'From the glowing embers of a Shakespeare play at St Peter's Hall last night emerged a performance by an amateur actress which has set new boundaries to the local stages . . . a warm-hearted confidence that proved wholly successful and absorbing . . . Her performance, linked with John Fulcher's customary skill and pleasing appearance as Romeo, made this foundling of the tragedies the greatest pleasure to witness'. He then gave Shakespeare a rather luke-warm notice for his contribution to the proceedings and continued, 'But presented by the Southsea Actors, and produced by the seemingly indefatigable K. Edmonds Gateley, to whom Portsmouth owes so much, it is an experience not to be missed by any lover of the theatre'. If one is tempted to dismiss this lavish praise as being provincial nonsense, perhaps it will deserve more respect if one bears in mind that this same critic had been the scourge of *Doctor Faustus*!

Audiences poured in! I had decided not to act in this one so that I could enjoy playing at being a theatre manager again. I actually had to turn people away from every performance except the first and even that was almost full to capacity. On one particular night I felt a great sense of achievement when three women begged to be allowed to remain outside the doors of the auditorium so that, as they put it, 'We can simply listen to those marvellous words'. It confirmed what I had always hoped, and that was that we were not just a group of self-indulgent amateurs amusing ourselves but that we were seriously accepted as bringers of Shakespeare's plays to members of a public that really wanted them.

Anne and her fiancé, Eric Nicolle, originally from the Channel Islands and eventually to become a valuable member of the company himself, especially in his capacity as a calm and astute businessman, had planned to get married in June, three months before the production of *Romeo and Juliet.* However, so that she could play the part, the wedding was postponed until October. The press loved this and brought us some highly desirable publicity. She was interviewed at her home by the Daily Mirror and the London Evening News. The fact that it was Juliet of all parts gave the situation that sentimental and romantic touch which is meat and drink to the popular papers. 'The wedding waits—show goes on', was the headline in the Mirror. In the other paper, there was quite a large photograph, and in both the company was named and the dates of the performances given. I rubbed my hands together with delight!

Whilst we were in rehearsal, eleven of us went in a party to London for the day to see the same play at the Old Vic. During the morning, whilst we were all strap-hanging in an Underground train, we saw Anne's photograph upside down on the folded-back half of a newspaper that a seated man was reading. We were very excited and must have been an odd sight as we all turned our heads upside down to try to see it better. As soon as we got into the daylight again, we rushed to the nearest newsvendor and bought up eleven copies!

That day in London was to be of far more significance for me than I realised at the time. It marked the beginning of a friendship that I may guess will be life-long and which, through its strength, would sustain me in difficult times that lay ahead and contribute greatly to the happiness of the easier ones. John Fulcher, although 15 years my junior, was now an adult and he and his girl-friend, Sunya Grant, eventually to be his wife, were amongst the party on this day. Somehow, we three continually seemed to find that we were together and clearly enormously enjoyed each other's company. Soon after that day we started to meet regularly outside the framework of the Southsea Actors. They were both fond of going to the theatre and this was still the great era of cinema-going. John also became a motorcyclist and before long I had got them interested in Stratford. They paid their first visit in 1954 and from the next year onwards we frequently went there together. When they were married in 1955 I was John's Best Man and I became the godfather of their two daughters, Cordelia and Marina (good Shakespearean names) when they were born some years later.

Prior to *Romeo and Juliet,* there had been four of us who had never missed being present at, and taking some active part in, every performance that the company had so far given. Prue had been a scene shifter when she was not being an actress, Melita Moon was both Box Office and Front-of-House Managers, Eileen Hall was Wardrobe Mistress and I was Lord High Everything Else. Melita unfortunately had to spoil her record at this point as the need to have a surgical operation caused her to drop out very briefly. However, so great was the devotion of the hard-core members such as herself in those days that when she returned for duty I was appalled to see how weak and tottery she still was. I am sure she was there against her doctor's orders.

Wolfit did not approve of my being out of the cast. 'Why don't you play the Apothecary in *Romeo?*' he said. 'The best star part ever written!' He followed that up with a postcard which read, 'You play the *Apothecary* and watch the *first half.* Don't be *out* of the cast and don't get depressed with what you do see. Serious advice from your patron! D. W.' After that came a letter. Here it is in full.

> My dear Peter,
>
> My main reason is that you have made yourself a "star amateur" and it is not good for you to be out of a play from now on. The public expect to see you—it is the penalty you must pay for creating an interest—and you are not as old as Nugent Monck yet!
>
> The Apothecary would give you the chance to do the gracious in front before the show—that was my main reason.
>
> All amateurs are inadequate in one sense or another and you are beginning to look at your people with a professional eye—and your productions too. It isn't good for the captain to be in the pavilion!
>
> I didn't explain myself clearly but you see what I mean.
>
> Yours, D. W.

During the summer, I had made five solid-looking trees by mounting chicken wire on to wooden frames and then covering them with papier-maché. These were for *A Midsummer Night's Dream,* the second play of the season, and they were draped with dark blue-black shot taffeta slashed into tatters to provide foliage. Together with the cut-cloth that had done sunny duty in Arden, but which had now been painted black, they made up a suitably dense and mysterious moonlit Athenian wood. Bill Smith was to have played Bottom, hopefully a good follow-up to his very successful Stephano, but found that the pressures of work and marriage were too much and so he had to drop out. Ron Mills took over. I played Oberon and found that wonderful lyrical verse almost played the part for me. This, too, was a great box-office success and again people were turned away.

Two years earlier, Stratford had staged its splendid cycle of four history plays from *Richard II* through the two *Henry IV*'s to *Henry V*. They had used a permanent Elizabethan-type set of heavy weathered timbers by Tanya Moiseiwitch which I had greatly admired. When I came to do *King Richard II* early in 1953, I made two big mistakes. I still had the music of Robert Harris's voice in my head (he had been the Stratford Richard in 1947) and so when I played the part myself I did, as I had done with Faustus, what felt to me like an impersonation. The result was as lifeless as before, though this time R. T. was a little less harsh. The other mistake was filling up the stage with a massive array of dark brown rostra and steps so that movement of the quite large cast was very restricted. Coloured banners were moved about and there were many lights changes but these were not enough to compensate for the heaviness of the stage picture and the overcrowding. Fashionably the front curtain was kept up throughout but nothing could have been less like the Tanya Moiseiwitch set which had inspired all this lumber. I was copying again and that way dead wood lies! Jack Lewis had met the London critic, Alan Dent, and had persuaded him to come to the matinee. It was bitterly cold and St Peter's Hall had such a high roof that it often seemed to be unheatable. Alan Dent stood, leaning against one of the gas radiators, throughout the entire afternoon, and afterwards wrote to Jack in French for some reason that none of us could understand. Perhaps it was to disguise the fact that it had all been too awful to write about straightforwardly in English! I was not mentioned and the set was described as 'fort formidable et fort gauche'.

As the last play of the season, *The Winter's Tale,* opened on the day on which Queen Mary, greatest of royal theatre-goers, died, I asked the audience to stand in silent memory for a minute before the performance began. This has always been a favourite play of mine and Leontes a part with which I have what might seem to be surprising sympathy. Although the near-tragic beginning is set in Sicilia, I always feel that it should symbolise winter visually and so, when the audience came into the hall, the curtain being up, they saw that, by an electrical effect, snow was falling against the dark sky and that a brazier burned in the foreground.

The production was only a moderate success. Nora played Hermione with a quiet dignity and was beautiful as the statue. Bill Smith returned to give us a splendid Autolycus (one of Wolfit's best parts at Stratford in 1937) but my young lovers, though they looked quite well, were rather ponderous and dull. R. T. found it 'soporific' until we got to the sheep-shearing feast.

People who knew nothing of the technical side of staging the plays often said that it would be so nice if we could play in somewhere better than this hall. I had now got everything running very smoothly and all our scenery and other equipment fitted that stage. Jack Lewis had drawn for me a scale plan of it and I was able to work out my sets to the inch. In any case, storage space was limited and bigger stages would call for bigger flats and a higher and wider sky-cloth.

Besides that, there was no management to interfere at St Peter's Hall and so all things were well under my control. The Pier would not take us as they were still only prepared to have the musical comedy people, the Portsmouth Players. The King's Theatre was ridiculously out of the question. It was much too vast for our small sets and, in any case, they would not consider having amateurs. One silly woman even suggested that she would like to see us on the stage of the San Carlo Opera House in Naples! Although my original dream, whilst I was still in the Army, was that we should use the Pier Theatre, experience had convinced me that it would be much too big, both for our productions and our audiences. When I had started the company, I still had ideas of building an Elizabethan theatre—in Portsmouth as opposed to the wild hope for one in the Cotswolds—but by now that fantasy had evaporated too. No, I was very satisfied with things as they were and had no desire to change them.

The trouble with blowing up a nice comfortable balloon of self-satisfaction is that someone always comes along to stick a pin in it. This was 1953, the year of the Queen's coronation and special events to celebrate it were being thought up in many quarters. Our publicly friendly rivals but privately arch enemies, the Portsmouth Arts Theatre, who alternated our high culture at St Peter's Hall with their copies of popular West End successes, suddenly announced that the Pier Theatre had opened its doors to them and that they would stage Hugh Ross Williamson's *Queen Elizabeth* there in May. Hell and damnation! However, why should we worry? We had no intention of moving and, perhaps surprisingly, the rest of the company seemed to agree that we were better off where we were. The Arts Theatre had been going for longer than we had and they were very much mixed up with members of the City Council. Harry Sargeant was the City Librarian and they still had their stores and rehearsal rooms under his library which was, of course, Corporation property—and the Pier was run by the Corporation. However much I sought to dismiss the whole matter as unimportant, I had to admit to myself that I was green with jealousy and that I was so largely because I did not think that I could cope with the Pier even if they would change their minds and have us there after all.

When the time came, I went to see the Arts play. Their sets looked rather dumpy on the very much larger Pier stage and they tended to use footlights and overhead battens too much for my liking. Even at St Peter's Hall, their lighting was still what I regarded as old-fashioned although they, who had seemed to scoff at my methods when I began, now used spots which they installed themselves, as we did, each time they used the hall. However, all went very well and the audience looked smug and comfortable in the crimson plush tip-up seats. The house was only about half full but it had that pleasant atmosphere which is quite different from when it is described as being half empty. From that time onwards, they did two plays a year at the Pier: one at the beginning of its season and the other at the end, each an adjacent week to the appearance of the Portsmouth Players. Their remaining two plays each year were still at St Peter's Hall in the intervening winter months.

I received a different sort of Coronation invitation from the Portsmouth Corporation. Alex Kinnear was the Director of Entertainments for the City and he asked me if I would call and see him in his office. I went and he said that he would like me to stage a set of tableaux, all illustrating events in Portsmouth's history, as part of a large and spectacular tattoo that was to be staged on the pitch at Fratton Park, the home of the Portsmouth Football Club. I was to be paid a fee (a professional of a sort at last!) and I was to have a reasonably free hand with the City's purse. I accepted and wrote six brief episodes which would be acted out whilst my voice spoke the commentary over loudspeakers. In between would be the usual sorts of things that can be seen at most tattoos such as marching and countermarching by massed bands, the RAF physical training team and the inevitable final firework display.

My episodes dealt with such events as Richard I granting the City its first charter, the arrival of Catherine of Braganza to marry Charles II, Nelson falling at Trafalgar and Charles Dickens writing the Portsmouth Theatre scenes in *Nicholas Nickleby*. I designed a large stage to be erected at one end of the pitch, thus leaving the centre for the other displays. It had four levels and, with the aid of hired professional stage scenery, proved to be very versatile. For example, with masts, billowing sails and a barrage of explosions and smoke, it served very passably as HMS Victory. The members of the Southsea Actors mimed all the leading parts but I had a lot of other people, particularly men from ex-service associations, to make up my crowds. Members of the local branch of the Dickens Fellowship appeared as the Crummles company rehearsing, whilst one of the Actors, spotlit out of the darkness that enveloped another part of the multiple stage, was seen as Dickens, writing and seemingly thinking up the scene that was being acted.

The whole thing was an extraordinary experience! I would never do it again but I would not have missed it for anything. (Rather like the war!) I had a cast of 120 and in three nights we performed before a total of 41,400 people! It was rough, ready and vast but it was very exciting to be an important part of a show that had a total cast of about 500. Two moments, both a million miles away from my Shakespearean ideals, live in my memory. One episode showed a local villain named Jack the Painter (whose mummifed finger converted into a tobacco stopper in the Portsmouth Museum held endless fascination for me when I was a schoolboy!) was seen setting fire to the dockyard, being brought to justice and then finally being hanged.

On the second night, when they came to put Jack's head (John Fulcher's in fact) through the noose, it was found that overnight rain had shrunk the rope. A raucous voice from the crowd got a big laugh from the rest of the audience of some 14,000 by shouting out, 'Big 'ead!' The other vivid picture I still have is of the finale on the first night. All 500 members of the cast were assembled, including the massed bands of the Royal Marines, the Royal Dragoon Guards and the Royal Army Ordinance Corps and all my 120 in their costumes dating from Richard I to the 19th century. All eyes were on two hugh golden gates as, up steps on either side of them, came the two previous great queens in our history, Elizabeth I (Nora Turner) and Victoria (June Vaughan Sherrin) to open them and reveal the new royal cypher of ERII. This was immediately followed by the massed bands playing the National Anthem whilst an enormous firework set-piece of the new queen's head burst into a great display of coloured sparks and smoke. At that moment, the rain, which seems to be an inevitable part of any outdoor event in this country, even in August as this was, came down. Victoria, in a white crinoline, was extremely *décolleté* and the one thing that I watched amidst all this huge spectacle was the cascade of rain running down her bare shoulders and bosom into her cleavage! It suddenly all seemed so ridiculous.

In the previous April, I had made another professional appearance. Florence

Greaves, a local soprano and the organiser of the Portsmouth Musical Competition Festival, loved a social event. She therefore put on a dinner with a concert to follow and persuaded most of the local socialites to come to it in all their grandest evening finery. I was to act as compére and also to do some verse speaking. My fellow members of the cast were the soprano, Astra Desmond, the pianist Maurice Cole (whom I already knew because he married a friend of mine) and Carl Dolmetsch with members of his family. It was all a bit too starchy and social for my taste but I enjoyed appearing and mixing with such distinguished artists who treated me as one of themselves instead of, as they might well have done, an interloping amateur. Over the next few years I appeared in more of these concerts and had the honour (and I do not use the word sycophantically) of appearing with artists of the calibre of Isobel Baillie, Marie Wilson, Heddle Nash and Robert Keys. I always claim that Heddle Nash gave me my one and only singing lesson. He praised my speaking voice quite extravagantly and refused to believe that I cannot sing. After I had protested that this was so, he asked me to sing a scale after him. I did it to the best of my ability. He winced and then, after a pause, said merrily, 'I see what you mean!' End of singing lesson!

Round about this time I was kept very busy with many other public appearances outside the Actors. I adjudicated verse-speaking and reading competitions and gave lectures in schools. I also frequently talked to adult groups varying from the Soroptimists, a collection of formidable top women who were the liveliest and most intelligent of audiences, to Townswomen's Guilds who, as I expounded about the world theatre's Greek origins or the physical structure of the Elizabethan playhouse, clicked away at their knitting whilst they wondered if next month's talk on jam-making would be more their cup of tea.

However, there was a new season to be staged at St Peter's Hall. We began with *Julius Caesar* which went reasonably well largely because many experienced members were willing to be in the crowd. All too often this consists of the dregs of any company; in one amateur production that I saw, they looked like a group of young people who had strayed from a very respectable fancy dress party. I did not believe in them for a moment and they were not the slightest danger to anyone. For this 1953 production, I had now had some half-round columns made and these were used with scarlet and gold Roman standards againt a simple pale blue background. Ronald Mills was Caesar and during one of the performances nearly made an unscheduled entrance which would have considerably altered the plot. He was standing in the wings at the point when Cassius dies and, for some reason, thought that the curtain had come down at the end of the play. He made a dash to go on for the curtain call, still wearing his glasses. Fortunately, several of us saw him in time and dragged him back. The appearance of Caesar at that moment would have been unorthodox to say the least! The Saturday matinee was extremely trying as a young petty officer in the Royal Navy, who was playing several small parts, found that he could not get back from his ship, which was out in Spithead, in time for the performance.

Understudies were not practicable in a company such as ours and so we had to do an alarming amount of improvising as we went along. I played Casca and so was free to do at least one of the missing actor's short parts in the second half. I managed fairly well until I found that I did not know the line that would get me off the stage. I am sure that 'I will go and find Brutus' must have sounded very un-Shakespearean! The most unhappy feature of this production was a car accident. Prue had a vintage Austin 7 to which she was devoted. It looked to the layman's eye like a very old pram that had its own means of locomotion. It was called 'Emma' but, alas, on the Saturday night before the play opened, Prue was in a collision. The car was a write-off and Nancy, my splendid Rosalind, who was one of the passengers and a member of my Roman mob, had her collar bone broken. The next production of *Julius Caesar* nine years hence would also be dogged with misfortunes which would include broken bones. Contrary to superstition, this was a much more unlucky play for us than the Scottish one.

I was getting more and more worried about the amount of money that we were spending on costumes with still practically nothing in stock to show for it. I asked Donald Wolfit if he knew of any company that would make some cheaply for us. 'Nathan's charge £80-£90 to put in a new costume nowadays because of Purchase Tax', he said, 'so I doubt if anyone would consider your suggestion. If I decide to get rid of any of my stock in the next year or so then you would be the first people I would write to to make an offer. Certainly the present system is all wrong for you. You are buying over and over again but would you be content to play all plays Elizabethan—that is the answer'.

It is said that the Lord helps those who help themselves. Almost immediately after we had decided to make some of the costumes ourselves for the next play, *The Merchant of Venice,* (deliberately left as long as possible after Ron's pre-Actors production in 1947 in order to minimise comparisons) Donald wrote again. His attitude had changed and so had ours. Eileen Hall had given up as Wardrobe Mistress and been replaced by June Vaughan Sherrin and Nancy Glenister, who were both very keen to make as many costumes as possible. Donald said, 'I have decided to get rid of some of the wardrobe. There will be a large basket which will contain *The Merchant of Venice* production, made by Simmons and designed by Shiela Jackson—some 33 costumes in all. Added to this will be some dozen to 15 costumes from *Volpone.* It is, of course, all excellent material and I propose to offer it to you for £1 per costume; that is, as you will realise, an absurd price . . . you *must* let me know before Monday at the latest'. I did not hesitate and when the skips arrived there were at least 60 costumes. Nonetheless, he charged us only £50, which meant that each garment, many of superb pre-war silk velvet, cost us just over 80 new pence!

They did not arrive in time for our *Merchant* but we were able to use them for the first play of 1954 which was one of those that everyone had said that we could not possibly do, *King Lear.* My Venice and Belmont before then, however, were deep cream with pillars, gondola poles and other trappings in red and gold. In time for this production, I had also bought some more tabs to relieve the monotony of front scenes always being played against black. One of these new sets was rust-coloured with a pattern of acanthus leaves on it but the other two pairs were plain red and blue respectively. Nancy was again excellent, this time as Portia, and Ron scored one of his successes as Shylock in spite of coming on in his first scene one night and beginning with the line, 'Three thousand dollars!'

King Lear hit some of the worst winter weather of the century! All the pipes of St Peter's Hall were frozen solid but the minute amount of warmth that was produced during the dress rehearsal must have melted an already burst one somewhere. When the hall was opened the next morning, it was found to be devastatingly flooded! I cancelled my patients and went to view the emergency. There were icicles several feet long over the stage door where the water had poured through a window and the dressing rooms were literally lakes several inches deep. All the shoes and boots that had been left on the floor were saturated and the girls' dresses and men's long gowns and cloaks had soaked up the water like sponges.

The Vicar, the Rev Jack Smithers, and his wife worked like Trojans to get rid of the water and to dry out our wardrobe before the evening's performance. Footwear went into the oven at the vicarage and every possible source of heat was put into use. One of the nicest sights was the dress of Goneril, wickedest of women, laid out lovingly to dry in front of the fire in the vicar's own study! We managed, however. Most of the costumes felt damp when we put them on—indeed, several were quite wet—but we got through the play. As one member of the cast said, it was a wonder we did not all go down with marsh fever!

Audiences rewarded our efforts by turning up in remarkably good numbers. Most of them brought thick rugs to wrap around themselves and many came equipped with flasks of hot soup. Where did I find an actor to play Lear after all? Does my reader really need an answer? I cannot resist quoting from the press notice: 'It is doubtful', it said, 'whether the standard of any future Southsea Actors production will surpass that of *King Lear* . . . Mr Gateley gives the performance of his career in the monumental title role . . . One feels that every member of the cast from Lear himself down to the Second Servant has been caught up in the sweeping maelstrom of this tremendous play'. Charles Biggerstaff, Ron's original Shylock, came in for great praise as Gloucester as did John Fulcher's fiancée, Sunya Grant, who played Cordelia.

We ended the season with *King Henry IV, Part I*. It had to be small scale but then so had the production by Robert Atkins been at the Vaudeville Theatre in London during the blitz. Kenneth Barnard, a big man with great relish and a strong voice, was one of my best Falstaffs. With amateurs I discovered that one must always start with a man who is physically already part of the way there. In my experience, it is the most difficult of all the parts for an amateur. Only amongst professionals does one normally find actors of sufficient power and expansiveness for it. I gave Hotspur as much dash as I could muster and Prue played Mistress Quickly. The King was Leonard Russell who had started with us in the tiny part of Bernardo in *Hamlet* but who had soon graduated to a run of noble types including Brutus, Macduff, Duke Theseus and Cominius. He, too, was a well-built man and, in fact, did not look unlike Donald Wolfit. He was a great enthusiast and, at the time, still had some of the bravura that had rubbed off on to him during his wartime service in the RAF. He became our resident Henry! He had played Bolingbroke opposite my Richard II and so had ascended to the throne as Henry IV then. During the rest of my time, he never left it! Nearly every leading actor in the company seemed to find one part that would become almost his own personal property. With John Fulcher it was Romeo, with Prue it was Juliet's Nurse and with Len it was Henry IV. In time, there would be another part, a much more important one, that he would add but that was still in the future. During the previous autumn, many of us had gone up to London to see Wolfit's Falstaff in this play at the King's Theatre, Hammersmith, where he was having a very successful season. We all went round backstage afterwards to meet him. These mass invasions of theatre dressing

King Lear St. Peter's Hall, 1954

King Lear (KEG) and the Fool (Alan Robson)
'Mr. Gateley gives the performance of his career in the monumental title rôle' (1954); '. . . the eventual madness scenes are superb' (1962); 'a towering performance' (1972) *Portsmouth Press*

rooms are always rather sticky affairs and can be embarrassing but it would have been unthinkable not to have gone. In any case, many of the company had not met him or Rosalind and were anxious to do so.

I was still worried that the Arts Theatre would do a Shakespeare play. Because of the very novelty of the other company doing it, there would be invidious comparisons. In any case, I felt very possessive over my friend, William Shakespeare, and I did not want trespassers into what I regarded as very much my private property. I had been entitling each recent season *Plays by Shakespeare* as a broad hint to possible invaders to keep off my ship. I now made my most positive move: I changed the name of the company by inserting an extra word. Henceforth we should be *The Southsea Shakespeare Actors* with, whenever I was feeling particularly vulnerable, the last two words printed bigger than the first two. Wolfit questioned the wisdom of the move. He wrote, 'I suppose you are right to change your title but of course it won't stop Sargeant from doing a Shakespeare play if he wants to—and it *does* limit you to the Bard, doesn't it?' Later in the letter he said, "Success always brings opposition and malice, especially in the non-professional theatre. I could have wished that my old friend Sargeant had joined you but obviously that is not possible'. He finished with a nice touch, 'Yours patronically, Donald'! Shortly after, there were more costumes on their way. The letter referring to these begins, 'Dear Peter, Exuberant letter to hand! Let's be *practical.* How many do you want and what can you afford?'

During the summer of 1954, I went to Italy for the first time. The Shakespearean and the Elizabethan in me had always yearned to go and at last it was possible. Nancy, Prue and I went together to Verona, one of the loveliest cities we could possibly have chosen for our first visit to that beautiful country. I fell in love with it as deeply as I felt sure that I would and my passion for it has never diminished. From Verona we visited Padua and Mantua and, most wonderful of all, Venice. When I first set foot in that incredible fantasy, the tears ran down my cheeks.

Our original flats, with their canvas that had previously been Naval mattress covers, had done sterling service for seven seasons and had been repainted over and over again. Now, at last, I decided the time had come to have some new ones professionally made. The number was increased but they were basically the same sizes so that I could still create my sets on the 'Lot's Bricks' principle of everything fitting. Some while before, Donald had offered me some of his scenery but I had refused it because I thought it would upset my scheme. In any case, it would undoubtedly have been too big for me to be able to store.

The first play for which the new scenery was painted was that other so-called impossible one as far as we were concerned, *Antony and Cleopatra.* By this time, I had no hesitation in offering the part of Egypt's queen to Nancy and she was remarkably good. The part is always considered to be so difficult because it embraces such a variety of facets of character but, for an amateur, Nancy had an amazing range from the languorously sensuous to the spiteful and terrifying wildcat. I played Antony and discovered for myself what Wolfit and many other professional actors have found; that it is even more tiring than Hamlet or Lear. Considering the limitations of the small stage, I think that I achieved quite a spectacular production. Mostly in black and gold, my set had converging lines to suggest a perspective and this helped to make it look bigger.

Our second play of the season was *Love's Labour's Lost* and my solid trees, now repainted to look summery and with fresh green tattered taffeta for foliage, made their reappearance. I played the King and John Fulcher spoke Berowne beautifully and had all the sparkling virility for which the part calls. The weather on the first night was described in the national press the next day as 'Freak' and 'A minor tornado'. This did not help a play which is never a good draw to bring in more than a very few people. The Lord Mayor, a builders' merchant by profession, who came to the first night, very generously bought up some seats for the workers in his business to help us but, sadly, many of the tickets were not used. The chief blight on the box office was something that was going to have an enormous effect on theatre and cinema attendances all over the country. It was the arrival of television!

This new form of entertainment had just become available in our area and the long march back to spending evenings at home began with a vengeance. Those who had not immediately bought sets went to the houses of those who had. The great post-war boom of going out to be entertained started to decline in that autumn of 1954.

On 2 February, 1955, the 353rd anniversary of its earliest-known performance, we opened in *Twelfth Night,* our first play to have a second production. I had much more control over my actors this time but the Sir Andrew went too far the other way and was rather dull and unfunny. My sets were the simple cut-outs against the sky-cloth which I should have used before and my street scenes were suggested by a single panel on which I did formalised line drawings of buildings I had seen in Verona the previous summer. Geoffrey Eagar, who had been so good as Petruchio and Shaw's Simpleton, was an excellent Malvolio whilst I contented myself with the tiny part of the Priest. Ken Barnard, my Falstaff, was Sir Toby and Prue again played Maria.

The final play was *King Henry V.* I appeared in the title role and went all out for the romantic approach in the pre-war manner. The modern muddier look had already come in but we did not want to spoil our costumes and our new professionally-made armour just for one production. The set, all swirling banners painted in deep blue and black, had been created in the drive at Crossways as usual. Throughout the whole period of the work, the weather had been bitterly cold. My sister, Gwen, was now usually my one assistant but this time I worked alone and, once again, several times amongst falling flakes of snow.

Ron Mills had been increasingly dropping out of our activities. For one thing, I had not had much to offer him this season: only Lepidus in *Antony and Cleopatra* and he had turned it down. When the season was nearly over, he decided to resign from the company. The Committee elected him to be an honorary life member and I made a suitable speech on the last night as he was in the audience. The title, 'Assistant Director', had never meant much, even in the earliest days. I had not intended to have such a post in the first place and so I now had no hesitation in letting it lapse. Ron and I continued to be good friends and the company went on using the flat over his own for rehearsals. Our pounding about on his ceilings must have made him feel that he was still very much involved with us!

I then made a momentous decision. It was that we should go, if they would have us, to the Pier Theatre after all! I discussed it privately, as I did so many things, with my two closest friends, Prue Higham and John Fulcher. The former was cautious and alarmed but John applauded my enterprise. I was encouraged by the knowledge that I was already on good terms with Alex Kinnear and I knew that he had liked my contribution to his Coronation Tattoo. He was not an intellectual himself but he respected what I was doing and admired my productions which he thought were an asset to the City. I approached him and he arranged a meeting with David Evans, whom I did not then know but who was the manager of the Pier itself. Melita Moon and I duly attended; I with my heart very much in my mouth! Evans was a stocky, hard-headed, Welsh business man who was running the Pier very efficiently at that time. Popular entertainment was more of a money-maker than culture and he was determined that the Pier should be as profitable as possible. The Players did musical comedies and the Arts offered West End successes but we were Shakespeareans and that might well be a very different matter. I need not have worried: both Kinnear and David Evans were very keen to have us and seemed to feel that we might bring some prestige. The terms were many times more expensive than the hiring of St Peter's Hall but the two of them seemed confident that we should play to larger audiences. I hoped that they were right but I was doubtful.

I had now so firmly set my heart on our going to the Pier that I would probably have accepted even higher terms. Details were soon agreed and our first week was to be the opening one of their next theatre season which would be in May, 1956. What play could I offer them? '*Hamlet*', I said, 'with myself in the lead'.

Before I made it public, I gave the news to several members of the Shakespeare Actors when we were at a friend's house one evening for drinks and a chat. My happy bombshell fell like a lump of lead! Almost everyone there greeted the news with the longest of faces and declared that the move to the Pier Theatre would be a great mistake. We were alright where we were and, if we tried to expand in this way, they feared that all that I had built up would collapse. We were amateurs, they said, and a professional theatre would only accentuate the fact. They were all sorry that I had not had the strength, as they saw it, to resist the temptation to copy the Arts Theatre.

I stuck to my guns and went ahead. Time would prove that I was right to do so because the next 11 years turned out to be, for the Southsea Shakespeare Actors, their Golden Age.

ACT TWO
The Pier

CHAPTER 13
On board a professional theatre

The South Parade Pier at Southsea was one of the grandest of its kind. The splendid pavilions that house the theatres on those piers that have them are usually right at the end, as far out to sea as possible. Visually this can provide an enchanting fantasy but, if the night happens to be wet and windy, it can make playgoing a very unpleasant business. The intending patron, if not deterred altogether, arrives soaked and storm-battered. Programmes extra but oilskins included in the price of the ticket! When you book your seats, take out an insurance policy against your hair-do being wrecked as you struggle along the pier to the theatre!

Sensibly, all the buildings on the South Parade Pier were at the shore end. The glass roof of the entrance area extended across the promenade and the broad flight of steps up to it from the road, to form a large canopy. Once inside, one went through the Minor Hall into the theatre foyer. From there, one could go either straight ahead into the back of the stalls or up the curving staircases to the circle. As on most piers, the auditorium was long with a U-shaped circle but it was richly decorated and very well kept. It was as lush as many a playhouse on land and had none of the tattiness that is so often associated with pier pavilions. The magnificent baroque proscenium, that I so loved as a child and which strongly influenced many of my designs, had long since gone.

Visiting touring companies had always found that the stage was very shallow. When a taxi that was used in one scene of *77 Park Lane* had to be concealed in the wings, I cannot imagine how they coped with it. Musical comedies, too, with their choruses and several sets, must have found it incredibly difficult. That they managed, I can bear witness, but in 1933 it was decided to enlarge the stage. This decision was forced upon the Corporation by the fact that the theatre did not conform with the fire regulations: there was no safety curtain! What is more, there was no stage tower to accommodate a solid one—which also meant that all scenery such as back and front cloths had to be rolled in order to be taken up out of sight. My beloved proscenium, therefore, was demolished. Today, no doubt, it would have been taken down very carefully and re-erected in the new position but in the 1930s everything that was ornate in the Victorian or, as this was, Edwardian style was detested and the sooner it was destroyed the better.

In the winter of 1933-4, the new proscenium was built some five or six metres in front of where the old one had been; thus adding that much depth to the stage and shortening the auditorium by the same amount. Both changes were improvements. A high stage tower was also built which not only accommodated the new iron safety curtain but also a grid housing counter-weighted lines for scenery. This meant that almost everything could be taken up out of sight, smoothly and without rolling up, so easily that one girl could operate the line in question. The new proscenium was rectangular and in the thirties style of the cinemas being built at that time and so did not match the roccoco plaster work round the front of the circle. The crimson velvet curtains were re-cut so that instead of being gathered up into great swags at each top corner, they were drawn electrically straight to the sides.

Now, over twenty years later, the Pier was thriving. No longer did the summer season consist of touring West End successes preceded by a few weeks of concert parties. Now, each year there was a resident summer show on the lines of a lavish revue and starring some of the biggest names of the time. Peter Sellers, Harry Secombe, Tommy Trinder, Jimmy Edwards, Yana, Bob Monkhouse, Tommy Steele, Max Bygraves, Terry Scott and Hugh Lloyd are only some of the artists who appeared either for whole seasons or individual weeks. Even Sunday nights saw the theatre packed out for concerts by visiting bands or a home-grown talent show called, *Palm Court.* There was dancing in the Minor Hall at night after it had done duty during the day as a café where holidaymakers could sit and listen to popular music churned out on an organ. On the deck outside, there were various entertainments including beauty contests, open-air dancing and every Wednesday night, after the theatre had emptied, a firework display. Bands played at the end of the pier during the day time and there was a large and noisy bar in the sea end of the pavilion beyond the back of the theatre stage.

It was into this teeming and highly commercial, professional entertainment centre that we were on the point of catapulting ourselves from the dark and dusty church hall in the backwaters. No wonder some of the old hands were nervous. The rank and file of the company, on the other hand, were thrilled and excited. In the meantime, however, there were three more plays to put on at St Peter's Hall and a great many things to do before we could transfer to the bigger and more demanding stage of this professional theatre.

Three factors needed to be taken into account. The first and most obvious one was that all the scenery would have to be bigger. The second was that we should now have part of our audience up in the circle looking down on to the stage instead of being, as they had been at St Peter's Hall, all below it and looking upwards. This meant that the tops of things, which were previously ignored, must in future look as well designed and painted as the rest. Up till now it had been possible to put only two sides of a seemingly solid structure, like a tomb, at right angles to each other with the point downstage towards the audience, to provide a piece of scenery that was totally convincing. No one sitting below the stage could see that it did not possess a top or the two upstage sides. Henceforth, all such objects would have to have four sides and a top. The third change would be an improvement in quality and standards generally. We had been very slack

South Parade Pier Theatre as it was after the stage had been rebuilt in 1933-4
(The SSA's 1957 *Romeo and Juliet* set on the stage)

about the fireproofing of odd properties and extensions to flats such as architectural details or overhanging foliage. These had often been simply cardboard but when adequately painted they had looked strong enough and were in fact sufficiently so to last the one week. From now onwards they would have to be of hardboard or plywood and everything would be thoroughly fireproofed. Not only would the city's fire officers come round to make inspections but the management of the theatre would insist upon such things.

A few years earlier, a Portsmouth man named Laurie Upton had set himself up in business as 'Southern Stage Supplies'. From his youngest days he had been a professional backstage worker and the atmosphere of the theatre had soaked into the very marrow of his bones. He was a small, balding man with a slightly apologetic air, a shaggy moustache, a perpetual battered cheroot and great enthusiasm. Above all, he was a very skilful manufacturer of any sort of scenery or properties. He had already made us our new flats, new rostra to replace the originals, superb brass crowns with jewels mounted on them and enough metal armour to equip our armies in *King Henry V*. Sometimes I would want, for just one play, a property that I did not wish to keep afterwards. The attics at the dental practice and the garage at Crossways were already getting too full for me to want to store items that might never be used again.

Egyptian long-handled, imitation ostrich fans, for *Antony and Cleopatra,* had been a case in point. On those occasions, I would supply him with a design which he would carry out with amazing fidelity. We would then use the properties for the week of the production and afterwards he would take them back and put them into his own store to hire out to other amateur societies. I not only designed all my own scenery and props but I prided myself that my ideas were always absolutely practical. It is no use dreaming up a piece of scenery unless one knows for sure that it will not only stand up but will fit into the set correctly. All my sketches for Laurie were done to scale on squared graph paper and the floor plans of the sets on the stage were worked out to the inch. In this way, I was able to visualise every aspect of my productions without having to rely on other designers who would inevitably produce something different from the picture that I had created in my own head. By the same token, Laurie could be relied upon to make for me exactly what I had put down on paper.

Being unable either to store in my garden shed, or to manhandle when painting alone, flats taller than those that we already possessed, my first job was to get Laurie to make removable extensions of a little over a metre in height for the existing ones. The half-round pillars also had to be made longer but their extra length did not matter as they were stored in the roof of the seven-metres-long garage. I had had that equipped with several sets of pullies and ropes for such things as those and the skycloth rolled on its battens. This last item had to be replaced by one that was both considerably wider and higher. I knew that the Pier Theatre had its own black borders, those overhead strips for concealing the upper workings of the stage, and so I had some of ours recut and sewn on to our set of black curtains, the much-used 'tabs', to make them big enough for the Pier, too. No wonder that by the time we actually went there, the 'National Debt' owing to me had risen to £800—at 1956 values!

The season opened at St Peter's Hall in the autumn of 1955 with a new production of another play that we had already done, *Much Ado About Nothing*. The set was based on the previous one for this comedy but somewhat elaborated with pale blue arches. These sported their new extensions and suddenly I saw that my sets had all grown up! Everything looked rather big for the church hall stage but it gave me a vision of what lay ahead. Nancy was a delightful, willowy Beatrice and I contented myself with Don Pedro for a change. Bill Smith was excellent as Dogberry—a performance based, as his Stephano had been and his Bottom would have been, on George Rose's Dogberry in the marvellous Gielgud production at Stratford-upon-Avon in 1949-50, which we had seen together.

My father, now aged 85, had been operated on for cancer twice during the preceding year.

Just after the rehearsals had begun for *Troilus and Cressida,* the next play, he died. I am sure that he had always been very fond of me and that he was proud of my achievements, such as they were, in the fields of both dentistry and the amateur theatre, but our relationship had always been a little remote. He was perhaps more grandfatherly than fatherly but the loss of a parent is always one of the most fundamental breaks in anyone's life. Donald Wolfit summed the matter up well in a letter that revealed his own feelings. It began,

> 'My dear Peter,
>
> I am so sorry to hear your news of your father. I know what a wrench this is—life is never quite the same afterwards. I never had a great affection for my own but he grew in my respect and memory when he had gone. I always feel there is a strong Roman influence in this country in our respect for fatherhood, don't know why'.

Shortly before, in response to an urgent telegram, I had lent him two of the baskets that he had previously given to us. He was now returning them and his letter about my father continued,

> 'The two baskets are due to be sent to you in a few days. I have given the orders and many thanks for the loan of them. I had a stupid stage staff at first but I sacked them and have an excellent man now'.

He finished,

> 'Great fortune to *T and Cressida*—it's a very hard one to tackle. Yours as ever, Donald'.

My first difficulty with the play was a sudden shortage of available cast. For various reasons, hardly anyone seemed to be free. One probable cause was that they all wanted to be in the first Pier play and so those who could manage only one part during the season plumped for that. The situation was so bad that one whole rehearsal became a discussion about how we could scrape a cast together. I was determined that we should manage it somehow and we did. We could not possibly cancel a production simply because of shortage of people at a time when we were planning to enlarge into bigger and better things than ever before. It was a very trying time for me as I had problems at home as well.

Throughout my father's long illness, particularly during his spells in hospital, I had been running the household because my mother, now 76, was becoming increasingly arthritic and infirm. Fortunately, my sister, Gwen, was now living at Crossways and so she was free to cope with the nursing.

As well as the costumes that Nancy and June had made, our wardrobe had been augmented with a lot more from Wolfit. We were now very well stocked with Elizabethan and mediaeval garments of all kinds. So far, though, we had nothing for ancient Romans, Greeks or Trojans and I felt that we had more than enough extra expenses and possible financial risk with our move to the Pier without the added cost of developing in that direction. I thought of Chaucer's *Troilus and Criseyde,* on which Shakespeare based his play, and decided to do it in the costumes of his period. In any case, the author visualised it as being in what were to him contemporary clothes and so English mediaeval was, I felt, completely justified. The reference to a glove would no longer be an embarrassment as it is when the play is dressed in costumes that Homer would have recognised.

Again I was delighted with the new height of the flats and joined a number of them together to form a solid backcloth. This worked excellently because it meant that it could be painted in sections, in the garage if necessary, and so the old problems of the former real cloths had been eliminated. This one was in black, purple and grey and had stormy clouds, severe 'topless towers of Ilium', tents and a distant bay filled with black ships. I played Pandarus and enjoyed making him as lecherous and obscene as was considered reasonable in the fifties. John Fulcher scored one of his greatest successes with a very moving Troilus. When he came to wonderful lines like, '. . . scants us with a single famish'd kiss, Distasted with the salt of broken tears' he seemed to be speaking from the depths of his heart, as I am sure Shakespeare was when he wrote them. I gave the part of Cressida to a completely new girl called Mavis Giles. This was a bit of a risk but it paid off. She was small and dark with a laughing face and dancing eyes and she probably acted instinctively. In the coming years, she would prove to be almost incapable of ageing and, as her technique developed, she became a delightful and very talented actress. Ten years later she was still looking young enough to be a lovely Juliet! Leonard Russell continued to be noble and wise: this time he was Ulysses. The mediaeval costuming softened the play slightly and emphasised the domestic rather than the martial side of it. This was a blessing because of the small cast as it helped to conceal our inability to make much of a display with the battle scenes. As I was so short of men, I had a female Chorus. This would normally be an odd thing to do as the lines are all about war but I dressed her in metal armour to suggest Athena.

Some time prior to this, a new name had appeared in the Hampshire Telegraph, a weekly paper published by the same firm as the Portsmouth Evening News. It was that of Charles Green, a great theatre enthusiast whose *Amateur Stage Spotlight* column became the most important local critical writing about our affairs for the next two decades. If he had a fault, it was, perhaps, that he was inclined to be too kind but he was a welcome chronicler of production and characterisation details. He was a small, mild man looking remarkably like the bust of Shakespeare in the Parish Church at Stratford-upon-Avon. He became a much valued friend of the company and also a personal one of mine. For him *Troilus and Cressida* did not seem to have lost its flavour. Under a headline of 'Poetic Pearls in Play of Lechery', he used phrases like 'diseased and flea-bitten' and he felt that the play was 'written at a time when Shakespeare was afflicted with a disgust of life'. The Portsmouth Evening News very generously gave us a half-page spread with photographs but, as usually happens with this play in the professional theatre too, it failed to draw. This was no surprise, of course, and the profits on plays like *The Merchant of Venice,* which always fill the house, were set against the losses on these rare ones. That I was able to do them at all was one of the joys of the whole venture.

King Henry VIII, which followed in February, 1956, did considerably better in spite of the fact that the Daily Telegraph reported on the day after our first night that 'Freezing winds yesterday from East Europe kept most of the country in the grip of the worst freeze-up since 1947'. This was becoming a bad habit!

Again I used a collection of our extended flats, battened together, as a backcloth and produced a set that was mostly old gold. On the left was a dais backed by Henry's Tudor rose and on the right a group of pillars and draped scarlet curtains. The background showed receding Tudor arches, one behind another. I am sure that earnest scholars often find motives and subtleties in the works of Shakespeare and other creative artists which would amaze their originators. 'Oh! Really?' one can hear them saying, 'Did you think that I thought that? Not a bit of it; I put it in because it felt right and I thought it would be effective'. In a much lesser way the same thing happened to me over the set. A party of intense students came from Winchester and said afterwards that the scenery was very clever because I had obviously put the Tudor rose on the left to indicate Henry's leftish views (breaking away from the Roman church and abolishing laws that did not suit him). The scarlet curtains on the right represented the Cardinal and his extreme Right conservatism'. Nothing could have been further from my mind. I did it because I liked the look of it and because that arrangement met the needs of the production.

The great processions had to be cut but I retained the gossipy citizens. Tyrone Guthrie in his masterly production of the play at Stratford in 1949-50 had been the first person to see how easily those three can be played for comedy. I followed his example but was criticised by Charles Green for doing so. He pointed out that the Chorus had said that he came 'no more to make you laugh'. He guessed my reason, however, for having the King himself, standing in the famous Holbein pose, speaking that opening speech. 'I felt he had Charles Laughton in mind', he said, 'when he announced his intention of not making us laugh'. That famous comedy portrayal was still very familiar to audiences at the time. Leonard Russell played Henry and looked remarkably like the famous pictures. The public probably knows more how that particular king looked than any other historical personage and this is one of the great problems of the part. He must *look* absolutely right. Often playgoers have preconceived notions of how characters like Shylock or Hamlet *should* look but everyone knows exactly how Henry VIII *must* look! Nora played Queen Katherine splendidly and the mature, noble qualities that Wolfit had felt were wrong for Isabella, were ideal for this part. I wish he could have seen her play it. My Wolsey was an actor of rather saturnine temperament who was not always easy to direct, but he was good. I became thin-lipped and icy-eyed as Cardinal Campeiius.

Another of the production problems of this play is the vision that the Queen sees shortly before she dies. The text refers to 'personages clad in white robes wearing on their heads garlands of bays'. If carried out too literally, the effect can be like the worst sort of Victorian view of Heaven. In recent years, I have seen amateurs attempt to do as their author told them and the result was ludicrous: they looked like young women in nightdresses who had come up from the dancing school in the village to perform before 'M'lady in the big house'. Tryone Guthrie had the whole thing in Katherine's mind. She sat in her chair and then appeared to open her eyes whilst still asleep; from the expression on her face we could guess at the wondrous vision she alone could see. I curtained off part of my stage with black tabs which, as she fell asleep having called for soft music, faded away into darkness. After they had opened surreptitiously, lights upstage came slowly on to show an angel and two cherubs with bright golden wings, and holding mediaeval song books open in their hands, against a pure blue sky. The lights faded again, the black curtains closed in the darkness and the former gloom returned. The aim had been to show a few moments of a tableau suggested by the golden angels rejoicing in the sky in Botticelli's *Nativity* in the National Gallery.

The costumes for Katherine and the Cardinals had to look as right as Henry's and so these were hired from Nathan's. The rest of the cast were dressed from our Elizabethan wardrobe. This seemed to be reasonable as the original actors would have been in their Jacobean costumes of the time.

It is not enough, especially with amateurs, whose average throughout the cast is never as good as the better professionals, however highly they may judge themselves, to concentrate solely on acting. By its very nature, the theatre is theatrical; too unadorned a performance might just as well be on a concert platform. I have known those who have put on visually dull productions and justified them with the declaration that they wanted them to be very simple. In my experience this is usually a cover-up for a poverty of ideas. Simplicity, like the little black dress, has to be stunning in its effect—a single scarlet figure, perhaps, spotlit alone in a vast, empty, white set or something else that hits the audience with its essential theatricality. It has to be served up consciously; to leave it to itself makes it look as if you do not know what to do.

Examples from these last two plays will give some idea of the way in which I tried to cope with the purely theatrical side of my productions: translations of aspects of the play into visual terms. After a good deal of downfall, death and general gloom, *King Henry VIII* ends with a joyous scene of the baby, Elizabeth, being christened. The costumes and the set had been rich and eye-filling but, by this time, the audience had been looking at them for a long while and so there would be no novelty when seen yet again this late in the evening. On the other hand, the economics were such that any late reviver of the audience must not be costly. The last but one scene had been played before the tabs and when they opened to reveal this final celebration, the stage was packed with every character who had managed to remain alive, each holding a tall gold staff from the top of which cascaded a cluster of white silk bows and streamers. It was not a visual distraction but it set the new mood that the play takes on at the end. The 'silk' was the cheapest taffeta whilst the gold paint and the wooden poles also cost very little. It was minutely spectacular and was a legitimate part of what must be added to a play when it is realised in the theatre.

Troilus and Cressida had a few lines cut at the end so that, for a proscenium stage, there would be a striking final moment on which to bring down the curtain. Hector's bleeding body was left in full view with Troilus, heartbroken and with the glove that the perfidious Cressida had given him as a pledge of her undying love still in his hand, standing dejectedly looking at it. The coughing, decaying Pandarus pointed to this sour outcome of the vile events that had made up the play and snarled at the audience, 'Good traders in the flesh, set *this* in your painted cloths!' Curtain.

When I came to direct *Hamlet* for the first time, I found it to be such a cerebral play that I had the greatest difficulty in making both production and design theatrical in the way that I have been describing. Looking back, as I can now, on the whole canon, I am quite sure that for me this is the most intractable of all the plays to make *visually* striking. It almost takes place in Hamlet's mind and so a black-suited prince with a black mind seems to call for almost unrelieved blackness and yet when Stratford did a production in such a setting, the effect on the spectator was distractingly and depressingly dreary. I suspect that it is because of this problem that I seem to have heard more coughings and fidgetings from audiences at performances of *Hamlet* than any other of the major plays.

I had been in it twice before, as I have recounted, but in other people's productions. This did not seem to help. Quite apart from my usual desire to realise the author's intentions, as nearly as I could discern them, on a modern stage, I wanted this first Pier Theatre production to be a real stunner. I could not achieve that if it all looked dark and drab.

The situation is primarily that of a black, mourning figure set against a bright, colourful, and mostly unfeeling, court. This, then, should be the keynote of my production. I devised a set of blue, streaked flats, heavily studded, with a rostrum across the back and a wide opening to the skycloth in the middle. To the left, there was a high alcove of deep red with a large cross mounted on it as the play abounds in Christian references: the King's prayer, the problems of Ophelia's burial, Hamlet's own belief in the divinity that shapes our ends and the reference to the cock crowing throughout the night at Christmas. The costumes should be our most lavish and all the state scenes would have attendants with massive satin flags of scarlet, emerald and yellow emblazoned with black and gold. These should be swirled spectacularly as their bearers came on or went off but held utterly still during the action of the scenes. For the exteriors, such as the battlements, the skycloth was open and plain but for the royal court I built a large screen, like a huge decorative railing, to stand in front of it. Now that we had a stage with a high tower and counter-weighted lines, this could be taken in or out (that is, brought down from the flies or taken up into them again) in a matter of about five seconds. For the graveyard, I designed a huge Saxon cross which Laurie Upton made for me in hardboard. With this I also had many yards of dark green hessian slashed in a herring-bone fashion to simulate—which it did very effectively—heavy, hanging foliage. True to my tenets, the audience should constantly have new things to catch its eye without them being in any way distractions. As everyone wanted to be in this first production in a professional theatre, I had no shortage of people to walk on as courtiers or soldiers.

The strolling players ought all to be, as they were in Shakespeare's own time, men and boys. However, like most amateurs, I had more women in the company than I could use. I decided, therefore, to make the players a troupe of the *Commedia dell'Arte* who happened to be visiting Denmark: a bit of a stretch of credibility, perhaps, but it enabled me to have at least the Player Queen and the Prologue performed by girls as well as several non-speaking members of the group. They were dressed in brilliant colours and had an orange satin banner suitably inscribed. I was always very fond of using heavy theatrical satin for flags and banners wherever possible as it catches the lights so beautifully and produces such rich, gleaming colours. The entrance of the Players was, therefore, yet another eye-catcher to keep the audience alert in case it was beginning to get tired of listening.

Even more care and hard work went into the rehearsing and the scene-painting than usual and, by the time those matters were in hand, even the timid conservatives had forgotten their misgivings and everyone was very excited.

Prue had become quite an expert fencer and so she directed the final duel. Poor girl! To try to teach me even one short fight is about as heart-breaking a job as anyone could wish to tackle! Perhaps it is because I am an abyssmal dancer but I just never seem to be able to do it more than passably—if that! John Fulcher was my Laertes in Ron Mills's production and he nearly lost an eye on several occasions! Now an actor named Edgar King was playing the part and for him the experience was just as hair-raising—perhaps even literally at times when I 'cut' too high! He had made his first appearance as Alexas in *Antony and Cleopatra* and had gone on to play Captain Gower and the Greek Ajax. He was well-built, good looking and, besides wearing costumes exceptionally well, moved excellently. He became a most devoted member of the company and a tireless worker in various departments. He was one of several young men who joined us round about the same time and who, because they were all good actors and keen company workers, gave the organisation great strength and solidity during the coming decade. Eric Greenwood, Brian Hillier, Douglas Bray, Geoffrey Douglas and Clifford Allen were other names—just names at this point in the story but all, especially the last, to make their mark in various ways in the years ahead.

Old hands filled many of the leading parts. John Fulcher was my Horatio this time, Nora was my mother and Leonard Russell added yet another to his list of kings by playing Claudius; a part for which he was ideally suited as he had the strength and authority to make it quite clear that, murderer or not, he would make an efficient, powerful and ruthless king. Nancy looked decorative as a member of the *Commedia* troupe and Bill Smith was back in padding to give his George Rose performance as the First Gravedigger. Sunya Fulcher played Ophelia and Prue was the Player Queen.

From the poster days of my childhood, I had always been interested in publicity. However, there was something quite new in this line that I enjoyed enormously although nothing could have been further from my ideals. It was the Pier's overall folder telling holidaymakers of the joys in store throughout the summer season. It had a photograph of Tommy Trinder looking through a ship's porthole on the front and Miss Southsea of 1955 wearing a sailor's cap. 'Come aboard, You Lucky People, for a wonderful time', it said. 'You Lucky People' was Tommy Trinder's catch phrase and was the name of the resident summer show in which he would be starring. Inside there were gaily printed advertisements for bathing beauty contests, ballroom dancing, steamer excursions, the pier orchestra on the deck, the cinema organ in the café and—THE SOUTHSEA SHAKESPEARE ACTORS in *HAMLET*. This may not have been how Stratford would have done it but, by Heaven, it was professional!

There was a marvellous feeling of enthusiasm amongst the permanent staff of the Pier, both those involved in the theatre and the rest, and one sensed a great love for the structure itself. If someone wanted to know if another person was on the Pier, he or she would invariably ask if that person was 'on board'. They treated it as if it were a land-locked ship and indeed that is very much how it felt. Edgar King later invented the phrase, 'On board a professional theatre', which neatly summed up its unique atmosphere. A man who appreciated this even more than most was Arthur Goodfellow, the resident stage manager. He immediately became a great friend to us. Always known as 'Buster', he was tall, very muscular and had the round face and rosy apple cheeks of a merry farmer in a children's book.

Moving in and setting the stage was going to be very different from how it had always been at St. Peter's Hall and I was alarmed in case we should look too amateurish when we actually got to it. Hitherto, on the Monday morning the removers' men had collected all the scenery, props, costume skips, lighting and other stage equipment from Crossways, our headquarters over Ron Mills's flat, the attics at the practice and any other address where they were stored. Early in the afternoon, one of the dental technicians from the practice and I would arrive at the hall and spend until about 5.30 or 6 o'clock on our own, unpacking and setting up as much as we could. From then on, the rest of the stage staff—by now consisting of most of the dental technicians—having arrived, they would join in and finish the work. Not only did the scenery have to be set up and the tabs and cloths hung, but also all the lighting equipment had to be installed. I knew exactly where each spotlight or flood was to go and what I wanted it to do but, none the less, the setting of all these took a long time. Quite early in our history we had given up trying to have a dress rehearsal on this day as well. It was bad enough when we began but by now our productions and their trappings had got so much more elaborate that the Monday had to be devoted entirely to technical matters. On Tuesday we had now just the one dress rehearsal.

As we were opening the Pier's season, the theatre was out of use during the few days before our week. The floor had been used for ballroom dancing through the winter and so all the stalls seats were having to be put back. They were comfortable tip-up ones, as in any other theatre, and as all the rows had to be screwed down to the floor, the job was a big one. Our equipment was delivered on the Saturday morning before our opening the following Wednesday. At least this time, I thought, as it will be our first summer production, we shall avoid the terrible weather that has so often hit our first nights. However, when, later that same morning, I took a stroll along the sea front, I saw something very strange that could only be an omen. It was a beautiful May day with bright sunshine sparkling on a gentle sea but, by a freak of the climate, the Pier itself, especially the theatre, was shrouded in an oasis of sea mist. We had brought our own weather with us! On the first night, the rain poured in torrents!

Every member of the cast who could so much as lift a finger was encouraged to come to the Pier on the Sunday morning to unpack and to set the stage. The cry was, '9.25 at the turnstiles, please'; an expression that became a tradition whenever there was a stage to be set, even when we were not on the Pier. We were met at 9.30 by Buster and escorted along the deck and in through the stage door. I was terribly nervous!

It was very exciting to be working in a real theatre and everything was immediately so different from the hall. That had a dank drabness and was utterly lifeless apart from our own activity. Here on the Pier we were aware at once of the almost pulsating bustle of a professional entertainment centre going on all round us. Even as a small child, I had loved its uniquely theatrical smell which was a mixture of scene paint, wood and make-up spiced with the beery fumes from the bar beyond the back of the stage. At St. Peter's Hall, on these occasions, I used to become terribly exhausted. I worked extremely hard at the jobs that only I could do but I also had to give instructions to half a dozen other people, each doing something different and then keep six eyes on them to make sure that what they were working at was being done properly. Now, suddenly all that was over. Buster was in charge and was exceptionally efficent.

He had his professional staff there and all I had to do was to tell him where everything had to go. Our own people were simply assistants to his. The Stage Electrician had their and our lighting equipment in position in no time. Everything was so very much easier than it had ever been before. We broke for coffee in mid-morning and went to the café where it felt marvellous to be on the inside looking out at the public. That night our set was used for the *Palm Court* concert with which the season officially opened and David Evans, now Entertainments Manager for the City as Alex Kinnear had just retired, pointed it out to the full house and recommended the audience to come and see us. I would have guessed that not many of the patrons at a jolly seaside show would have taken his advice and returned to see classical tragedy a few days later. However, one never knows.

On the Monday afternoon, Buster, his electrician and I had a session setting the lights in the correct positions to achieve the effects that I wanted. Again, it was so comparatively easy: the professionals did it all and I only had to say what I wanted. We had two dress rehearsals this time as it was such a special production. Instead of one dreary room with only one mirror, one wash basin and no hot water, for each sex at the hall, we now had six proper dressing rooms with enough chairs—a new luxury—and lights over the mirrors for everyone. When we were making-up and putting on our costumes for the first night, we knew that the front of the house would be ushered by uniformed attendants, people would be going to the bars in the interval and that we were surrounded by the liveliness and activity of a real theatre. The difference in the atmosphere from the hall was far greater than any of us had expected. On the opening night we invited the City Council and various big-wigs such as head teachers. From this time, these official guests became a permanent feature. We did it on the advice of David Evans who thought it would be a good advertisement and help to make something of an occasion of the first night. On the Thursday, we had in our audience a party of eight young Russians who were spending a fortnight as guests of the City's youth organisation. They were the first such visitors to come to Britain from the Soviet Union since before the war and our performance of *Hamlet* was part of their official programme. They came on to the stage afterwards to meet the cast and to be photographed with us. Both sides beamed with *bonhommie* as we did our best to improve Anglo-Soviet relations. As a dentist I could not help but notice how ugly the gun-metal crowns on their teeth were and took some pride in showing my perfect uncrowned English ones as I smiled on being presented with a couple of small medals.

Some of them had a few words of English but most of the conversations were conducted through their leader, a powerful and bossy girl with a square jaw and muscular shoulders, who acted as interpreter. On the Friday night, there was another civic party present: this time, guests of the Lord Mayor. They were delegates from a Youth Employment Officers' conference that was taking place and, again, coming to see us was part of their official programme. Things were certainly looking up and we began to feel rather important.

If I was nervous when we went on to the Pier to set the stage, on the first night I was positively terrified! I was not alone because all of us felt quite sick as we made-up in our spendid dressing rooms, especially each time another novelty happened: the Stage Manager's voice coming through the Tannoy saying such things as, 'This is your half-hour call'. When I made my entrance with the court

Hamlet Pier Theatre, 1956

First Player (Alistair Crowley-Smith) performs for Hamlet (KEG seated on steps). *Others L to R:* Polonius (Charles Biggerstaff), Second Player (David Whiteside), Players (Prue Higham, Mavis Patton and Nancy Glenister), Rosencrantz and Guildenstern (Colin Denyer and Clifford Allen) in the second scene, I was struck by a powerful and almost overwhelming atmosphere of Theatre. Out there, in the great black void beyond the proscenium arch, besides the dazzling miniature suns of the spotlights on the ends of the circle, one could just make out the rows of dim blobs that were faces of people above us as well as in the stalls below. There were also the green Exit signs glowing and adding yet another feature that made this night of intoxication feel a thousand miles away from the church hall. It was not too bad whilst Claudius and the rest were on the stage with me but, when they had gone off and left me alone for my first soliloquy, I was trembling so much that I was afraid it would show. In any case, that speech can be very hazardous: it is all too easy to turn it into a *Perpetuum mobile.* The phrase, 'Within a month . . .' occurs twice and if one is particularly nervous, or not concentrating as hard as one should, it is extraordinarily easy to go back to the lines that follow the first reference after one has spoken the second. If that happens, there is no reason why the speech should ever end! However, once through it, I became so absorbed in this wonderful part that my nervousness subsided to that desirable degree that still keeps an actor on his toes.

Hamlet is said to be Everyman; certainly he is the man who plays him. This is probably why, although the part is very tiring, if only because of its length, it is such an exhilarating one to play. In my experience, no character is easier to perform as if it were oneself expressing one's own feelings. In 'To be or not to be . . .' one has really only to try to produce those lines as if they are being freshly minted in the brain. 'What a piece of work is a man . . .' is another speech that I felt I was speaking as much for myself as I was for Hamlet. The identification was both astounding and total.

In due course, I reached 'O, what a rogue and peasant slave am I!', the most theatrical of all these great soliloquies; it, more than any other, is essentially an acting passage. On and on we went: the Play scene, the Closet and so to the banishment. Back in Wolfit's purple-lined black cloak, which he had lent me once more, I eventually came to the last of the solos, 'How all occasions do inform against me!' This, for me, is always the most moving of them all; perhaps because I lived through a world war and this speech so marvellously epitomises the folly and waste of it all. Certainly the irony and drama of hearing it in the Lyceum on that night only two months before war was declared in 1939 imprinted its awful meaning ineradicably in my mind. After that comes the rest that Shakespeare nearly always provides for his leading actor. Then back into action again for the Graveyard and on through to the wonderful simplicity of the profound, 'If it be now, it is not to come . . .' Two of the most important words in all this vast part are the last ones of that speech, 'Let be'. If they are spoken with deep feeling, resignation and an intensely serious optimism—a big test as there are only two syllables—almost all of Hamlet's, and indeed Shakespeare's, philosophy can be condensed into a moment. I threatened the stage staff with boiling oil and worse if they gave the cue for the trumpets and the opening of the tabs too soon and so cut off those two words. At last we came to the final scene and the duel—which I got away with!—and the end of the play when my body, arms outstretched in a cruciform pattern, was carried up the steps to the rostrum at the back by the four captains whilst all the gorgeous flags were lowered to the ground and impressive chords of Mussorgsky brought down the crimson velvet curtain that I had loved since I had seen it over 30 years before when, as a child, I paid my first visit to any theatre.

All seemed to be well. We had a house of about 400, which was more than the church hall could hold, and clocked up a total of nearly 2,400 by the end of the week. That was almost double the best we had ever achieved before. We had given only four performances, not having dared to risk a matinee, as I had not expected that we should do as well as this. In future there would certainly be matinees and, in fact, before much longer there would be extra nights as well. The press was most helpful. Under a headline of 'Southsea Actors' Splendid "Hamlet" ', was a notice which began, 'Last night, K. Edmonds Gateley gave a tremendous performance as Hamlet. In three hours of brilliant acting he held the rapt attention of a large audience at the South Parade Pier, Southsea'. It went on later with such comments as, 'The sets were excellent and the colour and magnificence of the costumes added lustre to an already polished production by this talented company'. There were one or two minor criticisms but, for the most part, it was paean of praise. It may have been a wild exaggeration to help us on our reaching this important milestone but it was a marvellous advertisement.

The Wolfits, sadly, were unable to come at the last minute because of an unexpected television commitment. However, their telegram giving me the news wished us, 'Tremendous success'.

I was quite sure that when Melita and I had our meeting to arrange this first visit we had also booked the last week of the season for a return in the autumn, although, admittedly it was not mentioned in any of the confirming letters. However, when the Pier's folder of the whole season's attractions came out, I saw that we were not in fact down to appear again that year. I bearded David Evans about it but he denied all knowledge.

The week that we would have had was already booked for a Rotarians' conference and, for it, all the stalls seating would have been removed again. I argued from every possible angle, including suggesting that we would pay to have it put back again for just one week afterwards, but he was adamant. The conference, which was, I have no doubt, a very paying proposition, had been booked and was immovable. That was the only time that David and I ever crossed swords. He was a person who made a devoted ally but could be a formidable enemy. He got very heated at this latest meeting and I feared that perhaps I was burning my boats by being too insistent and not a little angry. I need not have worried: I realised afterwards that he had accepted me as a friend whom he wanted to help and I think now that perhaps his respect for me was actually strengthened by this little battle. In any case, I could not take it too seriously because of something of which he was totally unaware. He was in a dinner jacket but was wearing a clip-on bow tie. One of the clips had come undone and the tie was waving about secured only on one side. No man can retain his dignity, especially as he becomes increasingly agitated, if part of his formal attire is behaving in such an absurd way. The future of the Southsea Shakespeare Actors, whether it progressed at the Pier or retrogressed back to St. Peter's Hall, probably hung on whether or not we remained friends after that night. I have a feeling that it was saved by that one clip that was still doing its duty.

CHAPTER 14
The knell of St. Peter's

As soon as I had made the decision to move to the Pier Theatre, a whole year before we actually opened there, I suddenly felt that everything we had done up to that moment had been only an apprenticeship. For all our pride in our superiority, perhaps it had only been 'church hall amateur dramatics' after all. We were to put on our productions in a professional theatre and I now had no desire ever to set foot in St. Peter's Hall again.

Even so, I realised that we should have to continue there in between our Pier visits. In any case, there had been the three plays that we had put on between the making of the decision and the staging of *Hamlet.* Now that productions were to be bigger and more demanding, it seemed to me that we had better reduce the number each year to three. We could do ones that were good box office 'draws' at the Pier in the spring and the autumn and, in between, one rare play, which would inevitably attract much smaller audiences, at St. Peter's Hall. The discovery that we had not got an autumn booking to follow *Hamlet* was a great disappointment. We should not be able to return to the Pier for a whole year and I felt very frustrated because this meant that the first two plays of the tenth season would have to be back in the church hall. The autumn one at the Pier was to have been *As You Like It* so I decided to delay that until the spring so that it would still be our second play in a real theatre. The season opened at the hall with *Othello* in October and this was followed early in the New Year of 1957 by *Pericles, Prince of Tyre.*

After the vitality and colour of the Pier, the church hall was dispiriting and dreary. *Othello* went well, in no small part due to the quite exceptional performance of the title role by Leonard Russell. Hitherto he had given sound performances as Bolingbroke and much of the nobility but in the Moor he found the part that would remain his special province so long as he chose to play it. I tackled Iago again and Nora repeated her Emilia. Anne Nicolle, our brilliant Juliet of some years before, had now returned to the area and reappeared with us, after too long a gap, as Desdemona. Perhaps things were not so bad at St.

Othello St. Peter's Hall, 1956

Iago (KEG) and Othello (Leonard Russell)

Peter's Hall after all! Whether they were or not, we could hardly wait to get back to our real theatre. What was more, members of our regular audiences were already saying, 'We'll come and see you at the Pier where there are comfortable tip-up seats, a bar and a nice theatre atmosphere but, we are sorry, we can't face St. Peter's Hall any more'. Could anything be done about this? To do only two plays a year would be too few to keep the company united and sufficiently occupied, I thought. In any case, I very much wanted to go on staging the rare plays and I just did not dare to risk them at the Pier. No, there was no alternative: two plays a year at the Pier and one at the hall would have to be the formula.

No avante-garde director, whose Juliet enters on a motorbike into a set constructed of rusty bedsteads hanging upside down in a supermarket and wearing canvas clothes, is ever short of a justification for his excesses. He is usually rebelling against those boring, reactionary productions which suggest that Shakespeare knew what he was talking about. He invariably uses that pretentious cliché, 'I want to make it relevant for our time', and he never lacks supporters amongst the inexperienced. 'One touch of nature', says Ulysses, 'makes the whole world kin'—they will always prefer a bit of glittering new gilt to real gold with a little dust on it. I remember hearing a lecturer talking very loudly after a disgraceful performance of *King John* at a university in the south of England. This sombre, dramatic and intensely serious play had been turned into a pantomine, with the king played as a knockabout clown, by the RSC's touring group then known as Theatre-go-round. This young man praised it to the skies and condemned the great Stratford era of the 1950s, when John Gielgud, Peggy Ashcroft, Laurence Olivier, Tyrone Guthrie, Anthony Quayle and Glen Byam Shaw did much of their greatest work, as 'the bad old days'. He was, I believe, five years old when that decade began and was still a schoolboy of 16 when it ended. So much for his judgement!

The truth behind that sort of nonsense is that, just as a puritanical exterior sometimes conceals a ravening sensualist within, many directors find themselves bursting to outshine both author and cast. The temptation to shock the audience and show off one's own inventiveness is enormous. A Shakespeare play, in all its complexity, is an ideal framework on which to perform one's high jinks—and it has the great advantage that the author is too long dead to be able to complain. Ideally I like my Shakespeare played in the costumes of his own time and in a setting that is at least derived from the Elizabethan theatre but even a purist like myself has a directorial whizz-kid under the skin. It is a consuming desire to commit the eighth Deadly Sin—self-indulgence.

All of which leads me to *Pericles, Prince of Tyre*. I was delighted that I had reached a stage in the company's development when I could risk putting on such a great rarity. On the other hand, I knew that this would draw only the minutest of audiences. I had been dying to attempt a way-out production to display, as I hoped, my own cleverness but my love of Shakespeare had always kept me in check. Here, however, was a text which, although in the second half there is some great Shakespeare, contains much inferior work—the first two acts probably being by someone else. In any case, if a wildly unusual production caused a bit of a local sensation, it might bring the cash customers to the box office in larger numbers than it would otherwise have done. My publicity therefore announced: 'REAL THEATRE-LOVERS will want to see an UNUSUAL PRODUCTION OF A RARE PLAY'.

In spite of everything, I did still want to be true to the spirit of the work and to embroider it to its limits rather than to distort it. I had in the company at that time one of the very, very few amateur actors whom I would ever have backed for a successful career in the professional theatre. He was a master at Portsmouth Grammar School, where he had directed the boys in a most remarkable production of *Coriolanus,* and he had already played Buckingham in *King Henry VIII* and the Ghost of Hamlet's father for us. His name was Trevor Conway and I cast him as Pericles. He had looked forward to playing the part but was appalled when he knew what I was going to do with the play. We discussed it for several hours after I had outlined my production to the cast. We stayed on in the rehearsal room and then went for a long walk in the dark along the sea front. He threatened to give up the part unless I would do a more conventional production but we wrestled mentally and eventually I won. In the event, he gave a beautifully spoken and most moving performance and he very gracefully admitted afterwards that, to his great surprise, the production had worked very well and that he was glad I had stuck to my guns.

The story of the play is essentially a moral lesson and so, when the audience reached our high-vaulted church hall—after coming up the dank, concrete stairs past the dripping and rather smelly lavatories (oh! how we yearned to be back in our splendid, glittering theatre on the Pier!)—they found a school blackboard on a rostrum to the left of the proscenium. Chalked on the board were the words, 'Today's Lesson: the joys(!) of being virtuous'. The play began with the sounding of a school bell and, as the curtain went up, Gower, in the gown, mortarboard and shabby suit of a 'Mr Chips'-type schoolmaster, came forward and took his place on the rostrum. The stage had a bare skycloth with the usual black wings and borders. Three white ropes rose from the stage with three white slats fixed across them near the floor. These were intended to indicate the passage of time: after the interval, during which Marina had grown up, the number of cross-pieces had considerably increased in number.

Gower brought on with him a large volume with the title of the play clearly on the cover. Before he opened it, he blew a cloud of dust off it. This was not just a funny gag; it was intended to suggest what we were about to do with this neglected play. Antiochus and his incestuous daughter (the latter played by Nancy in her Cleopatra vein) entered with an executioner who carried a bloody sack. She looked inside it and sighed: she was already carrying two skulls in her hand. They were the 'fearful objects' to which Pericles refers. When he had returned to Tyre and, ill at ease, complained, 'Here pleasures court mine eyes, and mine eyes shun them', he was leaning on a cabinet with a picture on it that just happened to be in a frame that was recognisably the shape of a television screen.

One of the most successful devices, I believe, was my representation of the starving city of Tarsus. Dionyza and Cleon sat dejectedly on the floor beside a flat on which was painted a structure that was outlined with roofs, turrets, towers and arches. In the centre of it were roughly-shaped rectangular niches housing empty pots and dishes. From behind the flat reached out twelve live human arms; their hands groping and reaching into empty space in vain. This really was most effective from the front but the sight from the wings was quite hilarious. The six actors, whose arms only were visible to the audience, had various parts in the play, mostly in costumes that had sleeves. The half-dressed, half made-up, motley array, jammed out of sight, reaching their bare arms outwards, was a vision of absurdity to be treasured. When Pericles arrived with the corn for which they were all starving, the hands took it in and disappeared.

When Pericles was washed ashore, he emerged from a group of black and white cubical rocks backed by an abstract of curling waves and further cubes. The fishermen had silver fish hanging from necklaces and the grandeur of Simonides' court was simply suggested by four vertical battens of decreasing height, to suggest a perspective, each covered with glittering crumpled gold foil paper. The tournament was in the form of a simple courtly dance. The general costuming throughout, with the exception of Gower, was from our mediaeval wardrobe and for both ship scenes a scarlet sail, caught up in decorative drapes, was slung at an angle without any suggestion of a mast.

I wanted to be in the play but decided to content myself with one of the smallest parts. I played Leonine, the man who fails to murder Marina because pirates arrive just in time to carry her off to the brothel. This establishment was represented by a single red lamp and a sign which read, 'Visit our Messina branch'. This was a topical pun because at that time the papers had been full of accounts of a prostitution scandal involving some men whose name was Messina. These low life scenes have the true Shakespearean ring and went down well with Prue playing the Bawd and giving a nice Rabelaisian performance. She excelled in parts like this, Mistress Quickly and Juliet's Nurse; she would have loved to have been as good at romantic juveniles but she was so much better in these robust character parts and in low comedy.

The great recognition scene between Pericles and Marina, which as a piece of writing is worthy to stand beside much of Shakespeare's more highly esteemed work, was very movingly played by Trevor and Helen Williamson, a very pretty, slightly-built girl who had made her debut with us as Anne Bullen. I used a shimmering lighting effect, hired from Strand Electric, on the vision of Diana but parodied the opening of the final scene in her temple. A new moon hung between two tall candles to suggest an altar and a list of hymn numbers, exactly like the kind that one sees in a modern church, was prominently displayed. The assembled cast, after the scene had opened with English church bells, sang a version of one of the drearier Anglican hymns. Clifford Allen, who played Helicanus, was much involved with his local church and was quite an authority on the worst aspects of the subject. He imitated the inevitable bad, loud singer in every congregation who is just a little ahead of the rest. At the end of the play, schoolmaster Gower joined the cast to speak the Epilogue and then rang his bell to signal the fall of the curtain and the end of the night's lesson in morality. All in all, with the possible exception of the suggestion of a television screen and the final mocking of the aspects of many church services that deserve to be so treated, it turned out to be only quite a mild exercise in avant-gardeism after all. The reason was, of course, that my love of Shakespeare and my ineradicable desire to try to realise the author's intention, proved to be too strong to let me overstep the bounds more than a very little. It played to nearly 750 people, a figure which would have been considered to be rather good only seven or eight years before, and drew Shakespearean performance collectors from London and Stratford who wanted to 'clock up' one more play that they had not by then managed to see.

The spring of 1957 not only brought our return to the Pier but was a landmark in the company's history. 'Completion of Ten Seasons, 1947-57' proclaimed the advertisements for *As You Like It.* It was a great joy to be going back to our

Pericles, Prince of Tyre St. Peter's Hall, 1957

The starving city of Tarsus. The Governor, Cleon (John Usher), and his wife, Dionyza (June Vaughan Sherrin) in despair

bright and lively theatre and the company was at the peak of its achievement; a level it would manage to maintain for at least the next ten years. We had all learned a great deal from working together for so long and the company was now well stocked with remarkably talented amateur players. Some of them had reached their high standard by learning their craft during their time with us, but others, who had already proved their worth elsewhere, were keen to join us because of the high reputation that we now had. I had been professionally trained by Nugent Monck but also more than 30 years of avid theatre-going, including a quarter of a century's devotion to Stratford, had taught me a lot more. My teaching of acting and stagecraft in Norfolk during and just after the war had given me some very useful practice in that field and I like to feel that the level we attained was in some part due to my ability to pass on to the regular members of the SSA, as it was now often known, some of my experience, my imagination and my dreams. We had a party to celebrate the completion of our first decade and during it I was presented with a solid silver cigarette box which had been subscribed to by as many as 62 past and present members of the company. Prue was the person chosen to make the presentation and it was accompanied by an illuminated address done by Leonard Russell who, when he was not being Bolingbroke, Othello or a schoolmaster, was very clever at that sort of thing. The words on it included, '. . . our admiration of your manifold artistry, our respect for your devoted energy, and our affection for being—our Peter'. I was very moved by this as I was also by Wolfit's saying, 'Such a feather in your cap and such a sincere decade of inspiring and unselfish work; we do congratulate you'. It was very nice indeed to have these things said.

In a letter written a year before from the Haymarket Theatre, where he had been appearing in *The Strong are Lonely,* Wolfit had said, 'I am not surprised you did not do so well with *Troilus, Much Ado* and *Henry VIII.* They are all the most difficult box office draws and if you have kept your head above water you are very clever'. Never having thought of myself as any sort of a business man, I was quite pleased to have it pointed out to me that I was not doing too badly on that side of the organisation as well.

Every now and again, a Shakespearean director or a scholar points out something that should always have been obvious but somehow, up till that time, just does not seem to have been noticed. When Glen Byam Shaw directed his wonderful *As You Like It* at Stratford in 1952, he not only had lovely sets by Motley, but he illuminated then, and for me for ever, one of those truths. He set the first part of the play in the winter! Spring and summer only came when love began to blossom and all those previously unheeded references to the 'winter wind', the 'bitter sky', the 'bleak air', the 'icy fang' and shrinking 'with cold' that haunt the first two acts, disappear from the text. My 1952 Forest of Arden had been all in the bright greens of high summer but this time, Oliver's orchard had a stile and a dovecote that sparkled with a film of snow and the court of Duke Frederick was suggested in black and white on two large two-fold screens. The first scenes in the forest were played against a bleak sky broken by a snow-tipped bare tree and a holly bush bearing outsize spiky leaves and clusters of big red berries. My summer forest was very lush and I reused many parts of it in future such scenes. Out of slender tree trunks, made of hardboard and wood, long graceful curving branches of cane, with individual stiffened canvas leaves wired on to them, swept in great arcs in all directions. The idea was based on the Motley sets that I have mentioned and they really did produce a lovely feathery effect. These were made for me by Laurie Upton but I did a lot of the rest of the set myself. I cut out hundreds of leaves of green cloth and tied them into dozens of metres of artificial silk cushion-edging cord. Clusters of these hung together looked like weeping willow. I also greatly increased our stock of hanging dark green hessian that had been cut to hang like heavy foliage. To reach right up out of sight on this larger stage, lengths of five or six metres were needed and I should think that I did at least ten of them. First of all, they had to be cut in long slits of varying lengths and then all the edges had to be further cut in a deep herring-bone fashion so that, when hung upside down, all the small strips so produced would curl backwards like masses of leaves. The result was splendid but my hands were almost bleeding with blisters and my lungs choked with the harsh hessian dust by the time I had finished. This was a very real case of 'suffering for one's art'!

Nancy played Rosalind again. Perhaps, with her long legs in tights and her rather neat doublet and hose, she looked a little too much like the traditional Principal Boy of pantomime. Perhaps, too, she was rather too feminine but she had considerable beauty and a certain sparkling grace. Donald Wolfit, commenting on a photograph of her in the previous production, had said, 'Your Rosalind looks a sweet girl'. I played Jaques, which I found enjoyable, and the Celia was a merry little lady named Mavis Patton. She was one of Nancy's colleagues on the staff of Portsmouth High School and she became known as 'Flo' because no one, least of all Prue, seemed to like her real name! She had helped with the Wardrobe for some time and when, after *Hamlet,* June and Bill Vaughan Sherrin had dropped out of their posts of co-Wardrobe Mistress and Stage Manager respectively, she joined Nancy in June's place. Receipts at the box office were even better than for *Hamlet* and on the last night we had a Lord Mayoral occasion with a party afterwards to mark the actual completion of our first ten years. After five years I had produced the little photographic booklet which I have already mentioned but this time I thought we ought to have a souvenir programme. It was quite a grand affair and was paid for largely by selling advertisement space in it. The main feature was a four page insertion of photographs of previous productions on glossy paper.

I had always hoped that there would be plenty of activities for members of the company between the production periods but few of the events arranged seemed to create much interest. I would have liked them all to have been deeply involved in Shakespearean and theatrical affairs but the only ones that seemed to be at all popular were the purely social ones without any such connections. We tried garden parties in midsummer in the early days but these were not very successful, especially after the organiser of one of them had used a whistle to call order for each game or other activity when it was ready to start.

Arranging these affairs had been yet another job on top of all those that I already had and so, in the summer of 1956, just after *Hamlet,* we had a General Meeting so that we could elect a Members' Sub-committee to take over this side of the SSA's life. One proviso was that I must be a permanent member of it: I was to be a silent observer and the possessor of a possible power of veto in case anything was proposed that I felt was contrary to the proper image of the company. The meetings were always very jolly occasions and it was alleged that I was not usually as dumb as I was supposed to be! A very good start was made and the first year's programme of inter-play activities included two particularly successful and well-attended events. One was a visit from Richard Blore of the famous make-up firm of Leichner, who came to give a talk and demonstration; and the other was a three-and-a-half hour session with Frances Mackenzie from the British Drama League. She gave a session on stage movement and had us all exercising a great many muscles that most of us did not realise we possessed. However, as is so often the way with these things, interest tended to flag somewhat after the first year and once again it became a problem to know which sorts of events the members really did want to support. The actor, Hector Ross, of whom more anon, came to give us a talk and only five people turned up.

The mention of his name brings me to a theatrical event in Portsmouth which not only created quite a stir at the time but did in fact start a trail of events that would revolutionise the whole Portsmouth and Southsea theatre scene during the course of the next two decades and more. The Theatre Royal, which I had so loved ever since I was a child, had come to the end of its sixteen years as a rather shabby cinema in 1948 when the decision had been made to use it again for live performances. Unfortunately it was also decided to redecorate it in a sort of beer colour and light blue instead of the original ivory and gold. (However, the curtain and the draperies of the boxes were very properly red—as they should be in such a theatre). It was not just nostalgia; this really was a most beautiful building in spite of the new colours. The plan was to reopen it as a twice-nightly variety house to replace the bombed Hippodrome which had been nearly opposite. The sailors' music hall, the Coliseum, which had been renamed the Empire, was still going strong less than a quarter of a mile away. Incidentally, it did occasionally have a brief respite from nude revues and stand-up comics. In December, 1956, the performer of a Dickens reading and the compére in a concert that starred the tireless reviver of shows like *The Desert Song,* John Hanson, was none other than myself! A year later, I appeared in a similar concert there; that time with Tudor Evans, who had been in the original production of *Kismet.* These were Sunday evening affairs and I hasten to add that, contrary to the traditions of the house, I did keep my clothes on! It was quite a nice little theatre with only two circles and four little boxes that looked rather like teapots with lids on. However, to return to the Theatre Royal.

By 1956 the decline of variety theatres was more or less complete and just after commemorating its centenary with a visit from Max Miller, the Theatre Royal, where Irving had played and Eva Turner had sung with the Carl Rosa Opera Company, closed its doors. Lovely old theatres all over the country were being pulled down at an alarming rate and so I immediately wrote to the local paper. Across three columns ran the bold headline, ' "Royal" must not be demolished'.

Predictably, my letter began, 'Here is one of the few ancient buildings left in the City, a fine playhouse full of real theatre atmosphere with that essential intimacy . . .' etc, etc. I then went on to point out that some of us had dug deeply into our own pockets to provide the citizens with some culture and that here now was an opportunity for the City Council to start paying for something better than 'tripper pleasures' and follow our example. 'If they will acquire our beautiful and much-loved Theatre Royal and preserve it as a civic theatre, as other lesser cities have done . . .' and so on. I finished by saying that if they would do this they would 'go down to posterity as the Councillors who were not just profit-mongers but men of foresight who gave their City something for its mind as well as its coffers'.

This produced an absolute torrent of letters to the press. What is more it initiated a controversy that would rage for many years to come and which would involve the City Council and the Department of the Environment as well as dozens of passionate people who knew a lot about theatres and an equal number who knew nothing but were just as vociferous. The Portsmouth Evening News gave the matter considerable coverage and the letters represented every possible point of view. Many supported my view intelligently, others wallowed in nostalgia in a way that did not really help, Councillors got touchy about the implication that they were only interested in making profits out of lowbrow catch-pennies, and the eternal irate ratepayers, who always seem to imagine that a city is run on thousands of pounds when in fact they should be thinking in terms of millions, protested at the idea of the City's paying out money for anything as useless and outmoded as a theatre. However, whatever view was expressed, the star name that was bandied about by everyone was mine! 'Mr K. Edmonds Gateley's plan . . .', 'Does Mr Gateley think . . .', 'It's all very well for Mr Gateley to suggest . . .': at once my name became almost synonymous with the Theatre Royal; certainly it did with the desire to save it. What is more, it opened the eyes of the majority of the people to the fact that here was indeed an architectural treasure that they had never really thought about before. I am sure the publicity did the Southsea Shakespeare Actors good though this was certainly not my reason for stirring up such a hornets' nest. If I have ever been altruistic about anything, it is certainly the Theatre Royal. The affair gave me personal publicity and thus the company too because many people thought of the SSA as being so very much my own project; though I doubt if many of them went as far as Dr Louis Marder, the American scholar who now edited the Shakespeare Newsletter in Chicago, who referred to the company in one headline as 'Gateley's Southsea Shakespeare Actors'.

None of this stopped the theatre's closure, of course, but it did prevent its being stealthily bulldozed into rubble overnight. However, it was not closed for long because, in the summer of 1957, shortly after our *As You Like It,* Hector Ross and his wife, June Sylvaine, arrived on the scene to reopen it as as repertory theatre. Needless to say, I rushed in and offered help. I was their first Founder Member and, in no time at all, was elected to be the Chairman of the Theatre Royal Club which was formed, not only to encourage support, but to provide social occasions and Sunday night entertainments in the theatre. One of the members of my committee was Harry Sargeant, Wolfit's old friend from his schooldays and the Business Manager of the Arts Theatre. In spite of the rivalry between the two companies, Harry and I always got on very well. We had a great mutual respect and seemed to be able to stand outside our two societies and view their weaknesses and strengths dispassionately. We were also equally keen to save the Theatre Royal. Amongst the members' occasions that we arranged were visits from Sir St. Vincent Troubridge, one of the Lord Chamberlain's 'readers' (these were still the days of censorship), who gave us a witty and quite brilliant talk about his job, and Rosalinde Fuller, the delightful actress who was then specialising in her one-woman show. There was also a Brains Trust which I chaired. It was good to be involved in a professional theatre and in this one in particular. It was my job to wine and dine people like Sir St. Vincent and his wife before the performances and to be in evidence in the club bar and at the various events. I also enjoyed appearing on the Theatre Royal stage to make speeches of welcome or thanks to these visitors and whenever it was necessary for me to preside in any way as the chairman.

The newly-knighted Donald Wolfit was as interested in our affairs and as keen to help in 1957 as he had been in 1947. 'I am glad to hear of your great activity for the Theatre Royal', he wrote. 'Troubridge is great fun, isn't he? The best informed man on the theatre I know, with a wonderful library—and a great enthusiast'. He went on with several suggestions for the future of the Royal. 'I should say that a non-profit company will ultimately be your' (note the 'your'!) 'best answer to the T.R. It will take time but you mustn't stop Hector Ross thinking he can make a fortune—private enterprise is the best answer after all, if it's possible'. Some while later he wrote, 'I should arrange, if you can, four shows a year on the Pier and leave St. Peter's alone—*unless* the Corporation take on the T.R., which I hope they do, and let you and Sargeant as joint trustees run it for the city. That's what you ought to do if you can'. What a splendid idea that was! Unfortunately, no one else seemed to agree.

Running my company in the way that I did, doing practically everything from painting and designing the scenery to directing and acting in the plays, as well as working full time at the demanding job of being a dental surgeon, just about filled every day already and left me very little time for relaxation or socialising. This extra involvement was really too much and I could not have continued under such pressure for long. As it happened, these early days turned out to be merely the honeymoon and the marriage did not last. I began to feel unhappy about the situation when Hector said that they intended to do a popular Shakespeare play each year for the schools. If they did that, I knew that our life blood would be drained. We were not particularly cheered, either, when he said that he would like the Southsea Shakespeare Actors to play the very small parts and the walk-ons.

Our autumn play, which was at the Pier, was *Romeo and Juliet.* I felt sure it would be popular as it had been such a marvellous draw when we had done it at St. Peter's Hall and I wanted John Fulcher to have a chance of playing the part again. The repertory company at the Theatre Royal chose the same week to do Peter Ustinov's *Romanoff and Juliet.* They said that they did it because they felt it would make an interesting contrast for the public and that it would stimulate them into coming to both. I always doubted the sincerity of that and Wolfit seemed to as well. 'Yes, I think the clash a pity', he said, 'but it is pro. v. amateur. Remember that most pros don't like amateurs'. How true that is and how few amateurs realise it! No expert in any field, naturally enough, has much time for the dilettante. We did not have a particularly good week at the box office although it must be admitted that this was probably partly due to a spell of cold weather and a minor epidemic of 'flu.

Artistically I was, on the whole, well satisfied. John, now aged 25, had continued to mature as an actor and still looked lithe and handsome in a slightly Italianate way. His warm and generous personality came over very strongly on the stage and made him as good a Romeo as one could ever hope for in the amateur theatre. He conveyed the feeling that he really was in love and his final scene had great depth and passion. His Juliet this time was the very pretty, slim girl who had played Marina, Helen Williamson. She fell a little short of John in talent and lacked the great professionalism of Anne Nicolle (then, Martin) who had played the part before. However, she looked ideal and had a very touching fragility about her. I designed both their costumes and Nancy and Flo (née Mavis!) Patton carried them out beautifully. John's was a short scarlet mediaeval tunic with sleeves puffed near the shoulders whilst her's was white with a high waist from which a trail of tiny flowers wound its way round her full skirt in a single spiral to the hem. Prue repeated her Nurse and she, too, had benefited from the experience of several years and many plays. I played the Prince, Bill Smith was an excellent Capulet with Nora as his Lady and Clifford Allen was Friar Laurence. I took the music from Constant Lambert's ballet, *Horoscope*.

Once more I seemed to have settled into a comfortable plan. The Pier suited us ideally but we could go there only twice a year. Never mind; St. Peter's Hall would do well enough for our one rare play in the winter. The Arts Theatre were in much the same situation except that they were doing, I think, two plays each winter at the hall. In this autumn of 1957 they did the comedy *As Long as They're Happy* there and then suddenly it was announced that Mrs Sperring, the Chairman of Portsmouth Theatres Ltd., and one of the Arts Theatre's horde of vice-presidents, had invited them to repeat it at the King's Theatre. The King's Theatre! That large Edwardian No. 1 touring date that had seemed as remote as the San Carlo Opera House in Naples that a fool of a woman had suggested for us many years before! I remembered what happened when they moved into the Pier and we had temporarily shut our eyes and protested that we were snug enough at St. Peter's Hall! This time I was not so ostrich-like: I immediately realised that we would have to follow suit in due course if we were not to lose prestige. I had no idea how it was to be done but suddenly I became certain of something else that I had been tossing over in my mind for most of the year—our next play at St. Peter's Hall would be our last one there. We still had ten of the very rare plays to do to complete the staging of the whole Shakespearean canon. What an achievement it would be if we could accomplish that! Right from the start I had always hoped that I might stage all the plays but it was only round about this time that I was considering it as a real possibility. Now the damned Arts Theatre had started at the King's it looked as if my hopes were futile. If I could not afford to risk these bad box office draws at the Pier, I most certainly could not at the bigger and more expensive King's Theatre. In any case, how would I ever cope with the three parts of *King Henry VI*? How would I manage to stage them even at St. Peter's Hall? I had always realised that these three unknown and, to the general public at that time, thoroughly unattractive plays would probably be the ultimate barrier that would prevent me from staging the whole canon.

On New Year's Eve we had a giant party in the Theatre Royal. There was dancing on the stage to two bands; there was free champagne cup (more cup than champagne!); a treasure hunt, which I enormously enjoyed laying all over the theatre; and various other delights. At first, it all looked absolutely lovely and the tall, ornate drum of an auditorium, with its boxes and three circles, appeared dark and golden again as it had when I was a child. Everyone seemed happy but, as the hours passed, some of the rowdier elements became increasingly alcoholic, late walkers from the turned-out pubs gatecrashed and it all finished in a rather sordid fashion. A few days later, there was a dispute between my committee and the repertory company management over the money we had taken. The result was a parting of the ways between my club committee, which was dissolved, and the professional actors, not without some acrimony. It was all rather a pity but it did at least mean that I was free from this extra burden for which I really had not enough time on top of all that I was already doing.

To fit in with the Pier Theatre's seasons, it seemed that it would be a good idea to run our own within the calendar year in future. Up to this point we had opened in the autumn of one year and closed in the spring of the next. *Romeo and Juliet* was therefore tacked on to the Tenth Season as an additional play and so the Eleventh began in the February of 1958 with our final week at St. Peter's Hall. The play was *The Two Gentlemen of Verona* and, ironically, it was one of the most satisfying productions that I ever staged there. Perhaps it was because there was now no need to show how big and professional we thought we were. Whatever the reason, I did it very simply; it was as if, subconsciously, I was scaling down to the small stage. In a totally black surround, I had a small square flat towards the left. It was pale grey and had on it two Elizabethan ruffs, one black and the other white, to symbolise the two gentlemen of the title. To the right, at first, I had a much larger square flat with a huddle of Verona buildings on it sketched in grey, white and black. This was replaced later by an equally large yellow square with two plain, practical archways in it. This was Milan. Finally, there was a third square with an abstract of entwined, prickly branches in grey and white for the final forest scene. Leonard Russell and I, with Terry Salmond, the Volscian soldier who had gone back for his cloak during my fall in *Coriolanus* years before, played the three noble Outlaws with the accents of retired wartime RAF officers, still then something of a topical joke. Edgar King, who had survived playing Laertes opposite my swordplay as Hamlet, was Valentine and Geoffrey Douglas, one of the many keen and reliable stalwarts of the time, played Proteus. Eric Greenwood and Brian Hillier, both naturally very funny men, were Launce and Speed and the inevitable show-stealer, the dog, was Eric's shaggy Pippin. We even advertised that the cast would include our 'Adorable four-legged star'. Within the bounds of good taste, I have always had sufficently the instincts of a showman to be able to cash-in on anything that will help the publicity. I am sure that too austere a display of intellectual superiority borders on superciliousness and costs money in the form of unsold seats! I am also equally certain that comedy parts must be played by people who have a real sense of humour and who are capable of being witty and amusing in conversation. This is not to say that they should be like W. S. Gilbert's 'funny fellows, comic men and clowns of private life'. Many great comedians are, in fact, very serious, sometimes even solemn, men but they must have the natural gift of humour. I have failed to laugh at too many professional performances, much less amateur ones, by normally unfunny actors who have believed that their technique was all that was necessary to enable them to play comedy, to doubt the truth of this. *The Two Gentlemen of Verona,* gentle, charming and full of pre-echos of enchantments to come in greater and later comedies, needs, I think, only to be played simply and straightforwardly to work beautifully. I believe that most professional directors feel that, because it is so uncomplicated a play, they must 'do something with it' and so, consequently, most productions that I have seen give the impression that a slender vessel is sinking because it has been overloaded. B. Iden Payne, Rosalind Wolfit's father, did a production at Stratford in 1938 that for me has never been equalled. It was very simple and the Launce was the former music hall comedian, Jay Laurier, who amply proved my point about naturally funny men as Shakespeare's clowns.

I spent much of our last night of this play prowling round backstage saying with some relish and not a touch of regret, 'Well, tonight another provincial theatre is closing'. Actually, St. Peter's Hall was not closing by any means; it was

The Two Gentlemen of Verona St. Peter's Hall, 1958

Launce and his dog, Crab (Eric Greenwood and his own dog, Pippin) with Panthino (Kenneth Marchant)

just that we were giving our last performance there and the conceit, to use an Elizabethan word, amused me. Not even the most sentimental and conservative let fall a tear: the chrysalis had shed its skin.

Whilst I was still Chairman of the Theatre Royal Club, I felt that it was my duty to mingle with the members and their guests as often as I could in the club bar. I met a great many people and forgot most of them almost as soon as I had parted from them. However, one evening, in the midst of the noise of conversation, the cigarette smoke and the crush of people in what had been the old Pit bar, I was introduced to a man and his wife who obviously made a deep impression on me because I still remember that meeting so clearly. He had a smiling mouth and a soft, rather sibilant, voice but his eyes seemed to express a different mood. They did not smile but had a penetrating quality which seemed to suggest that there was a seriousness of purpose beneath his otherwise relaxed expression. His wife had great charm in an excitable, actressy sort of way; she had clearly been a very pretty girl and was now a strikingly handsome woman. They were a Commander and Mrs Reginald B. Cooper and I remember that they were extremely interested in all that we were doing at the Theatre Royal. He was a wealthy industrialist and she had indeed been a professional actress. Their interest certainly did not fall on stony ground because, in the space of the next few years, these two were destined to become so influential in the city's theatrical circles that the fates of both the King's and the Theatre Royal, and even, to a certain extent, the Southsea Shakespeare Actors, would rest in their hands.

CHAPTER 15
New homes for old

1958 was the Golden Jubilee of the South Parade Pier and we reopened its theatre after the winter recess with the second play of our own season. Our choice was happy enough for us but no believer in theatrical superstition would have chosen it either to open a season or to mark a celebration. It was *Macbeth!* As it happened, no particular disaster seemed to befall either the Pier or us—at least, not until so long afterwards that I am sure this production can be absolved of any blame.

Charles Green wrote in the Hampshire Telegraph, 'The producer, K. Edmonds Gateley, loves colour . . . with a simple set, symbolic of stone walls and wooded land, brilliantly designed, and lighting that was wonderfully varied in colouring, Mr Gateley lit the sombre tragedy with a romantic glow which deserves, literally, the word colourful. The many-coloured hues of the lighting changed the set magically so that, almost without realising that we were looking at the same set, we were transported in and out of the Castle . . . It was, in a word, an artist's *Macbeth* . . . With a flair that can only be called brilliant, ultra-modern, barbaric-sounding music was used in as exciting a way as the lighting to underline the mood, to heighten a situation . . . In the midst of all the business of selecting and designing, of creating scenic and musical atmosphere and producing the play, Mr Gateley found time to pay attention to making the character of Macbeth grow and develop and bolden in evil. His playing of the central character was authoritative: small, weak, almost timourous at first, not without conscience: later, emboldened by his wife, man changed gradually into monster by ambition and suspicion. Nancy Glenister was Lady Macbeth, magnificent, proud, cruel as the blade of a sword, wicked as Jezebel . . . and then in the sleep-walking scene . . . her hair wild and unkempt over her shoulders, distracted, neurosis-ridden, near mental derangement'.

There were also criticisms and these help to give authenticity to the praise. He found the first scene with the witches too dark and, whilst he liked Clifford Allen's Banquo when he was alive, he thought he was too 'corporeal' as a ghost.

He did not care for the Lady Macduff but he did heap praise on to Bill Smith, back in his Dogberry and Stephano padding, as the Porter and on to Leonard Russell for a 'most moving' Macduff. Eric Greenwood, as good a straight actor as he was a natural comedian, was also something of an authority on make-up—in fact he and his wife, Barbara, ran a theatrical shop called the Stage Door. He played the Sergeant and Charles Green's comments are worth a further quotation. 'With make-believe blood oozing from his eye and down his cheek, Sergeant Greenwood coughed and spluttered out his lines in great agonized gasps. This was no romantically wounded soldier but a terribly mangled one'.

The News critic mentioned that the Lord Mayor of Portsmouth was present at the first performance and at the civic reception that we held in the Circle Bar afterwards to celebrate the opening of the Pier's Golden Jubilee Season. This was not only a nice excuse for a party but, more important, it was good publicity and helped our prestige. 'The Lord Mayor', wrote the critic, 'described Mr Gateley as a perfectionist'! I took that as a compliment though most people seem to regard it as a dirty word.

The fact that we were now doing only three plays a year instead of four or five, as we had done during our first nine years, did not mean that I had any more spare time. The whole structure of the company had become so much more complex, and the bigger productions were needing so much more thought and preparation, that the pressure was, if anything, greater rather than less. However, although I virtually ran every department, by this time I had been persuaded by the Advisory Committee to do a certain amount of delegating. From *Macbeth* onwards, I now had a Personal Assistant for each production. He or she was selected from the Committee and was always a member of the cast of that particular play. The P.A. had nothing to do with the actual directing, or producing as it was still then called, but was a general dog's body to relieve me of some of the tedious, minor jobs and also, usually, to help with the painting of the scenery. My stage management was in the hands of Bryan Tozer, a delightful, breezy tower of strength who had been at school with John Fulcher. His assistants were our four technicians from the laboratory at my dental practice and they made a marvellously relaxed but efficent team.

My partners had by now realised that the theatrical invasion was irresistible and so had docilely accepted that patients would often find themselves meeting pieces of scenery on the stairs and that Prue, the lads in the laboratory and I would be far too concerned with the theatre during the week of a play to give much thought to dentistry. At home, it was much the same. My mother, whose word in the house and garden had always been law, likewise gave in before the lava-flow of scenery and other Shakespearian trappings that seemed more and more to be taking over. Our stage management team of five worked in perfect harmony with Buster and his professional staff at the Pier.

Similarly, the carriers-out of my lighting instructions were so good that I had no worries there either. Our Electrician was Bryan's large, drily witty and impeturbable brother, Charles. They were the sons of a tall and burly police inspector and would themselves have made good natured and impressive policemen! Buster was by no means dwarfed by them and this squad of humorous and extremely competent giants gave me great confidence and relieved me of many worries when I was on the stage trying to act and did not want to have niggling thoughts about the scenery or lights in the back of the mind at the same time. Charles worked with the Pier's electrician as smoothly as Bryan did with Buster. My Sound Operator, working with reel to reel tapes, instead of marked 78 r.p.m. discs, from *Macbeth* onwards, was a calm and gentle soul named Gwynne Jones who was just as efficent as the others. A marvellous team: so much of the success that the company achieved at this period of its history was due to them. Whatever shortcomings there may have been on the acting side, and there will always be some in even the best of amateur companies, at least the staging was extremely professional. That it should appear to be so had always been my aim and I am convinced that if one is going to take the public's money for performances in professional theatres, this aspect of the work is very, very important.

Prior to this time, I had packaged and delivered all the posters and other publicity material myself. Now we had a Publicity Distributor. I still insisted upon designing all the printed matter, because this was something that I particularly enjoyed, but it was a great help to have someone to take it off my hands when once it had arrived from the printers. Geoffrey Douglas, who has been mentioned as one of Verona's *Two Gentlemen,* took on this rather dull chore. He was tall and could easily have been taken for a young Naval officer. This meant that he looked well in parts like Bassanio and Malcolm but, on the other hand, his rather 'Silent Service' reserve restricted him to the more outwardly respectable, unemotional characters. He was one of our most willing helpers on the business and social side of the company. All these delegated areas of activity were, in a sense, self-contained departments within the organisation. Each had its own leader but they all functioned under my overall direction. One of the earliest to be formed, it will be remembered, was the Wardrobe and this was now running very successfully under Nancy Glenister and Flo Patton. They had plenty of helpers, although they seemed to prefer doing most of the work themselves. This was something that I well understood: there were still many jobs that I did not delegate because either I enjoyed doing them or felt that they would only be carried out as I wanted them if I did them myself. Nancy and Flo produced some beautiful costumes and their work of alteration or refurbishing on the existing ones was absolutely first-class. Eric Greenwood's wife, Barbara, arranged the dances that were required in some of the plays and had a particular talent for getting adequate performances out of actors who appeared to have two left feet and no sense of rhythm. This was a department where I was wholly reliant on its leader but, none the less, I controlled even this one because it had to be I who would say how long the dance was to last, what music would be used and what style was required to fit in with the production. At the Wardrobe ladies' request, there was one further post created. It was that of Armourer! They were happy to stitch and cut and sew but they drew the line at fitting what Buster always referred to as the tin men!

Even members of the company used to say to me after a production had ended that it must be nice for me to have some time to rest. I doubt if anyone, even Prue Higham and John Fulcher, who were my closest friends, really knew just how much work I did between the plays. I was always far ahead of myself in that I was doing the preliminary thinking about a production one or even two plays in advance. It usually began with a vague, still picture in my mind of how it would look. The details of the possible set were blurred but the colours in which I saw it were very vivid and positive. Often the finished result would be quite different as further consideration, and various modifications that the action of the play would impose upon it, caused the mental picture to change. I had to get the overall shape and pattern of the play in my mind at a very early stage. As in the execution of a major musical work, I am certain that a basic plan or outline must be found and kept to rigorously. Whatever details would be etched in during the rehearsal period, they must not blur this. If the two needs clash, then it is the detail that must go in the interests of the total form.

Having reached this point, I would then design my set and work it out on my architectural plan of the theatre's stage. How it would be lit was already in my mind but the actual, practical details of this would come later. If I did not already know the play very well, and there were not many that I did not by this period, I would read it again several times. My first work on the text would be to decide what to cut. Unless a Shakespeare play is being performed by top professionals, nearly always it is much too long. Beyond certain limits, the less amateur players have to do, even those of the highest standard, the better they will do it. This stands to reason: they have less to memorise and more time in which to rehearse and so will produce a more expert result. Likewise, the audience at an amateur production, even though they may be watching one of a very superior quality, tires easily. The leading players may, perhaps, be of professional standard, but much of the cast will inevitably fall short: it is impossible to be as gripped throughout a long performance by such a cast as it is by a good professional one. The danger comes when amateurs, a notoriously self-sufficent lot, cannot or will not see this. Although I devoted most of a lifetime to this work, I was always a bit ashamed of being an amateur. Perhaps this was why I was able to keep my eyes widely open all the time to our obvious inadequacies. There are, of course, many lines in Shakespeare which are obscure even to scholars with time to consider them in the study. How, then, can a largely lay audience expect to understand them in the length of time it takes to speak the line? Those passages were my first to go. Nugent Monck used to cut very heavily indeed and so did I in the days when our audiences in the church hall had to sit on hard chairs. In these later years, I tried to reduce the shorter plays, such as the comedies, to about 2,200 lines and the tragedies and histories to about 2,500. On average, I found that round about 900 lines take an hour to play.

For economy reasons, we had complete sets of the plays in the Everyman edition. Some people bought their own copies but the rest borrowed them and handed them back after each play. My sister, Gwen, transferred my cuts to all these 20 or so books: it must have been an extremely boring job but she never complained and it did mean that each actor had his text already prepared when he received his book.

With both the text and the set that I intended to use now fixed, the next thing was to work out the production. As I have said, I was much influenced by the methods of both Komisarjevsky and Nugent Monck in this matter. I had visualised the whole production before I gave my exposition at the first rehearsal and had put it down in minute detail on paper. I have always had a strong sense of the visual effect in the theatre and even when I am acting in a scene on a crowded stage I know exactly what it looks like from the front.

Before getting my production down on to paper, I prepared tiny squares of coloured card for each character and moved them about on my scale plan of the set. I was thus able to plot all the moves of the cast and be sure that, at every moment of the play, the audience would see groupings of characters and visual effects that would not only interpret it but would be pictures worth looking at in their own right. I interleaved an exercise book with pages of the text and recorded all my moves and ideas on little sketched plans and in notes on the blank page opposite the printed words. This all took very many hours and, although I enjoyed thinking out the production, the actual recording of it on paper was very wearisome.

At the beginning of each season, I sent out Membership Forms on which were questionnaires about availability for the plays that I was announcing. No one could be expected to know his or her total commitments for the whole year but, within reason, I had a fair picture of who would be available for the coming production. Sometimes a play would be chosen with a particular actor or actress in mind but usually it was a case of choosing the best and most suitable available. Casting often took a long time as one could not invite everyone at once. If A and B will play X and Y, then I shall cast C as Z. However, if A decides that he is not available after all, then I shall move B up into the part of X and C will have to play Y. Sometimes they were slow in letting me know their decisions and this meant that it took several weeks to get to the casting of the lesser parts. When eventually they were asked, some of these minor members had occasionally assumed that there would not be anything for them after all and had gone off and become involved in something else—even a bigger part with a lesser society. One of the bugbears of the amateur theatre is the fact that most actors prefer to be big fish in little ponds to being little fish in big ones. We tried to combat this by making it a point of honour that we had no stars and that those who played the leads in some plays were equally happy to appear in small parts in others. This worked well up to a point and did help to ensure that some of the minor roles were also strongly cast. Our Othello was content to be the Boatswain in *The Tempest* and my first Juliet was prepared to endure a prickly beard as the Third Witch. The only snag was that those who were only fit for small parts felt that it should also work the other way round. I could not afford to be as egalitarian as all that! Had we been doing it solely for our own amusement, we could, perhaps, have been more democratic. As it was, if we were to take the public's money and time, then we must offer them only the best that we could manage. We should have been short-changing them very badly if we had given them inadequate performances simply because we wanted to be kind to members who, although they themselves would never ever realise it, were pretty bad actors.

Having completed my casting, I then had to prepare a rehearsal list. I divided the play into five groups of scenes, each as nearly as possible the same length. I tried also to restrict each character to as few of them as I could. If, for example, I was able to fit all Rosalind and Celia's scenes into four groups, it would mean that they would have one rehearsal night in five off. The rehearsals consisted of an opening Exposition followed by four cycles of the five groups. After the first two of these, books were forbidden. The cast was not expected to be word perfect but it had to manage without reading from the text. It is impossible to develop a character or to get either the moves or the body movements right if one is still clutching a book. The groups were followed by four nights of complete runs-through of the whole play with incidental music and sound effects. Everyone was exhorted to be free for these last four, very important rehearsals. They usually were but inevitably there were occasions when someone had to miss a night. The rehearsal list was often a terrible headache to work out. If, for example, Othello could not manage any Wednesday or Friday until the week of the whole plays and Desdemona had a commitment every other Tuesday, the situation was almost insoluble if they were both in all five groups. Perhaps Cassio would be away for one of the weekends and might not be back until too late on the Monday. When, at last, this conundrum had been solved, I had to lay the rehearsal programme out, get it duplicated and then post it to all the individual members. Did not the Secretary do this, it may well be asked? The answer is no: I am sure she would willingly have done it but it was easier and quicker, I thought, to do it myself. The total rehearsal period was five weeks; which meant that there were approximately five rehearsals a week. Sometimes there was an extra group for the dance or the fights or whatever special feature needed a separate set of rehearsals.

Well before rehearsals began, two other things had to be done. First of all, any extra pieces of scenery that were required, such as trees specifically designed for that particular set or architectural units of one sort or another, had to be drawn accurately on squared paper and sent to Laurie Upton so that he could make them. The raw powders for the various colours of the scene paint had to be ordered from London together with a sufficent quantity of emulsion medium. My other task at this stage was to make a complete list of all the characters, with details of what I wanted them to wear, for the Wardrobe Mistresses, Nancy and Flo. Sometimes I asked for individual costumes that I knew we already had in stock but the rest were general requests. I knew what types of costumes I wanted and what sorts of colours; these were important, not only for the characters themselves but for the overall colour scheme that I had in mind for the production. The two of them would then look out what they thought might be suitable or else would decide that in certain cases new costumes would have to be made. Shortly after, we had several meetings to discuss these matters and to look at possible materials and designs for the additional ones. The first rehearsal evening was divided into two parts. First of all, for almost an hour, I gave my talk in which I explained my set, gave my account of how I saw the play and said what I hoped we were going to be able to do with it. Afterwards, the Wardrobe girls took over and tried as many of the costumes as they could on the various actors and actresses. In some cases they would be a perfect fit but, in others, our original ideas could be seen to be so wrong that we had to decide then and there either to use something quite different or else to make a new costume for that character as well as those already planned.

We three, fortunately, had a sound knowledge of historical costume. All too often amateurs choose simply what they think would 'look nice' without any relation to period accuracy. They have little idea which items and styles are correct for each social and age group and innocently produce absurdities which any member of the audience who has a grain of knowledge of the subject will find ridiculous. Even a wildly imaginative variation must be derived from correct foundations.

Posters had to be designed and copy sent off to the printers in Stratford. Proofs would be corrected in due course and in the meantime the material for the programme had to be written. Each one contained an essay of some 250 words by me on the subject of the play and in later years there was even a half-page of chatty gossip under the heading of 'SSA News'. More proof checking to be done and more writing when notices were to be sent out to the schools to try to entice them to come to see us. There was also publicity material to be written for the local press to publish in advance and at least a couple of photographs from leading members of the cast to be collected for printing in the paper also. All this could, and perhaps should, have been done by someone else but it was not. I had a duplicated list of some eighty jobs that I worked through each time. To this were added about another twenty which were special to that particular production. These hundred varied from items as lightweight as 'Post: rehearsal lists' to such huge understatements as 'Scenery: painted'. That last job, albeit assisted by my sister, Gwen, and the Personal Assistant—both of them usually only semi-skilled labourers who coped with the base colours and certain very simple details—took up most of the weekend afternoons throughout the whole rehearsal period. It was still done in the drive and garage at Crossways and had to be tackled whatever the weather. The only parts of the set that were done completely under cover were any rostra that had been set up in the headquarters for us to rehearse on. These were painted on the last non-rehearsal evening before we moved into the theatre. One item that I did not include in my list, although I might well have done as it was very time-consuming, was, 'Five full working days of dentistry each week: done'!

My list did, however, cover two more very big aspects of my work for each production. One of them was the sound. First of all, I had to work out a complete column of all the passages of incidental music that I would require, as well as all the fanfares and sound effects. I had to choose a major work from which I would select the first group, usually by far the largest. I did it instinctively: I would think of the play in terms of music and eventually a work would suggest itself to me. Then, on one of the non-rehearsal nights, I would start to select the various bits that I needed and record them on tape in the order in which they would come in the play. The tape then had to be marked where each recording began so that the place could be found again with absolute accuracy. Finally, a copy of the play had to annotated for the Sound Operator to give him all his cues in such detail that each sound would come in on the exact second required. I was very fussy about the precision of the recordings and the whole operation took two or three evenings to complete as there were often as many as thirty to forty sound cues.

In the same way as I could visualise what the groupings would look like, so I was able to plan my lighting with reasonable accuracy. Some alterations were always necessary when my plot was put into operation at the dress rehearsal but usually they were few and minor. I could think the lighting out in the way that a composer can think out his music without actually having to hear it. I knew what lights placed in which positions, and with what colours in them, I would need. I worked out all the various cues to produce the complex effects that I so enjoyed creating. Sometimes there would be sixty or more light changes in the course of a play and every dimmer involved had to be recorded on the cue sheets. Another lengthy and tedious job: the planning was a joy but the paper work a necessary bore.

Our rehearsals lasted from our punctual start at 7.15 until about 9.45. These alone, especially when I was playing a leading part like King Lear or Hamlet as well as directing, were very demanding. How I managed them on top of all that I have already recounted, I do not know now that I look back. Towards the end of the rehearsal period I made lists of the properties and other items of equipment, such as our own special lighting, and the chests of things connected with stage management, that had to packed up for the removers' men when we transferred to the theatre. I also had to make careful schedules for the removers' men themselves as they had to go unsuperintended into most of the places from which they were collecting. We could not be there ourselves to guide them as they did the work at a time of the day when we were all earning our own livings. We could not afford to arrive on the stage on the Sunday morning to do the setting-up only to find that some important item, or for that matter even a trivial one, had not been collected.

After the Saturday night performance, everything had to be packed up again for the return to store. Within an hour of the fall of the curtain, the stage would be piled with stacked scenery, chests (which had been old Army ammunition boxes bought from a surplus store) containing props and equipment, and large theatrical skips full of costumes. The removers' men would then arrive at about 11.30 pm and pack them all into their huge lorry parked outside the front of the Pier. During the following week we had the depressing business of unpacking and stowing everything away again. What had been colourful and exciting when the play had been in preparation, now became as grey and cold as dead things.

Shortly before *Macbeth,* sixteen of us had taken part in a good will exercise with the Arts Theatre. They invited us to visit them and give a play-reading. We prepared a programme of scenes from six plays with the opening Chorus from *King Henry V* to start it off and the Epilogue from *The Tempest* to complete it. It was a pleasant evening and we all worked very hard at liking each other. In their news-sheet published afterwards our visit was politely described as the 'highlight . . . undoubtedly' of the second half of their season of play-readings. Which of us were the Americans and which the Russians, I am not quite sure.

After *Macbeth* we had more serious matters to cope with. We were in two senses homeless! We had now given up St. Peter's Hall and needed a theatre for our winter production. I approached Mrs Sperring, the Managing Director of the King's Theatre, and without any difficulty we arranged a week for our debut to take place there in the following February. The terms were more expensive than the Pier but I was determined to risk it. Henceforth we should have two weeks at the Pier each year and one at the King's. This meant that any hope of staging the rest of the rare plays had now gone. A week of something like *Timon of Athens* at either of these expensive, professional theatres would have spelt bankruptcy for us and would have been greatly disliked by the two managements. Only a few years before, any idea of appearing at the big King's Theatre would have been absolutely laughable and yet, here we were, taking it on without a qualm.

That settled the question of the first of the two new homes that we needed.

The matter of the other was of greater moment. For some reason, the details of which I now forget, the new Rent Act forced us to leave our headquarters in the attic flat which Ron Mills sub-let to us over his own rather grand one. We had to be out by a few weeks after our autumn play. Our needs were almost impossible to satisfy. We wanted several rooms including one that was at least six metres square for the rehearsal room itself.

Our stock of costumes, hats, haberdashery, armour, lighting, stage-management equipment and properties varying in size from huge banners and the witches' cauldron down to golden goblets and bloody napkins, had bred like rabbits and needed more and more space for storage. We must have somewhere really large and preferably in a locality where the noise of rehearsing battle scenes would not disturb the neighbours. Above all, we could afford only a nominal rent. As usual, the local press were most helpful and gave us a lot of free publicity. It was based on the theme, a perfectly valid one, that if we could not find anywhere to go we would probably have to close down. 'Now Rent Act Hits the Bard' said one headline. The popular phrase was, 'Villian Rent Act'. John Fulcher, who being a quantity surveyor knew a good bit about property, and Geoffrey Douglas, who was in the local government offices at that time and therefore had his ear to the most hopeful sort of ground, undertook the search for premises. There was a good response to the publicity and we had a lot of offers. Most of them were quite impossible. They varied from two little back bedrooms in small semi-detached villas to a filthy, derelict and almost inaccessible bakery. One of the most likely, which we very nearly took, was a complete basement of a very sleazy so-called seaside hotel facing Southsea Common. As far as we could see, it was being run single-handed by a shabby, fat old man who was the proprietor. It appeared to be deserted except for one commercial traveller although we visited it during the holiday season. There was a great deal of floor space and he did not want much rent. The great snag was that the ceilings were low but we were used to that as throughout the seven years that we had been in Ron's attic the same problem had existed. It was as well that we did in fact turn it down as during the very weekend that we should have been moving in, the old man was murdered on the floor above. He had his head smashed in with a wash-basin. I have often amused myself since with imagining what might have happened if it had occurred whilst we were rehearsing down below. Would the police have rounded up such eminently respectable ladies as Nancy, Flo and Prue as possible suspects? I still chuckle over the thought of them being bundled into a Black Maria like street-walkers in an American film!

At last, when we were beginning to despair of success, an estate agent put us on to the accommodation that we decided to accept. It was the seventeenth place that we inspected and was far nearer to the ideal than our previous sixteen disheartening experiences had led us to hope for. It consisted of two rooms over a motorcycle shop in Elm Grove, the road in central Southsea where, many years before, Conan Doyle had practised as a doctor. One of the rooms measured about six metres square but the other was, by our standards, blessedly enormous: it was at least ten metres long by six wide. Almost more important than this splendid amount of floor-space was the fact that the ceilings were nearly four metres high. Not only would we have a reasonable amount of room to rehearse horizontally but we should, at last, be able to work vertically. What a luxury to be able to practice our sword fights, or even to wave banners, on the tops of high rostra when we needed to do so. Prior to this we had not even been able to stand upright on them, much less perform anything vigorous. This new height would also be a great benefit with regard to storage: the ceiling could be the limit and it was all more space. John Fulcher, Edgar King, two of the dental-technicians-turned-stage-staff, Cliff Burrows and Brian Coggins, and others of us had formed ourselves into the thriving, but unofficial, extra-mural activity, the Southsea Shakespeare Actors Motor Cycle Club. Needless to say, we all thought that the very location of the new headquarters was a bonus in itself. What better than to be able to gaze at the gleaming new machines in the windows below when arriving for Shakespearean rehearsals? Most of the company thought that we were either frivolous or just inexplicably barbaric! How can you mix culture and motorbikes? Very easily, actually.

Our new landlord, Leslie Kiln, whose father had founded the motorcycle firm, was keen to help us and charged only a very modest rent. Our neighbours, on the other hand, especially his manager who occupied one of the flats that adjoined our new premises, did not really enjoy our presence at all. His complaints, and to a lesser extent those also of the other residents around us, sometimes made life there distinctly uncongenial. We did our best to keep the noise down, of course, but how can a performance which is designed to be heard at the back of a large theatre be rehearsed without disturbing neighbours who are only a wall's or ceiling's thickness away? When all is said and done, the premises were let to us for that particular purpose. Small comfort that was, however, for the victims: I must admit that I should have been equally unhappy if I had been in their shoes. It was, perhaps, fortunate for us that Mr Kiln himself lived just out of earshot!

There was one more play to be rehearsed in the old headquarters before we moved. It was *The Tempest;* a play which, like any of Chekhov's, must have a director who is on its mystical wavelength. I remember the production at Chichester in 1968 when it was performed in a bare white set. It was as explicable and clinical as an experiment carried out in a scientist's laboratory and, because of its insensitivity to the play's mysticism and magic, had a sterile atmosphere which killed it stone dead. I believe that it is not enough to convey that sense of unfathomable mystery, which is the very heart of the play, through the acting alone; it is necessary also to employ the artifice of the theatre to accompany the performance with visual beauty and wonder. This is not to say that it has to be loaded with acres of painted scenery—the mistake I had made in 1950—but the eye should, by more subtle means, see something of what the text implies.

Against the sky-cloth, I set, towards the audience's left, a cluster of rocks on which was a pile of heavy books and, on a pedestal, a celestial globe. (This particular prop had originally been made to give an air of learning to the King of Navarre's park in *Love's Labour's Lost*). This area was Prospero's cell and it was canopied by a battered sail which hung by means of creeper-entwined ropes from a leaning mast that had been saved from the wreck. Elsewhere, voluminous nets were draped from the flies and these, too, had been invaded by strands of foliage. The picture was completed by two gaunt cacti and a giant fern that had been converted from one of the *As You Like It* trees. A screen of hanging branches, made from dark green hessian, slashed into strips and streaked with deep crimson, could be lowered to conceal the cell area and so suggest other parts of the island. It also hid the chess players in the last scene and could, as it were, be removed by magic to reveal them. The play opened with a huge sail and a red lantern swinging violently to and fro on a very dark stage. In front of it were the characters on the ship and at their feet, like waves, were Ariel and two sea creatures swaying backwards and forwards in time with the sail to suggest that they were creating the storm. They had a purely practical purpose as well: they could see the sail whereas the king's company and the sailors could not! This meant that if the latter kept a watchful eye on the Ariel 'waves', they too could sway in time with it and thus produce a rhythmically realistic effect of the ship rolling on an angry sea. I also had one of the sailors swinging on a rope ladder on the same batten as the sail and bravely, at one point, even climbing right up out of sight into the flies! All this was, of course, accompanied by the usual thunder and other storm noises. Unfortunately, I had to bring the curtain down at the end of the scene so that we could clear all this away very quickly before we revealed the island set which was to remain permanent for the rest of the play. Violent music, again Ravel's *Daphnis and Chloe,* bridged the short gap but when I did the play again nine years later, I devised this better and was able to avoid the break.

I again played Prospero, one of my favourite parts, and John Fulcher's wife, Sunya, was Ariel. She was not always easy to cast as she had a slightly plummy voice and, although she moved with the grace of a dancer, had, contradictory as it may seem, a certain gauche quality. Ariel suited her as ideally as Romeo did her husband. I made, as I am sure Shakespeare intended, as big a spectacle as I could of the masque of the goddesses. A local department store had had a big display in which they had used some delightful lifesize papier-maché mermaids. I managed to borrow these in return for an advertisement in the programme, and built up round them a big framework of golden leaves which came down from the flies to form a canopy. Iris and Ceres had two huge golden staves to carry, the one entwined with diaphanous, rainbow draperies and the other with fruits of the harvest. The sudden appearance of Ariel as a harpy after the creatures of the island have tempted the king's company with a banquet was another scene that seemed to work well. By means of an electrical device hired from Strand Electric, I plunged the whole stage into an inferno of red flames and equipped Ariel with large wings of glittering gold.

Once again, we had a very good local 'press'. 'Owes its success not only to some fine acting, but to spectacular stage effects which must surely be the most ambitious attempted by an amateur company in the area', said the Portsmouth Evening News. 'The magical effect of the scene where fairy food is snatched from the shipwrecked victims to be replaced by a flaming cavern', it went on, 'was unforgettable'. The Hampshire Telegraph also praised the 'flaming cavern' but added the 'spectacular shipwreck' and 'the calm sunshine of the enchanted island'.

On the Sunday after the last night, 41 members, friends and relations met in the old headquarters for a picnic lunch. Our last rehearsal there had ended very appropriately with my speaking of Prospero's farewell to his magic island as we came to the end of our final run-through of the play. Now we had other work in hand! With the aid of one estate car and five family saloons we set about the task of clearing out all our wardrobe, props, equipment and other trappings that we had collected over eleven years and transferred them to the new premises. We worked with tremendous vigour for three hours and eventually it was done. At the end we gathered in a tired huddle amongst the new chaos; we were all dirty and it looked very depressing. However, this was only the prelude; there was a great deal to be done before the place would be usable.

Being a quantity surveyor, John Fulcher worked with architects and so had a wide knowledge of their field as well as his own. He undertook the task of planning our new headquarters and produced a scheme that utilised every inch of space in a quite brilliant way. It was decided that the ten-metres-long room was a luxury that we could not afford and, in fact, did not need. The removal of one-third of it would still leave us with a sufficently spacious rehearsal room. A wall was therefore erected to form a third room which was itself sub-divided into a connecting passage, with storage for such items as spears and banner poles overhead and for lighting equipment and bulky standing props alongside, and a room for the Wardrobe. In this latter, gas piping was erected to form four sets of rails on which costumes could be hung, one pair over the other thanks to the remarkable height of the ceiling. This was also equipped with chests of drawers and various shelves for a multitude of boxes, hats and crowns. The other smaller room, the entrance in fact of the premises, was to be the 'Gossip Room' but even this had a section walled off to make a prop store with space over the top for the other large items. When all this was completed, everywhere then had to be attractively decorated. The Gossip Room was mostly grey and white with scarlet doors and the rehearsal room was pale duck-egg blue with one wall only a deep maroon. Set in the middle of this area of dark colour we put a huge photographic blow-up of the Droeshout portrait of Shakespeare from the First Folio.

Before *The Tempest* we launched an appeal for funds to carry out all this work and the public responded magnificently. The list of contributors was headed by the Lord Mayor of Portsmouth and included the heads of schools and colleges, David Evans of the Pier, our own members and many of our regular supporters. The Portsmouth Players sent a donation and several came from members of the Arts Theatre. To our great delight we found that we had sufficent money to do the job really well. John Fulcher did much of it himself but the bulk was done by a professional jobbing builder.

Whilst all this was going on, the repertory company at the Theatre Royal found itself in financial difficulties and the Commander R. B. Cooper whom I had met in the bar there one night, stepped into the breach. The local paper said that he had 'now taken the theatre over, as a private individual, on a long lease'. We did not give the matter very much thought, however, as we were fully occupied with getting our new headquarters ready in time to start rehearsing for our debut at the King's Theatre with *King Richard III* in the following February. I had been through all the usual routine of working out the production, designing the set and casting the parts when I had an unexpected visit to my practice in the middle of an afternoon's surgery from Mrs Sperring, the Chairman and Managing Director of the King's. She was in great distress and told me that there had just been a directors' meeting and that they had decided they could not have us after all on the terms which she and I had arranged. The King's, like the Royal, was in financial straits and would want something of the order of three times the amount of money that we had previously agreed upon. There was now no question about it as far as we were concerned: we just could not think of paying as much as that. Immediate cancellation was the only answer. I was determined not to return to the church hall but Mrs Sperring suggested an alternative: what about the Theatre Royal? This seemed a marvellous idea and so she got in touch with Commander Cooper for us and told him what had happened. He said at once that he would like to help and I went to see him. Unfortunately, he also wanted more than we could afford even though his figure was less than the new one required by the King's. He was very persuasive and had firm ideas about what we should or should not do but, none the less, I knew that I must resist his blandishments. The outcome was that for the first time there would be no winter production and also for the first time there would be only two plays in the year.

During that autumn of 1958, I went for my last stay of the year to Stratford-upon-Avon. One evening, as I stood on the terrace of the theatre during the interval of the play, someone asked me if I had heard that Nugent Monck had just died. No, I had not but if I must hear such sad news, then where better to hear it than there? At such moments one remembers usually the trivial but endearing touches about the life that has ended. I saw, 'in my mind's eye, Horatio', that half wistful, half cynical smile and heard what we at the Maddermarket used to refer to as 'the patter of little feet'. I remembered how, some ten years before, he had completely fooled my mother and my sister a mere hundred metres from where I was then standing. He had been our guest at lunch and was on the point of departing when he discovered that we were going to take the car on a jaunt to Kenilworth. He obviously wanted to join us but I thought that the other two might get bored with him over so long a time and pretended not to notice. He so outrageously out-did Charlie Chaplin walking sadly away into the sunset that my mother and sister begged me to run after him and invite him. I did and of course he accepted. They were really quite moved by his pathos but I had seen it all turned on far too often in Norwich to be taken in. I remembered him as witty and altogether remarkable. I recollected, too, how we at the Maddermarket had often been cynical ourselves and wondered what was so special about him. Since I had left there I had never stopped marvelling at my good fortune that had enabled me to receive his three years' training. The longer I ran my own company, the more I realised my immense debt to him. As I watched the swans on the dark water and looked down the river to the barely-visible spire of the church where Shakespeare's bones lay quietly, the atmosphere was so theatrical and emotional that I felt I wanted to say dramatically to the evening sky, "Thanks for everything, Moncklet'. If I had done so, I am sure that I should have heard the Little Man's voice saying mockingly, 'That was much too stagey'.

An event took place just before Christmas which was as merry as the other had been sad. Some while before, Eric Greenwood had formed a concert party called the Southsea Shakespeare Follies. He was principally abetted by Prue who, deep down, had the soul of a low comedienne in spite of her ladylike education and a 'Naval Officer' background that had more than a little of the Edwardian twilight about it. They gave little shows at our parties and between the matinee and evening performances on a Saturday when we were having our tea and hanging about between the departure of the first audience and the arrival of the second. Now Eric had been really ambitious and had written and produced a pantomime, for the private consumption of our members and friends only, called *The Aladdin Story*. About eighteen of our Shakespearean players were in it and the performance took place in the back room of a pub. Eric, who, as I have said before, is one of the most naturally funny people that I know, had written a script which I thought was delicious fun. It was full of 'in' jokes, of course, and it managed to be satirical without being unkind.

This capacity for the enjoyment of simple fun, the ability to laugh at ourselves and the absence of highbrow stuffiness were all vital ingredients of the company's strength and vitality at this time. However hard and seriously we worked towards our ultimate goal, which was the best possible staging of the plays of Shakespeare, it was all immensely enjoyable. When in the course of time this fire began to die down a little, then the fortunes of the company began to wain as well.

For the present, however, we were on the crest of a wave. By February our new headquarters was ready for an official opening with a party. After our builder had gone, members of the company worked hard to clean up and make the whole place sparkle. The result was a suite of rooms that were brightly lit and fresh with new paint. It was all very exciting and in astounding contrast to the picture we had left behind us on the day that we moved in. Then two depressingly shabby rooms had been piled high with what most people would have regarded as grubby junk—for that is what theatrical equipment looks like when it is out of context. Charles Green, who was one of our guests at the party, quoted me in his next article as having described myself as 'an unpaid labourer' and he went on to mention that 'fair Shakespeare ladies scrubbed and scrubbed and scrubbed'. John Fulcher's design had produced an ideal workshop for our productions.

Apart from our necessary equipment, we had also managed to find space for such things as bookshelves and an exhibition frame which could house collections of photographs of past productions that would be changed from time to time. These had been transferred from the old Gossip Room to the new one but had been repainted and freshened up during the journey. In the Rehearsal Room, the big new blow-up of Shakespeare faced signed portraits of Sir Donald and Lady Wolfit on the opposite wall. All three of them, we felt, smiled benignly down upon us whilst I proposed the toast of the new headquarters when the party was at its height.

Proceeds from the pantomime, and from a repeat performance of it shortly afterwards, helped the funds for this splendid new step. Abanazar must have asked at some point for 'New lamps for old'. We had asked for a new home in exchange for our old one and had got it. The problem yet to be solved, however, was where we should find that other new home that we also needed: a theatre where we could put on our third play each year? We had thought that it was going to be the King's but that had now unexpectedly been snatched away from us. As far as we could see, there was no answer to this problem at all.

CHAPTER 16

Tonight, the comedy; tomorrow, the tragedy

Day after day of dazzling sunshine gave us a sweltering July in 1959. For two very trying weeks of it my sister and I took turns to sit by the open windows of our mother's bedroom waiting for her to die at any hour. With increasing arthritis and a dimming of her lively mind, her health had been failing for some time. Having been a rather forceful personality, these transformations frustrated her and life at home had not been easy for several years. Suddenly she had collapsed and her doctor pronounced that she was dying. However, perhaps because of the warmth of the weather, she rallied and lingered semi-conscious for a further fortnight.

Fortunately, one is usually left with memories of the best of times; the mind conveniently hides away the things it does not want to remember. Our relationship during my younger years had been a splendid one and, although I was strictly brought up, I have no complaints. She introduced me to all my earliest theatre and music and happily encouraged my ever-growing interest in such things. She infected me with her own great love of gardens and fine furniture and, perhaps above all, I cherish the memory of our mutual joy in Stratford over almost a quarter of a century. As early as 1940 we had said, as we strolled one evening in the garden at the back of the theatre there, that if we could we would visit Stratford every year in future. We had started in 1934 and only her having become so infirm made her decide to stop after 1957. Since the war, I had made many visits with various friends, and even alone, but at some point each year I had found time to go up there with my mother. The only years we missed were 1936, which was because the family had other plans, and 1944 when the war was at its climax and I could not get leave from the Army. She was devoted to me but did not over-indulge me either materially or with adulation. She was frequently critical and I always maintained, perhaps with slight exaggeration but certainly some truth, that her comment on every one of my productions was the same. I would get home at night after the performance she had seen and be greeted with, 'Very good, dear; now come and have your supper'. I could echo Antony after the death of Fulvia, 'There's a great spirit gone'.

The first of our two plays that year had been the only one of my productions that my mother had missed seeing. It was *The Merchant of Venice* and it opened the Pier's summer season. Doing that had now become a routine and it suited us very well. As we moved in during the transition from ballroom to theatre, there was no question of our having to squeeze in after the departure of the previous production and this gave us extra time for setting up. We had to do that with our other Pier play, which came at the end of their season each year, but then we always occupied the last week and that had an advantage, too. The later in the year the play was put on, the less chance there was of my finding that actors would not be available because they were still having their summer holidays.

I believe that Shakespeare intended *The Merchant of Venice* to be accepted as a romantic comedy about a man who crosses a villain but is rescued by his friend's wife. It is easy to unearth all sorts of dark corners; to condemn Bassanio as a worthless scrounger and Jessica as a thief, to see Antonio as a rampant homosexual and even to damn the whole play as a disgraceful piece of anti-semitism. That there are foundations for such views, I will not deny but I think they are accidental. I always feel that Shakespeare had reached a stage in his writing career when he found to his delight that he could run off yet another new play with a facility that amazed perhaps even him. I think that the first three acts are just such a piece but that he got carried away with the writing of his villain and that he found he was putting more of his heart and soul into the trial and the final moonlight scene than he had imagined he would need to do when he started with Act I. The result is an uneven play; perhaps his most banal until we reach the Court of Justice when suddenly the Master shows his skill.

My curtain went up in a black-out and then a voice could be heard saying, 'This is the story of Antonio'. Through gauze, the solitary figure of the man appeared in a spotlight and the recorded sound continued, 'And this is Antonio, a merchant of Venice'. The stage was then fully lit up and the gauze disappeared. I framed the sky-cloth with two pillars that had thin strips of gold, silver and dark grey twisted round them. Venice was all sunshine with gondola posts hanging apparently in space but Belmont was always seen at night. There, against the deepest of blues, glowed three poles: one encrusted with glittering gold leaves, one with silver and those on the third were dark grey. At the end of the play the three pairs of lovers came downstage and left Antonio by a group of foliage-hung romantic arches, upstage centre. Music was heard and the lights faded until only he was lit and the rest were in silhouette against the night sky. The gauze then came slowly down and the solitary man, about whom the play had been, was much as the audience had first seen him.

Anne Nicolle brought her striking presence and considerable Webber-Douglas-trained talent to the part of Portia. The Nerissa was Marie Seaborne, previously a professional actress but now making her debut with us. Short, fair and full of sunshine, she was a great acquisition to the company. One night, Anne had one of those hideous moments that every actor or actress dreads! Normally word perfect, she 'dried' in the famous 'Mercy' speech! All our hearts bled for her! Those terribly well-known 'purple passages' are an awesome responsibility. It is the knowledge that every dear old soul in the audience has been waiting for this moment ever since she sat in her seat, and that all the school-kids there know the speech down to the last comma, that makes it so terrifying. Bill Smith forsook his padding to give us a very believable Jew, both in appearance and voice, but his performance was rather more bland than I had tried to get. I tackled Arragon this time and played him as a sad, aged, effete dandy. Whether or not I succeeded, I am not sure; it is a difficult part to make much of without indulging in a lot of irrelevant business. Talking of business: ours was splendid! We broke all previous records by playing to a total of 2,581 people; a far cry from the 549 who had come to our last play at St. Peter's Hall!

Morocco was played by Clifford Allen who had first appeared as Borachio in the 1955 *Much Ado About Nothing*. He was very talented but, like the rest of us, he had his limitations. He was an unromantic, rather dry and spiky actor and some of his 'old men' characterisations were amongst his most successful. His enthusiasm was always enormous and he was destined to become, many years hence, one of the most important personalities in the company's history.

Clifford was one of those people who are so single-minded about the theatre that one often wonders if any slight interest they ever show in any other subject is more than lip service. Off-stage it seemed to us that he was so inclined to dramatise his own situations that he sometimes did himself a disservice.

At that time he was working for the Portsmouth Water Company whose offices were only a stone's throw from the Theatre Royal. He had approached Hector Ross and had soon found himself playing small parts with the repertory company as it was so easy for him to pop across the road at lunchtime to rehearse. Whether it was by art or hap I cannot say, but he had a way of being noticed and whilst appearing at the Theatre Royal in the part of the priest at the beginning of *On the Spot* we were able to use an example of this as publicity. We were rehearsing *The Merchant of Venice* at the time and each night that he was required he was rushed by taxi, in full costume and make-up, from the theatre to our headquarters. On the basis that even little tit-bits like this are valuable in helping to keep the name of the company before the public, we saw that it was reported in the press.

This was the first play to be rehearsed amidst the bright lights and shining paint of our new headquarters and we felt very pleased with ourselves. The local press added to this feeling by saying that if we continued to 'lavish such devoted care' on to our productions, 'Portmuthians will have no need to go to Stratford or London to see good Shakespeare'. This was nice to read providing we did not take it too seriously; I hoped, however, that the paper's readers would! Welcome adulation also came from the Education Committee of the Portsmouth City Council. At their August meeting they expressed their 'warm appreciation of the very high standard of the work of . . .' etc, etc. The Chairman sent me his 'personal congratulations' and also the 'good wishes and best thanks' from his Committee. It was a modest dose of civic recognition which it was very gratifying to have.

Whilst we were rehearsing our autumn production, the one of *King Richard III* which had originally been intended for the King's, Commander Cooper decided to close the Theatre Royal. He transferred the repertory company and his other employees from there to the King's and, according to the Portsmouth Evening News, 'the present manager and staff of the King's Theatre' had 'been given notice'. He was certainly making his mark on the local theatre scene very rapidly. It seemed that Mrs. Sperring and her directors were handing the entire management of the King's over to him, especially in view of the fact that their staff was being given the sack, presumably to make room for his. Once more I became worried for the future of the actual building of the Theatre Royal. Was it again in danger of demolition?

A Shakespeare history, even one as vivid as *King Richard III,* can provide a long and heavy evening if it does not have pace and does not provide an ever-changing picture to interest the eye. Nugent Monck had been almost obsessional about pace. Jokingly he sometimes said, as a performance was beginning, 'Well, we have got their money so let us hurry up and get through it as fast as possible so that we can all go home'. Beneath this quip was his completely serious spur to us to keep the pace going and to beware of letting it drag at any point. I am sure he was absolutely right and, to return to my previous musical analogy, not only must a play have shape in the way that a work of music should, but also it must have a strictly controlled tempo. The great virtue of Shakespearean productions since Granville-Barker and Poel has been the elimination of gaps, as far as possible, between the individual scenes. With a play like *King Richard III,* speed and continuity are essential and so, in my production, props and changable items of scenery either came down from the flies in full view or else were set whilst a smaller scene was being played downstage of black tabs. I had a basic set of grey walls with steps up to a large central platform and further steps up to a higher one behind that. This gave me three levels on which to work.

Amongst my decorative features was a black gauze which hung from the flies and had painted in gold upon it the 'Sun of York'. This not only illustrated the second line of Richard's opening speech but provided somewhere for Margaret to hide behind on her first entrance. She was believably concealed but was, of course, fully visible to the audience. On the death of Edward IV, I invented a symbol of mourning. A bell tolled and the Duchess of York was followed back on to the stage by Dorset bearing a very tall black pole surmounted by black plumes and from which trailed an immensely long streamer of black gauze. It was not an irrelevant effect: it did provide food for the eye but it accented the essence of the scene. Wherever possible there were gold screens or displays of vividly coloured banners and flags. Stage battles are always a problem, especially when one's means are as limited as ours were. If realism is attempted, then one needs all the resources of Stratford: anything less will look embarrassingly amateurish. I did our battles with twelve characters all in our metal armour. Two had banners, one with the White Rose on it and the other with the Red; two had impressive tasselled and fringed flags on great gold poles and the rest were armed with swords. To crashing music and amidst smoke, they went through an elaborate mime of fighting positions intermingled with dramatic arrangements of the flags and banners to try to create the groupings that one sees in battle paintings.

The tents were stylised and consisted of two identical decorative tops from which hung red draperies for Richard and blue ones for Richmond. At the end of the play, Richard died on the central platform and Richmond went above and behind him on to the other. The banner holders stood on either side of him; the rest of the characters were grouped below. Each banner was, when unfurled at this point, seen to be ten meters long. The one with the White Rose on it was red and the other had the colours reversed. As Richmond's accession was proclaimed and the union of the two roses announced, these immensely long banners were criss-crossed over each other down to the front of the stage over the body of Richard. It was one of my most spectacular finales but, again, it illustrated the text at that point and was not just a display for its own sake.

King Richard III Pier Theatre, 1959

KEG as Richard

I played Richard again: one paper thought I was 'magnificent' but the other did not think I was as good as last time. Ah! well! Generally I had a very strong cast with Nancy as Margaret, the new Marie Seaborne as Lady Anne, Prue as the Duchess of York, Len Russell as Buckingham, John Fulcher as Richmond and Clifford Allen as Clarence: all of them on top form. I loved my part, of course: it is one of the richest and most rewarding to tackle. My medical knowledge helped me to know how to stand and in what ways a humped back affects movements. Even professionals sometimes think that it is enough simply to be padded in the right places. It is not; the whole body must behave in a special way when the spine is as distorted as Richard's is supposed to be. I always believe implicitly in the character that I am playing and Richard was no exception. I felt quite hurt, therefore, when people said how evil I was as Richard. I usually manage to work myself into a state of mind in which the character's actions are to me fully justified. I hope that psychoanalists would confirm that this ability possibly saves me from behaving like a Richard or an Iago in real life!

Do I believe in Richard as Shakespeare drew him historically? Very largely, yes. I know all about the White Rose whitewashers and I was not convinced by Josephine Tey's *The Daughter of Time*. It is said that the account of Richard's life by Sir Thomas More (from whom Shakespeare's source, Holinshead, got his information) was untrue Tudor propaganda but, as the great American scholar, Professor Arthur Colby Sprague, (of whom more later) pointed out to me, More was a man so totally honest that he preferred to go to his death rather than give support to something in which he did not believe. More was born five years before Richard's death and must have known many of his contemporaries. Anatomy Professor William Wright's examination in 1933 of the bones of the two children found in the Tower in 1674 is amazingly persuasive—even to the historical fact that one of the princes had toothache when arrested and one of the skeletons has a dental abscess. From evidence of teeth (and now I am on my home ground) those two children had reached the right stages of development to be the ages that the princes were in 1483—the year in which More says that they were murdered; 2 years before Richard's own death. Most convincing of all seem to me to be the memoires of Richard's contemporary, Philippe de Commines, who lived from 9 years before his birth until 24 years after his death. He stated categorically that it was known that Richard had had the princes killed and that Charles VIII would have nothing to do with him because he thought he was 'very cruel and bad'.

In December came a letter from Commander Cooper's General Manager at the King's Theatre asking me if I would consider the SSA's putting on a play there in the following February. By this time, it was too late: I had already hit on an answer to our problem of how and where to include a third play in the season again. After pointing out that the notice was much too short to give me time to prepare a production in the way that we did things ('fresh and original . . . from the bare text') I went on to say that, as the King's had 'let us down badly' a year before, we did not feel inclined to risk them again. I wrote to Harry Sargeant of the Arts Theatre and he agreed that 'it would be foolish for either of us to enter into any engagement with the King's'. They were doing their winter play in the Royal Marine Barracks Theatre.

I had always been fascinated by the idea of repertoire (as opposed to repertory). I loved the Stratford method of doing one play today and a different

The Taming of the Shrew Pier Theatre, 1960

Sly (Eric Greenwood) on his raised bed watches the 'play'. Nathaniel (Chris Bloxsom) and Gregory (Barry Wilkins, on the floor) unsuccessfully attempt to serve Petruchio and Katherina (Leonard Russell and Nancy Glenister). *Far L:* Peter and Philip (James Whitehouse and Alan Butland). *Far R:* Grumio and Curtis (Terry Salmond and Kenneth Marchant)

one tomorrow. How delightful to arrive at the theatre and be able to say, 'Let's see; which part do I make-up for today?' They had a repertoire of half a dozen plays but could we possibly do it with two? It would be tremendously exciting. An actor who had a big part in one play could appear in a small one in the other. If we could do it, we ought probably to rehearse for about 12 weeks: it would be better to extend the period to more than double the usual length as we should be rehearsing both plays at the same time. If it succeeded, this idea would provide answers to our two big problems. Firstly, it would keep us occupied through a reasonable part of the winter months and, secondly, it would mean that the two visits a year to the Pier would be enough after all and so there would no longer be any need for a second theatre. As we opened the Pier season we could simply move in a few days earlier than usual and have a longer run of performances. In the autumn we would return to doing simply our one play as usual. Hey, presto! Problems solved—if it could be done.

Now that the company had settled down to the idea of acting in the Pier Theatre, this idea produced a new stimulus that helped to prevent enthusiasm going off the boil. Everyone seemed very thrilled with the project and the two plays announced for the *1960 Southsea Shakespeare Festival,* to last for seven nights, (no matinees were risked but it was our longest run so far) were *The Taming of the Shrew* and *Titus Andronicus*. The other great advantage of this new plan was that we were back in business as far as presenting the rare plays was concerned. Swings and roundabouts; the week should be economically sound as the very popular comedy would pay for the rare tragedy. There was more fun for me ahead in the designing of new style posters and also throw-away folders giving the day-to-day programme of plays. A basic set of rostra could be permanent for both of them and the lighting would be planned so that no positions of spots or floods had to be altered whichever we were doing.

The rehearsals were as exciting as we had hoped they would be and the whole thing was a great success. We opened on the first Saturday with *The Taming of the Shrew* and repeated it on the following Tuesday, Wednesday and Friday. The dress rehearsal had been on the Friday before and the one for *Titus Andronicus* was on the Sunday morning after our first night. It was a wonderful experience to find ourselves putting on a second play when we had launched the first one only the night before. The tragedy had three performances: Monday, Thursday and Saturday. We played to a new record total: 2,878, of whom over 1,000 came to see *Titus*. The famous Peter Brook production at Stratford, with the Oliviers in it, had opened only five years before and had put this previously ridiculed blood-bath firmly on the map as a considerable play that can be very moving and which contains some magnificent scenes. I played the old warrior himself and John Fulcher scored one of his major successes as the heartless moor, Aaron. The scene where he chops off Titus's hand held the audience in a most flattering utter silence and did, in fact, make some of the squeamish feel sick as we did it so realistically. A concealed bunch of twigs, when hit with the sword, produced the necessary crunching sound of chopping through the bones of the wrist! The basic set had two great monoliths: on one was engraved a live hand pierced with darts and on the other a dead one.

The production that I did of *The Shrew* seemed to work so well that when I came to do it again eight years later I more or less did a carbon copy. More of that anon. Nancy brought both her glamour and the tiger-cat performance that had been so good in her Cleopatra to Katherina and Len Russell was Petruchio,

Titus Andronicus Pier Theatre, 1960

Aaron (John Fulcher) with his and Tamora's baby, keeps her sons, Demetrius and Chiron (Chris Bloxsom and David Lippiett) at bay. (Mavis Masters as the Nurse)

a nice change from his run of kings. I simply walked-on as the Stage Manager of the players who do the play within the play. Anne Nicolle was well employed as a quite dazzling Tamora in the other play.

In the autumn, our one offering was *A Midsummer Night's Dream.* I chose this because I felt sure that it would bring in a lot of money; we might be very much in need of it if the Festival failed. It had broken our records when we first performed it and now it did the same thing again, 3,336 people came! With a little rearrangement and some dark blue and black paint over the bright green leaves, the *As You Like It* forest of cane and canvas trees produced a very pretty effect. I played Bottom but was doubtul if I could manage the bucolic quality needed. 'Of course Bottom is your part', said Wolfit, 'he is just Hamlet in reverse and he is a great part, not just a clown'.

The Fairy Kingdom, with the exception of Oberon, Titania and Puck, often appears to be populated either by the corps-de-ballet from *Les Sylphides* or else nothing but children. I wanted to make mine a reflection of the mortal world and so they were put into translucent Elizabethan doublet and hose or farthingales made of black gauze touched here and there with silver. They thus appeared as odd, pixilated creatures with blue faces who ranged in age from the apparently young to a gnarled duenna and a bent major-domo.

On the last night I indulged in a piece of the most disgraceful amateurism and the sort of thing that I had fought against ruthlessly when I had seen other people do it. In the last scene, I suddenly decided that, as the audience was laughing marvellously at our antics, I would insert some unrehearsed improvisations to spin it out and milk more laughs! I was not funny and I have been deeply ashamed ever since! One night we had a power failure in the middle of the performance. Something had to be done to keep the audience occupied during the enforced blackout, especially as there were a lot of children present who might have panicked or stampeded if they had tried to get out. Eric Greenwood volunteered to go on with Moonshine's lantern and give an impromptu concert of community singing in the dark. This both delighted and distracted the audience for about a quarter of an hour: he brought it off with great skill—an example of the versatility and talent that not only he, but others in the company at that time, had.

My father's estate, which had been held in trust for my mother during her lifetime, had to be divided according to the terms of his will now that she had died. My sister, whose needs were greatest as she was a single woman again, was generously provided for and my brother and I shared the rest. My portion consisted mainly of the property of Crossways. I had known that this was going to happen and I was delighted because I have always loved the house and its garden and looked forward to running my own establishment in my own way without interference. My sister, nearly a generation older than me, could easily have assumed my mother's mantle as she had often done when I was a child. I had already lived, almost too long, tied by ageing and ailing parents and I now wanted to be free. It is often not realised that a bachelor son can be as trapped by a demanding homelife as the more traditional spinster daughter. My sister therefore left Crossways, where she had lived since her divorce, and moved into a flat of her own. It was quite close and so we were able to continue to see a lot of each other and communicate easily in any emergency.

One of the first social occasions in what was now my own house was a party for the Wolfits. This was in the autumn of 1960, just after they had returned

A Midsummer Night's Dream Pier Theatre, 1960

Starveling (Clifford Allen), Snug (Leonard Russell), Snout (Eric Greenwood), Bottom (KEG), Puck (Terry Salmond), Flute (John Pearce) and Quince (Brian Hillier) in one of the sets that included the cane trees and the slashed hessian foliage

from a world tour doing a double-act Shakespeare programme. They brought it to the Portsmouth Guildhall for one performance and the SSA supported them in force. Earlier in the day on which it took place, Rosalind and Donald took me out to lunch at Murray's Restaurant in Southsea where he was presented with the distinguished patrons' autograph book by the head waiter. He took one glance at the page and saw that he would have to sign three-quarters of the way down under Harry Secombe. With a merry smile and a knowing look he said, 'I hope you won't mind if I start a new page and then I can sign at the top!' After the Guildhall performance, he and Rosalind came back to Crossways for a quiet supper in my dining room before joining a large party of our members who were waiting for them in the sitting room. They went on far into the night, holding court as before and delighting everyone with their warmth, their brilliant conversation and their rich personalities.

In January, 1961, came another letter from the King's Theatre again asking us to do a play there. Again I refused and again I pointed out that, in any case, the notice would have been too short. I explained that unlike companies doing modern plays, we did not work from other people's 'Acting Editions' and our wardrobe did not consist just of our own present day clothes. I also went on at some length about how good David Evans and Alex Kinnear had been to us at the Pier and that I did not want to upset them. Now that we had started doing the spring Festivals we could not manage a winter play at the King's as well without dropping one of our Pier bookings—and that we had no intention of doing. The repertory company not having lasted long there, the King's had soon returned to being a No. 1 touring date.

Our 1961 Festival included the first play that we had done for the third time, *Twelfth Night.* We opened, however, with the one that seems to be not only about the rarest but also the most unpopular, *Timon of Athens.* This had only three performances (the first Saturday night and the following Tuesday and Friday) whereas the comedy was given five times. This was an eight-performance run this time as we had a matinee on the second Saturday. Audience figures went on mounting: 3,661 this time. Only 645 of those came to the rare tragedy and this was a marvellous justification of our new policy. We could not possibly have stood a run at either the Pier or the King's of just that one play but by backing it financially with *Twelfth Night* we had managed to stage it without worry.

Clifford Allen, who could make himself like Dickens' Mr Grewgious, 'an angular man', was a perfect casting for Malvolio. Much as I should have liked to try it again, the part obviously fitted him so perfectly that it was to be his for life in the way that Romeo was John Fulcher's and the Nurse was Prue's. Anne Nicolle was a particularly beautiful Viola and the whole production was one stage nearer still to my ideal of this wonderful but elusive comedy. I managed to get some of the Chekhovian melancholy that I had grown more and more to see in this play. My two best comedy actors, as opposed to clowns or even comedians, also gave strength to the cast: Eric Greenwood was Feste and Brian Hillier Sir Andrew. Both were very professionally self-disciplined and they were also both capable of conveying a deep underlying sadness. The sets were Tudor brick, against which thin black branches, with a few yellow leaves clinging to them, framed cut-outs of formalised autumn trees and box hedges in different designs of Elizabethan topiary.

Just as *The Merry Wives of Windsor* is as near a picture as we can get of

Twelfth Night Pier Theatre, 1961

Fabian, Sir Andrew and Sir Toby (Kenneth Marchant, Brian Hillier and John Fulcher) hide whilst Malvolio (Clifford Allen) reads the letter

Shakespeare's Stratford, so *Twelfth Night* is an eye-witness account of life in an Elizabethan country mansion. I hoped that my use of Tudor brick would contribute to the illustration of this: I have always felt that the great house at Compton Wynyates—or perhaps, closer to home, Charlecote—must have been the sort of location that Shakespeare had in mind for Olivia's domain.

I decided not to be in this play at all and spent much of my time at the back of the circle watching my own production. Especially as this was the Pier Theatre, my very first all those years ago, and as the stage looked so small from where I was standing, I felt that I was playing at toy theatres again. There was the stage and there was the scenery that I had drawn and painted. There were the actors moving as I had directed them and speaking as I expected them to. I had never really stopped playing with my toy theatre: here I was still doing it and I was loving it just as much as I had done when I was six.

In the other play, I tackled the very rewarding part of Timon. He has all the heart in an otherwise heartless work and has a wonderful range of passions to express. I see the play very much like the two parts of *Oedipus; Oedipus Rex* is the drama of action and the succeeding *Oedipus at Colonus* a melancholy meditation on what has gone before. The two parts of *Timon of Athens* seem to me to follow the same pattern. I staged it very simply with latticed, gold screens in the first part and a rocky arch against the cyclorama in the second. Wolfit had staged the two *Oedipus* plays at the King's, Hammersmith, several years before and had let us have his costumes for them. Since we had started our own wardrobe there had been a famine of Greco-Roman plays in our programmes but now there was to be an absolute glut of them. *Titus* last year; *Timon* this spring and *Antony and Cleopatra* was lined up for the autumn. At last we had some classical costumes: everything before had had to be either Elizabethan or mediaeval. Hence, it will be remembered, the mediaeval *Troilus and Cressida.*

Although the standard of local press criticism was now on as high a level as we could hope for, there were occasional lapses when mere reporters were sent instead of the usual critics. Invariably they would be youngsters with virtually no knowledge of Shakespeare—possibly even without a taste for the theatre—and so their judgements were valueless. Worse than that, they could sometimes even be harmful because their readers took their nonsense as gospel. As with many of the people in any audience, it would too often be a case of 'He's for a jig or a tale of bawdry, or he sleeps'. Antony and Cleopatra can act their tragic hearts out but it will always be the comic countryman who brings in the figs who will get a round of applause. The difficult *Timon of Athens,* which really does need an expert assessor, had the benefit of the critical opinion of a lass of 17 who had only just started on the paper!

During this Festival, John Fulcher had coupled Sir Toby Belch and Apemantus whilst David Lippiett, a fairly new, keen, romantic actor, had played both Orsino and Flavius. These are just two examples of the possibilities that were available to us and it was a very exciting experience to be able to play such different parts on roughly alternate nights.

Since I had started living alone in my own house, I had been able to develop my social life. Now that I was no longer part of a family circle, I found myself depending to a much greater extent on the support and companionship of my closest friends. Prue Higham and John Fulcher were, in a sense, my new family but I was also very attached to Nancy Glenister. She and I had gone to Italy again after that first trip to Verona in 1954. Accompanied by Flo Patton, we had

Antony and Cleopatra Pier Theatre, 1961

Cleopatra (Nancy Glenister, on the altar, *centre*) and her attendants. *2nd from L:* Charmian (Sunya Fulcher) *2nd from R:* Iras (Mary Hodgkinson)

returned to that city, and then gone on to Florence, a year or so later. Matchmaking gossips had frequently put our names together but by the autumn of 1961, although my bonds with Prue and John were growing even stronger, a chill wind seemed to be stirring between Nancy and myself.

The next play was *Antony and Cleopatra* with the two of us again in the leads. When we had played the parts before we had seemed to have little difficulty in generating the right sort of warmth but this time it was not so easy. Critics are inclined to complain that Shakespeare drew this great play on too vast a canvas. They often imply that this was a fault that he could have avoided. I believe that the absolute reverse is true: he wanted to make it as grand and spacious as he could. The text abounds in tremendous sweeps of magnificence whether it be referring to 'the wide arch of the ranged empire' or to the splendour of Antony's and Cleopatra's way of life. To try to subdue these or to pretend that they are unfortunate excesses that would be better omitted is to deny the very essence of this spectacularly sumptuous play. When Peter Brook directed it at Stratford in 1978, he had, I think, over-intellectualised it to such a degree, and was so anxious that it should not look like *Aida,* that it was as if he had boiled all the flavour out of it. Set against a modest group of frosted glass screens and dressed in a way that contradicted the descriptions that we heard in the text, he reduced it, to my mind, to a provincial affair taking place in an hotel sun lounge at an English spa with everyone clothed in remnants from the local drapers.

Although our means were of necessity limited, I attempted to make my production as magnificent as possible. It was certainly the most spectacular that I ever did. Within a frame of massive granite blocks and against the sky-cloth, I achieved a series of rapidly changed sets by using the Pier Theatre's counterweighted lines system to the full. Some of the scenes in Cleopatra's palace were in a Temple of Knons with a three-metres-high reproduction of the bust of the god that had been found at Karnak and with bowls of smoking incense on tall stands. The dim and smokey picture was lit by mysterious shafts of amber light. In other parts of the play, different Egyptian gods were seen painted as if incised on panels of pale green marble and Cleopatra's Monument was flanked by huge figures copied from the statues in the Temple of Amon at Luxor. Rome was usually represented by a great golden Roman emblem, draped with a voluminous swag of rich purple material, hanging against a black background. Laurie Upton had made us some splendid gold and scarlet Roman armour and Nancy and Flo, although not conveying as much as usual of their delight in what they were doing, created some spectacular costumes. The cast of 27 was very strong with Clifford and Len giving particularly good performances as the cold Octavius and the soldier Enobarbus respectively. Attendance figures dropped to fractionally under 2,000 and because of the feeling of there being something of a rift, the atmosphere throughout the company was not as happy as it had been. Artistically we were still on the crest of our wave but the sea was getting rough!

The plays for the 1962 Festival were *Julius Caesar* and *The Comedy of Errors.* I was a little afraid that the latter would fall flat on its face and be singularly unfunny. 'Don't despise *C. of Errors',* said Wolfit, 'it plays *so* well—*audiences love it*'. At the same time he said, in response to my having complained that *Antony and Cleopatra* had not had such good houses as we had hoped, 'Ever heard of Gadarene swine? Antony *is* unrewarding and so tiring to play—strange that you should find that out in so short a time. Big money loser'.

My production of *The Comedy of Errors* was inspired by, but not copied

The Comedy of Errors Pier Theatre, 1962

Antipholus of Ephesus (Eric Nicolle), held by the First Merchant (Chris Bloxsom) and Balthasar (Peter Blackburn-Stretton), is arrested by the Officers (Leonard Russell and KEG). *Others L to R:* Dromio of Ephesus (Clifford Allen), Adriana, Luciana and the Courtesan (Stella Miller, Mavis Whyte and Nancy Glenister), Dr. Pinch (John Pearce)

from, Komisarjevsky's at Stratford in 1938. The set consisted of a huddle of bright, pastel-coloured houses with such light-hearted touches as the sign of a mermaid over the Courtezan's house and a notice outside the priory which announced that young girls were 'taken in'. We dressed the cast in whatever style the character suggested. For example, the Duke brought to mind the noble peers in *Iolanthe* and so he was costumed like one of them. The jealous wife was seen as a tragedy queen and her sister as a Victorian coquette with pantalettes and a saucily-used sunshade. The Goldsmith was in the modern morning clothes of a gentleman of Hatton Garden whilst Len and I appeared as twin (yes, making the pairs up to three!) pantomime policemen. Nancy looked very glamorous as the Courtezan in fishnet tights and a flame-coloured skirt tucked into her waistband on one side to show her very shapely leg. When Dromio of Syracuse had prepared for setting sail with his master, he donned an admiral's cocked hat and entered with a lifebelt bearing the words, 'South Parade Pier Southsea'. There was much new business to be invented, of course, and this included having a sit-down strike by the cast when Aegeon announced that he had *bought* the babies who grew up to become the Dromios. A banner appeared as from nowhere with a symbol on it designed to look very like the Nuclear Disarmament one (very much in the news at that time) and bearing the words, 'Ban Baby Buying'. Another device, which was not done solely for fun, was that if any late-comers walked in, the comic policemen would blow their whistles and the whole cast would stop the play and watch them into their seats. Prue and Geoffrey Douglas stood by to act as stand-in latecomers if there were not any real ones. I used Wolf-Ferrari's wittiest and gayest music and Charles Green commented, 'Mr Gateley has an unerring ear for just the exact music for the mood of a play'. He thought the whole affair was 'glorious' whilst the other paper said that 'Once again' we had 'proved that amateur stage can still be among the tops in entertainment'.

Knowing how awful most amateur stage crowds are, I planned to do *Julius Caesar* entirely in a series of formal patterns of grouped characters. At times the crowd would be in a triangular formation and at others in either a perfect semicircle or in diagonal lines. I played Caesar and worked out a dramatic fall when I was killed that strained the hernia that I already knew that I had. I staged the first part of the play in a receding avenue of statues that formed a perspective leading to a giant one of Caesar in the centre background. In the second half, I used a similar idea but this time it was done with stylised leafless trees that each looked like the stretched tentacles of an inverted octopus. The tent was shown in outline and was made up of two diverging poles, a decorative top and graceful swags of material.

I think the performances were strong and effective but the whole production was a most unhappy affair as far as the cast was concerned. John Fulcher, who was playing Mark Antony, fell and broke his wrist about a week before we opened and had to have his costumes cunningly draped to hide the plaster cast on his arm. The atmosphere of dissention, which had been growing since the previous autumn, was now very strong and it infected the whole of my crowd. This made them seem to be disagreeable and unco-operative and resulted in my becoming irritable and aggressive. We had designed some additional Roman costumes that were variations on authentic ones, both in colour and line, so that the cast would not look, as it too often does in this play, as if it is cooling off after a sauna. The togas of these kept slipping off the shoulders with the result that several of the actors became angry and temperamental at the dress rehearsal. Nancy and Flo retaliated by blaming the wearers for their inadequacy rather than themselves as the makers. I had been sure that we would have large school audiences but this time they kept away and the houses were comparitively poor. Nancy and I had become distinctly antagonistic and I was in a highly emotional state. I was upset by the bad atmosphere in the company and worried by the thin box office takings. They were not, in fact, too bad—2,784 came to the whole Festival, a figure which had been beyond our dreams only a few years before—but I had become intoxicated by the rocketing numbers of the recent years and these showed a set-back. The match was finally put to the touch-paper when I asked Nancy during the practically empty matinee of *Julius Caesar* on the last Saturday if her school had sent its usual large party. She said that they had not; they had gone instead that very afternoon, in the charge of one of her closest friends, to see the same play at the Old Vic in London.

I exploded with such anger that I hardly knew how to get through the rest of the two performances. Even the press notice had been headed, 'Small audience sees remarkable "Caesar" ' and each night I had made a whining speech pleading for support, especially from the schools. On this last night, (and hindsight shows how ironical it was that it was *The Comedy of Errors*!) I made a bitter speech and told the audience what her school (without mentioning its name) had done. She was, of course, standing in the line behind me throughout it and her headmistress was in the stalls. I was distraught, savagely angry and deeply disillusioned but, none the less, I knew the very moment that I had done it that I had probably never in my life made a greater mistake. The effect was electrifying! Nancy immediately came to my dressing room in a towering fury, as well she might be, poured out her feelings and, of course, instantly resigned from the company. The packing-up and the striking of the scenery that followed was agony: no-one knew what to say to anyone and the atmosphere was hideous. I felt almost suicidal and no one seemed to be capable of speaking to me naturally: it was as if I were white hot and they dared not touch me in case they got burned. I knew at once that the company was rent in two. All the teachers in it, and there were many, sided with her and felt that schools in general had come under attack. The total destruction of the company was a very real possibility. One of the members who had been in the company longest, himself a teacher, came round to my house the next day with his letter of resignation. I told him that I did not think that this was the sort of stuff that old friendships were made of and he soon tore it up. Prue said with heart-warming strength, 'I think you were wrong—but I will support you to the death'. John Fulcher and Clifford Allen both immediately said much the same thing and affirmed their total support of me and their determination that the company should not be weakened. Melita Moon sent me a deeply felt and very understanding letter in which she said that she, too, tended to over-react in similar circumstances and that she probably knew better than most what had been going on inside me. My strongest allies were making no bones about their support of me and other stalwarts soon made it clear that their allegiance, too, was undimmed. Another boost came when Flo, Nancy's closest friend and fellow wardrobe mistress, told me that she would continue alone in that department. Although I had not asked for money in my curtain-call appeals, a remarkable number of people sent cash because I had said that we were 'in the red'. My fear that schools and educational bodies generally might, as a result of this upheaval, break off all connections with us and thus perhaps lead to our ruin, was dispelled by the fact that the first of these donations to reach me came from Stanley Hall, the head of the City's Education Department.

We would survive.

CHAPTER 17
Shakespeare 400

Some months before the troubles of the 1962 Festival, a rather more benign schism had occurred. Len and Clifford had telephoned me one evening to say that they were planning to form a new company that would run in conjunction with the SSA. They promised me right from the start that it would not clash in any way with our Shakespearean activities. It was to be known as the Arena Players and it was hoped that it would correspond to the SSA in the way that the RSC's London productions related to their main work at Stratford. The intention was to stage arena productions of modern plays starting with John Osborne's *Epitaph for George Dillon.* I gave them my blessing and soon began to refer to them as 'The Aldwych Branch' after the London theatre that the RSC used prior to the opening of their new one in the Barbican.

In my heart I had considerable misgivings. Even though their productions would not interfere with my own, what if people started to say that they would not be available for mine because, if they could manage only one in a certain period, they had chosen to do an Arena play instead of a Shakespeare? I was already finding it difficult again to get big enough and strong enough casts. *Antony and Cleopatra* had been a great problem and my crowd in *Julius Caesar,* as I have already said, was not exactly bubbling over with joy and enthusiasm. I knew, too, that human nature being what it is, if they scored a particular success, their high principles about not clashing with the SSA could all too soon evaporate. Amateurs have poor heads for the intoxication of adulation! For the present, at any rate, all was well. Arena productions had suddenly become fashionable, especially as this was the year of the opening of the Chichester Festival Theatre. Like teenagers discovering sex and thinking they have invented it, these new exponents of open staging, both amateur and professional, seemed to give the impression that they thought they were the first in the field. When all is said and done, it is a form of theatre that goes back 2,000 years, and I could not help smiling wryly when I remembered the considerable amount of arena work that Jack Mitchley and I had done in King's Lynn and elsewhere as long as 14 years earlier.

When we gathered for the autumn production after the cataclysm of the spring, we all seemed to be chastened. There was a new spirit abroad: a fresh and bracing air had blown away the previous tensions and divisions. The play was the one that for me is the greatest of them all, *King Lear*. I staged it this time in an abstract set that suggested a ravine of dark green, jagged rocks. Stella Miller, a girl with the serious face of tragedy, even though off the stage she had a good sense of fun, played Goneril and Prue, with an edge usually unsuspected in one so naturally warm of nature, was first rate as Regan. David Lippiett, an obvious romantic lead who had shown in that most touching of parts, Flavius in *Timon of Athens,* that he was an actor worthy of more than that, proved to be an excellent Edgar. Clifford gave one of his very finest performances as Gloucester and the scenes that he and I had together were a joy to play; they were duets in perfect harmony. I had always imagined that Lear would become my favourite part and this second attempt only confirmed my devotion to it. We had been extravagantly praised by the press in 1954 but now the Evening News headline read, 'Triumphant Lear Even Better'. Charles Green went so far as to say, 'Lear is one of his finest portrayals—indeed of the whole production, one member of the audience said afterwards, "I don't see how the play could possibly be done better". I agreed with her'. It is easy to be bowled over by this sort of thing but I kept reminding myself that, however well I might have done, my amateur performance, even at its best, could be only a pale shadow compared with the towering professional Lears at that time—Wolfit, Gielgud, Redgrave and Olivier. Such heady praise had to be taken with care!

I had been worried for some time that the schools' support was so very fickle. Several of them were most faithful and came to everything that we did and they were the salt of our earth but others did not come even to the most popular ones unless they were working in that particular term on the play that we were doing. One would have thought that all of the few really top favourites would have been virtually obligatory as part of general education. If we did happen to be putting on a play that was in the curriculum of many schools at the same time, then we would be besieged by teachers, all too many of whom would be bossy and dictatorial. They must have the best seats and all sorts of privileges including booking arrangements being as they wanted them and not as they were. That particular play, they seemed to think, was obviously being staged solely for them and the general public, our main and regular supporters, were hardly to be considered. The sort of outrageous attitude that we sometimes had to battle against can be demonstrated by what one headmistress said at a head-teachers' meeting. 'I propose that the productions of the Southsea Shakespeare Actors should be *boycotted*' (yes, she actually used that word!) 'as I cannot get my girls off the beach after the performances!' Every year I asked the schools which plays they would like us to include in the season's programme and I was usually lucky if I got as many as a dozen replies to over 100 letters. Often requests came for the play that we had just done and every year *The Merchant of Venice* and *Macbeth* were the most wanted. We did all we could do to be co-operative but, with the exception of our faithful few schools, we often found our efforts were blunted against magisterial attitudes or sheer indifference.

Because of this unsatisfactory situation, a meeting between members of the Education Committee and myself was called at the Portsmouth Guildhall to thrash the matter out. It was chaired by a Lord Mayor who confessed that he was not interested in Shakespeare and who shortly after disappeared from the area following stories about him in the News of the World. The only two people who spoke any sense were Stanley Hall, the Chief Education Officer and a great personal supporter of ours, and a vigorous City Councillor named Mrs. Mack. The rest were either woolly-headed or else self-righteous and pompous. After idiot remarks like, 'People will say, "Who is this Mr Gateley to tell schools which play they are to see?" ' from one of the latter, I felt like saying, 'Don't bother; this is just a waste of time'. However, in the end it was decided that the Corporation would buy 1,000 seats for one play a year and sell them to their own schools. If they did not dispose of them all, then the loss would be theirs, not ours. This was, in effect, a subsidy at last. The choice of play was still to be our own as it was quite obvious, even to the dimmer ones there, that we could not keep doing the same two favourites every year and that there were other considerations to be gone into besides the needs of the schools. As it happened, when the new scheme came into action, they often did not sell all of their 1,000 tickets but, rather than be unfair to those who had already paid, they threw the unused, but paid-for, tickets into the waste-paper basket. Personally, I always thought that such an action was a great deal more unfair to the several hundred children who might have enjoyed a free night at the theatre but who were robbed of the opportunity by this supposedly egalitarian policy.

The whole business of the subsidy and our need for cash created quite a stir. Somewhat surprisingly, the BBC gave it nationwide coverage by reporting it in their main radio news. We were even described as being 'one of the most celebrated amateur companies in the country'. The Hampshire Telegraph gave us a very flattering banner headline, no less than five columns wide, which read, 'We don't want to lose the Gateley Shakespeareans'. It was all very useful free advertisement.

The 1963 Southsea Shakespeare Festival opened with *King Henry IV, Part II.* Whoever was the Lord Mayor of Portsmouth at the time now regularly came to our first nights. This time, however, he brought with him Brigadier-General Hartono, Commandant of the Indonesian Marine Corps, and his entourage. It was not that they, as far as I know, were notable Shakespearean scholars, but it does indicate that by then we were considered to be of sufficient significance to be used for a local State Occasion. Whilst I was being sociable with these prestigious customers afterwards, David Evans whispered to me, 'If everything goes according to plan, you'll be putting on your plays in the Theatre Royal this time next year'. This prospect filled me with great delight, of course. The Portsmouth Corporation were, he told me, negotiating to buy it as a civic theatre. Alas, the discussions broke down not long after and so 15 and more years of acrimonious wrangling over its future started their weary course.

The general opinion is that *Part I* is the better of the two *King Henry IV* plays. Not so for me. The autumnal quality of *Part II,* with its atmosphere of decay is, to my mind, so much richer and more interesting than the vigour and drive of the first half. I love *Part I,* of course; the Falstaff of that play is an incomparable creation but he does not *move* me as much as he does in his decline in the second piece. I am at a disadvantage, too, I suppose, because I do so dislike Hotspur. His red-blooded ebullience may be attractive at a distance but how utterly I detest people like him in real life—and Shakespeare invests him too realistically with flesh and bone for my comfort. He is the intolerant, arrogant, hard-drinking, philistine hearty that I met so often in the Army and who can be found in clubs and pubs anywhere throwing his weight about. In *Part II,* Hal undergoing his transformation into the model king is, for me, infinitely more fascinating than the earlier wastrel and, above all, there are those marvellous scenes in the Gloucestershire countryside with Justice Shallow and his cousin, Silence. To me they are amongst the most lovable passages in the whole canon. Do any scenes in the first part catch the throat in the way that the duologue between the new king and the Lord Chief Justice does in *Part II* or is there anything in it as disturbing or moving as the final rejection of Falstaff?

The production was my most Brechtian up to that point. It was directed as if it were being played on an open platform stage; the set being a simple central platform backed by a semicircle of arches of rough-hewn timbers—Gothic ones on the right to suggest the court and those on the left representing the tavern, the streets or rustic Gloucestershire. When the audience came in, the front curtain was already up and in the middle of the set were two collections of symbolic objects spotlit on wooden stools. Those on the Gothic side were various pieces of royal regalia and the others were tavern chattles. I was being much influenced by the new Chichester theatre with its open stage and also by the similar methods which were current at Stratford-upon-Avon in what had been renamed the Royal Shakespeare Theatre two years before. I cut the opening scene with its account of the aftermath of the Battle of Shrewsbury as it is only relevant if one has seen *Part I* at the previous performance.

We had the best Falstaff of my entire time as Director; a man who physically was already part of the way there. He was a major in the Royal Marines with a full, rather red face and a plumpness which meant that he did not need as much padding as some actors might have done! His name was Ben Keen and he was a splendid actor who was greatly helped in the playing of this part by his having the natural military heartiness of the almost traditional stage senior officer. Prue continued her masterly study of Mistress Quickly and Clifford Allen, with a thin and slightly upturned nose, gave a quite brilliant performance as Shallow. Being a rather earnest person, his occasional attempts at comedy were usually not very successful but this type of thing, where the humour emerges from the creation of a character rather than the putting over of funny lines or situations, he did remarkably well.

Len Russell was, of course, the king once more—thus completing his overall portrait from the first appearance in *King Richard II* to the death—and John Fulcher made a strong and virile Hal who was believable as the future Henry V. I, having enjoyed being Cardinal Campeius seven years before, played another nasty churchman, the Archbishop of York.

The other play in the Festival was our second one to be done for the third time, *Much Ado About Nothing*. I cast myself in the part that I had played as long before as fourteen years, Benedick. The confirmed bachelor is reasonably mature and so I was not pretending that I could still get away with juveniles! David Lippiett was Claudio and looked a good deal younger than I did even though with careful make-up and a very handsome dark, wavy wig I believe that I made a reasonably dashing figure. I suffered a good deal of leg-pulling from the older members of the company—I had by now achieved a status which made the younger ones a bit afraid to risk tweaking the lion's tail—but a good wig does help. I kept looking in the dressing room mirror and telling myself, to the hilarious disgust of everyone within earshot, that I looked a hell of a dog! This was not vanity; it was simply applying one of Stanislavsky's methods. It does not

King Henry IV, Part II Pier Theatre, 1963

Prince Hal (John Fulcher) tries on the crown whilst his father, Henry IV (Leonard Russell), sleeps

always work: I have seen others try it and fail dismally even though their egos probably told them otherwise! I hope mine told the truth!

No play of Shakespeare's shows the various levels of society more clearly than *Much Ado About Nothing*. This polished comedy of the High Renaissance so often suffers nowadays because it has become popular to downgrade all the characters socially. There are four distinct levels and one loses much of the play's essence if one pretends that, in a twentieth-century sort of way, they do not really exist. First of all there are the Nobility who do not work but who have arrived to take a holiday in a household of the Gentry. These latter perform ladylike and gentlemanly occupations and mingle freely with the Margarets and Borachios who are on a lower social level still. They need to be employed but are not low-life servants. They would probably have been impoverished, youngest members of middle class families. (It should be remembered that Maria in *Twelfth Night* 'can write very like my lady'). Lowest of all are the bumbling burghers, mostly illiterate (though it must also be remembered that Hugh Oatcake and George Seacoal can both write and read) who form the Constable and his Watch.

This production was romantically lush with giant flower sprays on pillars of white gauze for the garden and a wedding procession for Claudio and Hero moving slowly round under a canopy of golden leaves to the accompaniment of gentle organ music. The Watch scenes came off particularly well with Eric Greenwood and Brian Hillier as Dogberry and Verges and a collection of watchmen that included Douglas Bray, a large actor who would attempt Falstaff himself in due course, and Barry Wilkins, a very small one who was destined eventually for Puck. Audiences for the whole Festival clocked up 3,240 which was a considerable improvement on the previous year even though it did include several hundred tickets that the Education Committee had bought but thrown away. In a city with a population of about 200,000, it seemed pretty feeble not to be able to find 1,000 children to use the tickets that the ratepayers had already paid for. In the days of the Portsmouth Teachers' Dramatic Society, which our company seemed to have killed off, several thousand children were taken to each of their Shakespeare productions. Was that solely because they did some of their performances during school hours? I think not. However, we did not have to rely solely on these particular schools: there were also all the various independent ones in the city and a remarkably large area outside, as well as the many state schools under the county authority.

After the 1962 Festival, when I began to panic over our financial losses and moaned about what I saw as a falling-off of support, I had some very sound words again from Donald Wolfit. 'If I may venture', he said, 'do remember that amateur or professional you are the servant of the public and must always play to as many as care to come. Nothing is certain in the theatre and from the public aspect your losses are not their concern as you have no salary list and do it for artistic pleasure and recreation for all. Perhaps a tactful letter to the press may regain you the friends you feel you have lost. Console yourself by reading *Troilus and Cressida* with its bitter advice . . . I went to Cardiff last Saturday—the capital of Wales has NO theatre at all—all are closed. Imagine you were a professional and think upon that!' I am glad to say, by the way, that his remarks about Cardiff did not remain true for long but at the time they made their point very strongly. A few months before, my old friend from my Guy's days and now a very distinguished specialist in actors' and singers' throats,

Norman Punt, had heard a recording of a curtain speech that I had made after one of the performances of *King Lear*. In it, I went on at some length about how much deep satisfaction the play had given us to do. 'What you all feel about it', he said, 'is of no interest to the audience at all. They only care whether or not they themselves have enjoyed it'. I suddenly realised how right both he and Donald were. It is a bore and an impertinence to pour out one's own feelings to an audience; we are their servants if they have paid good money to come and see us and we must accept that they have the right to choose whether they will do so or not. As far as they are concerned, there is no 'ought' about it. If what we have to offer does not attract them, we must not blame them: it is up to us to make our wares more enticing.

For some time I had been thinking about 1964 which would be the quatercentenary of the birth of Shakespeare. We must make it a year of celebrations, but how does a Shakespearean company do something special other than by doing what it always does—stage the plays of Shakespeare? Whatever risks I took, I must have one certain financial backer. I asked the Education Committee early in 1963 what play the schools would most like in the following May. The answer was the usual top favourite, *The Merchant of Venice,* and so I agreed at once with them that a new production of it would be in our Quatercentenary Festival. On the back of the programme in the autumn of 1963 I announced that we were already making plans for the great year and that this play would definitely be part of them.

The autumn brought back *Othello* as I particularly wanted Len Russell's fine performance of the title role to be seen in a real theatre. I was anxious to play Iago for the third time, too. The play's chief problem arises because black men were a great rarity in England in Shakespeare's time and he seems to have been somewhat confused. Moors are by no means black and yet the very darkness of Othello's skin is constantly stressed. The African negro does not, to my mind, appear to be the answer as his warmth and amiability ill sort with the character that Shakespeare drew. I see him as being in temperament much more like an Arab. 'I fetch my life and being from men of royal siege', he states. This was a quality that Godfrey Tearle, the greatest Othello of my time, got so well at Stratford in 1948-9. This, too, was where Len Russell scored heavily: he brought out the aristocratic breeding of the man as well as the passion. I tried to make Iago an Italianate figure with a black leather tunic and short cropped black hair and beard: an unsmiling man who wins respect because he never indulges in insincere social tricks. He could therefore expose his villainy to the audience or to Roderigo without any great change—still an unsmiling man who keeps very much to the point. Charles Green's headline was 'A Cool Iago'. Prue, who always did well with warm-hearted, earthy characters was an excellent Emilia and Anne Nicolle, fresh from giving us a beautiful Beatrice in the previous May, was a Desdemona strong enough to have stood up against Venetian opinion. I enclosed the whole drama in a claustrophobic brown box with a stylised suggestion of webs in the decorations of the walls.

Whilst I knew that the management of the King's Theatre increasingly wanted us to move over to them, it came as a great shock to read in the Hampshire Telegraph in the November of 1963 the following announcement:

> 'The professional theatre's
> contribution in Southsea to the
> next year's Shakespeare

> celebrations may be a production of "The Merchant of Venice", starring Donald Wolfit, at the King's, if Commander Cooper follows up an idea of his'.

If this were true, it would kill our financial backer, the same play, which had already been planned and announced. Donald? Could he really be doing this to us? Surely not. I wrote at once and his reply read, 'This is all news to me—no one has made any approach and I don't know Cooper. In any case, I don't think I could contemplate it at that time, so don't worry. *Do let* Cooper know you are doing it'.

My next move was to try to get in touch with Commander Cooper. This proved to be difficult but eventually, a fortnight after the press announcement, he telephoned me at my surgery. Even though it meant leaving a patient stranded in the middle of treatment, the Commander and I argued for a very long time. He was extremely anxious that we should appear at the King's that year but I pointed out that our plans were already made, that we could not manage a fourth play and that I had no intention of deserting the Pier management who were such good friends to us. He seemed to use every line of argument that he could think of to try to get me to change my mind. The professional *Merchant of Venice* at the King's, though now with a different star in the lead, was still planned for just before our production. The whole conversation, sadly, was an unfriendly business and the outcome was that I said that we would go ahead with our amateur production and risk the competition from his professional one.

In due course, the following appeared in the local press:

> 'Patrons of the King's Theatre, Southsea, may have wondered why they are having no Shakespearean play to mark the quatercentenary year. In fact, Jean Kent and Peter Murray had been booked to appear in "The Merchant of Venice" but the management decided to leave the way clear for the amateur productions by the Southsea Shakespeare Actors at the South Parade Pier'.

Even so, less than two months before our Festival was due to open, I found myself writing again to the Commander. 'Our telephone conversation of this afternoon has both surprised and disappointed me', I began. 'Last year you told me that you had definitely decided to cancel the visit of the professional "Merchant of Venice" company . . .' This was obviously a misunderstanding, however, as the professional production had indeed been cancelled a long time before but relations were not good. Wolfit, interested and helpful as ever, wrote, 'I don't like your controversy with the King's but I can see your point of view and I have never heard a word from them on the subject. I am sure your terms are better on the Pier but I wonder if *once* a year you should do a big production at the King's and give them a look in on a guarantee'.

To Shakespeareans, 1964 was a wonderful year and amongst all the excitements these contentions were soon forgotten. Stratford not only put on a dazzling exhibition of priceless Tudor treasures in a series of brilliant theatrical settings of Elizabethan England but also there was the great cycle of the Shakespeare histories from *Richard II* to *Richard III* at the Royal Shakespeare Theatre. Several of us Southsea Shakespeareans were able to be in Stratford for the exciting events on the actual 400th Birthday as our own Festival did not start until a week later. In the previous autumn, the Royal Shakespeare Company had staged the *Henry VI* trilogy as two plays in preparation for the full cycle in the following year. This brought these daunting works into the public eye and so it seemed to me that if ever I were to put them on, now was the time. The Stratford versions included a deal of rewriting by John Barton to fit them into the overall pattern of the full cycle and when the Old Vic did them in 1957 as part of their five-year-plan to stage the complete First Folio, they edited them to such an extent that there was hardly any of *Part I* left. They had also reduced them to two plays whereas the Antioch Theatre in Ohio, USA, when they had done all Shakespeare's histories in 1952, had compressed the trilogy into one play. By 1956 they were proclaiming that they had presented the 'Complete Works'. It was quite clear that when a company staged a Shakespeare play no one ever expected that every word of the printed text would be spoken. I wanted to be able to claim, as these others already had, that I had staged every one of the plays, albeit pruned to meet the exigencies of the theatre and the company. I therefore decided that our chief contribution to the quatercentenary celebrations should be a condensation of *King Henry VI, Parts I, II and III* into one vast play. Unlike the Old Vic's text, each Part would finish up with approximately the same number of lines and unlike Stratford's, there should be no rewriting. The total length that I aimed at was about 3,000 lines which meant that, with one ten-minute interval, it would run for nearly three and a half hours. This was going to make strenuous demands on both actors and audience but there seemed to me to be no other way of doing justice to the trilogy and thus being able to claim that all three plays had been staged.

The task that I had set myself was enormous and I realised that I must have an even more positive plan than usual when I worked on the cutting of the text. Most of the weakest writing in this, the earliest of Shakespeare's works, is in the huge multiplicity of battle scenes. I decided, therefore, to concentrate on the human interest and to reduce the war passages to the absolute minimum. The whole play must flow swiftly with as few blackouts and other gaps as possible whilst props were set or scenery changed. Whenever a battle sequence occurred the backcloth immediately blazed with a projection of flames and smoke and simply the relevant moments or speeches were acted out without introduction or delay. The only important character to disappear completely was Talbot as he was solely involved in battle scenes. Joan la Pucelle, played by Mavis Whyte (my Cressida of 1955, now married and therefore with a different surname) was the central figure of the wars of *Part I.*

All the plays with huge casts have a large number of characters who appear very briefly and, although what they say matters, who they are does not. My final version had a total of 47 speaking parts but 21 of them were these very ones who do not really need names. There were also 19 different sorts of crowds or armies and the whole span of the play covered a period of 50 years. I would have needed what Hollywood has always referred to as 'A Cast of Thousands' and each character would have been constantly changing his make-up to indicate the passage of the years. My treatment of the battles was an artificial convention and so too should be the effect of time on the actors: they would not change their make-ups; the half-century should be ignored and it should all be treated as if the time scale were the same as in most other plays. The 26 important characters were historically dressed but I also had a large Chorus clad in identical black uniforms with the gold masks of drama on them. They could be soldiers, courtiers, street mobs, anything, and usually appeared simply in their uniform costumes but sometimes had additions such as helmets and weapons. There was no need to change their make-ups or appearances as they were without individual identities and corresponded very much to the Property Men of the Chinese theatre. They completely solved the problem of the many speaking parts that had to be filled. They were able to come on just as they were—it mattered not whether they were Tom, Dick or Harry—to make brief appearances as if they were characters without names or identities.

I had never forgotten that, to the casual playgoer who does not pretend to be a Shakespeare specialist, one might just as well announce *Henry III, Part IV* as *Henry VI, Part II* or even *Henry IV, Part I*. When I put on the two *Henry IV* plays, I made a point of including in all the advertisements the phrase, 'The Great Falstaff Comedy' and usually contrived to add somewhere, 'Complete in itself in spite of its title'. As *Henry VI* was likely to be even more meaningless, I gave my adaptation a new name altogether, *White Rose and Red*. The expression, 'The White rose and the red', occurs in *Richard III* and 'The red rose and the white' turns up twice in *Henry VI* and so it seemed to me that a shorter adaptation of those lines not only made the play sound more attractive but also happened to be apt. I had plenty of people available as this was such a special occasion and still had a very efficient backstage staff. Tony Copsey had taken over from Charles Tozer on our switchboard and a more devoted and perfect electrician I could not have had—a description that could have equally well applied to Charles. There were 82 light changes in *White Rose and Red* and there was not a single mistake at any performance. Flo Patton had by now given up the job of Wardrobe Mistress and Prue had replaced her. She had two excellent assistants: Buster's wife, Susie, who ran a professional theatrical costumier's in Southsea; and Edith Wilshere, who had two additional advantages on top of being a first-class seamstress. She was a trained nurse, which was very useful if there were any backstage accidents, and she had a husband, Teddy, who was a professional artist and who made nearly all our small props and head-dresses most beautifully. There must have been between 75 and 100 costumes in the whole Festival and quite a few of these were new ones specially designed and made for these productions. A total of 57 members were involved on or behind the stage on top of the front-of-house and administrative people such as the devoted Melita Moon.

Staging this very big production could well have been an exhausting business in itself but we were, of course, rehearsing *The Merchant of Venice* at the same time. We moved into the Pier Theatre on the Tuesday and worked through the whole day setting the stage and the lights as well as unpacking and ironing the costumes. On Wednesday we had the dress rehearsal of *The Merchant* and on Thursday the one for *Henry VI*. The Festival opened on the Friday with the

King Henry VI, Part II. (White Rose and Red) Pier Theatre, 1964

The Cade rebellion. Jack Cade (Edgar King) and his mob (played by the Chorus in their black and gold uniforms) prepare to hang the Clerk of Chatham (Michael Bird). Smith the Weaver (Eric Nicolle) holds the rope. Dick the Butcher's Wife (Nora Turner, *3rd from R*) stands ready to assist

comedy and was followed on the next night by the first performance of *White Rose and Red.*

I had consulted the Lord Mayor some time before about the possibility of making this performance the City of Portsmouth's official celebration of Shakespeare's 400th Birthday. He very readily agreed and it was proclaimed as a Civic Night. Evening dress was requested and the City Council were apparently 'very enthusiastic' about providing a reception at the back of the circle after the performance. Anne and Eric Nicolle's daughter, Sarah, presented the Lady Mayoress with a bouquet of red and white roses on her arrival and, by provincial standards, it was a grand gala occasion.

What of this vast and sprawling play? Had I overstretched myself this time and was it going to be an embarrassing disaster? I was absolutely terrified when the curtain went up to reveal gold masks of Shakespeare's head on either side of a black inner proscenium which also bore the dates 1564 and 1964. My recorded voice spoke out of the darkness: 'The Southsea Shakespeare Actors salute the 400th birthday of William Shakespeare', and then slowly lights came up behind a gauze to reveal the purple-draped coffin of Henry V and we were off. Would it be much too long and the audience be in revolt at least an hour before the end or might the constant coming in and out from the flies of pieces of scenery and the rapid interchange of crowds with banners and spears flounder into chaos? It was too late; we had already started on what I believed could well be the great fiasco of my life. The set, a framework of dark Gothic arches without columns to support them and intertwined with long swags bearing the scarlet, royal blue and gold of the Arms of England, looked well, but what of the events that were to take place within it? It is not really for me to judge: I will let the press do that for me.

The Portsmouth Evening News described it in its sub-headline as a 'Resounding Triumph'. The notice began, 'Southsea Shakespeare Actors paid tribute to the Bard on Saturday night with a tremendous "White Rose and Red"—a roaring triumph, as resounding and shattering as any 21-gun salute'. The critic, Bernard King, said that it was to me as 'the man who has piloted the Actors to their high position on the amateur stage that most of the praise must go. He attempted the impossible and as near as makes no difference, brought it off'. Charles Green in the Hampshire Telegraph found it a 'single, exciting, easily comprehensible play', thought that the staging was 'flawless' and added, 'I say, without reservations, that a kind of genius has been applied to this project'.

I had a marvellous cast. Ian Burton, who was with us all too short a time, played Henry VI astoundingly well. He and Trevor Conway, who had played Pericles for me seven years before, were the only two actors in all my time whom I would have unreservedly backed for successful careers on the professional stage. Stella Miller, the girl with the tragic face, was strong and colourful as Margaret; whilst John Fulcher as York, Clifford Allen doubling Duke Humphrey and Young Clifford (very aptly!), Len Russell as Warwick, Eric Greenwood doubling the Dauphin and Richard Crookback, Edgar King playing Bedford and Jack Cade, with David Lippiett as Suffolk and Louis XI are only a few performances out of so many that I treasure in my memory. I did the evil Cardinal Beaufort but returned as the Messenger to the court of Louis XI so that I could be able to say that I had acted in *King Henry VI, Part III* as well as *Parts I and II.*

We gave four performances of this play, including the matinee on the last

Saturday, and five of *The Merchant of Venice.* Our total audiences rocketed to an all-time record, 4,251, of whom not far short of 3,000 came to the comedy—a gratifying advance on the average of 893 who came to the plays in the first season.

Anne Nicolle again played Portia but this time the Antonio was John Fulcher. Bassanio was David Lippiett and I tackled Shylock for the first time. My sunny set had a great expanse of sky against which floated a skeletal cut-out of domes, towers and a bridge for Venice with gold, silver and leads cupids for Belmont. The caskets were carried before Portia's wooers by three tiny girls looking enchanting in Elizabethan dresses. Bill Smith's daughters were two of them and the third was Sarah Nicolle. The masque that ends with the flight of Nerissa was a blaze of cerise and purple dominoes with amber lanterns carried on tall poles; once again I had gone all out for a romantic approach without the darker undercurrents which can, but I think should not, be unearthed.

Earlier in the year, I had suggested to the Portsmouth Corporation that they might like to borrow my collection of Shakespearean books, playbills and prints to put on an exhibition in one of their art galleries, Cumberland House. They agreed and it was filled out with a host of photographs of our productions and a display of our costumes. Major Clarke-Jervoise, a local landowner and art connoiseur, lent some of his own collection and the result was quite good. However, we felt that far too much of the material that we supplied was never shown. Perhaps if the museum people had been a little more enthusiastic, the exhibition could have been quite a lot better.

To end the season, which had been labelled 'Shakespeare 400', I devised something which I hoped would be entirely original. The audience was greeted on its arrival by the sight of a completely empty stage, open to the back wall. The performance began with my walking down the centre gangway of the stalls and up on to the stage. I was in casual trousers and an open shirt and, in dialogue that I had written myself (the only time William and I shared the audience's attention as authors!), I pondered on why it was all so dead. I called for scenery to remedy the matter and black curtains came in from aloft and dressed the stage. I then called for lights and they came on, too. I said that I needed actors, and a team of eight men and five girls entered in the black and gold uniforms that the Chorus had worn in *White Rose and Red.* They struck postures typical of various aspects of drama—love, hate, murder, comedy and so on—but they remained mute. I then protested that they needed voices and words; above all, the theatre's greatest, Shakespeare's. From that point, all fourteen of us (I having rapidly changed into the black and gold uniform) proceeded to trace Shakespeare's career with a series of extracts from over a dozen of the plays. We showed Launce and his dog, Lear being rejected by his daughters, Henry V philosophising before Agincourt, the Box Tree Scene from *Twelfth Night,* the Shrew being wooed and even gave some of the Sonnets. It had been difficult to know what title to use and Eric Greenwood, with his wry sense of humour, had suggested *Where There's a Will.* I do not think it was a particularly good idea but it was what we did indeed call it. Was it the type of programme, was it the not very explanatory title or were people simply getting tired of the whole 400th birthday business by the autumn? Whatever it was, audiences plummeted down to a mere 1,097. That would have been splendid in the church hall days but now it was a near-disaster! Having been on top of the world over the marvellously successful Festival, I was now down in the depths and started to complain in my annual letter to the members that they were not being sufficiently helpful and keen. Why did they not sell more tickets to their friends and how many of those who were not in *Where There's a Will* bothered to come and see it?

Was I beginning to feel sorry for myself or was it simply that I had been working too hard? Was it even possible that our golden vein had already been slightly over-mined? Our reputation had never been higher in the public's estimation but internally the going was getting tougher. The youthful high spirits of the first seasons were as long as sixteen or seventeen years ago and we were all that much older. Those who were in their mid-twenties and fancy free then were now round about forty and had family and business ties. The newer, young members already belonged to a generation that was marrying earlier, or becoming more involved in further education, and so was not prepared to devote itself to the company as totally as its seniors had done. The quatercentenary had been a great goal to stimulate interest but just ahead lay an even more important one for us. We now had only two Shakespeare plays to do to complete the staging of the whole canon and this would mean the achieving of world records. We must drive on! Was I so obsessed by the productions that I was becoming a little blind to the strong devotion of the great majority of the actors or was it that enthusiasm really was getting more difficult to work up? Was it even that the new Arena Players were diluting interest in the old Shakespeareans? These were some of the questions that I asked myself. I have a feeling that I did not bother to think about the answers.

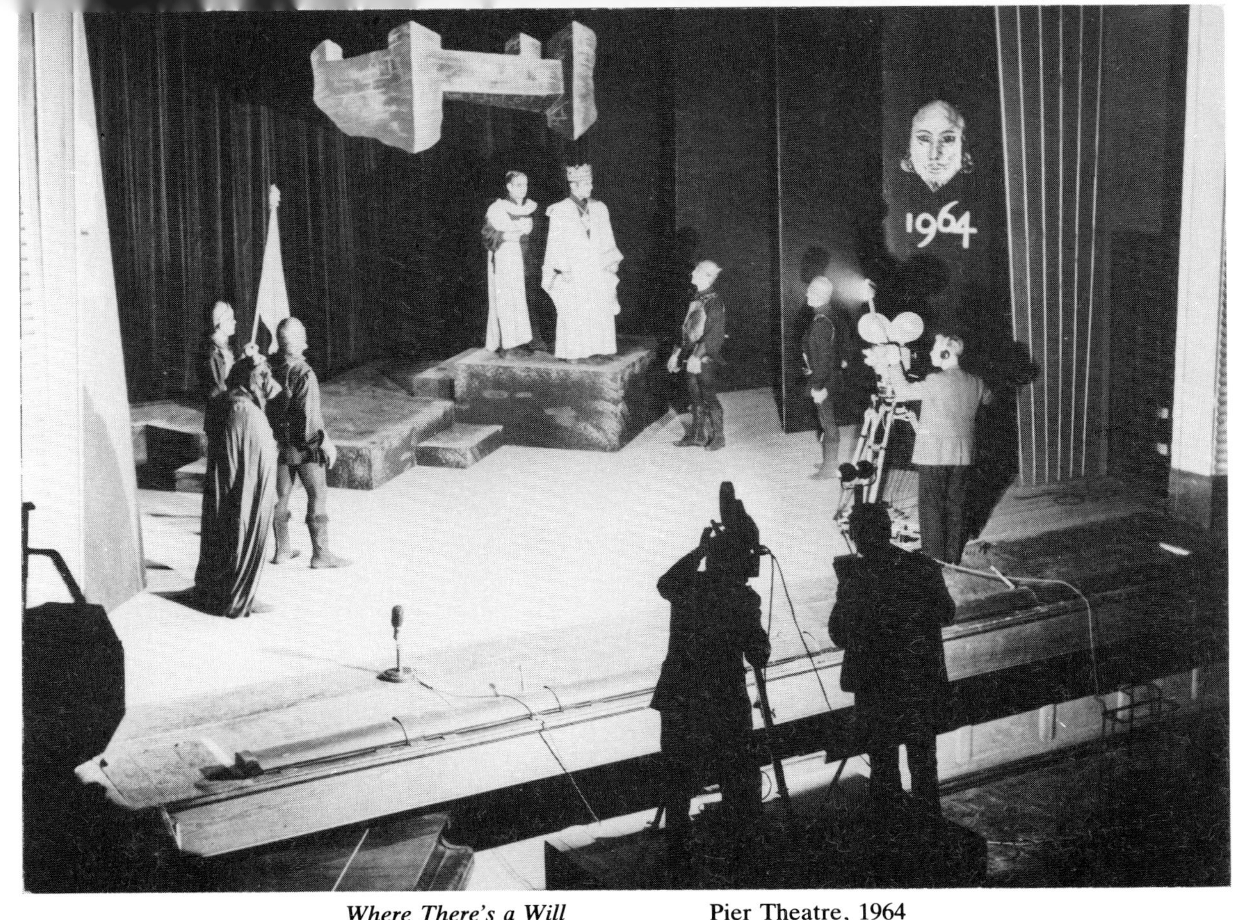

Where There's a Will Pier Theatre, 1964

BBC Television filming Richard II (David Lippiett, *right*) and Aumerle (Chris Bloxsom) on the battlements of Flint Castle. Northumberland (George Metcalfe) faces them from below

ACT THREE
The King's

CHAPTER 18
The next move

There were two moves to be made. Though one was political and the other physical, both had the same objective—our appearance, at last, on the boards of the King's Theatre. Commander Cooper's and my tug-of-war in which *The Merchant of Venice* had been the rope, subsided into a breather for both teams when I agreed that, later in the year, we would discuss the matter again 'over a glass of sherry'.

The 1964 Festival, with the massive production of *White Rose and Red,* had proved to be monumentally tiring for the whole cast who were only called upon to act. For me, with two plays to direct, scenery to paint and all the masses of other things that I still did for every production as well as playing Cardinal Beaufort and Shylock, it was almost too much. We had done five very successful two-play festivals, a notable achievement for an amateur company, and they had culminated in this very special one. This, I thought, was the time to stop and revert to doing three separate plays a year again. The Arts Theatre and the Portsmouth Players having long established themselves at the King's, I had to admit that it would be rather nice to appear there. What is more, it would end the bad relations between us and its management. As we had only two more rare plays to perform to complete the canon, we could perhaps risk them at the Pier now that our audiences had grown so much. I decided, therefore, that I would do something about it during the reception after the Civic 400th Birthday performance. Commander and Mrs Cooper with whom, in spite of our disagreements, I got on surprisingly well socially, were amongst the official guests.

Immediately after the curtain came down on that night's *White Rose and Red,* there was a rapid changing into dinner jackets and evening dresses before the cast mingled with the guests at the reception. As we stood there, twiddling our cocktail glasses and blushingly receiving the inevitable plaudits—who can say they hated it on such an occasion?—the Coopers greeted me like a long-lost friend. This was the moment that I chose to say that we would be happy to come to the King's in the coming winter if they still wanted us. Had there been fatted calves available amongst the canapés, I am sure they would have been produced at that moment.

There had been rumours that the Arts Theatre did not have the freedom at the King's that we were used to. There was talk about interference over the choice of play and of having dress rehearsals without the proper lighting or being allowed to use the curtain. I was determined to get all these matters ironed out before I signed anything finally committing us to going there. One summer evening I went to the King's and had a business meeting with the Commander and his manager, James Holland. I took with me John Fulcher as support and also as a second pair of ears in case of 'If you said so, then I said so'. Indeed, the play selected was to be *As You Like It.* Commander Cooper was at his most relaxed; that night the astute business man had become tweedy and boyish. He flung his arms wide and said, 'Just tell us what you want' in a tone that suggested that nothing that I could ask for would be denied. We discussed possible financial arrangements based on a guarantee to them and a percentage split of the rest of the box office takings.

The meeting was perfectly amicable and we were soon in complete agreement. All my requests, such as the need for a full stage staff at the dress rehearsal so that scene changes, lights and curtains could be operated precisely as they would be at the performances, were granted without demur. I was most anxious that we should still be responsible for all our own printing as we were at the Pier. This was accepted and so too was my insistence on their standard programmes being suspended for our week and their using our own Stratford-printed ones.

There was no doubt that the idea of going to a full-scale theatre was a great thrill. We loved the Pier and it suited us very well, better perhaps than the King's ever would, but a pier theatre, even one as splendid as ours, cannot ever really match up to a grand Edwardian playhouse with boxes and three circles. The King's, like some other theatres designed by Frank Matcham, has a wide auditorium. The boxes on each side turn away from the line of the front of the stage at such a big angle that they face the opposite ends of the dress circle. At the Theatre Royal, basically C. J. Phipps's plan of 1884 but enlarged by Matcham in 1900, they embrace the stage and draw the audience in to it as they do in the most intimate of London's older theatres. At the King's, the actual openings of the boxes, two on either side with an unusable balcony over them, are small in proportion to their architectural setting which is rather heavy. There is also a fairly massive marble proscenium arch. Every theatre has its own odd characteristics and the speciality of the King's is that it is at its best when it is packed to capacity. Unfortunately, we were unlikely to see it in that state very often. It is decorated in cream and gold with a crimson velvet curtain and draperies in the boxes to match. The best arrangement for the size of house that we were expecting would be to use only the stalls and dress circle. When these are occupied, the fact that the upper circle, the gallery and the very back stalls are empty does not seem to show. When we had a special schools performance and expected a big crowd, then the upper circle could be open, too.

Surprisingly, the stage of the King's was not so very much bigger than the Pier's. The proscenium was less than a metre wider and the depth only two metres more. On the other hand, it had a huge amount of space in the wings in comparison and much greater height. The call for manual labourers from amongst the cast to assist their and our stage staffs at the setting-up on the

King's Theatre, Southsea, with the SSA's winter forest for their 1965 *As You Like It* on the stage

Sunday morning was, as usual, '9.25 at the turnstiles!' In this case, it was the stage door in a back street but the expression had stuck.

To borrow and adapt a favourite phrase from the world of boating, those who enjoy 'messing about in theatres' find them to be in many ways just as exciting when they are grey and cold as at performance times. Indeed, it was very thrilling to walk on to that bare stage and to look out at the auditorium and see the three circles and the boxes towering above us. After getting used to the long U-shaped auditorium at the Pier, the front of the dress circle felt very comfortably close. The Stage Manager was a man who had been much loved and greatly respected over the years but by now was a tired invalid nearing the end of his time. It was difficult for us to appreciate what others before us had revered. How desperately we missed Buster's brisk efficiency as we found ourselves back almost in a St. Peter's Hall situation. We had to do practically everything ourselves and it was a big and heavy stage for amateurs to cope with. Bill, a lean, quiet man, who was to be a friend of ours for many years, was in the fly gallery to haul all the cloths, borders and spot-bars up by means of ropes. No counter-weighted system of flying here. Not only did this make the setting-up a much more cumbersome business than we had grown used to but it meant that I must avoid too much visible flying in and out of items of scenery during performances as the handling of the hemp lines was jerky and bottom edges were seldom horizontal as they swayed in and out. It was all much harder work than it had been at the Pier and it lacked some of the joy in spite of the increased prestige.

Once again, there was little difficulty in assembling a strong cast as the members wanted to be in the first King's play in the way that they had rallied for parts in the debut at the Pier. Anne Nicolle, a treasure of an actress for any of Shakespeare's great leading ladies, was superb as Rosalind and John Fulcher matched her marvellously as Orlando. It was interesting to see my youthful Romeo and Juliet of thirteen years before playing these lovers of another sort. They had both shown a remarkable amount of talent then but now had matured into very professional players. Chris Bloxsom, who had made my scale plan of the King's stage for me and was one of the most devoted members, played Charles the Wrestler with a shaved scalp that Eric Greenwood, with his expertise as a make-up artist, managed to create. By this time, the Theatre Royal had been leased out as an all-in-wrestling arena! What a tragic loss of dignity for a once famous theatre but at least it kept it from being demolished. We enlisted the services of one of the wrestlers, Roger Green—known jokingly in the company as 'Basher'—to teach Chris and John how to do the fight. This was well worth the effort as the result was most expert even if I did have to X-ray John's front teeth at my surgery on the morning after one of the performances! Eric was a wistful and sagacious Touchstone: a difficult part to make both worldly-wise and funny. I think that one must always be able to look at Shakespeare's professional fools, even when they are not putting over their actual comedy material, and be able to understand why their masters employed them to amuse. I have seen Touchstones that, if I had been Duke Frederick interviewing them for the job, I would have said to them, 'I am sure you would make a reasonable footman but you are the last person on earth I would employ to make me merry!'

Clifford gave us another of his hard men as Duke Frederick, Len slid right down the social scale to play a lively Corin and Brian Hillier exhibited a professionalism that I never stopped quoting to undisciplined youngsters for ever after. He followed a gentle and moving Adam with a very funny sketch as the dilapidated hedge-priest, Sir Oliver Martext. The character has only about four lines and many directors use him as an excuse for a wild bit of farce. Brian gave an enchanting old alcoholic who managed to produce a musical note by blowing across the top of his bottle just before he went off humming a hymn. For all the praise and laughter that he earned, he never varied his performance in the least. If he had done so, he would have spoiled it and the temptation to embroider it must have been more than most amateurs could have resisted.

To be fully understood, I think that this play must be related to the great variations in living conditions that occurred between one season and another in Elizabethan times. Even nowdays, with all the luxuries of central heating and double-glazing, we complain about the differences between winter and summer. We tend to forget how immense that contrast must have been in Shakespeare's time, especially to someone like himself who was used to half-timbered houses in the country. Intellectuals and actors—though I am not suggesting that it is not possible to be both at the same time!—are inclined to be superior about the Shakespeare properties in Stratford-upon-Avon as if they are simply tourist traps. This is a great mistake: the Shakespeare Birthplace Trust is run by distinguished scholars and the furnishing and preservation of the Birthplace, Anne Hathaway's Cottage, Mary Arden's House and Hall's Croft, as well as the information given by the staff at each one, are impeccable. I frequently revisit them as they give me such a real feeling of how life was lived in houses of that kind. They are an invaluable aid to an understanding of the exposure to the elements that was an accepted part of Elizabethan life. The bitter cold from the uncontrollable draughts, the shortage of fresh food and the long, dark evenings with no more than a candle or a rush dipped in household fat to provide a pathetically dim light must have made them yearn for the warmth, the extended hours of daylight and the comparative ease of summer.

Shakespeare never tired of bringing this part of his experience of life into the plays. He seems to have been fascinated by the extremes of the two most opposite seasons, winter and summer. 'Now is the winter of our discontent made glorious summer . . .' and the line and a half from the fifth sonnet, 'Never resting Time leads summer on/To hideous winter' are only two of countless such comparisons. In the same way, he appears to have had a continual desire to bring these contrasts into the construction of some of the plays. As early as *Love's Labour's Lost,* he took the tremendously daring risk of changing the mood of a play as fundamentally as the Elizabethan summer transformed itself into winter. After four acts of delightful house-party trivialities under the green trees of summer, sparkling in the sunshine, the mood instantly turns to one of romantic seriousness and melancholy with the unexpected entrance of the black courtier, Mercade. It was a brilliant stroke that came off miraculously. At the other end of his career, he took this dramatic trick to its ultimate limits in *The Winter's Tale* when he built the whole structure of the play on the idea. A melodramatic, even tragic, first half set in winter is suddenly transformed into a fairy tale and a pastoral full of summer warmth.

I believe that *As You Like It* was a half-way stage. Whilst not exhibiting so complete a dichotomy as *The Winter's Tale,* it is, none the less, a play of two distinct moods. The first two acts are sombre and wintery but the rest is a matter of 'sunlight tempered by forest boughs', as Dowden put it. One might say that the mood changes as love itself comes into leaf.

Dressing the bigger King's stage for this play was no great problem as all the scenery had been enlarged sufficiently when we moved to the Pier. Besides that, I had invested in an increasing number of very tall, black wing flats and so it was possible to produce a basic box consisting of black wings and borders enclosed by either the sky-cloth or black curtains across the back. Within this, anything, or even practically nothing, could be constructed using as many or few items of scenery as we needed. Indeed, as we stood on the stage waiting for the curtain to go up on the first night, Anne Nicolle looked round, enclosed within our own set as we were, and said, 'Here we are at the King's and, apart from the fact that it is bigger, we could equally well be at St. Peter's Hall!'

An abstract background, constructed with flats and suggestive of foliage, served for both my winter and summer forests, depending on how I lit it. For the former, the stage sprouted the stark, inverted-octopus-like trees from *Julius Caesar* but after the interval these had been replaced by my graceful summer ones with their long, curling branches of cane. I cast myself as Jaques again and as I sat speaking the famous soliloquy by a log fire from which a wisp of smoke drifted up into the winter's night, I could see the dim outlines of the ornate Edwardian architecture of the theatre. As I sometimes think that I have camera lenses instead of eyes, I revelled in the picture. Summer in Arden was all flowers and sunshine but it began in moonlight with Orlando's apostrophe to the 'Thrice-crowned queen of night'. (I can never understand why so many directors have that speech, so obviously addressed to the moon, spoken in stage daylight!) This was then followed by the dawn creeping up through the trees. It was not just a matter of bringing on all the lights very slowly, but of planning a realistic effect. The first primrose-coloured touches of light caught a few of the green leaves on the branches and then gradually the invisible rising sun cast brighter and brighter rays on to more of the foliage until the moonlight had dissolved away and sunlight filled the stage. This was the first point in the play when such warmth had appeared and it coincided with the flowering of Rosalind's and Orlando's love. Bernard King in the Evening News got my point about the two moods of the play but thought that this was a fault on the part of the author!

The production drew almost exactly the same size total audience to the King's as the same play had to the Pier. The prophets had said that the King's would attact more people but this proved not to be so. We had hated going back to the church hall after our baptism of appearing at the Pier but our debut at the King's produced no such reaction. Yes, we would certainly come back next year but we were happy to be doing our next play over the waves again. At least, we would be sure that our lighting would be carried out as I had planned it. Our clever Tony Copsey had not been allowed to work on the switchboard with the theatre's own somewhat disinterested electrician but henceforth this would have to be altered. It was—and Tony virtually did everything on the board from then onwards. There were no more mistakes.

Rumours about the Pier Theatre's future were, however, giving cause for alarm. The Portsmouth Guildhall, a large Victorian stone wedding cake, had been burned out during the bombing raids of the war. By 1959, however, the interior had been redesigned and built within the old standing walls. David Evans had been put in charge and it was the city's pride and joy. Before this time, he had devoted himself to making the Pier a great success but now he lost interest in it. His new toy was all that seemed to matter and so cries began to be

As You Like It King's Theatre, 1965

The weary travellers arrive in the forest: Touchstone, Celia and Rosalind (Eric Greenwood, Jenny Bloxsom and Anne Nicolle)

heard that the Pier was becoming increasingly unsound and uneconomic. In 1965, quite suddenly, it was declared that the summer shows with the big stars that had packed audiences in up till the previous year and had made profits, could no longer be afforded. A modest show without any names at all was put on and, to nobody's surprise, it played to small audiences and lost money. Already there was talk of converting the theatre into an amusement arcade or some sort of show bar. In a letter to me, David Evans had shown a change of course by referring to piers as 'relics of the Victorian era'. It began to look very much as if it was being deliberately run down both verbally and physically.

Did we perhaps add to the omens of doom by opening their theatre season with *Macbeth* for the second time? I think not: with hindsight it would appear that the die had already been cast. Whilst the Thane himself is a wonderful part to play, I suspect the reason that it is often unsatisfactory to audiences is because they are never given a chance to see the Macbeth that Duncan describes and everyone reveres. Within a few minutes of his first appearance he is telling them that his ambitious thoughts could include murder. He must earn the audience's sympathy in some way during the early acts and I tried to make him a deeply haunted man in order to do this. My Lady Macbeth was Stella Miller who had been so strong as Queen Margaret in the *King Henry VI* trilogy. This time she seemed less sure of herself though reports suggested that this was something of which she and I were more aware than the audiences. An actor named George Metcalfe, who had won 'golden opinions from all sorts of people' by his performances in other companies, had joined us for the Quatercentenary Festival. He played Macduff and it was to be the first of many major parts that he would tackle. He was a very thorough and precise actor: in fact, he was almost too perfect and this led to a certain coldness in his work. None the less, he was a great asset and—oh! blessed virtue!—utterly reliable.

Having a strong feeling for the supernatural, I always enjoyed creating productions that needed an atmosphere of magic and mystery. Directors who are not sensitive to the psychic usually leave both *Macbeth* and *The Tempest* completely earthbound. Critics are inclined to blame the author but I think they should address their strictures to the interpreters. One of the difficulties with the former play is purely technical, however. It is the question of how to stage the rapid alternation between the advancing army and the horrors within Macbeth's castle in the last act, without having gaps between the scenes. This time I designed a set that had a thick, curving wall that came down from the back of one side to the centre of the stage. Left and right of it could be used as separate areas for these scenes: they were lit alternately and the plan seemed to work. At other times, of course, the two halves combined to form the full-stage setting. The overall effect was of a jungle of iron bars, tangled muddy draperies, casually slung nets, dusty ropes and faded banners. By keeping it mostly dark and lighting only limited areas with greyish blues and touches of smoky red, I think that I managed to make the stage look evil and haunted—like the man that I was playing. Audience figures rose again encouragingly: 1,000 more people came to this play than had come to *As You Like It* and thus produced the second highest figure for a single play up to that time.

Success in the theatre is something of a halucinatory drug. During the week of each production we were usually 'high' on the effects of it. Ours was an enclosed world of excitement and nothing outside really mattered. We were convinced that what we were doing was not just for our own pleasure but was immensely important for the cultural well-being of the City of Portsmouth. I tried hard to keep a balanced view but some of the others got alarmingly carried away. One's sycophantic friends—often so because they have not either the courage or the necessary sadistic streak to be able to tell us how much they disliked it—have been round to the dressing rooms after the performances and have lavished praise on to us whilst we are still hot and sweating with the elation of it all. The press notices, too, at this time were so consistently good that it was very difficult to keep a level head. Seventeen years before, Donald Wolfit had bade me beware of 'a clique of self-satisfied amateurs who begin to think that they are more important than the play'. The News notice for *Macbeth* had said, 'Productions by the Southsea Shakespeare Actors start at a level of quality which other amateur groups often flounder in their attempts to achieve . . . Again it was shown that sheer competence and efficiency can be taken for granted—all that is left to the scope of the critic is the interpretation chosen by the director and to what extent the cast excels itself'. The 1960 *Midsummer Night's Dream* had received a banner headline which read, 'This Production Equals Old Vic Standard'. The *Julius Caesar* in 1962 had been described as, 'A remarkable performance . . . newcomers might well have thought they were seeing a professional company in action . . . Brilliantly directed and staged'. How does one live with this sort of thing without having one's head turned? Alas, all too few amateurs do.

For a long time I had referred to us as 'unpaid professionals' because I wanted the company to approach the work as if that was indeed what they were. The word, 'Amateurs' savoured of the excruciating, frequently prompted and badly acted efforts of untrained groups in little halls; the sorts of affairs that only friends and relations go to. The danger with our type of amateur theatre is that the word, 'Professional' is often taken too literally for the comfort of people outside the limited circle of the members and their devotees. Wolfit had often warned me, too, of the detestation that real professionals frequently have of amateurs who think that they are able to do their job as well as they can. Professionals are, in my experience, amongst the kindest and politest of people but it can be terribly embarrassing to see amateurs talking to them as if they were equals and not realising that they are being indulged. I am fortunate in that I have quite a number of very good friends who are professional actors and actresses. One of them is Douglas Fielding who created the two well-known TV policemen, Sergeant Quilley in *Z Cars* and Sergeant Quick in *EastEnders.* I remember him telling me once how, when he was on tour in *Suddenly at Home,* he was tackled by a boring amateur who had recently done the same play. The wretched man went on at great length telling him in what ways he thought that their amateur production had been better than the one in which he was playing. Douglas was obviously intensely irritated by such rudeness, if not impertinence, but the big-headed amateur, like so many of his ilk, remained, I am sure, quite oblivious to the fact, insulated by his own self-importance.

A letter which I received in the July of 1965 not only brought a scholarly accolade to our efforts but was to be the initiation of one of my most valued and enriching friendships. It began, 'From a Portsmouth scholar who was visiting Harvard University this summer I heard very pleasant things about your Shakespearean productions. Portsmouth is a long distance from London—and I am not young—but I am keen about the plays in "ungimmicky" productions and I am eager to know what you're doing this autumn. I shall be returning to the

United States, sailing from Southampton, November 10'. It was from the world's leading authority on Shakespeare in performance, the American author, Professor Arthur Colby Sprague. I already knew the name well as I possessed and treasured several of his books, especially *Shakespeare and the Actors,* the definitive history of Shakespearean stage business. Here, at any rate was someone who believed what he had been told about us even if I thought it prudent for ourselves to take it all with a pinch of salt. A great honour and a great thrill! I wrote immediately and we had soon made arrangements for him to come and see our autumn production of *All's Well that Ends Well.*

Rosalind and Donald Wolfit had never undervalued our efforts, either, and their support had always been a solid rock to cling to in the deceptive whirlpools of effusive praise. In the spring of that year he had offered me the last of his theatrical wardrobe and we made plans for a few of us to go over to their charming cottage at Hurstbourne Tarrant, near Andover in Hampshire, to fetch them. Prue Higham and John Fulcher were two who went and David Lippiett, fast becoming one of my group of close friends, was another. John's marriage had failed several years earlier and had been dissolved in the divorce court. Later he had met and married Ann Reed, a beautiful and vital girl with blue eyes of a strangely smouldering quality. On the Boxing Day of 1964 their first child had been born. This was Antony, the little lad whose visit to the pantomime I recalled at the very beginning of this book. In fact, he was born three weeks early: had he been three hours earlier still, it would have happened at Crossways where his mother and father had spent Christmas Day with my sister, Gwen, and myself! Ann and Antony made up the rest of the party.

Our visit to the Wolfits on that crisp but sparkling spring day was memorable and enchanting. They were such delightful hosts whether we were having tea together under the ancient beams of their cottage or strolling amongst the daffodils in the garden and admiring their three geese, Pyramus, Thisbe and Lavender, which they had bought to eat but had kept as pets because they had not got the heart to kill them. One of the great moments was when Donald suddenly took the four-months-old baby in his arms and sat at his own cottage door speaking the speech from *The Winter's Tale* with which the Old Shepherd addresses the abandoned baby that he has just found. John immediately took a photograph which Ronald Harwood, after Sir Donald had died all too few years later, included in his official biography of him.

Most of the costumes that we brought away in our cars had been designed, as had been the ones that we borrowed for our first *As You Like It* in 1952, by Max Reinhardt's designer, Ernst Stern. Several of the items that Donald gave specifically to me have gone into my collection of theatrical relics and included his own King Lear crown, royal hat, wig and beard; and the glass sceptre which Martin Harvey had used as Oedipus at Covent Garden in 1912. Another of my professional actor friends, Donald Sinden, is a great theatrical collector. He claims that he is very covetous of my Wolfit gifts and, in his capacity as Chairman of the British Theatre Museum, has accepted them and much of the rest of my collection on its behalf when I move off to the 'undiscovered country from whose bourn . . .' etc! With gleeful relish and a twinkling eye, he once said to me, 'We're only waiting for you to die!'

With its background of graceful, ageing characters, *All's Well that Ends Well* has, for me, the soft air of an autumn evening. We made a rough, trellis canopy that covered the whole acting area of the stage and laced both it and its four

All's Well that Ends Well Pier Theatre, 1965

The Countess of Rousillon (Anne Nicolle) and her ward, Helena (Mavis Whyte)

supporting columns with a large number of branches of autumn leaves. I know it is traditionally unlucky to use real plants on the stage but beggars cannot be choosers. We always used real branches for Birnham Wood and this time I cut foliage from my own silver birch trees and dipped them in rust-coloured paint. Through the leaves came the amber-tinted lights and the whole production was bathed in a dappled sunset glow. Very simple changing backgrounds against an autumnally-coloured backcloth came in and out smoothly on the Pier's counter-weighted lines. I enjoyed pottering on and off in the tiny part of the Countess's steward, Rinaldo, whilst some of our best people excelled themselves. Strange to say, everyone seemed to love this sadly neglected play and those regular members of our audiences who came to everything but were not in any sense scholars, and therefore judged each play on how they found it and not on its reputation, enjoyed it almost more than any.

Edgar King brought an easy charm to Bertram which prevented the character from appearing to be the prig and the snob that he really is. Anne Nicolle, playing an elderly woman for the first time with us (apart from having been the Third Witch in 1958!), portrayed the Countess with a graciousness that made me think of old silver. It was one of the loveliest performances that we ever had in any of our productions. Professor Sprague was captivated by her and has never stopped referring to it. Mavis Whyte, fresh from sparkling parts like Hermia, brought a lovely solemnity to Helena and both Prue and Eric gave the Widow and Lafeu much rich humour. John Fulcher, whose stock-in-trade had so often been sincerity with parts like Hal trying on his father's crown prior to becoming Henry V—to say nothing of his fine, tragic death scene as York in *King Henry VI, Part III (White Rose and Red)*—gave one of his best performances as the braggart, Parolles.

The Professor had told me how I would recognise him and so I had no difficulty when I met him at the station. He was a short man with a humorous face, pale mischievous eyes, rolling vowels, a remarkably large double chin and a rich sense of enjoyment. He began, as soon as we got into my car, to ruminate that to him Portsmouth meant Pompey—no, not the Naval port but the football team. I told him that I had no interest in the sport but he upbraided me with the comment that it was 'extremely dramatic'. He has always enjoyed telling a tale against himself which he denies with such a twinkling chuckle that I am sure it must be true. It is said that he got so excited at a football match on one occasion that he stood up and shouted out, 'Ambition should be made of sterner stuff'! Years later, I was having a pub lunch with him and Dr Gareth Lloyd Evans, another distinguished Shakespearean scholar, at Stratford. Gareth and I were discussing Shakespeare as was right and proper when the Professor interrupted us. 'I want to speak to Gareth about something *very* important', he said. I naturally assumed that he would start on some theory that would be beyond my Shakespearean studies but instead he began, 'Gareth, did you think that the goal that so-and-so scored last week . . .'! He soon became a very dear friend and a most welcome visitor to my house. I have always felt highly honoured that so learned and internationally revered a scholar should have so much respect for my own efforts and knowledge.

Our Nineteenth Season was to open with our return to the King's Theatre in February, 1966. Their pantomime that Christmas was due to run for six weeks as usual but, after four of them, it surprisingly transferred to the Theatre Royal which had been empty again for some time. The reason was that the King's had

Romeo and Juliet King's Theatre, 1966

The Prince (Kenneth Barnard) stands over the dead lovers (David Lippiett and Mavis Whyte). *Others L to R:* the Capulets (KEG and Mavis Patton), Balthasar, Second Watch and Page (Leslie Wright, Victor Bulbecke and Peter Jackson), Montague (Douglas Bray), Friar Laurence (Clifford Allen, behind Montague) and First Watch (Michael Pitt)

a chance of a four-week visit of *My Fair Lady* if the theatre could be free for it from the fifth week after Christmas. I was delighted to have a chance to go to a Theatre Royal pantomime again, especially as it was *Dick Whittington* which was the first show of any kind that I ever saw there. Any thoughts that there was a possibility of the Royal's making a come-back were soon dispelled by a friend who was a City Councillor ringing me up and saying that there was a plan afoot for it to be demolished. He was telephoning on behalf of several other councillors as well as himself to see if I would start a 'Save the Theatre Royal' campaign as my love for it was so well-known. I agreed immediately and set to work almost in a state of panic as I had visions of the bulldozers moving in within hours! I wrote literally hundreds of letters and, with Prue as my second-in-command, organised others to do so, too. Famous stars and champions such as Sir John Betjeman responded at once and the Guildhall was flooded with pleas that this lovely old building should be bought by the Council and run by them as a Civic Theatre and Arts Centre. There was the usual division into those who were for and those who were against the idea and, needless to say, the management of the King's Theatre opposed the scheme. When all was said and done, it savoured of competition in a city which was then not particularly noted for its support of any of the arts. It was in this contentious atmosphere that we took *Romeo and Juliet* to the King's!

As in my two previous productions, the basic colour of the set was blue. It is fashionable nowadays to show Verona blistering under the sun and using the line, '. . . these hot days, is the mad blood stirring' as the key-note of the play. This is to overlook totally the fact that the quarrels in the streets occupy only a very few scenes and that as much as half the play takes place in quiet locations at night. In 1952 I had to 'make do' with a cumbersome balcony made up of rostra but in 1957 Laurie Upton had made me a real one of a believable height that could be set or struck very easily as it was on casters. Then my set had consisted of pale blue wings separated by a thin, white skeletal structure, with a suggestion of Verona's forked battlements on it, against the sky cloth. This time the same balcony was still available but my scenery was realistic for a change. A courtyard, built of dusky blue stone, with a central archway backed by the sky cloth, dominated the right-hand two-thirds of the stage. The rest was concealed from anyone in that area by a vine-covered bastion. The set could therefore be used for a whole-stage scene such as a public square in Verona or the courtyard of Capulet's house during the ball; or else, the two sections could be used separately. If the courtyard had a window put into the arch, it quickly became Juliet's bedroom; and when the window was replaced by iron gates, it was ideal for the tomb. In that final scene, the area on the left of the vine-covered walls was perfectly logically the graveyard approach to the outside of the tomb. All too often its geography is distorted to fit it into a single acting area: there must be both an inside and an outside to the tomb. The result is otherwise always a muddle.

Mavis Whyte, who had been Cressida eleven years earlier, was an extremely good, petite Juliet and still managed to look young and innocent enough for the part. She was a remarkable little actress with the warmest of hearts and an outgoing temperament that endeared her to everyone. The Romeo this time was David Lippiett who looked well and, indeed, gave a very good performance but had a slightly sulky quality and lacked some of the dynamism that made John Fulcher's more Italianate portrayal so exciting. Clifford was Friar Laurence

Romeo and Juliet King's Theatre, 1966
The Nurse (Prue Higham) and Juliet (Mavis Whyte)

again—one of his down-to-earth older men that were his forte—and Prue, playing the Nurse for the third time and benefiting from past experience and maturer years, gave her finest performance. I tried Capulet; a part which I found very difficult to learn but this may have been largely because I was coping with, and worrying about, the Theatre Royal campaign at the same time. George Metcalfe gave a rather precise Mercutio who could have done with a little more of the 'mad blood'.

The spring saw our return to the Pier with *A Midsummer Night's Dream.* For me, this is a play—perhaps more than any of Shakespeare's others—that must *look* right. A stage setting can, of course, be anything from the totally abstract to the incredibly naturalistic. If it is going to be the former, then it must not be contradictory to the imagined location of the action. It would be absurd, for example, for a scene set in a supposedly dimly-lit coal mine to be played in a blaze of lights against a bright yellow background, however abstract and non-representational it might be. It would not be negative, as a true abstract set should be, but would quarrel with what the author and the actors were trying to get over to the audience: it would be atmospherically contradictory.

Peter Brook, in his famous production at Stratford-upon-Avon in 1970, staged this play in a plain white box, blazingly lit most of the time. He said, in effect, that people no longer believe in magic and so that side of the play should be presented as circus tricks—a sort of substitute for magic that we recognise as being contrived and therefore explicable. It was a dazzlingly exciting production, marvellously acted and perfectly spoken, but for me it missed the essential atmosphere of the play. It was another case, to my mind, of Peter Brook over-intellectualising his interpretation with the result that the basic ingredients had been boiled out of it. The very core of the play is that we do indeed accept, during the time that we are watching it, the concept of fairy magic. The dark mystery of the night is the absolute essence of it. As Mark Van Doren, the American poet, said as far back as 1941, this play is soaked with darkness, rain and moonlight. The white box was not neutral; it was a permanently visible antidote to the mood that the author had striven to create.

My new production was set in an inner proscenium of white gauze festoons entwined with rambling roses against an entanglement of black branches on the deepest of blue backgrounds. Within this, the Palace was represented by a gold outline of Tudor arches and Quince's shop by a sign board. My forest was indeed a place of mystery. There was a clump of ivy-covered, but otherwise bare, white trees in the centre whilst the rest of the stage was filled with layers and layers of dark hanging foliage which made tortuous pathways up into the depths of the wood. These were all flown on the Pier's counter-weighted lines and when the moment came for the change to the woodland scene, I had every one of them manned so that they could all move at the same moment. We effected a magical change to a really complicated-looking set in precisely fifteen seconds! When the stage had been set for the dress rehearsal, I did as I had always done whenever I had produced a forest scene: I sentimentally went up to the seats at the side of the circle and looked at it from where, as a child of about five years old, I had gazed in wonder at the first stage set that I had ever seen—the woodland in *Cinderella.*

When I had played Bottom in 1960 I had been miserable in the ass's head because I could not see where I was going. What is more, the traditional mask so muffles the voice that Bottom is inclined to lose his effectiveness during that part

A Midsummer Night's Dream Pier Theatre, 1966

Puck (Barry Wilkins, kneeling *far L*) and Oberon (John Fulcher, *R of centre*) watch Lysander, Helena and Demetrius (Chris Bloxsom, Jenny Bloxsom and Richard Cole) goad Hermia (Mavis Whyte). (New productions of plays that had already been staged, always had newly-designed sets. Compare the photograph on page 179)

of the play. I designed a new type of head: it was entirely realistic with the exception of the muzzle and this was simply a wire frame-work. It was in the shape of the animal but left the actor's face completely visible. It worked well and Len, who played the part this time, had no difficulty with it. I cast myself as Theseus and John Fulcher was a fine Oberon. Puck was delightfully played by Barry Wilkins, the small actor who had already shown a talent for comedy as one of the Watchmen in *Much Ado* and as Old Gobbo. Ironically, his passions in life are Wagner and mountains—neither of which is small or funny. In the years ahead we would become great friends but at this time I think he was a bit in awe of me! John Pearce, our splendid clown who dated from the night of our very first rehearsal nineteen years before, was again a perfect Flute with Clifford in his element as a bewildered old Peter Quince. Lysander and Helena were enchantingly played by particularly dear friends of mine, Chris Bloxsom and his wife, Jenny. Chris had first appeared as Donalbain in 1958 and had a long list of credits which included Ratcliff, Demetrius in *Titus Andronicus,* Diomedes in *Antony and Cleopatra,* Oswald, Borachio, Roderigo and, a year before this, the brother of his first part, Malcolm. Like the Fulchers, the Bloxsoms would, in the course of time, produce some wonderful godchildren for me!

It was a production that I was very proud of as I seemed to achieve the gaiety, the moonlight and the romanticism that are, for me, what this play is all about. Modern theories that it is riddled with eroticism and sexuality are, I think, rubbish; a view that, I am glad to say, Professor Sprague shares with me. It was, however, an unhappy production. There were backstage bickerings and one of the minor characters was played by a dark-eyed little woman who seemed to have a talent for leaving contention in her wake. Whenever there was an atmosphere of this sort, it upset me and made me querulous and difficult. This did not help to improve matters any more than Clifford's saying that he was having to defend me from a good deal of grumbling that was going on about me in the ranks. By this time, he was becoming a most valuable assistant in many directions and had been appointed as the company's Acting Instructor. In this capacity he could take beginners on one side and give them special tuition to save time during rehearsals and this had proved to be a great boon. The audience figures were very encouraging even if the atmosphere was not. This production achieved our all-time record for a single play, 3,517; which proved that, for us, this was the most popular in the canon. Each of our three productions of it broke all our previous records for any play.

In the meantime, John and Ann Fulcher had had another son, Richard. These four had become almost indispensibly my own family. I was deeply devoted to them and my relationships with them and with Prue were the great anchors of my life. I was a bachelor living alone and enjoying my freedom but the major part of my well-being was rooted in the warmth and companionship that I derived from these very special friends. One night in the June of this year, John gave me a large whiskey and then told me something which he knew would upset me and which he was dreading having to say. For various reasons, some of them economic, he and Ann and the boys were going to emigrate to South Africa for three years. The bottom fell out of my world; I could not imagine my personal life without them but also what a dreadul loss it would be to the company! By this time he was our Stage Director as Bryan Tozer was working away from the area; he was the manager of the headquarters, which he had designed; he was the person I consulted about so many of my problems, both in the company and out of it; he was an invaluable leading actor and he was one of my strongest allies whenever I was the subject of backstage criticism. His protest that three years would soon pass was no comfort. Would they, in fact, ever come back or would the golden rewards of life in South Africa tempt them to settle there permanently? In any case, I was sure that life for me could never be the same again—and it was not.

CHAPTER 19
Journeys end

The humble role of the Countess of Rousillon's Steward is not usually the sort of stuff of which theatre history is made. However, for me it was of some significance. When I had appeared in that part in the autumn of 1965, I had achieved the feat of performing in every one of Shakespeare's 37 plays. I was ahead of the company by one of them through having already acted in *Cymbeline* in Norwich. Now, a year later, this one play was needed for the SSA to become a record breaker. Several companies, including the Maddermarket, the Royal Shakespeare Theatre, the Old Vic and the Antioch Theatre in Ohio, had staged the full canon but all either partly or wholly with professionals. Although all the players in Norwich were amateur, Nugent Monck was a life-long professional director and he had used paid staff in many capacities, especially that of scenic design and painting. Now we were on the brink of becoming the first completely amateur company under one amateur director to have staged all the plays—a world record, no less. I, too, had my own world record to proclaim as well. This production would make me the only person, amateur or professional, who had ever, anywhere, directed *and* acted in *and* designed sets for, the whole Shakespeare canon.

It was not enough to trumpet these facts to the world; they had to be put to the test as well. I had studied the matter carefully and I was sure that our claims were valid but, like justice, these things also have to be seen to be done. I therefore wrote a circular letter stating our case in the fullest possible terms and sent it out to 14 of the world's leading authorities in such matters. As I expected, no one contested them. We were, therefore, able to go ahead and proclaim our exciting achievements.

The press took the matter up and gave us good coverage. Dr Louis Marder put us on the front page of his Shakespeare Newsletter in Chicago and produced another of his splendid headlines. This time it read, 'Gateley of Southsea Shakespeare Actors to Claim World Production Record'. The article began, 'Dr K. Edmonds Gateley—a dentist, not a professor—is about to claim . . .' etc. It was not correct to call me 'Doctor', of course, but dentists have that title in the USA. The City Council, through its 'Contribution to the Arts' Sub-committee, had started to give us a small annual subsidy (on top of the Education Committee's purchase of tickets) in the previous year. To our delight, they decided to increase the figure 'in commemoration' (as the press put it) of our completion of the canon.

The time was obviously ripe for another souvenir programme. Our normal one had started, it may be remembered, as a single folded sheet of rough cream paper with discreet black type. There had been a special souvenir for the completion of the first ten seasons but otherwise the format had not changed until the Festivals started. From then onwards, it was still a fairly large, single folded sheet but the colour was changed to a smooth white inside and a strong yellow outside. The modern 'sans' type, 'Univers', replaced the former 'Times Roman'. This latest souvenir, which would consist of eight pages, was to be different from its predecessors. The photograph of the Droeshout portrait of Shakespeare would be on the front, as it had been on the ones for the Quatercentenary Festival, but the rest of the cover was to be divided into a block each of white and yellow. Inside I had a photographic montage of a character from every one of the plays as they had been seen in our productions of them. Chris Bloxsom, who was playing Guiderius, had to be photographed in advance as his was the one character who had, in fact, not yet been seen. All our printed matter had a symbol on it but this, too, had changed over the years. It began as a crude device which I had dashed off hurriedly and which showed four different types of theatre stages. However, when we became wholly Shakespearean, this was no longer suitable and so we held a competition for a new design. Ian Bailey, a local architect, won it with one that had a dramatic mask hanging on a classical pillar at the end of a pavement littered with sea shells. Eventually, I decided that I wanted a symbol that included Shakespeare's head and so I designed yet another one myself. This has the Droeshout portrait emerging from an open book against a background of stylised waves and a sailing ship.

I had no shortage of photographs from which to choose to make up my montage. Early in 1948, during our first season, I had noticed that a new photographer was setting up in Portsmouth. His name was Kenneth Pratt and he was a chubby little man with one of the naughtiest grins that I know. He became our official photographer with *Ghosts,* only our third play, and he stayed with us throughout the rest of my time. He did beautiful work and was remarkably quick. When he was taking posed scenes for us, his familiar cry from the outer darkness of the auditorium of 'Absolute still now! Hold it! Thank you, relax!' must have been heard thousands of times over the years. In fact, it became one of the company's catch-phrases. He was marvellously patient with us and would come, without complaining, for photo calls which lasted into the small hours of the morning or others which involved his staying throughout complete dress rehearsals. Thanks to him, the ephemeral theatre, which evaporates into the night every time a final curtain comes down, is at least, in our case, preserved in a huge collection of photographs which I, for one, greatly prize. They have certainly travelled world-wide: I remember my delight at being sent from India a copy of the magazine, 'Theatre Arts', which was published in the USA. In it was a photograph of me as King Lear in our 1954 production. Professor Sprague initiated collections of our photographs and programmes in the Harvard

University Library in America and the Shakespeare Centre at Stratford-upon-Avon where, to use his own words, 'they will remain for all time, as they deserve'. The Birmingham Shakespeare Library also has a collection and the Shakespeare Quarterly, published by the Shakespeare Association of America Incorporated, published one of Ken's pictures of our *Timon of Athens* some years ago.

Many famous people, including Dame Peggy Ashcroft, whom I already knew, and the Oliviers, whom I did not, were invited to come to our great night. Hardly surprisingly, they all politely declined with letters that included good wishes and congratulations. The exercise had been a means of publicising our world records to the heads of the profession and so we were not particularly disappointed. One of the nicest of these letters was a wholly hand-written one from Miss Jennie Lee who was the Minister for the Arts at that time.

The local BBC station showed considerable interest. I went over to the studios at Southampton and recorded both television and radio interviews prior to their coming with their cameras on the night of our dress rehearsal. They roamed all round the theatre and made a splendid film which included shots taken backstage, in the dressing rooms and of the cast waiting about both in the auditorium and amongst the scenery. The completed programme, which we all watched on a specially imported television set backstage whilst we were getting ready for the first night, began and ended with me being interviewed in the studio. The middle was occupied by the film so that, in effect, my conversation with the interviewer continued through it as 'voices over'. This was our third television appearance. Previously, Southern Television, then the local ITV company, had interviewed me on the deck at the end of the Pier when we did our first Festival and then the BBC came and filmed some of *Where There's a Will* in the Quatercentenary year. On that second occasion, the company behaved, of course, very professionally and John Cox, the director of the film unit, told me that one of the cameramen had given us the highest possible accolade. Normally, I gather, they are extremely taciturn and hardly ever bestow praise but this one had said, 'They're alright, this lot' and apparently no one could hope for more.

The first night, 4 October, 1966, was, for me, a very thrilling occasion but one or two of the older hands appeared to be rather sardonic about it all. I found this disappointing and perhaps that was intended. Was it because the limelight was inclined to be focussed on me as the captain who had guided the ship into port? It may have been. John Fulcher and Prue were certainly not amongst them. The former played Posthumous Leonatus and the latter the wicked Queen. They were immensely enthusiastic and, like Nora Turner (who appeared in the tiny part of First Lady) and Melita Moon, were thrilled because they were the only ones besides myself who had been involved in the company's very first production nineteen years earlier.

Prue excelled herself as Wardrobe Mistress and the Elizabethan farthingale that she created for herself was one of the most superb costumes we ever had. The important thing about it was that it was heavily boned and corsetted as such a dress should be. One of our recurrent problems was getting some of our actresses to tolerate the discomfort that is often involved to achieve the right Elizabethan look. Sadly, visual correctness sometimes had to be sacrificed to female comfort to a production's disadvantage.

Nugent Monck had always maintained that the best way to dress the Roman

Cymbeline Pier Theatre, 1966

Iachimo (KEG) tantalises Posthumus Leonatus (John Fulcher) by showing him Imogen's bracelet

plays was to do them as they had originally been done—Elizabethan costumes for the civilians and the full Roman armour for the soldiers. The great Italian painter, Veronese, did just this and one has only to look at his magnificent 'Family of Darius before Alexander' in the National Gallery in London to see how beautiful the effect can be. I decided that this should be the style for our production of *Cymbeline* with its mixture of Romans who behave like Renaissance Italians, especially Iachimo, and early Britons who could hardly be more Jacobean. As the audience burst into applause every night when the curtain went up on the second part to reveal the splendour of Caius Lucius and his Romans before Cymbeline and his court, I think the idea can be accounted a success. Anne Nicolle was beautiful as Imogen, as we all expected she would be, and I played Iachimo ('With a Renaissance swagger—cunning, amoral and sophisticated, a playboy of the Italian world', said Charles Green). The chest inside which I hid in Imogen's bedchamber was the one that Wolfit had used in his own production and which he had given to me with the last batch of costumes. In fact, Rosalind Wolfit's father, B. Iden Payne, had staged this play in a similar Jacobean style when he directed it at Stratford in 1937 and so my idea was not wholly original. Anne brought off the pathos of Imogen's desolation after the departure of Posthumus and also when she thinks that she has found his decapitated body, most touchingly. ('A rare and moving beauty', to quote Charles Green again). The whole company, in fact, certainly rose to the occasion and Clifford as the King, Eric Greenwood as Cloten, with George Metcalfe, Edgar King and Chris Bloxsom as the banished Belarius and Cymbeline's two lost sons, all gave really excellent performances.

My set suggested the end of a Jacobean hall with a screen made up of an irregular mixture of decorative devices of the period, including that favourite of the Elizabethans, strap work, against a mottled background. Our vine grew over and through it and simple props, such as Imogen's bed with candelabra by it and an ivy-covered arch of rock to represent the cave, were set in front of it. Laurie made me a huge cut-out of a gold eagle for the vision of Jupiter and this appeared in a swirl of smoke and a shaft of amber light, but the ghosts were solely off-stage voices. Through the centre opening of my 'Jacobethan' (to borrow someone else's amusing word) screen, a large medallion that I had rescued from the great Stratford Shakespeare Exhibition of 1964-5, could be seen and looked very impressive.

The music was taken from Mahler's 1st Symphony and its romantic grandeur earned the comment from Charles Green that I had 'infallible taste in music' for the productions. He also said that I had an 'exquisite talent for creating a picture on the stage' but Bernard King in the Evening News spent half his notice saying what a bad play he thought it was. The big night was another occasion for a Lord Mayoral speech from the stage and also a reception for the civic guests afterwards. Unfortunately, the Wolfits were in Africa but they sent a message for the Lord Mayor to read out. It ran thus:- 'Greetings and congratulations from your patron and patroness on this tremendous artistic achievement and congratulations to Portsmouth who nurtured this great and ambitious scheme—Rosalind and Donald Wolfit'. The Evening News devoted the whole of its leader to us on one night and said, amongst other things, 'No other city in the world can claim the fine record being celebrated this week . . .' It went on, 'People with a great depth and breadth of knowledge of the theatre have been unstinting in their praise of the work of Mr K. Edmonds Gateley and his

Cymbeline Pier Theatre, 1966

Cymbeline's lost sons, Guiderius and Arviragus (Chris Bloxsom and Edgar King), with Belarius (George Metcalfe) outside their cave

company. In every enterprise of this kind there is usually one man whose personality, drive and enthusiasm are key factors. It is in no way detracting from the talent and skills of his company to say that Portsmouth owes a great debt to Mr Gateley for his devoted work in offering to the city, and particularly to the schoolchildren, the sparkling interpretations of the Bard's works which we have been privileged to see each year since 1947. Some cities, we think, would have made much more of this talented company'. The week ended with a party for the cast backstage and during it I was presented with a beautiful silver salver which had been subscribed to by the members of the company. This was a very moving tribute as, indeed, were three individual gifts that were also made to me. Melita gave me her late father's gold cuff links, Edgar King a delightful coloured porcelain bust of our author and Eric Greenwood, whimsically and enchantingly, a toy cannon on a plinth. As he gave it to me, he said guilelessly, 'You have completed the whole canon—so here it is!' In spite of the crabbed ones, and they really were only two or three at the most, it had all been very splendid. As Shakespeareans we had conquered the world! The great thing about being the first to do something is that you achieve a record that cannot be beaten. It may be repeated but no one else can ever be the first.

When Donald and Rosalind returned from Africa, I told them all about it and let them see the press notices. 'I am delighted it all seems to have gone so well', said Donald. 'The play is like *Troilus and Cressida* was twenty years ago—the press and critics will come to understand it *in time.* It cost me much money in my time'. Some months afterwards I was with him and mentioned that we had played to 1,714. I said that I thought that, for amateurs, that was not too bad. 'My lad', he said, 'for *anyone,* that is *very good* for that play!'

A week after the last performance of *Cymbeline,* David Lippiett and I had driven up to Heathrow with the Fulcher family to see them off on their plane to South Africa. I shall never forget the searing minute during which we watched the plane shrink in the sky until it had 'melted from the smallness of a gnat to air', as Imogen had said only seven days before. I had many other good friends, amongst the most important of whom were David Lippiett, whose companionship on that hideous afternoon had been a great comfort not to be forgotten, and Chris Bloxsom and Edgar King, with whom I spent the following evening, and, of course, my sister and Prue. They were all invaluable, as indeed were others. None the less, the departure of the four Fulchers left a void in my life. I, who had always thought of myself as being self-sufficient and something of a leader, discovered just how very vulnerable I was.

With the completion of our staging of the whole canon, some people asked what we were going to do next. I pointed out, with raised eyebrows in order to stress my surprise at the question, that we should do what we had always done—be a Shakespearean repertory company. The fact that we had now staged each of the plays at least once did not make any difference. When all was said and done, many of them had already had two and even three productions. In my heart, I knew that it was not as easy as that. The loss of John Fulcher robbed me of one of my two right arms and we had run out of stimuli. At first, there had been the excitement of getting it all going; then there had been the transfer to the Pier. After that we had built up to the Shakespeare Quatercentenary and the further move to the grandeur of the King's Theatre. Finally, our climax had been reached with our ascent to the peak of world records. What next? To be honest, there seemed to be nothing ahead except routine all the way to the horizon.

No sooner had our next year's programme of one play at the King's and two at the Pier been announced, than a blow fell which was not a complete surprise. It had been dreaded as a possibility ever since the denigration of the Pier had started two years before. The Portsmouth Corporation decided that its theatre should cease to be. It was to be converted into 'a floor show type of entertainment' and the Minor Hall would become an 'amusement centre with slot machines'. The Portsmouth Players, the Arts Theatre and we were up in arms immediately. In a bitter letter to David Evans, who was promoting this new use of the Pier, I pointed out that it was 'ironical that after all these years of back-slapping from so many of the City Fathers—during which they have said that everything must be done to help and encourage the City's remarkable amateur companies, etc., etc., etc.,—they have now taken away their only theatre. If they think that we can survive (or for that matter, wait) until they have built some pipe-dream of a civic theatre in half a generation's time, they are mistaken . . . The prompt purchase of the Theatre Royal would be the answer. Will it be sacrificed to the great god, Money, like everything else? If so, it shows what all that has been said over the years has meant'. I repeated much of this to the press in an interview and also told them that we had lost money on both occasions that we had been to the King's. It was quite logical, therefore, to assume that we would not be able to survive if that remained our only venue.

Only a few weeks after all this, there was a further announcement. One of the giant, multi-million restaurant and catering firms had made an offer to take over the Pier on a long lease. The City Council, with only one member against, accepted the scheme with amazing speed. How strange that an international company of such proven astuteness and business acumen should wish to take over a structure which we had been told was coming to the end of its days and which would, in the words of one City Councillor, 'fall into the sea within ten years'! There was some talk in the early days after the take-over that amateurs would still be able to use it as a theatre out of the summer season but it soon became clear that this was not going to be practicable. In no time at all, a huge bar had been built all along one side of the auditorium and a permanent store for it of the same length on the outside of the building. These totally blocked all the emergency exits of that half of the theatre. A hole, the size of a grave, was cut out of the centre of the stage to accommodate an illuminated fountain that, I was told, weighed a ton. The main dressing room became a boiler room and most of the previously permanent seating in the circle was removed to make room for fixed tables. Finally, the solidly-blocked windows that had ensured a total black-out in the auditorium were replaced with clear glass. Although the new management made statements to the press that these things could all be overcome, it was obvious that our battle had been lost before the smoke from our first shots had died away. It became a showbar called the Gaiety Lounge and it was never used as a theatre again.

Our record-creating presentation of *Cymbeline,* with which we 'gave the Pier a unique honour' (to quote Harry Sargeant in his history of the city's theatres which was published some years later) was thus the final production to be staged in its theatre. It is perhaps foolish to say, 'All those years ago I could never have guessed . . .', but I could not help thinking back to my boyhood and of those pantomimes, concert parties and touring plays that I had seen and which formed the foundations of my theatre-going. It had always been so pleasant when we put on our plays there, too. Not only were Buster, the stage manager, and Harry, the electrician, and all the rest of them such good friends of ours but the whole ambience of the Pier was delightful. Before performances, Prue and I would often take a picnic supper to the deck chairs at the sea end and relax there as the sun was going down over the Isle of Wight. The sound of the lapping of the waves against the beams of the underside of the pier and the sight of the occasional yacht, or even of a distant liner on its way to Southampton Water, were enchanting. In the theatre, I always had a place in the main dressing room near one of the windows because it had more space for my inevitable collection of folders and plans. On a nice evening, it was such a joy to have that window open and to look out, as I was making up for my part, at much the same scene now that the sun had almost set. Later in the evening, if it was warm enough for the window still to be open, it was equally delightful to come off the stage and to find that the strings of coloured lights round the pier deck had been lit and that happy-sounding people outside were wandering past below us. There was even the pleasing vanity, when we had been sitting in our deck chairs, of hoping that patrons who had arrived early and were taking a stroll round the deck before going in to the play, would be regulars who would recognise us. 'Look, there are two of the actors!' Maybe, they did; maybe, they did not. In any case, it was all part of the fun.

Commander Cooper kindly offered to have us at the King's for all three plays instead of only the one in February that had already been booked. Knowing the financial risks involved I decided to take up his offer as far as the autumn was concerned but to cancel the spring play altogether. This would, therefore, be another year with only two plays in it. I made this decision all the more easily because it gave me an opportunity to have a surgical operation that I should have had done years before. I was suffering from a bad double hernia which had started one night at the Maddermarket when I was scene-shifting. I felt it go! The operation was performed at about the time when we should have been doing our spring play. It was really quite severe and my friends rallied round to my great comfort. Prue took me to the hospital and brought me home again afterwards in her car and my sister was, of course, a daily visitor. Most of the rest of the company came to see me and there were flowers and messages from the Wolfits ('an enforced rest is often a good thing', said Donald on one of their cards) and Professor Sprague. The Fulchers cabled for news from South Africa and I had not felt so generally popular for a long time.

Strange to say, being something of an invalid for several months afterwards, helped me out of a purely social problem to do with the plays. Except on celebration occasions, we had never had 'last night' parties as we originally considered them to be the mark of the amateur. However, several close friends, such as John Fulcher, David Lippiett, Chris and Jenny Bloxsom and Prue, had started coming back to my house after final performances since we had been at the Pier. Gradually these gatherings had grown and more people descended on Crossways automatically every time. I regretted this, as I was usually very tired anyway, but the matter got out of hand and I did not know how to stop it. One of the unfortunate aspects of it was that the members, many of them very senior ones, who were not invited resented the fact and felt that there was an elite from which, unjustly, they were excluded. I was aware of this and sympathised with them but I was not prepared to throw my home, which I tended as meticulously as ever my mother did, open to the entire company. After my operation, I

King Richard II King's Theatre, 1967

Aumerle (Chris Bloxsom) tries to conceal from his parents, the Duke and Duchess of York (Prue Higham and Clifford Allen), that he is involved in a plot against the newly-crowned Henry IV

brought these unfortunate parties to an abrupt halt. I claimed that I was just not fit enough to cope. This was, in fact, true but I made sure that when I was fully back to normal they would not be allowed to start again.

The first play of the 1967 season had been *King Richard II* with David Lippiett in the title role. The 'minor key' quality which had just taken the edge off his Romeo was ideal for this part. He played it superbly and achieved the subtle change from unsympathetic profligacy to heart-rending self-knowledge beautifully. His verse-speaking was excellent, as was that of most of the principals, but it was again becoming difficult to find enough good actors to fill a large cast. A few of the minor parts were not particularly well done but George Metcalfe as a cold, hard-headed Bolingbroke, Clifford and Prue as a charmingly domestic pair of Yorks, with Chris Bloxsom as their son, Aumerle, were well up to standard. Richard's Queen was very movingly played by Chris Bloxsom's wife, Jenny, but after this play they were both lost to us as they moved away from the district—another great personal sadness only months after the Fulchers' departure. The set, dominated by a large, gleaming, scarlet, royal blue and gold shield bearing the Arms of England, was an enclosure of heavy brown walls with Gothic arches scrawled on them like white graffiti. The weather ran true to form: on the first night, the storm outside was so bad that the rain even penetrated through the window frames of the King's Theatre dressing rooms!

Again we lost money and obviously this could not go on for much longer. In my hospital bed I scribbled various worried notes which I sent to the King's asking for some sort of revision of our terms but nothing much could be done until I was on my feet again. One afternoon during the summer, Joan Cooper came to tea with me and we discussed several minor economies that we might make but did not achieve anything very positive. Shortly afterwards, we had an SSA Advisory Committee meeting and decided to form a supporters' club that should be known as the 'Subscribing Members'; a clumsy title for want of a better. Eventually, they inevitably became 'The Friends'. Ken Crago, a vigorous bank manager who had always been interested in the amateur theatre, kindly agreed to organise all this for us and did it with very welcome enthusiasm and efficiency. Our desperate cries for help appeared in the press under such headlines as, 'Save our Shakespeare Company', 'Actors in danger of "curtains" ' and even another leader, this time under the quotation, 'To be or not to be . . .'; and the money started to come in. The 'National Debt' owing to me had risen to its highest figure at the end of 1958 when it had reached nearly £1,000 (a figure that should be judged by the value of money at that time) but since then, in spite of all our financial 'alarums and excursions', there had been a small surplus each year and so the sum had been slightly reduced.

The autumn play was a production of *The Tempest* which was very similar to the previous one in 1958. The storm scene, with which the play opens, was almost identically done; even to having a sailor on a swinging rope ladder disappearing up into the flies. This time it was a totally unrecognisable Prue! I managed to avoid the short break between the first two scenes that I had disliked before. From the start, I had Prospero and Miranda faintly visible on the island behind the ship, watching the storm which he had created. The change of scene was effected simply by flying the sail and its trappings out of the set and bringing the lights up on the whole stage. Prospero was then immediately ready to pacify Miranda's distress at what the audience had seen her witnessing. The growing interest in open stages had so influenced Shakespearean productions

The Tempest King's Theatre, 1967

Trinculo, Stephano and Caliban (Barry Wilkins, Douglas Bray and George Metcalfe) are amazed to hear music played by Ariel (Sunya Webster) who, to them, is invisible

elsewhere that sky-cloths and cycloramas appeared to be in danger of becoming as old-fashioned as realistic painted back-drops. In any case, I found that an enclosed set was so much more satisfactory to light: an illuminated background often took away some of the effectiveness of front lighting. From now onwards, our sky-cloth was banished and the background for this production, composed of flats, suggested dense jungle greenery and rocks.

I again played Prospero, one of my favourite parts, and Sunya Webster, John Fulcher's first wife who had also remarried, repeated her brilliant Ariel. If Prospero is confidently in command of everything, the play tends to lack the conflict which is the life blood of all drama. In an attempt to avoid this, I tried to make him a man torn with doubts about the value of revenge and conscious of his own bitterness. Often the key phrase of a Shakespeare play is in a line of very few words—as when Mercade enters in *Love's Labour's Lost.* In this one it is surely the moment when Ariel says that, were he human, his spirits would become tender at the pathetic sight of the bewildered lords. 'And mine shall', says Prospero becoming, in an instant, very human and fallible. Those three words are the turning point, just as Romeo's 'Then I defy you, stars!' are his. I cast Barry Wilkins, who had been so good as Puck, in the part of Trinculo but it did not work as well. He seemed afraid of the audience and no comedian will ever get over to them if he shows that. I then realised what is the essential difference between the two parts. With the exception of his short epilogue, Puck is always completely within the action of the play and is therefore protected by being part of a company. Trinculo, on the other hand, often addresses the audience, especially in his first long speech, and so needs something of the music-hall technique of a stand-up comic. The latter part obviously needed a more experienced comedian than Barry was that time.

On the Saturday night before we opened, the King's Theatre celebrated its Diamond Jubilee with a champagne party, to which Prue and I were invited, on the stage. The SSA, therefore, began a new era for them. On our first night we received a delightful telegram which read, 'All good wishes for tonight so pleased you are starting the next 60 years, let us hope great times lie ahead for all of us—Joan and Reggie Cooper'.

So ended a rather bleak year. All too many journeys had been completed during the previous one and there was a sense of emptiness creeping in. In John Fulcher, the company had lost one of its most valuable originals and I had become painfully aware that the SSA was an increasingly heavy load to carry without his shoulder to lean upon. Prue was as great a consolation as ever but, even so, I felt that I lacked half of the support upon which I had depended so much more than I had previously dreamed that I did. The Pier Theatre had reached the end of its journey and thus our happy eleven years there were over and past. The climb up the mountain of the complete canon had been accomplished and, in spite of all that I had said, it was rather difficult to decide where we would travel on to from there.

The year had, however, started on a very pleasant note but that, too, turned out to be the end of another journey. ITV were running a series of quizzes between three members of a famous family and three of an unknown one. One of these was to be recorded in the Portsmouth Guildhall and on that occasion the famous family consisted of Donald and Rosalind Wolfit with his daughter, the actress Margaret Wolfit. To my delight, they made Crossways their base camp for the day. I gave them an evening meal before the recording and I remember Donald's asking me not to make it heavy. 'I must not cloud my brain with food', he said. Such sound advice to any actor: a big meal before a performance has a most subduing effect. He also retired to my bedroom and slept on the bed for an hour before he went. It was a memorable day of lively conversation and, for me, enchanting company. The television people sent a magnificent limousine, complete with uniformed chauffeur, to take them all in regal style to the Guildhall. Donald put on his familiar black trilby hat and heavy camel-hair coat, which he had bought many years before for a Canadian tour, and they made a marvellous exit, thanking me for my hospitality and frankly enjoying the splendour of their luxurious transport. It was such a very happy occasion and so great a joy to be able to entertain them under my roof again. How sad I would have been if I had known then that I should never see him again.

CHAPTER 20
Unlucky 21st — Part II

On a Saturday morning in February, 1968, the scenery, costumes, props and equipment for the opening production of our 21st Season were moved into the King's Theatre. Two hours later, Melita telephoned and said, 'Have you heard the news? I know it will upset you but, if you are quick, it is on the radio now. Sir Donald Wolfit is dead'. I switched on immediately and, of course, it was true. Unashamedly, I wept.

Nearly two years before, when we had been discussing the problems of transporting some more of his costumes to us, he had said, 'I regret to tell you I am far from well, under the doctor and due to see a specialist tomorrow and I don't want Rosalind worried with all this'. Though concerned at the time, I did not give it much more thought as he did not mention it again. What turned out to be his last letters to me were all concerned with our fund-raising and with the attempts to save the Theatre Royal. He sent his own vigorous pleas to the City Council and, in one of his letters to me, he asked, 'Tell me—does the bar still hold good about the King's Theatre having permission to allow professional shows at the Royal? There are many people asking me this question—including Brian Oulton who helped your campaign.' This referred to a covenant that the Coopers had put on the Royal, which forbade its ever being used again as a theatre, when they bought the King's from Mrs Sperring and her company in 1964. 'Why does the King's cost you £300 a week? How? . . . Shall I write to Cooper?' he asked in his last letter of all. His final communication was a postcard only six weeks before he died. I was on the brink of going to the Portsmouth Guildhall as part of a deputation, which included Anne Nicolle and Clifford, to make a speech pleading to the City Council that they should buy the Theatre Royal. He wrote in a shaky hand which at the time I attributed to haste, 'Dear Peter, I have written and I hope it gets in in time. Good luck to the deputation. Yours, D.W.'

In a curtain speech after our first night, only 48 hours after his death, I said, 'Sir Donald was the greatest man I have ever known and the greatest man I am ever likely to know'. Hosts of memories from our thirty years of friendship flooded back and one of the richest of them was of a day in 1955. Donald, Rosalind and I had lunch together at the Ivy, the restaurant that was famous for its theatrical clientele. That in itself was thrill enough but there was better to follow. In the afternoon we went to the St Martin's Theatre, just opposite, and saw Bernard Shaw's *Saint Joan* with Siobhan McKenna in the title role. When we came out, Donald took Rosalind and myself to the Garrick Club. To be shown round that immensely impressive building with its baronial staircase and great, dignified rooms lined with books and paintings, by no less a person than Sir Donald Wolfit was a tremendously exciting experience. The highlight of the day was when he showed me a framed letter that had been written by David Garrick to the patron of an aspiring player who obviously did not stand any chance at all in the profession. Donald put his arm round my shoulder and read aloud to me the words of England's most famous actor in the magnificent club that bears his name. It is no wonder that I treasure that moment as one of the supreme theatrical experiences of my life.

The play that opened our 21st Season was *The Winter's Tale*. My theories about it, which I have already explained, were stressed by the setting. I used a very bare stage and restored the skycloth to favour for just one more play. Framed by two large skeletal screens, made to look like old bronze, was a big square flat on which I had painted an abstract of a cool, winter sun set in icy blues and greys. As before, the audience found that the curtain was already up when they entered the theatre and that, by means of an electrical effect, snow could be seen falling against the dark skycloth. It stopped when the play began as so distracting a device would have been too irritating a background. The winter sun remained until Antigonus took the baby to the wild place and then it was taken up out of sight into the flies and storm clouds could be seen scudding across the sky. After the interval, they were still there. However, during the speech of Time, they faded away and were replaced by the serene blue of summer as another large square flat descended which bore a flaming sun in a setting of yellow and orange. It was this regenerating symbol that backed Hermione when she appeared as the statue. Irrespective of their locations, the two halves of the play were clearly shown to be representative of winter and summer.

The transformation of Leontes after the real death of Mamillius and the supposed one of Hermione is often said to be too extreme to be believable. I never found it so and I came to regard this part as another of my favourites. The possessiveness and the unreasoned anger struck a chord of recognition in my own soul as did the deep regret and lasting self-recrimination that follows. Scholarly analysts of drama are prone to worry about the causes of Leontes's jealousy, just as they are about Iago's. This always seems to me to be utterly bootless (a good Shakespearean word!) as surely Shakespeare's view is clear in the answer of the sensible, down-to-earth Emilia to Desdemona's complaint, 'Alas, the day! I never gave him cause'. She says, 'They are not ever jealous for the cause,/ But jealous for they are jealous: 'tis a monster,/ Begot upon itself, born on itself'. These things are often not understood because academics prefer to apply rules of literature to their study rather than to consider their own emotional experiences. Only in that way could they ever consider, as many of them do, that Leontes is not jealous right from the beginning of the play. This is one great advantage of examining them through acting in, and directing, them.

Anyone who has been inside the skin of Leontes knows that all those short comments that open his first scene, which Hermione describes as 'too cold', are cover-ups. His first open admission to the audience, 'Too hot, too hot . . . my heart dances; but not for joy, not joy' is not a sudden out-of-the-blue beginning as far as he is concerned: he could easily have said, 'I am angling now,/ Though you perceive me not how I give line' at the very beginning of the scene.

Prue, strong, warm-hearted and capable, was perfectly cast as Paulina whilst Marie Seaborne (now, Crispin, following marriage) was a lovely Hermione. Clifford was in his element as the Old Shepherd—at his best as a character actor, especially when playing idiosyncratic old men—and John Pearce, our resident clown, ideal as his son. Eric, with Touchstone, Lear's Fool and Feste behind him, came off very well indeed as Autolycus. The leading parts were all strongly played but the new people coming in for the lesser ones were fewer and most of them seemed to be less talented than the majority of the newcomers had been in our earlier years. *The Tempest* in the previous autumn had been even harder to cast well and we had finished with only three sea creatures for the dance of Reapers and Nymphs. On the other hand, the sheep-shearing jollities in *The Winter's Tale* were well enough stocked with delightful rustics and those scenes were very merry and looked pretty with their festooned strings of summer flowers and the bright sunlight.

Not only did the production open under the cloud of Sir Donald's death but, during the day of the first performance, the City Council were debating whether or not to buy the Theatre Royal. As so many of us had striven openly and hard to bring this about and the King's management was rootedly against it, relations between us were distinctly strained. The Coopers arrived back from the Guildhall just as we were preparing to make our first entrances and the atmosphere was very frosty. The Council rejected the idea by 35 votes to 17. The death of King George VI had caused the cancellation of the opening performance of our 21st production and the whole season in which it was included was fraught with misfortunes. Even greater unhappiness seemed to be blighting the opening of our 21st Season. It looked as if it was not *Macbeth* that brought bad luck in our case, but the number 21. Other events, as yet unborn and still in the womb of this strange year, would confirm the theory.

The plan for this season was to have three plays again. Now that our Subscribing Members were providing the necessary subsidy to enable us to put all our plays on at the King's, we were financially reasonably secure. However, my own next priority was the accepting of an invitation to go and stay with the Fulchers in South Africa. Prue wanted me to cancel the spring play rather than to leave it in someone else's hands for the first time since Ron Mills had directed *Hamlet* in 1951 but I decided to ask Clifford to do it. He had had quite a lot of experience of putting on modern West End successes with his church dramatic society some ten years earlier; he had shown a flair for teaching in his capacity as our Acting Instructor and he had become a passionate devotee of Stratford ever since I had first introduced him to it in 1962. The play was a difficult one, *King Henry IV, Part I,* but he accepted without hesitation. As far back as the 1963 Festival, when I was ill during the first few days of rehearsals, it had been Clifford whom I had asked to take them for me. I designed his lighting and the few fragments of scenery that he required under his instructions and realised for the first time that he does not know one end of a pencil from another. He cannot draw and it can be very difficult translating such a person's wishes as the picture

The Winter's Tale King's Theatre, 1968

The supposed statue of Hermione (Marie Crispin) is revealed to Camillo, Florizel, Perdita and Polixenes (Richard Cole, David Lippiett, Mavis Whyte and Edgar King, *left*) and Leontes and Paulina (KEG and Prue Higham, *right*)

in his mind is so much more vague than it would otherwise be. I did all my usual production and business management jobs before my departure and then left him to it.

Prue drove me up to Heathrow and I set off on my 14-hours flight, crossing the equator for the first time and being hardly able to believe my eyes when we came down for a brief stop at Nairobi and I stepped out of late winter into the equivalent at home of early September. John, Ann and the boys met me at Jan Smuts Airport and the four of them gave me a really wonderful month's holiday. We spent the first week at their home in Johannesburg and then they took me on a 4,000-mile tour. We crossed the desert of the Karoo, paused at Kimberley (which looked like the set for an American Western), saw ostriches and the fabulous Kango Caves and then unpacked for a rest at the beautiful Mediterranean-like souternmost tip of Africa, just outside Cape Town. Whilst we were there, we had the great thrill of going up Table Mountain before moving on along the Garden Route of the East coast, which was breath-taking, to Durban, which I found disappointing and uncomfortably humid. From there we went to stay in the Kruger National Park where the people are locked up in cages called cars in the daytime and rest camps at night whilst the wild animals roam free. Amongst the great forests and mountains of the Transvaal, post from home caught up with me and I was shattered to learn that Crossways had been broken into and that some vile burglar had robbed me, selectively and knowledgeably, of the treasures that my mother had left me and which I most prized. The curse on the 21st year was at its work again! However, John and Ann had also arranged countless other delights including a brief stay in the magnificent little country of Swaziland, a descent down a gold mine, penetrations into parts of the veldt where white men seldom go to see black African life in the raw and a personal tour of the Johannesburg Civic Theatre.

The more marvellous it all was, the more frightened I became that they would be unable to resist these golden temptations and would decide to settle there for the rest of their lives. I spent the month being constantly torn between joy on the one hand and my fears for the future on the other.

Clifford still had two weeks of rehearsals to go after my return from South Africa. I stepped into the small part of Northumberland and found myself hating it all just as much as I had done in the early days when other people had directed some of our productions. With a largely bare stage and with groupings set very much four-square to the front, it was clearly a copy of Stratford's recognisable style at that time. There was no doubt about it, he made a very good job of it. Why then, I asked myself, did I seem to see only those things that I did not like? My old possessiveness, I suppose, and my everlasting desire to run everything myself. None the less, the performances of the leading characters were not directed in the way that I would have done them. The Falstaff was a big man but as an actor he was what I have always called a behaver. He was splendid as himself in whatever situation he was put into but he was unable to assume any other character. His Falstaff was simply a youngish man who was heavily padded except, because he had not been properly costumed, round the legs. David Lippiett's Hal was ingratiating to Falstaff and his cronies—the last thing that he should have been—and George Metcalfe's Hotspur was efficient but too controlled. He lacked the raw rugger-player beefiness that the character requires. (Actually, I am sure that I did, too, when I tried the part in 1954!) The fierce Welsh warrior, Glendower, whose age was about 44 at the time of the action of this play, was portrayed by Clifford as a comfortable old man in a white wig. I could never understand why. He had been so anxious to have a huge cast that he had imported all sorts of people who were completely without talent. Most of them appeared as soldiers and ran about the battlefield in scanty black costumes. I unkindly christened them, 'The Mickey Mice'! Even Falstaff's followers had a tavern wench each in the Boar's Head. This savoured too much of operetta for my liking and Professor Sprague, who came down to see it, said to me in private afterwards, 'I could have done without the ladies in the town'. The box office was good for the King's—at an average of about 2,500, the popular plays were doing less well there than they had at the Pier. The general public figure was about the same as usual but the schools' support was particularly strong and pushed the total to just over 3,000. It was their choice for the year: for once it was not *The Merchant of Venice*! We had one special schools night of each production, with every seat at the same low price, and for both *The Tempest* and *King Henry IV, Part I* it was a complete sell-out of the whole house, including the upper circle.

I was greatly missing the Fulchers but their absence helped to highlight the closeness of the relationship between Prue and myself. We were both very independent and so our respective ways of life suited us remarkably well. I liked my freedom and she was happy living with her sister, Jill. In any case, we saw each other almost every day, as she was still the secretary at our dental practice, and, as our houses were fairly close to each other, there was no problem about being together at other times as well.

Shortly after the play, I was very thrilled to receive an invitation, topped by the royal cypher in gold, saying that 'The Lord Chamberlain is commanded by Her Majesty to invite' me to a Garden Party at Buckingham Palace in June. I accepted with delight but, as one of the snags of being a bachelor is that one is expected to attend such functions alone, I asked if it would be possible for me to be accompanied by 'Miss Prudence Higham'. I explained who she was and pointed out that her position in the SSA was both important and unique. I assumed that the invitation was in recognition of my work for Shakespeare. To our amazement, the answer was 'Yes'. When the time came, I hired the traditional grey topper and morning suit and on the great day itself Prue and I had lunch with Gwen and Norman Punt at their house in Kensington. After it, they very kindly drove us to the Palace where we found the whole occasion to be both glamorous and enriching. The Queen, the Duke of Edinburgh, the Queen Mother and Prince Charles were all there; the military bands played and after going through the gilded rooms of the Palace, we strolled amongst the elegant throng on the lawns and by the lake. In the evening, very appropriately we went to a show at Her Majesty's Theatre and then had a late dinner on the way home. It had been a very splendid day. Only a week later, there followed another one when we went, accompanied this time by David Lippiett, to Glyndebourne to see Mozart's *Die Entfuhrung aus dem Serail.* Gorgeous music, more strolling on lawns—in evening dress this time, of course—and dinner by that other lake at sunset. Prue and I were having a very good summer together.

Three weeks later she was dead.

She had visited a friend just north of Petersfield in Hampshire and was returning shortly after midnight alone. There was a head-on crash with another car in which were two young soldiers who had missed their turning on their way back to camp. She was terribly injured and the wreck of her own car had to be cut open before she could be released from it. After being in intensive care, she died a few days later.

What more can be said? Much of this book could be read as her obituary. For 22 years she had been one of my dearest friends, and, for almost as long, a keystone of the company who was just about as irreplaceable as anyone could be. She was the only person besides myself who had taken part, either as a performer or as a backstage helper in one capacity or another, in every single performance that the company had given in its 21 years. An old friend summed her up perfectly when he said that she was 'the most *improbable* person' to have died. To say that she had great warmth, strength and a 'common touch' which enabled her to win the trust and affection of people on all levels of society is not the cliché that it may well appear to be. The extraordinarily large congregation at her funeral and the amazing number of wreaths were testimony to the truth of this. She was equally at home in full evening dress at Covent Garden or in paint-stained trousers and an old pullover working as a scene-shifter in Southsea. Her last appearance on the stage was as Mistress Quickly in *King Henry IV, Part I.* Under my direction she had played the character in both Parts and also in *The Merry Wives of Windsor* as a tidy and housewifely person, not unrelated to her superb Nurse in *Romeo and Juliet,* but Clifford wanted her to be much scruffier in his production. She had not liked the idea but she had given him what he asked for without complaining because she was an artist and, both in the theatre and out of it, a great trouper.

I had long since realised that although my direction of the company was referred to as an 'amiable dictatorship', I relied so heavily on the support of John Fulcher and Prue that it was, at times, almost a triumvirate. I had now lost both of them within two years. The 21st Season had done its worst and the dictator was alone.

Maimed though it was, the company had to continue and I had to go on leading it. The replacement of Prue as Wardrobe Mistress was only one of several changes that were necessary round about this time. When John went to South Africa, Edgar King took over as Stage Director and Chris Bloxsom became the Headquarters Manager for a short time until he, too, left the area. He was succeeded by Eric Nicolle who also became the first occupier of a new office, Business Manager. He had a great gift for the cut and thrust of financial negotiations and the commercial politics involved. These matters worried me too much and I was beginning to develop an anxiety neurosis. Earlier in the year, Commander Cooper had called a meeting at the King's Theatre of 'All Chairmen of Amateur Dramatic Societies' who had put on shows there. I guessed what was in the wind and, as I had no intention of being harangued in public, got Prue and David Lippiett to go as my deputies. The gist of his message was that support of the Theatre Royal campaign was harmful to the King's and that he was planning to alter his terms for amateurs. In July there was to be a Government Public Enquiry about the future of the Royal but, shortly before it was due, Nick (as Eric was usually called) and I had to go to the King's for a further meeting with the Commander and his General Manager, now Michael de Barras. Had I gone alone I would have coped with it very badly and finished in a state of nervous exhaustion but Nick was superb and handled the situation for me. I sat back like a constitutional monarch and let my prime minister get on with it! The meeting was a tough one and unacceptable terms were presented to us. Above all, it was made crystal clear that support of the Theatre Royal was actually damaging business at the King's—an argument which I did not understand—and that, if I wanted to continue staging my plays there, I should desist. I had no alternative but to agree but I did point out that I could not be responsible for the actions of the members of the company and secretly I still intended to continue to work underground. I could not now take part in the Public Enquiry but I wrote as fully as I dared to the Inspector. His decision was that the preservation order that already existed on the Royal should remain in force and so prevent the theatre's enemies from pulling it down as they wished to do. Even so, we were still ham-strung by the covenant that the Coopers held which forbade its use as a theatre.

The third and last play of the 21st Season was in the autumn of 1968 and Christine Field, a teacher who had helped with many odd jobs previously, nobly stepped in and took over the wardrobe which, extraordinarily, Prue had only recently tidied and inventoried. The play was *The Taming of the Shrew* and so the task was not as big as it might have been.

Quite a few professional productions of it these days seem to be in the hands of unsuitable directors who start off with all the trendy clichés such as 'socially and politically aware' (a thin disguise for using a play that was not designed as such for propaganda) and 'relevant for our time', and then go on to say how much they hate it. I am sure that it is useless to approach this play from the late-twentieth century angle of assuming automatically that all under-dogs must be in the right and that anyone who is treated roughly is bound to be a nice but misunderstood person. Likewise, it is wrong to take it as a serious, social drama. First of all, the structure of its being a play-within-a-play is of the utmost importance and the audience must never lose sight of this fact at any point. This then makes it clear that the story being told is intentionally artificial and should be enjoyed for its fun. The treatment of Kate is therefore no more cruel than the caning of the robbers in the schoolroom scene in a *Babes in the Wood* pantomime. Another modern fault is the toning down of the shrewishness of the lady in question. She is obviously intended to be a termagant who is so wild and impossible to live with that, until she can learn to make herself pleasant, no one dares to get too close to her. Lastly, it must be realised that this farce was written for an Elizabethan audience whose feelings about it would be less squeamish than our own. In short, it must be directed as a play of Shakespeare's time and not, as it all too often is, as one of our own.

In my production, I wanted to stress two particular aspects: firstly, it must have all the fun and excitement of a 'show' in the modern sense of the word and secondly, as the 'play's' audience and its actors are on the stage together, they must be made recognisably different. To get some of the brash glitter of the former, I used the music from *Kiss Me Kate* and to achieve the other aim of separating the two groups, I put the characters of the Induction into modern dress and staged the play that they were watching in mediaeval costumes. This also had the effect of allying the stage audience with the real one in the auditorium.

The note that I wanted was struck immediately by the curtain's going up to the singing of 'Brush up your Shakespeare' from the soundtrack of the film. The troupe of players could be heard arriving in a motor coach off-stage and when they appeared they were in the sort of everyday clothes that actors would wear when travelling today. The Lord and his huntsmen were in the scarlet tail-coats, white breeches and shiny black boots of traditional 'hunting pink' and their entrance made a spectacular *coup de théâtre.* The 'actors' unpacked their skips on the stage to the blare of Cole Porter's racy tunes and set up their props in an angle of a large brown room that had patches of harlequin diamonds sketched on the walls. The whole production went at a great pace and included a free-for-all battle with apples and dishes at the end of the supper in Petruchio's country house and human trees that moved to and fro whilst the actors 'marked time' in the returning-home scene. It was full of fun, as I am sure Shakespeare intended it to be, and played to very enthusiastic audiences.

I used the epilogue, in which Sly wakes up and sees the actors disappearing into the night, from the old play which was Shakespeare's source, as it rounds it off so well. Sly, played by my big actor, Douglas Bray, and the huntsmen were on the stage throughout: he enjoying the comedy that was being put on for him and they his antics as well as occasionally finding themselves press-ganged into 'walking on' in small parts; a device which caused laughter through its incongruity but which helped me as I was again short of actors. I used, as Nugent Monck had done, the interruption by Sly from the source play that comes after Tranio has cried out, 'Send this mad knave to the gaol'. 'We'll have no sending to prison, that's flat', he protests: an Elizabethan tinker knew enough about the insides of such places for him not to want one in a play, not even as a joke. It is such an authentic touch that I could not resist including it. George Metcalfe brought an ideal rather brittle sparkle to the part of Petruchio and the infallible Anne Nicolle was beautiful and vivid as Katherina. Some of the small parts were not very well done and, as I had been under so much strain after Prue's death, this led to several outbursts of temper from me during the rehearsals. Some of the shortcomings were due to parts not being thoroughly enough learned and I was finding it increasingly difficult to tolerate those who were not prepared to work as hard as I did. Perhaps the casting of myself as the harrassed father, Baptista, was more apt than I had realised! I think that I had a reasonable skill at putting over witty lines but I was never particularly good at broader comedy such as this.

Our troubles were by no means over. Apart from the ceiling of our Gossip Room coming down during a rehearsal and only just missing one of the actors, we could not agree with the management of the King's Theatre over the matter of their new terms. Two months after *The Shrew* we had still not received our share of the money taken and were faced with a bill from them that we could not afford to settle because it was so much greater than anything we had been charged before. The idea was that we should virtually pay for the running of the theatre during our week and then, in Commander Cooper's own words, 'If at the end of the year's working, you are showing any trading loss . . . after taking into account any subsidies received, R. B. Cooper Productions will, within reason, meet your losses'. The outlay that such a scheme would involve, the gamble that those last eight words inevitably implied and the fact that henceforth we could never hope to do more than break even, made the arrangement utterly impossible as far as we were concerned. Any future productions at the King's would be out of the question until all this could be changed. The only thing to do was to look elsewhere. The Pier had gone, the Royal was unusable and I had no intention of retrogressing to a church hall. Those benevolent City Fathers who had declared year after year that everything possible must be done to help such talented assets to the community as ourselves, did, in fact, do nothing.

When Bernard Miles started his Mermaid Theatre, it took the form of a portable Elizabethan stage set up in a barn in the garden of his St. John's Wood home. Leonard Russell and I went to it and it was just the sort of thing that I should have liked myself if my old Cotswold scheme had ever materialised. However, now I wondered if I might have such a stage made and plant it in the vast concert hall of the Portsmouth Guildhall. I made enquiries but the idea was really a non-starter as our small audiences would have been lost in that huge space. In any case, it looked as if there might be licensing problems as it was not a theatre. I went further afield and asked the management of Southampton University's little Nuffield Theatre if they would have us. They said that they could fit us in for one week a year but I did not follow it up as it would have been absurd to expect our regular audiences and the entire company to travel 25 miles for each performance. The basic truth was that I was in a mild state of panic as there was just nowhere in the City of Portsmouth that was suitable for us. The financial tangle with the King's had reached a complete stalemate and so, for the foreseeable future, we were homeless.

After several more weeks, however, those wrangles were finally settled and both sides agreed to even more new terms. The first play of the year was therefore not staged until May: it was *Hamlet* with George Metcalfe in the lead. This was probably the finest performance he ever gave during his time with us. The analysing intellect of the character suited him perfectly and the quality of his verse-speaking was superb. He was well matched by Anne Nicolle who was a Gertrude that Professor Sprague, who came down to see this one as well, thought was quite extraordinarily good. This time I designed a dark grey set made up of draped nets against a sombre mottled background which had the merest suggestion of the eye sockets of a skull. I appeared as the Player King and tried to show slight disapproval when the amateur, Hamlet, tried to tell me how to do my job—even though that advice is the very finest that any actor could be given. It is surely Shakespeare's voice rather than Hamlet's. The houses were surprisingly poor and the press notices were only luke-warm apart from richly deserved praise for George and Anne. Len Russell had lost his ex-RAF panache over the years and his Claudius lacked the strength of his previous portrayal. Clifford gave a good bumbling Polonius but the critics wanted more depth. Charles Green complained that he had seen 'far more memorable productions' by us and Bernard King said, 'No doubt the production will pick up during the week, as it must if Mr Metcalfe's acting is to be given the support it deserves'. The real life dramas of the past 18 months, coupled with 22 years of running the company and my dental practice in tandem, were making me weary and it was presumably beginning to show.

Shortly after Prue's death we had decided that there should be some sort of memorial to her. We sent out an appeal to the members and the response was extremely generous. As she had been an expert fencer and had, for some years, arranged all the duels in our productions, it was agreed that the money should be spent on a set of first-class Elizabethan swords to be made by Tony Watts who, at that time, provided the weapons for the Royal Shakespeare Theatre. He made a beautiful job of them and I am sure that Prue herself would have chosen something practical of this nature if she could have been consulted in her lifetime. They were first used in *Hamlet* and they not only look extremely well on the stage but they are splendidly balanced weapons to use.

During the summer of 1969, Melita, who had been our Secretary since before there were any letters to write and Treasurer from the days when the bank account had not even been opened, decided to retire. Two years before, she had married and now felt that her new home life should be her whole concern. One can understand actresses working hard on every production for 22 years because there is excitement and a sort of glamour to be enjoyed on that side of the company but Melita's tasks were the exact opposite. Her contribution to the SSA was incalculable and a chapter of our history ended when she went. A piece of cut glass was presented to her as a farewell gift to remind her of us though I am sure there was no danger of either her forgetting us or we her.

Although we were doing only two plays during this year, other stage appearances had kept me quite busy. In the previous December I had performed for one night in a religious jamboree at the King's Theatre with Joan Cooper, the Bishop of Portsmouth, three choirs and an amateur orchestra. It was called *The Road to Bethlehem* and was one of the worst rehearsed and most pretentious amateur concoctions that I have ever been involved in. Immediately after the performance, all the sycophantic supporters of the organisations that had taken part came round backstage vying with each other to find the greatest superlatives of praise. I was so nauseated that I slipped away into the night as quickly as I could. Were those, I wondered, who praised the SSA just as misguided? I hoped not but it disturbed me.

I also made my debut on the concert platform of Portsmouth Guildhall. I was the compere for the Schools Music Festival. With two or three hundred children piled up in seried ranks already in position, I was announced like a visiting guest star and came on alone to great applause. I felt like a famous pianist entering to play a concerto but I think the hordes of teachers there all thought that the wrong part of the entertainment was being clapped!

The autumn play was *King John*. It was not put on until November as we had to move out of our original earlier booking because a large Rotary Club conference wanted to come to something merrier and easier! I liked playing the lead in this history as the character has a trait in common with me. The key to him is that he likes getting his own way and making opinionated statements but shies away when his adversaries retaliate. Like Leontes, he seems to some critics to have two aspects which they find almost incompatable. As with that character, I have never found this to be so: I see both their apparent opposites in myself and therefore have tried to play them with sympathy. I am a true Gemini and had Leontes and King John, as Shakespeare drew them, been real people I am sure that they too would have been born under that sign of the zodiac! Artistically this play went a good deal better than *Hamlet* had done. Anne Nicolle, to nobody's surprise, was magnificent as Constance. Eric Greenwood brought the wry humour that had been such an asset in parts like Feste to the Bastard and Clifford was cunningly imperious as Cardinal Pandulph in a cast that was generally stronger than we had been able to muster for some time. The plain, stark set was mottled white and consisted of two diamond-shaped blocks of rostra and steps backed by three thick monoliths in an otherwise black stage. With much use of large shields and banners, coupled with a wide range of lighting effects, this worked excellently and enabled me to produce some strikingly spectacular pictures. Not least of them was the entrance of Pandulph. The smell of incense pervaded the auditorium, plainsong could be heard and all the French and English towards the front of the stage were thrown into silhouette as the monoliths glowed with scarlet and purple light and the red-

King John King's Theatre, 1969

Cardinal Pandulph (Clifford Allen) arrives to wreck the new alliance between King John (KEG) and the French King (Edgar King). Onlookers include the Bastard (Eric Greenwood, *far L*), Queen Elinor (Stella Miller, *L of centre*), and Constance with the boy, Arthur (Anne Nicolle and Huw Tipler, *2nd and 3rd from R*)

robed cardinal appeared from amongst them at the highest point. I was determined that there should be no more 'Mickey Mice' and so all my soldiers were loaded to the eyes with helmets, heavy full-length cloaks, chain mail, gauntlets and boots. This came off as I had hoped it would and made them all look tough and bulky.

Eve Tipler, a keen helper and the mother of the small boy who played both Mamillius and Arthur, had joined forces with Buster's wife, Susie, and had costumed *Hamlet.* They were most anxious not to become the Wardrobe Mistresses on a permanent basis and so, just before *King John,* Anne Nicolle very kindly offered to take over the job. She really did not want to do it either, but she could see that we had been rudderless since Prue's death and so she offered her services very nobly for the sake of the company. I accepted most gratefully and she organised the department very efficiently; producing, with Eve and Susie as her chief assistants, some extremely beautiful costumes including a marvellous one for me as the king which was a long gown of gold brocade with great pointed sleeves that were turned back to reveal their linings of brown velvet.

Since Donald's death, the solitary name of 'Lady Wolfit' on our programmes as the one patron had looked very lonely. As a decent interval had now passed, I gave the matter some thought and then decided to invite a friend of mine from the professional theatre to make the number up to two again. He was a Shakespearean actor whose many brilliant performances at Stratford I had admired over the years and who had just scored a considerable success on television as Soames in *The Forsyte Saga*—Eric Porter. Since about the time of our world record he had taken a lot of interest in the SSA and, to the delight of all of us, he accepted the office. How, though, would the still deeply sorrowing Rosalind feel about someone being asked to occupy the position that only her husband had held before? 'I don't think there is anyone I should like better than Eric Porter to take his place', she said. 'He is an actor whom I greatly admire and I have been deeply grateful for the fine and generous things he has said about Donald'.

After too many tempests, we seemed at last to be heading for 'calm seas' and 'sail so expeditious' once more. We had a new and successful, if slightly unwilling, Wardrobe Mistress and another Patron of whom we could be very proud. The captain, however, was beginning to wonder how much longer the voyage would last. Even the Flying Dutchman came ashore every seven years but I had been at the helm for more than two decades already and could see no sign of landfall ahead yet.

CHAPTER 21

The escape route

John Fulcher's place on the Advisory Committee had been kept open for him all the time that he had been in South Africa. He was therefore the only survivor from the cast of the initial production of 1947, apart from Ken Barnard, the 1954 Falstaff, now retired from acting but enjoying being our front-of-house representative, and myself, still to be on the active list; although it had to be admitted that his being separated from us by 6,000 miles did make that rather more theoretical than practical. However, he had always held the concept and the realisation of the Southsea Shakespeare Actors so very highly that it seemed to me, perhaps for no better reason than that he was too far away to influence our affairs, that I owed a greater responsibility to him than to anyone else to maintain the standards and the output that he so revered. I felt that I must not let our quality deteriorate in his absence lest there should be reproaches when he arrived back.

It came, therefore, as something of a shock when the Fulcher family returned to England in April, 1970—having been away for six months longer than the three years originally planned—to find that, apart from still remaining as an adviser and consultant, John was not prepared to take any active part in the productions. He and Ann were now more sophisticated than they had been in the old days and were too busy working and bringing up a growing family—after two more months there would be a third son, Michael—to find time for the amateur stage. My sister, Gwen, and I went with John's widowed mother and Ann's parents just after dawn on a bitterly cold morning to meet the liner on which the family travelled. I did not realise at the time that I was welcoming home only my dear friends and that the actor and company worker whose return had been so anxiously awaited was not there with them after all.

From my own point of view, it was a pity that they had not arrived back in the previous autumn as I had been expecting them to do. My increasing boredom with the chores of preparing each production and the strain imposed by the theatrical politics in which I was involved, together with the emptiness that followed Prue's death and the Fulchers' exile, took their toll and I found myself getting into so highly neurotic a state that I had to consult my doctor about it. He put me on to tranquilisers but with the return of spring and my old companions, this happily passed. Had they come home sooner, I am sure I should have had a happier winter but also they would have been able to see what I regard as my very best production of all that I ever did. It opened our 23rd Season and was my fourth attempt at *Twelfth Night.* At last I felt that I really had achieved the atmosphere that I had been aiming at ever since the company began its life with this same play. I was influenced and helped by seeing John Barton's perfect Stratford production only the year before and I stressed so strongly in my programme notes that this was the nearest that Shakespeare ever got to writing a Chekhov play that Bernard King headed his review, 'Anton Shakespeare of Moscow-upon-Avon'.

My setting consisted of a complete enclosure of high, trimmed hedges and leafy arbours with a rustic, latticed canopy entwined with branches of real leaves over the whole acting area again. As in *All's Well that Ends Well,* when I had used one before, the overhead spotlights filtered through it and dappled the stage.

The interiors were produced by using Elizabethan screens made largely of painted gauze. When the lights were upon them, they looked like solid panelling but, when they were not, they became frames like ornamental iron gates. A pair of these did service, for example, as Malvolio's prison. Once again, Clifford's performance of that dry and uncomfortable character was first class. Indeed, the standard of the whole of the blessedly small cast that this play needs was astoundingly high. I cannot list them all but David Lippiett, a splendid character actor as well as a romantic lead, gave a Sir Andrew who was both funny and pathetic. Eric was Feste yet again and with the passing of the years had been able to bring an even finer technique and deeper feeling to a part he had always played so well. 'Let the woman ever taken an elder than herself', says Orsino and so I risked tackling the part myself. 'A man of maturer years', said Charles Green, 'rather than a dashing young aristocrat, and the unrequited love of a man of mature years is always infinitely poignant'. Recordings of a solo lute provided the only incidental music and Eric composed his own settings for the songs. Occasionally, in the past, we had had problems finding a singer but generally we were lucky. Eric had been our best voice for many years and prior to his time we had had a remarkable boy soprano named Michael Cunningham who had appeared in play after play. At auditions I always asked if there was an owner of a lute amongst the aspirants but there never was.

My Viola was Marie Crispin and she was such a sensitive actress that she contributed in very large part to the achieving of the right balance between the high comedy and the deep melancholy of this wonderful play. She had something of the quality of a September day with its subtle changes from golden sunshine to gentle rain. In the Barton production, the distant sound of the sea breaking on the shore kept stealing in during the emotional moments that involved the twins and unashamedly I copied this most evocative effect. Nora, my first Viola of over twenty years before, wrote that the production 'had the right magic' and that 'none of the comedy was forced and the note of sadness as well as gaiety added to the charm'. A local canon said, 'I cannot remember being more greatly moved by the concentrated pathos of the final scene . . . your interpretation was amongst the sublest I have seen and quite memorable visually as well'. Both writers were stern critics who were usually very sparing of their praise.

The production that was in fact the first that the Fulchers saw after their return was a largely disappointing one of *The Merry Wives of Windsor.* During the previous year we had done only two plays instead of three through force of circumstances but for 1970 I had decided that two would be enough. Casting was difficult and I was getting tired. The reason why we had not done a new production of this play for 22 years was not that I had grown to dislike it but that, Micawber-like, I had been waiting for something to turn up. It was not the arrival of a remittance, like that impecunious gentleman, but the reopening of the Theatre Royal. Some of the City Councillors had said so often, 'You just wait; it will be the Southsea Shakespeare Actors who will be invited to stage the first production there; it won't be long now', that I had believed them. They had started nearly ten years before but at last I had given up waiting. I love this comedy very dearly and I thought that it would be such a joyous piece for the rebirth of the splendid old theatre. I had been storing ideas for it in my mind all that time and so I had great hopes for its success when finally I decided to put it on at the King's instead.

The set was one of my all-time favourites and that, I think, can be accounted one of the successes of a very variable production. Half-timbered houses, reduced simply to their wooden frames, stood on either side. One was the Garter Inn and the other Ford's house. When gaily-coloured, painted curtains backed their lower beams, they became interiors. Likewise, when tattered hessians came down from the flies to conceal the roofs and gables, they turned into trees. The backcloth, which was again a huge screen composed of flats, was a jumble of Elizabethan gable ends, with black timbers and yellow, orange, red and rust infillings, framed by snow-tipped branches and a distant silhouette of Windsor Castle. Herne's oak was a huge, leafless tree, originally made for *As You Like It,* decorated with icicles and that final scene in the Park at midnight was completed by some outsize holly bushes loaded with big red berries.

Leonard Russell, as he had got older, had become restrained and schoolmasterly: characteristics which, alas, were not what were required for Falstaff. Like me, he had only a modest talent as a comedian and so, as I played Ford, our several important scenes together were rather tame. Ian Richardson, who, after my time, would become one more patron of the SSA and who had already been a friend of mine for several years, was dazzlingly funny as Ford at Stratford in 1968-9. I had hoped that I could copy him to some degree but my attempt was as much of a failure as my Robert Harris impersonations had been twenty years before. It is enough to say that Anne Nicolle was Mistress Ford—she was enchanting, of course. Clifford, who could manage a passable Welsh accent, produced another of his nice, fusty characters as Sir Hugh Evans but really only he, with George as a spirited Dr. Caius, Eric as Shallow and John Pearce as Slender gave performances that got laughs. Two of the leads had such difficulty in learning their parts—and Shakespearean prose is often very tricky to memorise—that their scenes were never adequately rehearsed. Nothing can be more fatal to comedy than that: it must always be smooth and effortless and too much of this production was neither. It did at least end on a happy note: I had the whole cast strolling off the stage, back home to Windsor and into the night, softly singing the carol, 'The holly and the ivy'. Would that the week had finished as merrily! Were the stage staff and their helpers particularly stupid and lazy when they struck the set and packed everything up after the last performance or was it just that I was bad tempered through exhaustion and disappointment? I fear that it was the latter but the realisation of that fact now comes rather too late in the day. However, I had certainly had good reason to be extremely angry during one of the performances earlier in the week even if I had no real justification on the Saturday night.

I had carefully checked with the Chief Education Officer that there was no problem about having a small boy, Huw Tipler, as Arthur in *King John* when we had done it a year before. I knew, therefore, that it would be perfectly alright for him also to appear as William in *The Merry Wives*. When one is giving a performance one is in a very highly-strung nervous state and so my feelings can be imagined when I was told, just as I was about to make one of my entrances, that the Child Welfare Officer or some such functionary had just arrived backstage and insisted upon seeing me to discuss the legality or otherwise of Huw's presence in the cast. To come at such a time was absolutely outrageous. I flew into so great a temper that I told the bearer of the messge to order him out of the theatre and added that, if he would not go, I would throw him out myself when I came off the stage. How I played the scene in such a state, I do not know. If this person was within his legal rights, then the law is indeed an ass. I am not sure how much of my outburst was conveyed but he had gone before I made my exit! The matter was coped with satisfactorily and correctly by telephone the next morning. We were entirely in the right and if the official had done just a little homework beforehand there would have been no need at all for his turning out of his home that night—unless he would have cared to pay his money and come to see the play.

During the previous summer, Portsmouth had commemorated the centenary of the death of Charles Dickens who was born there. Many people felt that it should have been done on at least a national scale but it was in fact left largely to local amateurs. I gave two performances of a one-man Dickens recital as part of the official celebrations. For some years I had occasionally performed readings to the Portsmouth branch of the Dickens Fellowship but this was on a grander scale. Some bright organiser thought that it would be appropriate for me to appear at the Charles Dickens School without realising that the public avoid entertainments in such buildings whenever they possibly can and that this particular one was so off the beaten track that most people did not know where it was. The press report said that the passage about David Copperfield's journey to Betsy Trotwood 'was so movingly read that some of the audience were reduced to tears' but, none the less, my houses were thin and included only two acting members of the SSA, though, to be fair, many of them were occupied elsewhere. If my lamp burned low, so did others, too. One, the Arena Players, went out altogether. After their start in schools, they had moved into the Minor Hall at the South Parade Pier. When that closed, they then set up their open stage on the floor of a large room in the Portsmouth Guildhall. It was there that they presented a short play by Dickens, called *The Strange Gentleman,* as part of these centenary junketings. After that, they disappeared. They had, in fact, never been a threat to the SSA, even though, round about 1964, it did look briefly as if they might be. The Arts Theatre celebrated their Silver Jubilee and the Dickens affair at the same time by putting on *The Only Way,* Martin Harvey's old vehicle which was based on *A Tale of Two Cities,* at the King's Theatre. After it, they decided that their financial state and their following were

The Merry Wives of Windsor King's Theatre, 1970

The permanent set

now too reduced for them to appear there again. Henceforth they would be seen only in church halls or, eventually, the new little, open-stage studio theatre of one of the local colleges. 'How are the mighty . . .'! They had lost their headquarters in the City Library two years before and were now faced with accommodation problems as well. The SSA had no intention of leaving the King's. The Portsmouth Players, too, were still thriving and, like most amateur operatic societies, were, in fact, playing to capacity audiences which included an extraordinarily large proportion of people who never went to the theatre to see anything else.

More contentions in the autumn only increased my sense of disenchantment. Late in 1957, Ron Mills's father-in-law had died and his place as our Honorary Auditor was taken by John Marshall, a bank manager who had been one of our leading actors during the first six seasons. He had now also become a city councillor and was, at that time, very anti-Theatre Royal. Ironically he has since changed his views and is now one of its strongest advocates. However, he had then made speeches in the Council Chamber about Theatre Royal supporters which we of the Advisory Committee felt were so antagonistic to us that we asked him to resign. Ken Crago, our Subscribing Members Organiser, then put in his resignation as a protest against our action. It was an unhappy business but was pure politics and, like friends on opposite sides of the House sparring in Parliament, it did not affect any of our friendships. It was soon over and our former happy relations were quickly restored. John Marshall became more and more of a supporter of the SSA; not least of all did the company find this so when he became Lord Mayor in 1984-5. In the meantime, successors must be found. Betty Nicholls, that great rarity, a woman bank manager, kindly took over the Auditor's job and Nora Alder turned her considerable energies to the organising of the supporters' group. I had known her since the Dickens Fellowship, of which she had long been a vigorous member, had helped to make up the cast of my historical scenes in the Coronation Tattoo.

At least all that was sorted out but I had begun to yearn for an escape route. It was as if I had pushed this truckload up the steep slopes and now, having come over the peak, it was running away with me down the other side. I must put the brake on but where could I find it? The season after next would be our Silver Jubilee and so surely that would be the ideal time to give up as it would be a landmark and the completion of a good round figure of years. I no longer felt the compulsion to keep it all going as it had always been. The few old hands that were left seemed to have lost much of their incandescence and the really bright enthusiasts, of whom Clifford was the undoubtedly the leader, were all comparative newcomers to whom the pioneering days were really just history of largely academic interest.

Whether or not I retired then, the present situation could not go on for ever and so the time was ripe to consider the future of the company. It so completely belonged to me that it would have been in my power simply to close it down and sell up but that would have been a very great pity after so much had been created. No, it must certainly continue, if possible, but under what sort of leadership? Having been run always only one way, I felt sure that a sudden change over to a democratic committee would probably be fatal and that, for a time at least, it should continue on much the same lines as during my reign. Who could, or more importantly who would, take over as a complete dictator-director like myself? There was only one possibility: Clifford, a bachelor who was even more blinkered and single-minded about the theatre than I was. His attachment to Shakespeare had not started as early in life as mine had and he was considerably weaker on the academic side but his passion for the plays in the theatre since he had started going to Stratford in 1962 had become almost obsessional. There was no doubt about it, he was the only person. If he refused, then the company would probably disintegrate very rapidly.

With this plan already forming in my mind, I had invited Clifford to direct the first of the two plays for the following year. *The Merry Wives of Windsor* had been my 77th production in 23 years: as many times as that I had been through my 80 to 100 jobs varying from struggling with the problems of working out a rehearsal schedule to making the packing lists for the removal into the theatre. It had become unutterably boring and so, too, had the recording on paper of every tiny production detail of the 70 of those that I had directed myself. Clifford had been Public Relations Officer since the summer of 1964 and that had relieved me of quite a lot of items but there was still a monumental amount of sheer drudgery to be done each time. Two of Clifford's activities in the past looked now as if they might prove to have been useful rehearsals for the future. I had been ill with 'flu on the night of one of the auditions and he, accompanied by Edgar, had conducted it for me. More important than that, however, was his taking part in a series of experimental acting sessions which he, Len Russell and Nick had organised over seven weeks during the summer break in 1966.

As usual, when I had SSA problems, I turned to John Fulcher for his views. I put my ideas to him and he agreed immediately. He said that he was delighted that I had made the decision, even though it meant the end of an era. He had a considerable talent for summing up a situation very neatly in a single short sentence. 'I am glad you are going to stop soon', he said; 'I was afraid that you would continue for too long and then go down fighting'. We both agreed that as my retirement from the directorship would not be for almost another two years, it was too soon then to make the announcement. We thought that the beginning of the final season would be ideal and so we would have to keep our secret for another twelve months. However, events in the following summer forced my hand to make the announcement earlier.

My annual letter that winter included the now frequent pleas to the actors not to be quite so often unavailable for productions and to support the social events between the plays more enthusiastically. I felt rather like the prefects in the school stories of my youth 'rounding up the slackers and getting them on to the pitch'. The trouble was lethargy rather than antagonism, I think, and I was able to use the excuse of appealing for support for Clifford as he was such a beginner in the field of Shakespearean production. I gave my reason for handing over another play to him as being my need to rest as, having done so many productions, I was in danger of running out of ideas and of getting stale. This was, of course, no less than truth.

The play was the schools' choice for the year, if one can regard 12 answers to 103 letters sent out as a true consensus of opinion! Yes, it was, of course, *The Merchant of Venice*! Clifford played Shylock and I was cast as Antonio which I found to be the most depressing part I had ever played. It is entirely in a minor key and after its spineless opening line becomes steadily more and more negative as the play proceeds. Marie Crispin was a small but charming Portia and David Lippiett returned to being a juvenile again by playing Bassanio for the second time. On Clifford's instructions I designed a plain semi-circle of simple arches for his set. The production lacked pace and shape and took half an hour longer to perform than my own had using the same length text. It was overloaded with comic business that held up the action and included a mock ceremonial for Morocco and an Arragon played like a comic Don Quixote who had endless trouble with an overlong lance. Charles Green's headline read, 'Farce overdone in excellent "Merchant" ' Clifford's own performance was very good and he directed himself as a plausible, but human, potential murderer. It was very much as it would have been under my direction except when he overplayed the melodrama in the Trial Scene. There was one touch straight out of the worst sort of old musical comedies, that I particularly disliked. He had two supposedly vivacious Venetian girls whose job was to stand about and give the exteriors the right atmosphere. This was a bad enough idea in itself but, unfortunately, he gave the parts to two very serious actresses who looked embarrassed and indulged in the awful old cliché of standing with both hands on the same hip! I nicknamed them, 'The women who kept the wool shop in Venice'! The director under my skin itched to get out!

Professor Sprague had told me that he so very much admired our work that he would like to make a special visit to us in order to give a talk on Shakespearean productions that he had seen. This was a very great honour and so a date was arranged without hesitation. He came down in May and, as always, stayed in my house. We hired a small hall and he gave us a superb lecture full of fascinating reminiscences after having started by congratulating us on our achievements. It was a marvellous occasion of peace and delight but it actually took place when the company was in a state of some upheaval.

Only three days before, Edgar King, complaining that my attitude towards him had become intolerable, had resigned from the company. I was appalled that inadvertently I had offended him but no amount of apology or regret on my part would mollify him. His friendship was one that I very greatly valued but I had been totally unaware that my behaviour had changed enough to cause a breach such as this.

John and I had thought that it would be unwise to ask Clifford too soon about his possibly taking over the directorship because, once he had said yes, assuming that he did, it would be terribly difficult for us to avoid giving the game away through careless remarks in conversation. 'Sometime later on in the summer or even the autumn', we had said. However, the Edgar affair made us think that perhaps we ought to move a little faster. As we felt that this was something that we wanted to do together, John and Ann invited Clifford and myself to dinner one evening about a fortnight after Edgar's letter had arrived. It was not until halfway through the meal that we started teasing Clifford by implying that he had been lured into a trap. Eventually, over coffee and brandy, I told my story and said that we would like him to replace me as the Director of the SSA after the last play of the 25th Season.

He was obviously very much shaken by my news that I intended to retire but, when the great question was actually posed, he went crimson and visibly sweated. All he could say was an anatomical oath which, had it not been in the plural, would have been a four-letter word! When, at last, he partially got his breath back, he was obviously torn between excitement and disbelief that it was all really happening. Not surprisingly, he needed time to think but quite soon, humbly and clearly somewhat in awe of the task ahead of him, he accepted. However, we still thought that it was too soon to make a public announcement about something which would not happen for nearly another year and a half.

Only a week later, another letter precipitated the matter still further. It would be truer to say that I received two letters for the price of one. It, or they, were from George Metcalfe. Four months before, he had composed one of them and had hoped that the members of the Advisory Committee would sign it before it was sent on to me. They had not done so for a variety of reasons—some had not even seen it—and so he was sending it now, unsigned, but with a covering letter of his own. This 'round robin' contained passages such as, 'We all acknowledge your ability . . . and the immense amount of work you have consistently undertaken . . . However . . . you have often exerted undue pressure on some of your helpers and have used the force of your personality and command of language to push them (with a growing sense of resentment) where they would willingly have gone, given a softer approach'. He went on, 'You have forgotten, or ignore, how sensitive some people can be, take little account of the damage hard words can do, and then expect nothing but willing compliance with your demands, not acknowledging that others are less committed than you are'. Another comment was, 'Your opinion virtually reigns supreme and every decision on every issue is yours'. I was assured that this was 'no revolt, no ultimatum, no challenge' and asked to mend my ways.

However much truth there may have been in it, the fact was that it had not actually been signed by any of the remaining 10 members of the Advisory Committee. The covering letter obviously expected a more violent reaction than in fact it got. He spoke of his fear of 'its miscontruction' and his possible 'ostracism' but hoped that only good would come out of it. My first move was to telephone John and to read it all out to him. I did not like the letters, of course, but I was not greatly disturbed as I knew that the machinery was already in motion for my release from it all at the end of the coming year. John once more used one of his short sentences to put the whole thing into a nutshell. With a sigh of sympathetic weariness, he said, 'Oh! Mate; you don't want to be bothered with this sort of thing at your age'. Indeed, I did not and that remark summed up the whole situation. We decided there and then that the news of my retirement should not be delayed any longer. First of all, however, I telephoned George and in a voice of calculated lightness I assured him that he should not worry as I was not upset by his letters and that I completely understood his motives. That was, actually, slightly double-edged because I had always felt that he and his wife, like lots of people who are strivers for equality, were not entirely without ambition for some of the power themselves. However, I asked him to be patient and I would deal with the matter before long.

There were two things to be done and they had to be timed so that, as nearly as possible, they coincided. First of all, I must write a letter to be sent to all the members and to the press announcing my retirement and Clifford's accession to the throne. Secondly, I must call a meeting of the Advisory Committee and break the news to them. The letters were posted on the day of the meeting so that everyone would hear either late that evening or early the following morning.

I gave no hint that the meeting was in any way a special one and, up till the moment when I produced my bombshell, I conducted it in a very low key. I dealt with George's letter, which turned out to be the first that some of the members had heard of it, with deliberate calm. Rather like a gentle father telling a child about things that he will understand when he is grown up, I explained the special circumstances of this company and under what pressure I worked and thus attempted to defuse that particular grenade without getting ruffled. I then said with studied quietness and benevolence what I had to say about my impending retirement and Clifford's subsequent taking over. I added that I would make a gift to him and the company of all the costumes, scenery and other equipment. As far as the 'National Debt' was concerned, they could pay that off if and when they felt like it but, if I died before they had done so, then it would be cancelled. The response exceeded my wildest expectations! There was total silence for what seemed like several minutes whilst they all looked as if they were recovering from bomb blast. Eventually, Ken Marchant, who had taken over as Committee Secretary after Melita's retirement and had been for many years a useful, if rather mild, actor, said slowly, 'It is like when someone has died; you wish you had been kinder to them when they were alive'! The incipient antagonism that I was sensing in some corners collapsed, at least temporarily, like a pricked balloon. The local press had a field day: 'Shakespeare "supremo" to retire' proclaimed the Hampshire Telegraph in a huge headline and the Evening News headed its article, ' "Exit" Mr Gateley, 25 Years Later'. Unfortunately the announcement really was too soon as many people thought that it was all going to happen after the next play instead of, in fact, after another three. However, we had really had little choice in the matter and, in any case, it would give Clifford more time gradually to take over the ropes.

Whatever George had hoped for from his letters or however he felt after my reception of them, he did indeed send me a most generous and amusing letter which he wrote as soon as he got home. It began, 'May I send you my congratulations on your conduct of tonight's meeting?' He continued, 'Quite apart from the superb stage management (my dear, the drama!) I feel that you have done a big thing in a big way, with a command and a generosity which quite obviously left us all floored—I am sure you enjoyed it all immensely! . . . The company will go on and I hope you will have some cause to be proud of it after you drop the reins. Nothing is more certain than that Clifford has a great legacy and is suitably aware of it . . . On a personal level, I owe you an apology for assuming you would not be willing to take criticism in a large dose (an assumption shared, incidentally, by some others—an index of our small-mindedness, perhaps)'. This had obviously been one of my most successful productions. The only pity was that Shakespeare had not written the script!

CHAPTER 22
The Pinafore captain

Every one of my Shakespearean productions was, for me, a mental battlefield. Both the opposing armies had right on their side and, although I like to think that the result was usually an honourable draw, I believe that neither of them ever suffered a downright defeat.

On the one hand I had the text of the play as it appeared in the book. There it was, on the page, in its purest condition obtainable and totally undistorted by either the distractions of a theatrical performance or the vagaries of interpretations by actors and directors. If only I could transfer this ideal form to the stage! The adversary was the desire and need to satisfy an audience with a presentation that was, in the fullest possible sense, a creation of the live theatre. The two seemed to be poles apart and yet the text was written primarily for actors and actresses to perform in a playhouse and somehow they must be so happily united that neither suffered or lost anything of its stature.

When I directed *Coriolanus* in the autumn of 1971 I made my boldest attempt to reconcile these warring factions. It was not entirely altruism: the play needed a huge cast and so I had to devise a scheme, similar to the one that I had used for the *King Henry VI* trilogy, that would solve that problem. I had always been determined that I would never fail simply because I had not enough people available. Many years earlier I had discovered the extraordinary Osiris Repertory Company which was run by a tough old trouper called Nancy Hewins. At the time they were presenting a three-week festival of plays at Chipping Campden in the Cotswolds. They performed in the vicarage garden in the afternoons and the church hall in the evenings or if wet. During their season there, they presented 23 different plays including four Shakespeare histories—*Richard II,* both parts of *Henry IV* and *Henry V*—all on August Bank Holiday starting at 10.30 in the morning! The programme, which I still possess, has a footnote which reads, 'Owing to pressure of bookings on tour, the Company will be unable to produce the three parts of Henry VI until the Autumn'. A huge, subsidised organisation? No; it consisted simply of seven women who travelled everywhere in an old motor coach. The plays were chopped to pieces, of course, and the doubling, trebling and quadrupling of parts was colossal. Miss Hewins, to whose cottage I once went to tea with Professor Sprague and his wife, herself also a professor—a fascinating occasion!—told me that during that festival she had some 40 parts and that the youngest member of her team had about 80. If they could do it, then, if need be, I could, too. Before I had decided how to stage the *King Henry VI* trilogy I had even toyed with the idea of giving one performance of each part with all the cast in evening dress and reading from scripts. Had necessity forced me to do that, the three plays could have been done with, perhaps, as few as half a dozen.

After I had cut my text, *Coriolanus* still had 46 speaking parts, 9 non-speaking and 14 crowds, some of whom were Romans, some Volsces and the rest just soldiers of either side. I managed to gather together a cast of 25. Eleven of these played individual characters and the remaining 14 formed a chorus who, as in my production of the *King Henry VI* plays, could be anything else; either complete as a crowd or in small parts that did not need to have particular identities. Again it seemed to me that some sort of uniform was desirable as otherwise the constant changing of 100 or more costumes would just not be possible. I hired from the RSC wardrobe at Stratford the sets of black trousers and crew-necked pullovers for the men and long plain black dresses for the girls that had been the basic costume for their 1962-72 *Comedy of Errors*. The 11 leading characters each had some minor Roman feature, such as a simple drape over one shoulder to suggest a toga. Black leather armour and shields were also hired from Stratford. The stage was bare except for the two gaunt bronzed screens that had been made for *The Winter's Tale*. I aimed to make the play timeless and even had Coriolanus shot by Aufidius's assasins to bring home to the audience the parallel with today's cowardly political killings. We still began with the National Anthem but before the public had time to sit down, the rebellious Roman crowd had erupted from various parts of the dress circle, the stalls and even one of the boxes. There was no attempt to change make-ups as in whatever scene the chorus appeared they could be accepted for what the text implied that they were at that point of the play.

David Lippiett (now with a delightful wife, Pam—and more godsons for me!) was Coriolanus and gave his finest performance; even better than his Richard II. His insolence appeared to be something of which the character was unaware, which I am sure is right, and his behaviour regretable rather than hateful.

Stella Miller, my former Queen Margaret in *King Henry VI,* brought the right steely quality to Volumnia though her now usual lack of confidence whilst rehearsing worried the rest of the cast as much as it did her. I played the one really likeable character in the play, Menenius, and came off quite well, I understand.

Mr previous production 19 years before had been an affair of shining armour and full Roman splendour but this looked more bleak than any that I had ever done. Then I had used a lighting effect to stress the political swing—the more dangerous the crowd became the more the stage glowed with red light—but this time no theatrical tricks were to be allowed to distract from the purity of the spoken text. I was delighted with the result but I was one of the few who were. Charles Green was surprised to find a production of mine that was not a blaze of colour but found it 'tremendously exciting'. Bernard King in the Evening News liked it, too, and finished by saying, 'As always, the director's scenery, lighting

Coriolanus King's Theatre, 1971

Tullus Aufidius (George Metcalfe) and Coriolanus (David Lippiett) in RSC armour over pullovers and trousers

and choice of music—Richard Strauss's *Death and Transfiguration*—is impeccable. A play for today'; thus, in that final phrase, echoing the one that I had used in our publicity. Charles Biggerstaff, Ron Mills's original Shylock before the SSA came into being and himself a distinguished Titus Lartius when we had done the play before but now long since retired, wrote in horror. 'Oh! Peter!!!', he began. 'The acting left nothing to be desired but the portrayal of the Glory that was Rome—oh! dear!!! Patricians, Senators, Tribunes, etc., dressed in grey flannel bags and pullovers! To one who, like myself, knew the resources of your wardrobe in Elm Grove, this was indeed tragic.' I am pretty sure that Professor Sprague, who paid us yet another visit, did not like it either. One can usually tell by what he does *not* say! Of course, it is by no means everyone's favourite play. Back in 1952, Donald Wolfit had said to me, 'I have never liked *Coriolanus*—but then I couldn't play him and I detest crowds'.

I have one particularly strong feeling about this play which is often described as Shakespeare's most political. I believe that it is not, in fact, about politics but is a study of people involved in them; a very different matter. Shakespeare steers straight down the middle and shows both Left and Right as having equal values. Neither side is presented attractively, even though astoundingly truthfully, and the outcome shows how destructive to society and to humanity extreme political action invariably is. In any case, party politics did not exist in Shakespeare's time and, as always, one can only reach the author's intention by starting to study the play from the Elizabethan viewpoint. It has been presented in the past as propaganda for both the extreme Left and Right and the National Theatre's dreadful production of it in 1971, an example of the former, was one of the worst of these distortions. Directed by two East Germans, the crowd became quiet and knowing whilst the patricians were almost cariacatured. It did, however, have the great benefit of one of the finest performances in the title role that I have seen. It was played by Anthony Hopkins whom I had the pleasure of knowing quite well at one time but, to my regret, we lost touch when he went to America and got swept up into the superstar bracket. David Lippiett alleged that Anthony Hopkins was the only person that he ever saw put his brandy glass on my stereo equipment and get away with it!

Another aspect of the play about which one must be very positive is the pronunciation of the title. Douglas Fielding comes down on me very heavily whenever I say 'Corio-lanus' and he is quite right to do so. He began his stage career with the National Youth Theatre and Michael Croft, its director, insisted upon 'Cor-eye-o-lanus' when Douglas appeared in his production at the Queen's Theatre in London. Granville Barker in his famous *Prefaces* is very good on this subject. That is the only pronunciation that fits the verse or sounds right in relation to 'Corioli' in which the first 'i' must again be said as 'eye'.

The great lesson to be learned, I think, from this production, which was for me an almost perfect realisation of my theories but a drab let-down to many of the audience, was that, however deeply thought out the conception may have been, it was pure self-indulgence to inflict it on to those paying customers who did not agree with my views. I see a parallel here between what I did and those Peter Brook productions that I have criticised. However learned and persuasive our arguments may have been, we probably only succeeded in enucleating those particular plays of the very qualities that give them the richness, colour and, above all, the atmosphere that are their basic essence. The result of my own production was that yet again I found myself saying that now I knew what was wrong, the next one would be absolutely right!

A crown on all the work, anguish and heartache that I had put into these 24 years of running the company was my being made an MBE in the New Year's Honours List of 1972. Being a great royalist and lover of English traditions and ceremonial, this was a tremendous thrill for me. I had been sounded as to whether or not I would accept it in November but did not know positively that it had been awarded until the announcement appeared in the press. By pure coincidence, I had arranged to go to London on New Year's Day with my sister and Clifford to see *Peter Pan,* my favourite book as a child, with Dorothy Tutin, who after my time would become yet one more SSA patron, and Eric Porter, who already was one, in the leading parts.

The Investiture took place at Buckingham Palace in February. One is allowed only two guests and so I invited my sister and John Fulcher to go with me. Once again, Gwen and Norman Punt lent us rooms in their house in which to change and then drove us up the Mall and through the great gates to our appointment. Afterwards they entertained us to a most splendid champagne lunch. As before, it was very exciting to be inside the Palace and going up grand staircases lined with tall immobile guardsmen in their gleaming breastplates and plumed helmets. After waiting, and being briefed as to what we had to do, we recipients of the honours queued nervously at the entrance to the White and Gold Ballroom with its six superb crystal chandeliers. The Investiture was held by Queen Elizabeth the Queen Mother as the Queen herself was on a tour of the Far East. Music from the Guards orchestra in the gallery of the ballroom made the occasion feel delightfully theatrical and, indeed, I felt very much as if I were making a star entrance as I walked along the crimson carpet to stand before that wonderful lady to make my bow. She did not chat with everyone but, to my great joy, she did with me. I was amazed just how much homework she had done as she seemed to know such a lot about the SSA. I particularly remember her asking if we had 'an enthusiastic following' and I was, of course, especially thrilled by the words, 'It gives me great pleasure to give you this on behalf of the Queen'.

Heart-warming messages poured in from all sorts of people. Rosalind Wolfit said, 'Congratulations, congratulations, I am so pleased and Donald would have been equally so'. Professor Sprague wrote from Canada, 'The award should have read, "For services to Southsea, England and THE BARD"; most cordial congratulations, I rejoice for you'. The Stratford-upon-Avon Herald Press, the Lord Mayor of Portsmouth, Harry Sargeant on behalf of the Portsmouth Arts Council (to which I had belonged in its early days but from which I had resigned when they failed to do anything about the Theatre Royal) and Dr Levi Fox, the Director of the Shakespeare Birthplace Trust, were only a few of the others who wrote or telegraphed. Eric Greenwood gave a party for me and several of the old guard of the SSA were there. Was it my imagination or were just literally one or two of them, as they had been at the time of the world record, the tiniest bit sour about it? However, they were so very few and so unimportant that I refused to let them tarnish the brightness of the general response. I could not help but remember the remark of an old friend many years before, 'If you are efficient and successful, no one will like you'. 'No one' in this case appeared to be simply these very few carpers of old.

Something quite different did, however, cast a heavy cloud over this otherwise exciting time. On Twelfth Night, Ann Fulcher had given birth to her much wanted fourth child; this time, to their great joy, a sister for the three brothers. I was very sorry that Ann could not come with John to my Investiture as I could have only two guests but perhaps it was as well that she did not. A matter of hours after John's return home, Sally, the new baby, developed meningitis and died four days later. She would have been another godchild for me and one whom I would have valued as dearly as I do Antony, Richard and Michael. This was the second time that the death of someone close to me had followed immediately after my going to Buckingham Palace; a strange and bitter-sweet coincidence.

Since the end of 1963, we had held an Annual Dinner and Dance at one of the Southsea hotels. We always had a notability to propose the toast of the SSA and I made a speech in reply. In February, 1972, we held the last one at which I should still be the Director of the company and so we invited again the people who had been the guests of honour at our first dinner: Leslie Evershed-Martin, the founder of the Chichester Festival Theatre, and his charming wife, Carol. In our different ways we had each brought into solid and successful realisation our theatrical dreams. I was especially delighted when he gave me a beautifully bound copy of his own book, *The Impossible Theatre,* in which he had written, 'To K. Edmonds Gateley; to celebrate the Silver Jubilee of the Southsea Shakespeare Actors, the company you founded and led with great distinction through 81 plays'. It was a nice start to the 25th season of a venture that had also been declared to be 'impossible' when it was first suggested. '81 plays' was a bit premature; there were still the two of the coming year to be done to complete that number.

The first of them was *King Henry V,* directed by Clifford and staged at the King's Theatre in June. This time, I designed for him a set that was intended to represent the stage of an Elizabethan playhouse. It was painted to look like heavy, weathered timber and had a gallery at the back and a canopy overhead. I was cast as the Chorus and, whilst I loved speaking that gorgeous poetry, I found it a very lonely part. One is never involved with the other characters and there are not even any cues to be given or taken. George was the King but did not bring it off as well as he had done Hamlet. The philosophy, the logic and the clear debates of the Dane had reflected his own temperament more obviously than Shakespeare's ideal soldier. Clifford tried out his Welsh once more by playing Fluellen but he hammered too hard at the part and missed the essential gentleness of the man. His production again owed a lot to the methods then current at Stratford with centrally placed thrones and front-stage line-ups of characters all facing straight out to the audience. Generally I liked the production and it moved at a better pace than his *Merchant* had done but moments such as when the French Princess flung herself into Henry's arms at the end of the wooing scene to a swelling upsurge of romantic music from Bax's *Tintagel,* savoured too much of the old Hollywood film technique for my taste and reminded me of the operetta touches in his previous productions. However, here was the new man establishing his pattern and I was on the way out. It was too late for me to complain. I was glad that this time there were no 'Mickey Mice' on the battlefield! All his soldiers were heavily clad and looked suitably muddy as they lumbered about in their chain mail and tabards amidst plenty of smoke. All that came off very well indeed and showed that he was learning fast.

A few days before the first night, I was visited at Crossways by 83-year-old Captain Colin Hutchison, DSO, OBE, RN with an envelope marked, 'Do not open until the gate is passed; then do so and read to all ship's companies'. The night before 'D Day' in 1944, when the Allied Forces invaded Europe to rescue it from Hitler and his myrmidons, he had led a group of ships out of Portsmouth Harbour. All their commanding officers had been given by him mysterious envelopes which were identical with the one that he had now given to me. 'We passed Spithead Gate at 22.00', he said. When they had then opened their envelopes, they had found that they contained the passage from *King Henry V* which begins, 'Now, lords, for France' the enterprise whereof/Shall be to you, as us, like glorious'. It included, 'Then forth, dear countrymen; let us deliver/Our puissance into the hand of God' and ended with, 'The signs of war advance'. Just before our dress rehearsal began, I asked the whole cast to assemble on the stage as we were on the point of 'passing the gate' into our reliving of Henry V's expedition to France. I opened the envelope and read the contents. It was variously received, especially as several of them were too young to have very strong feelings about something which happened before they were born. I know that I was deeply moved by it and thought that this fine old seadog had made a wonderful gesture.

On a Saturday afternoon at the end of October, exactly a fortnight before my last production as the Director of the SSA was due to move into the King's, Ken Marchant, the new Secretary, telephoned to tell me that the Theatre Royal was in flames. By the time I got there the fire was under control as more appliances had been sent to it than to any blaze in the city since the war. The air, of course, was filled with that awful acrid smell and I could see at once that the stage tower had been reduced to gaunt blackened walls and glowing timbers that looked from the distance like flickering red lights. Thanks to brilliant action by the Portsmouth Fire Brigade, the auditorium and all the front of the theatre were completely undamaged. The stage and the scene docks had gone but these are replaceable. The war was still on.

In the previous year, there had been a second Public Enquiry and once more the theatre had been reprieved. The Coopers' covenant was still effectively preventing any further progress, however, and although many people were continuing to campaign for its reopening, I, whose voice had been so loud in its behalf in the early days, had now had to become silent. A new impetus had come with the formation in May, 1970, of the Theatre Royal Society. At first I had kept out of it, not wishing to stir up the old troubles with Commander Cooper, especially as I had more or less given him my pledge not to preach the Royal Gospel whilst he was having the SSA at the King's and, according to him, losing money out of his own pocket every time we were there. None the less, when in January, 1972, I had been invited to be the new society's chairman, I had accepted. In the following July we had held a buffet luncheon at the Queen's Hotel, Southsea, and a garden party on the Common opposite in aid of funds. Amongst the guests whom I, as Chairman, had the pleasure of welcoming were Bernard Delfont, not yet a lord, Sir John and Lady Clements, Richard Chamberlain, John Neville and an actress who was to become a very dear friend, Doris Hare. Two days later, we had an offer from someone who wished to remain anonymous of a very large five-figure sum of money which would have been sufficient to purchase the theatre. Immediately, through our solicitors, we told the owners that we wished to buy and that we now had the money. After a long delay, they rejected us. It became quite obvious that they had no intention of selling to anyone who hoped to reopen it; they were only interested in demolition and the redevelopment of the site.

Although there would, no doubt, have been a good case for my going out on a merry note with one of the lighter comedies, I did, in fact, choose the very opposite for my retirement play. It was *King Lear* and I selected it because I wanted to attempt once more the part in which I felt that I had given the finest performance of any that I had ever played. I had no difficulty in casting all the speaking parts remarkably strongly but the representative half-dozen of Lear's hundred knights had to be, with a few exceptions, a pretty inadequate collection of inexperienced lads. I had hoped that Anne Nicolle would play Goneril but after *The Merry Wives of Windsor* she had decided that she was tired of acting and did not want to perform again. This was a great disappointment but, after pondering for some time, I had an idea. I wrote to Nancy Glenister, the beautiful Rosalind and Cleopatra of the late 50s and early 60s, with whom I had had such a blazing row. We had not spoken for ten years. Would she like to come back for my last play and take the part of Goneril? Could she not, after all this time and in view of the splendid friendship we had enjoyed years ago, forget our ancient quarrel? To my great joy, she said that yes she both would and could.

Since I had announced that I was going to retire, there had been a tendency to treat me gently. The work was getting easier all the time as Clifford was taking over more and more jobs in preparation for his succeeding to the directorship. It was good practice for him and I was only too glad to unburden myself of the routine tasks that I had grown to dread each time I started on a new production. Even so, there were still some people in the company who could be very tiresome and disruptive. In the early days it had been necessary to ask the men who were not being provided with wigs in the production to avoid having their hair cut but by now the reverse was often the case. Some of the younger ones who were in the Chorus of *Coriolanus* had such long hair that they would have looked ridiculous in Roman helmets. These I had to ask to go and get some of it cut off. One beady-eyed woman in the company who, to my face was as sweet as cake icing that has too much lemon juice in it but, behind my back, was dedicated to undermining my authority, was still working with undiminished vigour. 'He has no right to tell you to get your hair cut; don't you do it, if you don't want to', she was saying. Having to cope with the odd case of that sort of thing was another of the reasons why I could hardly wait to hand over to Clifford.

There was one person who had been in the company since the beginning of the second season, 24 years earlier, who was unique. He had to have a part in *King Lear* even though he was quite extraordinarily short of talent. His name was Victor Bulbecke and no one could ever have been more devoted and faithful. I tried him in small parts but he always failed and eventually he became reconciled to an endless succession of third halberdiers, fourth citizens and fifth servants. He was almost the company's mascot and we were extremely fond of him. He was plumpish and had a dumpling face which, to his endless delight, Wolfit had commended when he saw him as Friar Peter in *Measure for Measure* in 1950. In my final production, he was the Old Man who leads in the blinded Gloucester.

There were two people whose offer to work backstage for just this one production I accepted with tremendous happiness. They were John and Ann Fulcher; he to be Assistant Stage Manager and she the Sound Operator. The

Stage Director by this time was the hard-working Nick but our marvellous Tony Copsey had left the area and there was a new professional electrician on the switchboard who was inadequate. One night, during *Coriolanus*, he had become temperamental and walked out of the theatre, leaving the lights to our own amateurs who were by no means of the calibre of Tony. More headaches and worries from which I yearned to run away. I still enjoyed designing the printing and, of course, we had to have another of our souvenir programmes. The design was the same as the one for the world record but the page of photographs this time consisted of a dozen scenes from our productions over the years. A brief history of the company was also given and the information that our audiences had totalled over 116,000. The BBC became interested again and this was another activity that I enjoyed as I had never lost my love for that wonderful organisation and it meant that I was stepping into the world of the professionals. They brought a television unit over from Southampton and turned my sitting room into a temporary studio when they plugged in their powerful lights. I was duly interviewed and posters and photographs were filmed. I loved every minute of it!

My previous sets for this play, grey with suggestions of Fingal's Cave rocks on it in 1954 and streaked green in 1962, had both been frames for a skycloth on which storm clouds could be projected. By 1972, fashions had changed and I used an enclosed box set and the current techniques which had evolved through the increasing use of open stages. There was a square platform, set diamond-wise with one angle downstage centre. All was otherwise black save for a long avenue of stone blocks like the Easter Island statues that eventually disappeared into infinity. A vague outline of a Trojan helmet on one or a crown on another merely suggested the wide range of human activity. Brechtian conventions were used such as walking all round the outside of the platform to represent a journey or going up on to it to indicate entering a building. A few stark outlines in bronze or rough wood came in from the flies from time to time to locate particular scenes. Apart from the usual thunder and wind noises, the storm was suggested by constantly changing shafts of light from overhead spots piercing a stage filled with swirling white mist from a piece of stage equipment known as a smoke gun.

Anne was now tiring of the post of Wardrobe Mistress which she had taken on out of a sense of duty rather than desire. I was therefore even more than usually grateful that she made several new costumes including three for me. Mine were, unfortunately, not quite as I had wanted them but I judged that it would not be prudent to complain at that time. I had hoped that they would hang in long folds like those in Blake's illustrations to the Book of Job but they were rather stiff and bulky. I had expected a sparse, lank wig (my responsibility, not Anne's) but a concoction of white curls arrived that would have better suited Jupiter in a baroque opera. I roughly man-handled them all to try to improve them but I still felt that I looked like Father Christmas. However, for my first scene I wore the rich gold costume that Anne had made for King John with a voluminous white brocade cloak. To this, I added Wolfit's own Lear crown, which he had worn when he created theatre history with his shattering performance in the part, his Richard III chain and Martin Harvey's glass sceptre, and these were a great help. Even so, when I came to play the part on the stage, I found that I was tired, conscious that this was my finale and keen to be rid of the whole business. I think that additional years of experience had brought a deeper understanding of the part but I suspect that my 1962 performance was probably better. However, Charles Green said that I gave 'a towering performance' so perhaps I did not do too badly after all.

A perfect example of how the whole must be more important than the parts occurred during the rehearsals for this production. When Lear is unsuccessfully seeking refuge with Regan, to his utter dismay Goneril arrives. At that point I had Regan and Lear on opposite sides at the front of the stage. The centre was clear for Goneril to come slowly, inexorably, straight down the middle of the platform to the extreme tip. She was to be like a cold blade of the sharpest steel cutting relentlessly through the dead centre. It was very effective but Marie Crispin, who played Regan, felt that it would be right for her to go and greet her sister. Indeed it would have been if that had been what mattered most. In this case, it would have ruined the grand effect, which was part of the shape of the play, for a corroborative detail of character which was infinitely less important. This was one of the chief differences between Clifford's methods and mine: he would have concentrated on the detail at the expense of the major plan.

Lear would have been a very trying man to live with but this does not diminish the fact that the two elder daughters, however difficult they may have found him, are thoroughly cruel and evil women. This is the basis, surely, of the play and those directors who try to shift this balance are, I am certain, wrong. I tried to make Lear's chief fault his sudden and speedily regretted temper; not unlike a vastly more impressive version of Leontes. I copied Wolfit's trick of being about to strike the Fool with my whip whilst we were waiting for the horses but stopping just in time with a terrified realisation of my state of mind: 'O let me not be mad, not mad, sweet Heaven!' Again I had the marvellously sympathetic Fool of Eric Greenwood; bitter but believably able to make Lear laugh. George was a fine Edmund, charming and ruthlessly cold, whilst Clifford repeated his superb Gloucester. As before, my duet with this withered, blind old man was one of my most satisfying stage experiences. The ageless Mavis Whyte, 17 years after her debut as Cressida, was a joy to have as Cordelia. I had no difficulty in being deeply moved every time we played the awakening scene which was staged with a large white gauze curtain mistily protecting the king whilst he was still sleeping. David Lippiett and Len Russell repeated performances that they had done before; the former his excellent Edgar and the other a bull-headed Cornwall. Both Nancy and Marie looked beautiful and were splendidly vitriolic. It was nice to be surrounded by so many old friends for my farewell appearance.

There was a crescendo of excitement about the last night all through the week of the performances. I knew that there would be some sort of party after the final curtain had come down but it was all kept very secret. When I made my first entrance in the play that night I was suddenly so overcome, not with emotion or regret but sheer terror, that I stumbled over my first line and wondered with horror if I would be able to carry on. I felt as if I were going to my own public execution and that there must be many regular supporters out there in the black void of the King's Theatre auditorium who had come to see the axe fall. In any case, I knew that I had two pairs of friends in the stalls who had come down from London specially for the occasion and who would be particularly critical. They were Gwen and Norman Punt who, being regular West End first-nighters, had little time for amateurs, and John and Alison Kane. As John is a professional actor, he would be almost too observant, especially as he has worked with so many great directors. In a clown's baggy suit of bright

King Lear King's Theatre, 1972

The permanent set

yellow, he had achieved fame as Puck in Peter Brook's white box production of *A Midsummer Night's Dream* and during the rest of his several years with the Royal Shakespeare Company had been directed by Peter Hall, Trevor Nunn, John Schlesinger and other big names. Alison, for several years one of the Royal Ballet School's pianists, had also worked extensively in the professional theatre.

After a few moments on the stage, I managed to pull myself together and for the rest of the evening all was well. I gave a fairly long curtain speech at the end and was nervous as it was, in its way, something of an historic occasion. I made the point that, although all this had been amateur, we had never done it 'just for fun'. In fact, it had frequently been quite the reverse because we had worked so hard in our unceasing efforts to try to achieve professional standards. I ended with Prospero's valedictory lines about abjuring his 'rough magic', breaking his staff and drowning his book.

After the curtain had finally come down, I was detained in my dressing room for quite a long time. When at last I was released, I found that the stage had been cleared of all the scenery and had been reset for a huge party and that there were some 200 guests milling about all over the theatre. Many people had been involved in the preparation of this occasion but the chief organiser and worker had been Clifford. I was shepherded like a star up to the dress circle bar through a sea of faces that belonged to actors and actresses who had been in the company at all sorts of times in the past. When I arrived there, I suddenly saw a phalanx of people who had come down specially from Stratford-upon-Avon and I was almost speechless with amazement. There was Ken Boyden, the managing director of the press which had done all our printing for a quarter of a century, and his wife; Dorothy Withey from the Chaucer Head bookshop there; Roger Fox and his wife, Caroline; with Kathleen Hacking and Clare Tatum, two former Southsea teachers who had retired some years before to Shakespeare's town. They were all totally unexpected. It would be invidious to list all the old faces that had appeared from the far past but our Desdemona of 24 years before, a television executive who had been one of our spear-carriers when he was a schoolboy in 1950 and several of the original members who had been involved in the first production in 1947 were only a few of them.

There was plenty of food and drink and it all looked richly picturesque in the grand setting of the crimson, white and gold of Reggie and Joan Cooper's Edwardian theatre. It was a far cry from the functional church hall in which we had made our debut. On this occasion, the Coopers were merely guests but they seemed to be enjoying themselves as much as everyone else. There were greetings from very many people including Professor Sprague, whose Western Union cable quoted Touchstone and read, 'Salutation and greeting'; Frank Judd, MP; Eric Porter, Dame Peggy Ashcroft and Donald Sinden. John Fulcher had been chosen to make a complimentary speech and to present me with a cheque for £250 which had been collected from past and present members and various friends. He made the whole affair sound very venerable when he pointed out that the SSA was precisely half the age of the BBC! Ken Boyden had brought from Stratford a magnificent cake that had been made there and which had our symbol, complete with Shakespeare's head, open book and nautical background, reproduced on the top in yellow icing and chocolate. His wife presented me with a tribute from the Herald Press in the form of an original terracotta bust of Shakespeare which was a beautiful and witty cariacature of the one in the church at Stratford. It had been made by a young Warwickshire sculptor named Mark Jones. Roger Fox gave me the book, *In Honour of Shakespeare,* which was both by and from my old friend, his father, Dr Levi Fox, the Director of the Shakespeare Birthplace Trust. With the cheque, John Fulcher also gave me another book. This had been specially bound in leather and contained over 300 signatures which represented, as it said in a splendid illuminated address which had been done by Len Russell on the first page, 'the affection and gratitude of past and present Members . . . and Friends of the Company' that I had 'founded and guided through a quarter of a century of singular achievement in the staging of the Plays of William Shakespeare'. All this, needless to say, I found very moving.

My theme throughout the publicity of the change-over from myself to Clifford had been that it would be like the last scene of Gilbert and Sullivan's *HMS Pinafore* which happens to be set in Portsmouth. The captain and the able seaman change places, it may be remembered. After the speeches and the toast, I produced two decorated gift boxes which were a complete surprise to everyone including Clifford. One was for him and the other was a present, as it were, from me to me. As a result of help from a naval tailor whom I knew, when Clifford opened his box he found that it contained a Naval Captain's cap with gold braid on the peak. In mine I had put a sailor's cap which had in gold letters on its black ribbon, instead of the name of a ship, 'SSA Shakespeare'. The joke was a great success and soon Clifford and I, each wearing our respective headgear, were cutting the great Stratford cake together and being photographed by Ken Pratt, on hand with his camera as ever.

The party's merry babble of conversation continued until the small hours of the morning. Theatre people, whether amateur or professional, usually have plenty to say and that night was no exception, especially as so many were meeting again for the first time for several years. It was gratifying that the quarrel with Nancy had now been completely healed and I was particularly delighted to find that Edgar King and his chirpy wife, Betty, had come to the party. When we met again, all three of us were obviously so pleased to see each other that it was as if our breach had never happened. For me it was certainly a fairly tale night of everyone living happily ever after.

Clifford and I had agreed that the signal for his taking over as the new Director should be the descending of the curtain for the last time after that final performance of *King Lear.* I did not, therefore, even have to attend to the packing up of the scenery and other equipment as it was no longer mine. When the party was over, I was able to walk out through the stage door without even a touch of regret. I was a completely free man and my heart danced.

EPILOGUE
Exit Left

CHAPTER 23
The mother-in-law

Did I dream that my retirement from the directorship of the Southsea Shakespeare Actors would make them see me as a loved and beneficient father-figure sitting amongst the clouds like a mediaeval painting of God in a golden Heaven? Perhaps I did. In the cold light of the dawn I awoke to find that the reality would be very different. Clifford had worked like a beaver to put on that magnificent party and to round up all those people with whom we had lost touch. He had made me feel like a king but my reign was to be only 'a one night stand', as they say in the theatre. It was he who had succeeded to the throne.

Even so, the adulation did not die down the moment the presents had been given and the lights of the theatre had been put out after that splendid occasion. Clifford had a personal gift for me which I did not receive until some time afterwards as it had not arrived in time. It was the complete recording of *King John* with my old friend, Donald Wolfit, in the title role. Just before my retirement, Bernard King had interviewed me for the Portsmouth News (the word 'Evening' had been dropped by this time) and an article, which I found both flattering and exciting, was published which occupied the whole of the top half of one page and was headed in very large type, 'The Pride and the Passion'. The Portsmouth Arts Council, as long after as 18 months, said that they wished to make me a presentation and asked what I would like. I chose a first edition of Nathan Drake's *Shakespeare and his Times* which was published in two rather grand volumes in 1817. By strange coincidence, Harry Sargeant, who had now retired from his post of City Librarian, was similarly honoured at the same time. There was a formal occasion in the Lord Mayor's Parlour in the Guildhall when he and I, both Wolfit's old friends, received our awards. It was all slightly embarrassing as the Lord Mayor made the sort of speech that sounded as if it ought to have been addressed to a large crowd but which he spoke in the soft voice that people use at funerals. However, it was a tribute that I was very pleased to receive and the words inscribed inside the covers of each book make good reading: 'In commemoration of 25 years' service to the Arts in

Portsmouth'.

The most impressive tribute that was offered was an Honorary Fellowship from Portsmouth Polytechnic only a month after *King Lear*. This was bestowed upon me during the Degree Ceremony in the Concert Hall of the Guildhall. I was on the platform surrounded by all their most learned academics and facing a largely gowned audience of 1,000 or more. In the best university tradition, an oration was spoken before I rose to sign the Fellows' Book and receive my certificate. Thankfully it was not in Latin, as it would have been at one of the more senior seats of learning, but it contained, as is the custom on these occasions, a certain amount of scholarly humour. I remember that, amongst other things, it was said that I had popularised the name of Shakespeare so thoroughly in Portsmouth that it was almost as well known as that of the local beer.

In the early summer of 1974 I went to stay with John and Alison Kane, as I often did, at their cottage on the Isle of Wight. I was presented with a large piece of hardboard on which was scrawled in chalk, 'Remember Pete's birthday present'. On the reverse, to my amazement and delight, was a magnificent oil painting that he had done of me as King Lear. He had used a photograph as his model and it showed me in the gold and white costume that I wore in the first scene, complete with Wolfit's crown and chain as well as Martin Harvey's sceptre. Later my sister had it put into a encrusted gilt frame and it hangs today in my sitting room at Crossways as one of my most treasured reminders of my career as a Shakespearean.

The first jolt that I felt as my under-carriage touched the runway after these flights of lionisation came as early as the night after the party. Dorothy Withey had decided to delay her return to Stratford-upon-Avon for a few days and invited Clifford and myself to join her for a drink at her hotel on the Sunday evening. During the conversation she asked him if all the money that had been collected in my name had been given to me. With an air of slight embarrassment but also with the merest suggestion of a sense of new-found power, he replied with a very positive, 'No'. For a moment I felt like Samson without his hair. Why had some of it been kept back and what would happen to it? In time I would find out but for the present I felt just the least bit snubbed.

I had retired on 11 November, 1972, and Clifford's first production under his own flag was staged at the end of the following March. He chose *Much Ado About Nothing* and, although I thought it would look silly for me to act in it as I had only just retired, I designed the scenery and lighting and coped with the printing as usual. The set consisted of a frieze of swirling autumnal sprays that looked something like the crests of parrots, and two bulky bastions of Tudor brick. As a background we used a very useful addition that we had been able to make to our stocks several years before through the generosity of a local engineering firm. It was a very large backcloth made of fibreglass. We had painted it a mottled mixture of greys and black and because of the nature of the material its surface was always slightly crumpled. Thus, if we lit it flatly it looked flat but if we let light streak across it, it became deeply textured and looked like a very solid, rough wall. It enabled us to produce one more variation on our enclosed box which we formed with black wings and borders together with a background, which was the basis of all our sets on the large King's stage. It had been a very prominent part of my almost completely empty setting for *Coriolanus*.

My heart, however, was not in what I was doing. It was like trying to get off a bus after it has started to move away again: I had reached my own destination but now it was taking me on to someone else's which was no concern of mine. My first reappearance before the company was when I went to a rehearsal to watch the moves and groupings so that I would know what was required of my lighting. The moment I walked into the headquarters I sensed antagonism. The cast was cooly, almost patronisingly, polite but I felt that at any moment someone would tell me that if I thought that I could interfere then I was very wrong. It was almost like the sort of nightmare in which one is struggling to get along but cannot move; everything round me was as I had created it and yet someone else was in charge and I was powerless. Perhaps I was just being over-sensitive but when we reached the theatre it seemed to be worse. I had been so used to controlling everything during the Sunday morning set-up that again it felt to me as if everyone was making a special effort to show me that I was no longer in charge. True I was not; but it did not make the experience any less painful. For the most part, Clifford did not contribute to this attitude but he was in a rightful position of authority and was very preoccupied. I could not help but resent seeing him ordering about all those things that I had originally bought or designed or had made, even though I had been so very willing to hand them over. One cannot spend most of one's adult life creating a whole world in the way that I had done without feeling possessive about it after one has given it away.

The performances were agony for me. I wandered round the theatre each night, or sat concealed behind the curtains in one of the boxes, and was very unhappy. Just before the dress rehearsal I had suddenly seen it all in a new light. The revelation occurred whilst everyone was strolling about in costume and make-up, waiting for the press and front-of-house photographs to be taken and for odd last-minute technical matters to be adjusted by the stage staff. In a flash, the whole thing appeared to be so terribly silly and childish. A hideous realisation began to dawn: it was that I had wasted my life on this sort of thing. It was a terrible disillusionment. At the back of my mind, though, I knew that my love for the best of the professional theatre was still undimmed; this was something quite different. Shakespeare was still the glory of my life and Stratford one of my supreme pleasures; it had nothing to do with them. It was just that I felt a revulsion against all that I had created and against what was going on before my eyes at that moment.

I went to my usual confessor, John Fulcher. He thought that this was a perfectly natural reaction and that, when I got used to the new state of affairs, this strange unsettling attitude would disappear. However, he did point out that he had felt very much the same when he had given up acting to go to South Africa. After a while, I began to understand rather better the causes for my radical reversal of views. I remembered that, for one thing, it is always more difficult to accept actors who are friends as characters in a play than it is complete strangers. For this reason, I sometimes wish that I had never met any or ever been backstage as those playgoers who have done neither of these things can enjoy the theatre with an innocence that I envy. I was discovering from experience that when one leaves a company, those left behind in it become like creatures of another world when they are involved in a play. One finds that it is often embarrassing and upsetting to come into close contact with friends when they are in costume and make-up as they become inaccessible strangers. In a way it is almost as difficult to get through to them at such a time as it would be if they were drugged or hypnotised. The nearer that they are to one emotionally, the more frustrating this unnatural barrier becomes. 'That was why', John suggested, 'your mother never said anything about your performances after she had seen them. She was probably embarrassed and perhaps hated them'. What had been my way of life for a quarter of a century—longer if one includes the Maddermarket—had suddenly become alien.

John Kane was quite worried about what he called my 'withdrawal symptoms' and said wisely that being involved in the theatre was like pregnancy: one cannot be partly pregnant! In other words, I must be either as totally absorbed in the SSA as I had previously been or else keep out of it altogether. The mere suggestion of the latter course was a welcome comfort. Professor Sprague offered similar advice. He knew a woman who had made the creation of a library her life's work but when she had retired it became an anathema to her. This, then, was the course that I must take. I would drop out altogether.

All that I would need to do now would be to go to see each of the productions. Even this was not easy. Generally I went with my sister on the last night and sat in the stalls. I knew that there must be many people in the audience who would recognise me and who would look every now and again to see what my reactions were to my successor's work. Surprisingly perhaps, this was something that I hated: I wished that I could have gone into the theatre incognito and sat in a quiet corner. Our seats were always immediately in front of Joan Cooper's and she invariably invited us to her private room backstage for a drink in the interval. Not only was this very pleasant—and in spite of the ups and down of our business relations with her and her husband, socially we always got on very well together and I found her a most delightful and charming person—but it did save me from having to do a 'founder and father-figure' act in the bar. Otherwise, I was like a cat on hot bricks during these evenings and could hardly wait for the play to end. Even then there followed a few minutes of further torture. There would be a curtain speech from Clifford and either he would make me want to curl up by pointing out my presence to the audience or else he would go on too long pleading for funds and complaining about lack of support. The trouble was that it reminded me that I had done the same sort of thing in the past and I just hoped that I had been more moderate. After that, there was the obligatory visit to the dressing rooms. I used to confine myself to calling on Clifford but, as I disliked the gushing of the other backstage visitors, I usually managed to slip away pretty quickly after conventional congratulations.

All these unlikely tensions had really very little to do with the quality of the production itself. I was unable to judge that soundly as I was inevitably a 'back seat driver'. All through each one I kept noticing the things that I did not like and tended to turn a blind eye to most of the virtues. Clifford's productions invariably seemed to me to be too slow. His scenery, which after that first *Much Ado* I no longer designed or painted, often struck me as being rather old-fashioned and I found that, for my taste, his productions tended to be unadventurous.

He made one attempt to be avante-garde but his ideas were, I thought, misguided. He did *The Two Gentlemen of Verona* in modern dress. The set, an abstract background of a jig-saw puzzle, mostly in black and white and designed for him by Keith Berry, was one of his best but it is useless to present in the costumes of our times any of the plays in which a girl dresses as a boy. The trick only works if it is set in a period when female attire was never other than a dress to the ground. Only then can a boy's clothes indicate clearly that this must be a boy and nothing but a boy. In today's casual trousers and open shirt, Rosalind, for example, never changes sex for a moment and there is no reason in the world why Orlando should mistake her for a male. It was the same with Clifford's Julia and her complaint that she could not travel alone looking like a girl was nonsense when translated into the late twentieth century.

After two or three years, my violent antagonisms gradually melted away and almost disappeared. I still found going to the performances to be an uncomfortable business but eventually I reached a stage when I felt that I could accept Clifford's invitation to act again. I had refused for some time but a letter from Professor Sprague turned the balance. 'The unwelcome news', he said, 'is that you may not be the Wolsey to whom I had looked forward so eagerly in next autumn's *Henry VIII.* That's a blow. Do reconsider your decision. Your taking part would mean much to me and much (I speak with conviction) to the whole company, whom you created. I'll say no more'. Up till that time, my image as a father-figure had not materialised. I had soon decided that my role was rather more that of the traditional mother-in-law who always wants to interfere and is quite sure that the man who married her daughter was not good enough for her and is treating her badly. Now, at last, I did not mind much what Clifford did or which way the company went and they, in their turn, no longer seemed to be on guard against me. Nick said on one occasion soon after my retirement, 'Of course, Clifford has one great weight on his back that you never had—you!'

Both the rehearsals for my return to the boards as Wolsey in *King Henry VIII* and the production itself were a roughly equal mixture of pleasure and boredom. It was quite nice to be on the stage again, standing in the lights and facing the dark auditorium and speaking Shakespeare's wonderful lines out into it, but I had a new fear. I knew my part as well as I ever had but I kept worrying *in case* I forgot. As far as the company was concerned, I was at last being treated as a father-figure and I found that I enjoyed it. The publicity made a lot of my return to the stage and I got good notices for my performance. The Professor said, 'One last detail in your Wolsey I must commend: the shift to the quiet, sympathetic manner in your last speech to Katherine. It made her giving up at the end conceivable as it would not have been otherwise . . . It was an admirable performance'.

In the meantime, I had learned more about the money that had been collected as a farewell present for me and, as Gloucester says in *King Lear,* 'I have heard more since'. The appeal had included the words, 'Firstly, we want to make a personal gift to Peter . . . Secondly, we want to provide the Company with something rather special as a tangible reminder of Peter's 25 years as Director'. I felt slightly insulted as it seemed to me that they should not need to be reminded. 'I gave you all', said Lear; and Regan replied, 'And in good time you gave it'. I felt a little like a very miniature Sir Christopher Wren advising people to look around them if they wanted to see his memorial.

This may appear to have been an unreasonably sour response on my part but further information which I obtained only confirmed my feelings. The total sum subscribed was, I have been assured by the Treasurer, approximately £480; the £250 given to me was therefore only fractionally over half. I do not complain about this through greed—I would not have contributed so much as I did during my 25 years had that been one of my own deadly sins—but because it savoured of injustice. Virtually all the donors to whom I have spoken were under the impression that the bulk of what they gave had come to me. I gather that there had been those dampers of old amongst the elders, lurking as ever like the Eumenides, who deemed that £250 was 'enough'. The 'something rather special' never materialised. £60 went very soon into the general account and was absorbed into the running expenses. The rest dribbled away to pay for routine supplies and maintenance such as boots, a theatrical costumes basket, some cables for loudspeakers, a few cloaks and a small cassette recorder for use during rehearsals. I bought a new set of stereo equipment with my £250 as my 'tangible reminder' of them. Ironically I had to add nearly half as much again to get something that I thought was good enough. The finances had gone so well during my last few years that the 'National Debt' had got down to £330 but the company was spared inheriting that as the City Council generously made them a grant to clear it.

My appearance in *King Henry VIII* had been in November, 1976, and 18 months later I was on the boards of the King's Theatre yet again. This time it was my second attempt at Shylock. In 1964 I had played him as the traditional shaggy rag-bag but this time, with Clifford's agreement, I presented him as a proud, ruthless and austere man as I thought that thus he would make a more formidable foe to the Venetians. I based the character on his reference to his 'sober house' and his pride in his Jewishness. Professor Sprague, who, as I have indicated before, can be remarkably silent when he has not liked anything, wrote, 'And what a Shylock you were, a fine and distinctive performance!' There was much that he did not care for in the production and that was a view shared by many of the cast. Clifford chose to play Antonio as a man with more than his share of emotional problems and made a big display of his melancholy alone on the stage at the beginning and the end. 'I almost felt that Mr Allen thought that he was playing Hamlet . . .' said Charles Green. When Antonio knew that he had been saved in the Trial Scene, Clifford chose to give a realistic display of being violently sick. Not only did the rest of us all dislike the idea but it happened at the second climax of the scene: the moment when Portia calls Shylock back. Marie Crispin, who played the lady, and I had no alternative but to redirect that passage ourselves in an attempt to retime it so that our 'necessary business' would not be ruined. Clifford did not notice because he was too busy being sick! The Professor hated this moment and so did John Kane who also came to see the play. The latter took Clifford to task for it and also for fidgeting with white gloves that had sparkling jewels on them during my big speeches in our first scene together. Even though this was criticism from a trained professional Shakespearean actor, Clifford was unrepentant. There, in a nutshell, is the great weakness of an actor-manager set-up such as ours was. How often did I cast myself badly or do things in my own performances that should have been corrected?

I remember particularly disliking his coming forward out of the grouping to do 'All the world's a stage', rather in the way that opera singers position themselves for big arias, to act all the 'ages' as the Victorians used to do. Sometimes he would give under his own direction what appeared to me to be a series of unrelated reproductions of fragments remembered from different professional performances: his Richard III and his 1980 Malvolio were both spoiled by this tendency. However, I must take care not to paint too black a picture. There were many things which he did very well indeed. His production of *Love's*

Labour's Lost was first class and so, too, was *A Midsummer Night's Dream,* in which Barry Wilkins repeated his splendid Puck, even though I did not like the set with its amber moonlight. Anne Nicolle returned for two plays before retiring yet again. Her Lady Macbeth was superb, as one had guessed that it would be, and Clifford's own performances as Iago, Cassius and Buckingham were up to the highest amateur standards. After discovering that Clifford's reign was not going to be any more democratic than mine had been, George Metcalfe had written the same sort of letter to him as he had to me and then he and his wife had resigned. Their departure robbed the company of some strength but many of the other old hands continued to give sterling service and Clifford had several very talented additions to the company though I must admit that I do not count amongst them a Rosalind who would have been better cast as Celia and an Isabella who played the part like a mixture between Tosca and Lady Macbeth.

In 1979 I returned just once more. This time I played Leontes yet again but was about twice the age that he should have been. I am afraid that I was openly rebellious about many aspects of the production which I did not like but I dared to think privately that my own performance was really rather good! How much did Clifford enjoy having me back and how successful did the audiences consider me? The older members of the latter were extravagantly complimentary and sighed for the old days but I am not so sure about the rest. My irritation at some of Clifford's methods was probably exceeded by his at my attitude but he was remarkably patient. I knew now that I had had enough and I have no doubt that he was very relieved when I assured him that this really had been, at last, my farewell appearance.

Have I been too unkindly critical of the post-Gateley era? I hope not: surely I may now have the same privilege as any other member of the public to do as Rosalind advises in her epilogue, '. . . like as much of this play as pleases . . .' How often were my own bad performances the very ones that I had thought that I had done rather well? The dictator-director has no one to control his wilfulness or point out to him the errors of judgement of which he is unaware. In any case, even with a success one cannot hope to please everyone and each individual in the house has a right to his own opinion. Very few amateurs will ever believe that adverse criticism is justified. They are invariably deeply hurt by it and usually attribute it to spite, malice, ignorance or 'anything but to the purpose'.

Time, however, began to show that I was not alone in my disquiet. By 1978 Clifford was beginning to find that he could not muster enough actors to stage the plays adequately. *The Merchant of Venice* had been postponed for several months and a proposed autumn production of *King Henry IV, Part I* was cancelled altogether. It would be easy to attribute these troubles solely to less and less people wanting to be in his productions but that would, at this stage, be less true than it later became. He had had a harder row to hoe than I had as far as membership was concerned. Even towards the end of my reign, attitudes had changed considerably from how they had been in the earlier days and the situation had worsened during his time. In the years immediately after the war, people had given themselves more selflessly and whole-heartedly to companies like ours than they do today. Far more members began to belong to several companies at the same time than they had in our best years. They see no reason today why they should not flit from one to the other just picking up the bits of each that please them at the time. That is fine for them but it does reflect the frequently-held modern belief that one's own easy, self-indulgent wants are all that need to be considered. I know from long experience that a company cannot be held together unless it contains a strong body of chauvinists; it will not survive on a floating population of casual members.

In the SSA's case, it has to be admitted, though, that the new mood was in some small part caused by a stirring of restlessness, a faint feeling of rebellion against Clifford's inflexible authoritarianism and his inability to see that people were becoming increasingly tired of the old dictatorship. My methods had been tolerated because it had been accepted that the company was so essentially my own creation and toy. Clifford had, as they say in the Services, 'risen from the ranks' of themselves. Even so, the Metcalfe attempt to get me to be more democratic had been a sign of the times and if I had continued much longer I would have had to have changed my ways considerably. Clifford, however, did not see the writing finger and continued to pursue a rigidly unchanging policy which he always claimed was a copy of mine. To an extent it was but he did not seem to realise that it had grown out of date. His one major attempt to bring in a new idea was his announcement that the SSA would put on some non-Shakespearean plays at the little open-stage drama studio in the local Faculty of Education. In this he was copying the RSC's The Other Place at Stratford, of course. Twice John Osborne's *Hotel in Amsterdam* was announced but twice was cancelled. On one occasion it was because he was unwell but as it had a cast of only six this did seem to suggest that the actor-managerial belief in his own indispensibility was as strong as ever.

The new rot that had set in began to bite deeper. In 1980, Clifford had to go into hospital for a short time and there was talk of cancelling the already-advertised *King Henry V*. I visited him in hospital and begged him to let the production go ahead and to allow the company to run their own rehearsals until he would be fit enough to take over. When I left him I believed that he probably would do so but within 24 hours he had anounced yet another cancellation. The cast had met for the first rehearsal and they were extremely angry.

The ultimate responsibility for the company had, since my retirement, rested in the hands of a triumvirate of trustees consisting of Len Russell, Ken Marchant and myself. It had been formed in case of just such an eventuality and so that, if the company did come to an end or if he resigned from his Directorship, the stock and other assets would not be Clifford's own property. A meeting of the Trust was called to consider the future and Clifford did indeed threaten to resign. He went to the very brink and then changed course and announced that *King Henry V* would go ahead with a very small cast after all.

The autumn production of that year was *Twelfth Night* and these two plays formed the SSA's 32nd Season. Clifford had announced it as 'my personal Silver Jubilee with the SSA'. He went on to say, 'To celebrate this occasion our 1980 season will commence with a new production of the play which has often been used as a celebration play, *King Henry V* . . .' (Well, yes, for coronations and centenaries of national importance, perhaps, but . . .) All this was on the back of the last programme for 1979 and he continued, 'I will complete my celebration by playing . . . Malvolio . . .' This pronouncement upset a good many people, especially those who had been in the company longer than he had. It had an aroma of 'star complex' about it which only increased the antipathy towards him.

In 1981, he attempted to cast *Much Ado About Nothing* but he could not get enough actors to make up even an inadequate cast. In the January he came to see me one evening and told me that he had decided that he would have to postpone the production until the summer and that if he then still could not cast it, he would have to resign. I was very gentle with him and said that I would not press him either way: he must make up his own mind on this matter. He confessed that, having come to this conclusion, he felt strangely relieved and not nearly as upset as he had imagined that he would be.

Three months passed and the worst happened: he could not get anything like enough people to be in the postponed production. As usual I was amongst the last to be consulted or told and the first that I heard of it was that he was announcing that he was going to close down the company and that he had decided not to renew the lease of the HQ which would have to be done within a few weeks from then. That would have meant that all the company's vast wardrobe and stock of properties would have to be got rid of and quickly too. On a Friday afternoon he telephoned me and said that he would like to come and see me. I said that I thought that I already knew what it was all about as I had heard what he had been saying to other people. He replied that I was correct. He called on me, as arranged, the next morning. We were both rather artificially bright and, having been warned by his remarks three months before and by all that I had heard during the preceding few days, I accepted his resignation. Even during our telephone conversation the day before, he had suggested what he thought might be a good way of disposing of some of the wardrobe. I told him that the other trustees and I wanted the company to continue and that I was sure that the time had come when a democracy could make a success of it. This he opposed but I pointed out to him that the decision now rested with the Trustees.

The first thing to be done was to scotch the news that the company was closing down—news with which one member said to me, 'The town is buzzing'! Every pronouncement for years had been of gloom and doom and, presumably because the public was beginning to share my views about the productions, audiences had shrunk to sometimes close to half the numbers who had come to the same play in my time. The general opinion had been that the SSA was dying on its feet. This had to be reversed as quickly as possible and a General Meeting was called at once. Clifford took great exception to this and said that nothing should have been done until he had had a chance to send a farewell thank-you letter to all the members. From that point a rift gradually widened until it reached a stage when he would not have anything to do with anyone involved in the new plans. A present of over £100 was collected for him but he refused to accept it as what he chose to call 'disloyal' actors had contributed to the sum. One would have thought from his attitude that he had been sacked at the height of success whereas the truth was that he had resigned entirely of his own free will (and not on the spur of the moment either) when he had found that the company's activities had ground so completely to a halt that he could not continue.

In due course, the General Meeting took place and was highly successful. Fifty-two members came to it! The tide appeared to be in a great hurry to turn! I took the chair and, as all three trustees had agreed, made sure that apart from praise for all that Clifford had done, the business should be solely that of the future and that no opportunity should be allowed for anyone to criticise Clifford or to start recriminations. An elderly and devoted follower of Clifford got up and launched into a diatribe against how the press had treated him. I felt that he must be stopped but when I did so he announced that he regarded that as an attempt on my part to prevent him from 'defending' Clifford—which was nonsense—and he stumped out. The rest were excitedly in favour of the new autonomy and after a steering committee had deliberated, an Executive Committee was formed. The first Chairman, democratically elected, was the now-long-since-returned Chris Bloxsom which ensured the maintaining of strong ties with the company's past when many of the newer members were all for fresh starts in almost every direction. Old members who had grown dissatisfied and left, now returned and when an audition for the first production 'under the new management' (was the title, *The Comedy of Errors* ironical yet again?) was called, no less than 35 people came to it in search of parts. I was invited to become the President and so now perhaps I am, after all, sitting up in the clouds like God in a mediaeval painting. However, for whatever reason, I do now feel involved and wanted by the company in a way that I did not during the previous few years.

Clifford cut himself off even more from any of us who were involved in the newly constituted Southsea Shakespeare Actors. At first I could not help but have thoughts of Achilles in his tent and Timon of Athens in the last two acts but decided that these were unjust. He had become genuinely angry and embittered—justifiably as he saw the situation but without cause in our eyes.

The old dictatorships had run their course and died but the old company had come to life again and was all set for a new era full of fresh ideas. *The Comedy of Errors* proved to be highly successful and was acclaimed by Claudia Sherwood, the successor to Charles Green who, to our great sadness, had died in 1980, as 'something very special'; and by Chris Harrison, Portsmouth's Arts Administrator, as follows: 'This company in its new form is a force to be reckoned with . . . The Southsea Shakespeare Actors have re-emerged as a major force'. For my part, I hope it will continue long enough for its own chronicle to be written in the course of time but for the present I am going to leave them to get on with their work and create their own story.

Going back briefly to the old days, it may be wondered whether everything always went smoothly. Were there never any hitches or mistakes? Yes, there were plenty but I do not boast of them or find them funny as many amateurs do. When all is said and done, no cook ever brags about the time that he let a casserole burn dry, nor a runner laugh about the race that he lost because he had a stone in his shoe. There was, for example, a mishap when I played Henry V in 1955. As the warm-hearted young king, I brought on the wounded old Lord Salisbury and gently placed him high on a flight of steps to rest whilst I came downstage to make a speech. A moment or two later, there was an alarming crash but I carried on, fearfully trying to see out of the corner of my eye whether or not some of the scenery had fallen down. When, at last, I could turn round, I saw the poor old chap, for he was an elderly actor, crawling up over the top of the high rostra. I had put him down rather carelessly and he had immediately fallen over the back and disappeared from view. It must have been a hilarious sight but I am glad to say that no one laughed. Another occasion was when some flats were being flown out in a blackout during the 1957 *As You Like It* and one of them got entangled with a stage tree. To cover the time whilst the matter was put right, the banished lords, who had just gone off singing, had to go on with endless repeats of 'Under the greenwood tree'. Prue, as Patience in the 1956 *King Henry VIII* gave an encore of the song, 'Orpheus with his lute', because

Griffith, played by another elderly actor, had missed his cue. Nora Turner, who played Queen Katherine, had had to insert a completely new line, 'Sing again, girl'! Nick spent a whole scene in the 1968 *King Henry IV, Part I* hidden behind a flat, holding it up. In Clifford's production of *The Merchant of Venice* in 1971, one night I failed to come on altogether in a brief half-minute appearance. I would have murdered any actor who had done that if I had been the director but he was kinder to me than I deserved.

Looking back, the overwhelming impression I have gained as the only person who has ever acted in as well as directed and designed sets for the complete Shakespeare canon, is that here is so clearly a single mind at work. For all their diversity from *The Two Gentlemen of Verona* to *Antony and Cleopatra,* and from *A Midsummer Night's Dream* to *King Lear,* the same recognisable hand held the pen for all of them. When Heminge and Condell, Shakespeare's friends and fellow actors, published the plays in the First Folio in 1623 as being all his, they knew what they were doing and always seem to me to have been in a better position to judge than those latter day scholars who apportion off some of the lesser passages to inferior anonymous collaborators. The only one of the accepted canon that Heminge and Condell left out was *Pericles* and one can easily see why. Although the voice of my old friend, Will Shakespeare, gentleman of Stratford, rings out loud and clear in the latter half of the play, my ear tells me that it does not in the first part. They obviously did not feel that enough of it was by their 'fellow' (as they called him and he each of them) to warrant inclusion in their book. Admittedly a few of their texts are not the best available but they were Shakespeare's in the condition that they were in shortly before 1623 and—most important fact of all—not one of the pirated versions, the so-called Bad Quartos, which were known to be inaccurate, was included. That solo voice sounds to me so positively and steadily all through the First Folio that for me now that volume contains a single great work encapsulating all the plays.

During the span of 30 years since I started the SSA, there were, of course, many switches of fashion and attitudes. Henry V, for example, is no longer a romantic heart-throb but has become 'one of the chaps' and a modern man with a conscience about war. The greatest change seems to me to be the acceptance of Juliet's age as being only 14. In my youth, this was a great stumbling block; people tended to close their eyes to it as it was quite ridiculous for a child of that age to be in love in the way that Shakespeare shows her to be. Since then, youngsters have developed so much earlier that nowadays it never seems to occur to anyone to question it. There are plenty of Juliets of 14 in the news every week!

In 1980, two events occurred which round off my story almost too neatly. The major timings of my life have happened so pat that I have no doubts in my own mind about there being, for Heaven alone knows what reason (literally!), a plan or design for living that is imposed upon us. The revelation of Stratford and its exciting new theatre at the most impressionable time of my life; the discovery of the Maddermarket as an ideal and the miracle of my later going there at just the right time and for precisely the necessary length of years to be trained as an actor (Nugent Monck said three years and I was there for exactly that time); coupled with my passion for Shakespeare which had been inherited from earlier generations than my parents but not in any way even suggested to me by anyone during my childhood, are only some of the more obvious ingredients of the 'well made play' that has been my life.

The first of these roundings-off was the saving, at last, of the now partly ruined Theatre Royal. It was bought by a trust which had been formed allegedly out of the Theatre Royal Society (of which for eight years I had been, and still was, the Chairman) but which, in fact, had no closer connection than that two members were common to both organisations. To my disappointment I found that I had not been invited to be one of them or even to make a third. I was, I suppose, becoming something of a back number but, none the less, my work for the Theatre Royal in those early stages had been without question extremely valuable at the time when the theatre could easily have been bulldozed overnight. However, in 1985, a full five years later, when I had become resigned to my contributions being treated—as it seemed to me—as unrecorded prehistory, I was invited to become a Trustee after all. I accepted and found myself warmly welcomed; a pleasing contrast to the sense of rejection that I had, perhaps irrationally and unjustly—or perhaps not—felt during those five years. Shortly after the theatre had been purchased I had retired from the Chairmanship of the Society as its role would henceforth become simply that of a supporters' club. However, thanks to someone's on the spur of the moment suggestion, I became its President. Nonetheless, until I was actually invited to become a member of the Trust I had felt that I was on the outside all the time. I not only wanted to be on the management side of the fence, even if only in a fairly nominal back-bench capacity, but I also felt so strongly that I *deserved* to be there. Becoming a Trustee was very gratifying indeed: it seemed that at last I had confirmation that I was one who, in Enobarbus's words, 'earns a place in the story'.

My second special event was when my life-long passion for Stratford's memorial to Shakespeare on the banks of the Avon was rewarded later in the year by my being invited to join the Board of Governors of the Royal Shakespeare Theatre and the RSC. I could not possibly have been more thrilled and delighted. The privilege and joy of being able to say 'we' instead of 'they' was the fulfilment of half a century's yearning to be part of what I originally saw as the most exciting building site of my lifetime. I had been invited, as I was to be again those five years later with the Theatre Royal, *inside*. Small cog though I might be, I had become part of the management—always for me the vital ingredient. Membership of the RSC Board may not mean more to me than my MBE but, by Heaven, it runs it very closely!

Now that it is several years since I retired from the Directorship of the SSA, I can go to the theatre and enjoy my Shakespeare without analysing every technical detail to see if there is anything practical to be learned from it. Unfortunately, the older I get the more I hate crowds and, alas, that is just what audiences are! None the less, I am still the happiest of playgoers unless people round me fidget, flap their programmes, talk or rustle sweet wrappings. Generally speaking, at the Royal Shakespeare Theatre, at the National, at Covent Garden and a very few more, the bulk of the audience are well-behaved and considerate to those sitting near them. At the other end of the scale, I have given up the cinema altogether as the endless chatter and chewing make me so angry that visits to it are nowadays sheer purgatory.

No longer do I have to study the plays with a view to staging them and so I am able to read them straight through again for sheer pleasure as I used to do before 1947. In my younger years I would not have believed that it would be possible for me to do that now with even greater enjoyment than I did then. As my knowledge of them has increased, so my love for them and the happiness that they give me have grown ever richer, deeper and more wonderful. 'Age' certainly 'cannot wither, nor custom stale (their) infinite variety' as far as I am concerned. For me, Shakespeare more than ever 'makes hungry where most (he) satisfies'.

At the end of the day, few things delight me more than to be able to retire to bed with a particular leather-bound volume of the plays that my mother gave me 50 years ago or, sometimes for a change, a facsimile of the First Folio or of one of the earlier quartos. These latter act as a sort of magic carpet which carries me in imagination back to Shakespeare's own time. I can look at these reproductions of the original editions of nearly 400 years ago and see precisely what he (in the case of those printed before 1616) and his contemporaries actually saw. In a way they bring me even closer to that old Stratford friend who was born in Henley Street and is buried in the Parish Church than do modern editions. I get into bed and arrange the pillows so that I can sit upright because, as there is no one within earshot, I want to be able to read out loud. Thus in the tiny private theatre of my head I can not only be the actor of all the parts but be my own audience at the same time. There is so much extra pleasure to be gained from reading Shakespeare aloud; hearing the actual sound of those marvellous lines. My bedside lamp is on, brightly lighting my book and at the same time bathing the rest of the room in a comfortable golden glow. Which one shall I begin this time? A tragedy, perhaps? A comedy; or shall it be one of the histories? Ah! yes, that one, I think. It has always been one of my favourites—but which of them has not? I settle down, open the book and clear my throat. I start to read: 'Act I, scene 1 . . .'

POSTSCRIPT

1987 being the 40th anniversary of the birth of the Southsea Shakespeare Actors, the new democratic management, then in its seventh year, decided to celebrate.

40 years to the day after the first public performance, it held a successful party in the partially-restored Theatre Royal; a somewhat ironical setting when one remembers the role it has played in this story! Long-vanished members emerged from the past to mingle with the current ones. Donald Sinden came down from London to add some lustre and made a witty speech when it was announced that he had joined the SSA's list of Patrons. To my great surprise I was presented with a tall glass goblet beautifully and suitably engraved. As a cabaret the SSA presented *Hamlet* abridged to 15 minutes. This meant that the company had at last acted in the Theatre Royal after all these years but the play was, sadly, no funnier than usual simply because it had been reduced to a frantically guyed fragment.

Three productions were presented during the year. As a compliment to the pioneers, the first two plays of 1947, *Twelfth Night* and *She Stoops to Conquer,* were restaged. To make the third in some way different from their usual offerings, I was invited to return to direct and design a play again for the first time since I had retired 15 years before. As I had already done the whole Shakespeare canon, they asked me to tackle *The Two Noble Kinsmen* by Fletcher and in small part possibly—even, I think, probably—by Shakespeare.

I had misgivings about accepting but felt that if I did not, I would for ever after reproach myself. I decided to dress the play in the style of Veronese mixing scarlet and gold Roman armour with Renaissance costumes like Alexander the Great in the National Gallery.

I dreaded the project as the time to start rehearsing drew nearer but I was assured that I would be treated with kid gloves. However, I soon discovered from the gossips that things would be very much as they had always been. Early petulence over a trivial but unwitting solecism on my part brought rebukes from the top that were so badly and pompously handled that I nearly withdrew before I had even started.

A flattering number of old members, who had survived from my time, and new ones to whom I was something of a legend, wanted to be in the production. The former were no trouble to direct but the newer ones were less easy. My punctual and concentrated rehearsals were a shock to a company that had become used to late starts, long coffee breaks and more indulgent directors.

My production, with brilliant colours against a dark set of brown, black and gleaming beaten gold, was elaborate enough for the King's Theatre but was staged in the tiny Portsmouth Drama Centre which had become the SSA's usual venue at that time. I tried to get the newer people to play with style and a sense of period movement but I found that many of them seemed to think that only 1987 modern dress naturalism should be used for any period. Some told me that they were glad to have learned from me but a few, who thought they knew it all already and who clearly could see no point in some of the most basic, timeless rules of stage technique, called it 'old-fashioned acting'. The consequence was that the production largely lacked the polish and style it would have had in the old days. The quality of speaking was often poor but there was little that I could do about that in the time. Actually it went reasonably well and my Veronese look reminded someone of a Monteverdi opera and that pleased me. As usual, we were showered with praise and I was told that 'Prospero' had 'not lost his magic'. Drugged as one always is by the euphoria of it all during the run of the play, I wanted to believe it. Alas, the dream is actually never fully realised and when it is over, cooler reason reveals the truth about the shortcomings.

I am glad to have done it even if I did not greatly enjoy the doing. If this play ever becomes accepted as Shakespeare's 38th, even though his part in its writing could only have been so small, I can claim to have added it to the 37 that I have directed, designed—and, yes, acted in! To achieve that, I took over the part of the 4th Soldier on the last night!

THE END

INDEX

Numbers in italics indicate photograph pages